Gwyneth

Gwyneth

THE BIOGRAPHY

AMY ODELL

G

GALLERY BOOKS

New York   Amsterdam/Antwerp   London
Toronto   Sydney/Melbourne   New Delhi

G

Gallery Books
An Imprint of Simon & Schuster, LLC
1230 Avenue of the Americas
New York, NY 10020

First Gallery Books hardcover edition July 2025

GALLERY BOOKS and colophon are registered trademarks of Simon & Schuster, LLC

Interior design by Jaime Putorti

Manufactured in the United States of America

10 9 8 7 6 5 4 3 2 1

Library of Congress Control Number has been applied for.

ISBN 978-1-6680-0577-4
ISBN 978-1-6680-0579-8 (ebook)

For Mom

CONTENTS

INTRODUCTION

Gwyneth Paltrow may not have known, as she headed into Goop's weekly staff meeting at ten a.m. on Tuesday, January 17, 2017, that the company was about to find itself embroiled in one of its biggest controversies.

Goop, which Gwyneth had started as a newsletter nearly ten years earlier, sometimes tried to plant products that would draw headlines for being wacky or controversial, which tended to boost traffic and therefore sales. An "energy clearing kit" that went up for sale around this time—contents: a wooden box, a bundle of sage, a feather fan, a smudge bowl, and a "potion"—was a plant. But it failed to draw mass attention, and Goop only sold one hundred of them. However, the egg-shaped stone Goop had plugged in the newsletter five days before the staff meeting, and now sold in jade ($66) or rose quartz ($55), was an entirely different story. Gwyneth believed in the eggs, which Goop expert Shiva Rose had recommended inserting vaginally and leaving there for as long as a full night. Rose claimed in Goop that these yoni eggs could do everything from "increase orgasm" to "balance the cycle" to "invigorate our life force."

The media quickly noticed.

"It's no yolk! Gwyneth Paltrow's website Goop is selling eccentric stone sex eggs which 'improve orgasms and muscle tone,'" announced a *Daily Mail* headline. "Gwyneth Paltrow wants you to put a rock in your vagina. Seriously," offered Mashable. Writing on her blog, vocal Goop critic and ob-gyn Jen Gunter took a serious tone, accusing Gwyneth of "profiting from snake oil" and warning that the eggs could lead to bacterial vaginosis or potentially deadly toxic shock syndrome. Major news outlets around the world invited more doctors to speak against the eggs, which became a referendum on the entire premise of Goop.

Gwyneth—referred to as "GP" around the office—often drove to work in her white Range Rover and parked in her space, denoted by the sign RESERVED FOR G-SPOT. She regularly arrived damp-haired and bare-faced following her morning Tracy Anderson workout, wearing Goop's G. Label clothing brand.

Goop now employed around seventy people, and she stood in its newly annexed office space in Santa Monica, stylishly outfitted with Restoration Hardware furniture provided gratis in exchange for publicity. She delivered her weekly address as though nothing was amiss. "We are the number one voice in the wellness movement," Gwyneth told her team. "Goop defined the concept of modern wellness and created the language to describe it. Let's own it."

Goop had only ordered around six hundred eggs; as she spoke, two thousand customers were on the waitlist to buy one. Her message was that the company was winning—that the response was another sign that Goop was threatening the medical establishment, connecting women with forms of healing and self-care that traditional doctors either couldn't understand or, worse, wanted to keep hidden.

She went on to outline the brand's philosophy of merging consumerism with a state of higher being. Goop was the authority on what we put *in* our bodies (supplements), how we *treat* our bodies (sleep, detoxes, and exercise), and what we put *on* our bodies (serums and creams). All were product categories in the Goop store. The virality of the egg story showed, she added, that they could offer solutions to women's problems and educate them at the same time. This was proof of the might that came from telling consumers about things they hadn't heard of before.

"We have incredible power," she said.

Goop had long served as a platform for Gwyneth's favored gurus. Habib Sadeghi, for instance, had contributed an article suggesting (falsely) that there could be a link between bras and breast cancer. Linda Lancaster had proposed that readers undergo an eight-day raw goat milk cleanse to rid themselves of hidden parasites (this is not medically advised).

But those controversies had mostly just driven awareness of Goop. So as the egg story went viral, Goop's primary worry was keeping enough in stock. The following year, California district attorneys sued Goop over the health claims it had made about both the eggs and another product, the "Inner Judge Flower Essence Blend" of essential oils. At which point, Gwyneth said in one meeting, "Let's just not sell it [the egg]." But the company paid a fine, admitted no wrongdoing, and continued selling eggs into early 2025 without making the same claims.

Goop was a business, after all. "She is fucking borderline brilliant," a former executive said. "GP knows exactly what she's doing."

BORN TO A successful television producer and a Tony Award–winning actress, Gwyneth Paltrow had spent her entire life surrounded by the players and poseurs of the entertainment industry. Growing up in New York and Los Angeles, she had attended elite private schools and had been adored by her parents' famous friends since her days as an infant spitting up on her godfather, Steven Spielberg. As a teenager, she was welcomed into a film world eager to profit from her beauty, charm, and pedigree. An enviable acting career soon followed, along with an Oscar, and serious relationships with some of the world's most famous men. Gwyneth then channeled her notoriety into her own brand. Though her perceived relatability would be crucial to her success, she hadn't really lived a day as a "normal" person.

It wasn't that Gwyneth didn't try to understand average people. She simply had no point of entry into their lives. To her, they were always more like a theoretical construct. The idea of being "normal" became both a fear and a fascination. Her desire to translate her extraordinary life into terms her fans could appreciate gave rise to a second career recommending products and experiences as the face and CEO of Goop. Though staff wondered about her susceptibility to alternative health ideas that lacked scientific backing, she just hadn't faced many of the real-world problems that taught people to be skeptical of costly, easy solutions. Her statements about poverty, obesity, divorce, and nutrition revealed just how little she had in common with the masses, and at times seemed to make her one of the most resented celebrities in the world.

GWYNETH HAS BEEN admired and envied by a massive global audience for three decades. She felt destined for fame from early childhood. Her WASPy, sometimes anxious mother, Blythe Danner, and brash, sometimes narcissistic Jewish father, Bruce Paltrow, guided their firstborn to play bit parts in Chekhov plays and Greek tragedies as a child. They then steered her toward well-written, tasteful roles as her career took off in her late teens. Her first noteworthy part came in 1993's *Flesh and Bone*, when she was twenty-one. Practically overnight, she became known as a tastemaker and darling of Calvin Klein. She soon became a tabloid obsession thanks to her boyfriend, Brad Pitt, whom she started dating when the two played husband and wife in David Fincher's 1995 film *Se7en*. Her search for quality parts brought her to Miramax, where she quickly became a favorite of Harvey Weinstein, who gave her roles in highbrow literary fare, but also once sexually harassed her and treated her in a way that Gwyneth described as "abusive." (Weinstein disputed this characterization.) At twenty-six, she won the Academy Award for Best Actress in a Leading Role for *Shakespeare in Love*, famously crying at the podium in her pink Ralph Lauren ball gown and six-figure diamond necklace as her parents and Weinstein looked on. To many of the more than 45 million people watching, she appeared as a real-life princess without an ounce of relatability. And that dual fascination—hating her and wanting to be her—has persisted ever since.

In 2000, with her acting career at an all-time high, she told a reporter, "It's not like I go out there and say 'Will you please put me on the cover of the tabloids?' or 'Will you please mention me in every article about lipstick?' People just do that and it's beyond my control . . . I'm sick of this Gwyneth Paltrow person I see everywhere. I hate her and I wish she would go away. But there's nothing I can do about it." And the public sometimes seemed to agree. The more she talked, the more she revealed the distance between them and herself. And she talked even more once she pulled back from acting after having children and began Goop, sending the first newsletter from the well-appointed London home she shared with her rock-star husband, Chris Martin.

As fans and the media gawked at her missives, filled with expensive recommendations for sushi restaurants, handbags, and hotels, she doubled down, even as the economy crumbled and people lost their homes in the Great Recession. Gwyneth kept sending emails and kept talking to the press—"I can't pretend to be somebody who makes $25,000 a year"; "I would rather smoke crack than eat cheese from a can"; "I think it's incredibly embarrassing when people are drunk"—and she kept offending. She upset the medical community by promoting unsubstantiated health claims; mothers by saying, "To have a regular job and be a mom . . . of course there are challenges, but it's not like being on set"; and fat people, as when she starred in *Shallow Hal* and then said in a television interview that "every pretty girl" should be forced to try on a fat suit. There was often a seed of truth in her remarks. The medical establishment has failed women in many ways, parenting with any job is challenging, and pretty women probably would benefit from understanding living in a different body. But as a famous person bathed in adoration since infancy, she seemed to fail to see the massive gulf between herself and her audience.

IN 2022, I published a biography of Anna Wintour, exploring her impact as the editor in chief of *Vogue* and a cultural icon in part thanks to the film *The Devil Wears Prada*. When trying to think of another woman whose life and career had the same combination of public fascination and private complexity, I kept coming back to Gwyneth Paltrow. As a movie star in the nineties, she became a fashion icon whose every look was parsed. Building on this influence, she became the face of brands like Dior, Estée Lauder, and American Express. Before it felt like every celebrity had their own lifestyle or beauty company, she launched Goop. The brand not only has sold an untold number of $600 sweaters, face creams, and vaginal eggs, making Gwyneth synonymous with a certain upscale minimalist aesthetic, but also has helped bring the wellness movement and alternative medicine into the mainstream—to the horror of doctors and academics. Throughout her public life, Gwyneth has given a master class in commanding the attention economy that now rules culture. Hating on her with just the right bravado and contempt has boosted the profiles of her critics, one of whom wrote a book titled *Is Gwyneth Paltrow Wrong About Everything?: When Celebrity Culture and Science Clash*. Love her or hate her, for over thirty years, we haven't been able to look away. And she has used that power to commodify her taste and lifestyle and sell it back to us, even though her life is the very definition of something money can't buy.

Gwyneth strategically curated her public image by giving count-less interviews to friendly glossy magazines and talk shows, doling out "candid" statements and revelations when it served her project of the moment or elevated her brand. When I began my research for this book, I spent a year just reading thousands of such articles and interview transcripts, creating a detailed timeline of her life. I wondered if, after all that coverage, I would be able to uncover anything new. "My father always used to talk about the difference between the public perception of me and what I was really like, and how there was such a huge gap," Gwyneth has said. "He was like, 'You've got the whole country fooled.'" When I started interviewing people who knew or had worked with Gwyneth, I realized what he'd meant. She and her handlers have controlled her image brilliantly for decades, particularly when it comes to her middling run as the CEO of Goop. The company she founded in 2008 hasn't experienced sustained profitability, has allegedly suffered from a chaotic and sometimes toxic office culture, and has lacked a clear business strategy as it ping-pongs from one of Gwyneth's ideas to the next. As the main narrator of her own public story, Gwyneth has masterfully shaped our perception of her. She knows all her best angles. I interviewed more than 220 people from her childhood, her inner social circle, and the entertainment world—including directors, costars, crew members—and current and former employees from Goop. In writing this book, I set out to create a complete portrait of this somewhat elusive subject from all angles, not just her best ones. And to understand what that intangible quality is that exalts someone to an enduring level of status and fascination few ever achieve.

When I initially spoke to Goop's then-publicist, asking whether Gwyneth was willing to be interviewed or to participate in the research for this book by providing sources (like Anna Wintour had for *Anna*), she told me they would be happy to help. But then I'd reach out to potential interviewees, saying I'd been in touch with Gwyneth's office, and they would check with her about speaking with me and come back with a no or simply disappear altogether. I reached her uncle Robert Paltrow by phone in late 2024, and he told me he would be happy to help if she said it was okay. The next day, I received a text message with his regrets.

Around a year after our first call, the publicist told me Gwyneth would help with this book if I agreed to let them "fact-check" it.

Yet Goop had published many stories that were not subjected to any traditional fact-checking. I assured her this book would be checked thoroughly by a professional fact-checker. I told her Gwyneth was still welcome to sit for an interview, and we could fact-check anything used from that as much as she wanted. But I didn't get a straight answer about Gwyneth's participation—a tactic I had heard about from other journalists who'd requested interviews: first an encouraging, welcoming response and then silence. This tracked with what I'd been told by an old friend of Gwyneth's, who noted—as many people have—that she has long been ahead of the curve on everything from cuisine to fitness fads, and that she *invented* ghosting.

That publicist left the company when I was finishing up the book and her replacement finally declined my interview request on Gwyneth's behalf and made Goop's chief people officer, Djenaba Parker, and Gwyneth's friend Richard Lovett, the co-chairman of CAA, available for interviews. Yet, this publicist denied or ignored my requests to speak with additional sources who wanted Gwyneth's permission before doing an interview.

Many were terrified to talk about Gwyneth. Her Goop staff seemed cagier than many of Wintour's former employees. Many had signed NDAs. Some people I interviewed had seen her take action against people she felt had crossed her. ("I can be mean. I can cave in to gossip. I can ice people out and I can definitely harbor revenge," Gwyneth has said.) Yet I was still able to interview many people who had never spoken about her before. (Anecdotes were corroborated where possible; dialogue was re-created from memory and may not be exact.) Gwyneth has had a habit throughout her life of bringing people close to her, then cooling on them. Some simply move on, while others become dismayed and desperate to get back into her inner circle. One person who worked closely with her around the time she started Goop said, "She's very good at, 'If I'm going to let you into my world, you're going to pay for it.' Yet she wants to come off to most people as just being that simple girl next door who just gets you. But in reality, that's not her."

This is the first extensively researched, thoroughly reported biography to piece together the often-told and little-known aspects of her life, to follow the golden child of Blythe and Bruce from being an It girl through becoming one of the biggest and most polarizing cultural influencers of the twenty-first century. Thus, the book has also become a study in the power of media, from *Vogue* to *The Tonight Show* to Twitter/X, that anoints women like Gwyneth, and an audience thrilled by her takedown even more than her rise. My hope here is to tell her story in a way that begins with her strengths, her talents, her vulnerabilities, and her desires and shows how that inner life passed through the bizarre, often corrosive influences of fame, beauty, and privilege, to illustrate Gwyneth Paltrow as never before.

CHAPTER 1

Perfect Pedigree

[Bruce] was one hundred percent involved in being a success in the industry.

—Paul Michael Glaser

No one called it "wellness" back then.

Most mornings in the fall of 1977, the little blond girl would take her place on the floor of Miss Murdock's kindergarten class at St. Augustine by-the-Sea Episcopal school in Santa Monica, close her eyes, and begin her meditation. For fifteen minutes, she lay on the rug in the corner of the silent room with the others, focusing on her breathing, as the class rabbit, Sophie, hopped around the students. When time was up, Miss Murdock would retrieve Sophie and invite the kids to draw whatever images had passed through their minds.

The two-story school in a wing off a church sat a few blocks from the beach. Each grade consisted of just one class, and the kids grew up together through sixth. Among Gwyneth's classmates in those years were Abbie Schiller, whose father, Bob Schiller, wrote for *I Love Lucy*; Chris Levinson, whose father, Richard Levinson, co-created *Columbo* and *Murder, She Wrote*; Maya Rudolph, known then as the daughter of singer Minnie Riperton; and a light-haired girl about Gwyneth's size, Mary Wigmore, who would become a lifelong friend.

Gwyneth's teachers remembered her as a sweet, creative kid but not a standout. Like many of her classmates, she would sometimes tuck little notes into teaching assistant Jill Mackay's purse that read, "I love you, Jill."

Mackay one day noticed Gwyneth playing with something that wasn't hers. When she went over to investigate, she found that Gwyneth had been pinching pencils, erasers, and other small items from her classmates' backpacks. Mackay conferred with Murdock, and they decided to invite her parents in for a conference. Blythe, who wore her blond hair in a chin-length Farrah Fawcett–style bob and who had the same blue eyes and downward-sloping eyebrows as her daughter, arrived with Gwyneth's younger brother, Jake, around two years old, in her arms and Bruce by her side. Mackay and Murdock wondered, given their careers and a toddler, whether the couple's daughter was getting enough attention at home.

After the meeting, Bruce had to go to the school office, and Mackay escorted him. Known for being both animated and blunt, he turned toward her and laid a heavy hand on her shoulder before they parted ways. "Do you think my Gwynnie's always going to be like this?"

"Oh yes," she joked, "she's going to grow up to be a bank robber."

After the meeting, Gwyneth's stealing stopped. But as she got older, Bruce's worries became more pronounced—about her performance in school, her teenage smoking habit, her partying. She was always a daddy's girl, but also may have noticed early on that the world was eager to give her what she wanted, and she didn't need anyone's permission to get it.

BLYTHE WAS AROUND the same age as her pencil-stealing daughter when she announced to her father, an easygoing banker named Harry Danner, that she wanted to be an actress. "So," he said, "who's trying to stop you?"

The son of a milkman, Harry himself had been offered a chance on the stage, as a singer at New York's Radio City Music Hall, but he turned it down, around the time of the Great Depression, for a career in banking. Before meeting her father, Blythe's mother, Katharine, sang at supper clubs. Young Blythe was aiming for the stage career her parents had passed up, choosing instead to raise their children in a large four-story house in the suburb of Rosemont, on Philadelphia's Main Line. When they moved from Philadelphia to Bucks County for Harry's job, Blythe was enrolled at George School, a private Quaker institution where teachers emphasized peace, equality, social justice, and a simple life. After performing through high school, she joined the drama program at Bard College, a small liberal arts school around a hundred miles north of New York City, where she dated fellow student Chevy Chase, with whom she sang in a band (he played piano). She received offers during college to act professionally but completed her degree to please her parents. Despite her early success, Blythe could feel timid and full of self-doubt. In college, she fixated on how she was the only student in her program who couldn't cry on cue, which felt to her like a tragic flaw.

After graduating Bard in 1965, Blythe took random acting jobs, including small parts on the soap opera *Guiding Light* and the crime drama *N.Y.P.D.*, and as Miss Gum-Out at the New York auto show. She took what she called her "first real job" with the repertory Theater Company of Boston in 1966.* The company was looking to cast a slender, young German-speaking woman for a war drama called *The Infantry.* "I speak German fluently, and at the time I was disgustingly skinny. I doubt that any other girl who auditioned met both requirements," she said. *The Boston Globe* raved over the play and Blythe, who conveyed "a perfect sense of alienation." She was earning $60 a week (about $600 in 2025), which "meant no more checks from home," she said. "Having a father who was a Philadelphia banker makes you very proud of your

---

* Known as a highly creative group, the company's members included then-unknowns Dustin Hoffman, Jon Voight, and Robert De Niro.

financial independence." Her next few roles were "not just ingenues," she recalled, "but whores and innocents, crazy kids and characters." She signed with a New York agent in 1966 and received excellent reviews for her work in the Lincoln Center productions *Summertree*, *The Miser*, and *Cyrano de Bergerac*. She was offered her first Broadway role in 1969 but turned it down for a play called *Someone's Comin' Hungry*. Among the show's producers was Bruce Paltrow, the gregarious twenty-five-year-old son of a successful scrap-iron dealer.

BRUCE WAS THE kind of guy people either loved or couldn't stand. The second of four children, he was born to Jewish parents in Brooklyn and raised in Great Neck, Long Island. His father, Arnold, was a tough figure who went by "Buster."

In 1961, Bruce went to Tulane University in New Orleans to study painting, a subject his business-oriented family might have discouraged. He wore fancy loafers to class, and found himself a blond girlfriend who wasn't Jewish. He shared a house with a group who included Paul Michael Glaser, who would go on to play Detective Starsky on the seventies series *Starsky & Hutch*. The two were good friends, but Glaser remembered that the young Bruce "made himself a fair share of enemies. He had a very acerbic tongue, a very quick sense of humor, which I enjoyed. But he rubbed people the wrong way a lot of the time." Bruce knew this, too, but he refused to change. When one of their housemate's beloved pet rabbits died suddenly, Bruce said at its burial, "Can I have his left rear leg as a good luck charm?" The joke was not well-received.

Glaser saw a shift in Bruce around the time he became president of his fraternity, Sigma Alpha Mu. "It was very much a gesture for acceptance," Glaser said. "All of a sudden, Bruce walked away from the painting." If painting had been a way to reject the idea of taking after his father, who ran a lucrative business, and his brother, who by this time was a successful real estate developer, he was now falling in line. "There was a dichotomy. It was the artistic side of him that wanted to express itself, but maybe, because of familial pressure, he wanted to be successful as well, and the success won out."

A few months after graduation, Bruce was working back in New York as an executive assistant at Screen Gems, a television production company, plotting his ascent each day as he dined at the lunch counter at Hamburger Heaven near Madison Avenue. When his friend and fellow assistant Preston Fischer found a promising script for *Someone's Comin' Hungry*, he brought it to Bruce. The play told the story of a married couple, the husband Black, the wife white and pregnant, who shared an apartment with the husband's father. Edgy material for the time. Bruce liked it, and the two agreed to leave their jobs to take a shot at producing it. Fischer had experience in production and figured Bruce could help him raise the relatively small sum of $75,000 ($650,000 in 2025) needed to stage the play, since he'd come from money and likely had connections to people who could cut the $2,500 check they were soliciting from each investor. They each raised a share and had their sights on Broadway after Marlo Thomas and Bill Cosby showed early interest. But then, Thomas signed on for a final season of *That Girl*, Cosby backed out, and they downgraded to Off-Broadway.

Actor Burt Brinckerhoff came on board to direct, and the three men began auditions. Blythe Danner arrived as not quite a star but certainly a critical darling. Brinckerhoff, Fischer, and Bruce agreed she was the one. Bruce was immediately attracted to Blythe, whom he called the "blond shiksa." She was refined, talented, beautiful, and plainly on her way to stardom. He wooed her with a confident patter and a stream of old-fashioned jokes, among them the Spencer Tracy chestnut, "You only need two things to be an actor: Remember your words and don't bump into the furniture," and "Nudity is great—if you can't remember your lines." Blythe was charmed.

One evening after rehearsals, before they started dating, Bruce and Blythe were walking together when they decided to visit the resident fortune teller at the Fifth Avenue Hotel. As Blythe recalled later, she saw their future: She and Bruce would marry. As Glaser remembered it, Blythe was involved at the time with John Crowther, a Princeton graduate who had attended her same Bucks County high school and whose father, Bosley Crowther, was the *New York Times* film critic. But she quickly got together with Bruce. "[Bruce] did have a fabulous sense of humor. He was very, very personable. Everyone liked being around him. He came from money. I just think it was just one of those young, wonderful matches," said Fischer.

Blythe and Bruce were opposites in many ways but similar in one, Glaser noticed. Blythe was polite and kind but kept people at a distance. "That ability to do that could have been very attractive to Bruce, because he was really adamant about not feeling his emotions."

Someone's Comin' Hungry premiered on March 31, 1969, at the Pocket Theater on Third Avenue and Thirteenth Street. It ran for all of two weeks. *The New York Times* review stated, "The dialogue is all outline and no heart."

THE SUMMER OF 1969, Blythe landed the lead role in a comedy called *Butterflies Are Free*, playing a bohemian woman whose blind neighbor falls in love with her. She described the role as "grueling physically." The strain of this stage voice damaged her vocal cords, and she began losing weight. Bruce had already been referring to her as "the blond stick," but now her ribs started to show.

Two days before opening night and around seven months after they met, Bruce proposed. He thought it might ease her anxiety about her performance. *Butterflies Are Free* opened on Broadway on October 21, 1969, and Blythe's dressing room filled with friends, relatives, flowers, and congratulatory telegrams.

By the end of the night, Blythe Danner was a star.

THE NEXT DAY, a *New York Times* reporter interviewed Blythe at Sardi's restaurant. He wrote her up as "Broadway's newest, freshest, most-acclaimed young star." Similar profiles followed in newspapers across the country.

The thrill of this success splintered quickly into anxiety. Blythe didn't think she could possibly live up to the acclaim. She felt unworthy of it, and the play began to seem trivial—it's not like *Butterflies* was Shakespeare or Chekhov. She became, in her words, "terribly depressed."

She managed those feelings by turning away from the fame and the ensuing expectations. She imagined settling down with Bruce on a Connecticut farm instead of in a Hollywood mansion. "I don't think I ever will be a celebrity," she told an interviewer. "This will blow over. If everybody someday could recognize me, it would be a bloody bore. I remember a lot of people are heard about in one big show and then nothing happens again."

She replaced the star on her dressing room door with a peace sign.

Blythe got her wish. She was not a one-hit wonder, but she never became a mega-celebrity, perhaps partly because she never got comfortable with fame. She treasured privacy and loathed the exhibitionism of going on talk shows or press tours to promote a project. The fame that her daughter would wear so naturally, almost weightlessly, threatened Blythe's sense of herself. She hated watching herself onscreen, forcing herself to do it only to critique the work. She learned not to read reviews until a show ended. "If they're good, there's the danger they'll give you a big head; if they're terrible, you're going to slide into a deep depression."

THE AFTERNOON OF Sunday, December 15, 1969—a date selected so that she wouldn't have to miss any *Butterflies* performances—Blythe slipped into an ivory Empire-waist dress and walked with her father down the aisle of Old St. David's Church in Wayne, Pennsylvania, outside Philadelphia. Bruce wasn't religious, but his Jewish friends were surprised at just how Episcopalian it all was. The reception was held at a nearby golf club.

Blythe had been living in a sublet on Twelfth Street in Manhattan. After the wedding, she moved into Bruce's West Seventy-First Street apartment, which occupied a full floor of a brownstone. Friends had helped him strip the plaster off one wall, exposing brick, and he decorated the place himself with fashionable furniture. Bruce had been brought up knowing about good food and good clothes, and he had expensive taste. Like his peers, he wore a suit and tie to work every day. Unlike his peers, his ties came from Ralph Lauren, his suits from the upscale men's boutique Roland Meledandri, a favorite among high-status Hollywood types.

After the failure of *Someone's Comin' Hungry*, Bruce's ambition started to lead him, which strained his friendships. Glaser was in New York, too, struggling to make it as an actor. "I was going through all kinds of emotional turmoil," he said. "I always felt like [Bruce] kind of kept me at arm's length because he didn't want to deal with that side of a relationship . . . He was one hundred percent involved in being a success in the industry."

While Bruce was struggling to get his scripts produced, Blythe's career took off. She won the Tony in 1970 for *Butterflies*. When she walked onstage the next night, she received a standing ovation that made her so fearful of letting down the audience that she didn't think she would be able to go through with the show.

With her husband's career lagging behind and the spotlight now following her, Blythe chose to turn toward her family. "You can put things off while you build a career, and then it can all collapse," she said. It was also protective: She feared getting caught up in her own hype and didn't want to live and die by her work.

Bruce's career needed a boost, though, and around 1971, they decided to move to L.A., where he could better network and catch a break.

By 1972, Blythe was pregnant. A month before she was due to give birth, Bruce met a young director whose breakout film, about a murderous shark terrorizing a New England beach town, would be released in 1975. Bruce Paltrow and Steven Spielberg would be close friends for the next thirty years.

While Bruce thrived on the attention and praise of successful producers and directors in Los Angeles, Blythe seemed disinterested. "I don't want to denigrate his ability or his talent, but I always got the feeling that he was kind of riding on her coattails a little bit," said Glaser.

As her due date neared, Blythe thought about what to name the baby. If it were a girl, she wanted to give her a Welsh name. She considered Bronwen but decided in the end on the name of a childhood friend that had always stayed with her. Bruce was pushing for something less "airy-fairy," but he gave in. Blythe found doctors and hospitals on both coasts.

Gwyneth Kate Paltrow was born in Los Angeles on September 27, 1972. Spielberg became her godfather. In her first days as a mother, Blythe thought about not going back to acting but decided in the end "that I'm a better mother when I have an outlet for this particular kind of craziness—the desire to crawl into somebody else's skin."

CHAPTER 2

Nepo-Baby on Set

I've known my whole life that this was going to happen to me in some way. You don't think it really will, but then when it happens you're like, "I knew it would happen." I believe if you ask any famous person they will have known that they were going to be famous. It's like a predestined thing.

—Gwyneth Paltrow, *Vanity Fair*, September 2000

Gwyneth showed up on her first movie set at twelve days old. Her mother was filming *Adam's Rib*, and on breaks Blythe would carry her daughter around, and Gwyneth, ever the extrovert, would reach her little hands out to anyone who came near. But Blythe's workdays with her baby were the exception. Bruce had plenty of free time back then, so "I was the nanny," he said. "I would be with Gwyneth all day and night. And when it came time to feed, I would get Gwynnie out of her crib and bring her to Blythe, shooting movies or rehearsal. And she would breast feed and when she'd get done, I would burp her, I would walk her, and we would spend our days together." As an infant, Gwyneth stayed up all night, and Bruce would hold her in his arms and stroll around with her. Gwyneth developed a closeness with her father that she wouldn't feel toward her mother until much later in life.

Blythe, though happy as a wife and mother, still wrestled with anxiety and a sense of unworthiness. "Had I been more confident, I would simply have dealt with situations head-on. I think you really have to work at this very hard unless that quality is inborn. For example, I admire that trait in Katharine Hepburn, just knowing and not caring what anybody thinks about what you believe or feel," she said. "That is what I wish for Gwyneth." True to her mother's wish, Gwyneth would grow into someone who wasn't crippled by criticism that became intense and unrelenting, but that apparent apathy would surface in personal relationships as well.

So began Gwyneth's uniquely Hollywood upbringing: carried around Los Angeles in the arms of her confident father, rolling onto movie sets to meet her mother and be cooed at by the cast and crew. Blythe and Bruce sought to achieve something rather elusive in Hollywood, where long hours and seething ambition regularly tore families apart: They wanted to create a protected and normal world for Gwyneth and, eventually, her younger brother, Jake. Only that was impossible when family togetherness required hopscotching around the country to movie sets.

By 1973, when Gwyneth was one, the family had moved to a New England–style white clapboard house in Brentwood that Bruce had found, which they filled with antiques. Bruce, however, remained restless. His friends said his work was motivated primarily by money, and Glaser wondered if Bruce was ever truly happy with his career. "I feel like, no, he wasn't. He had a beautiful wife, and he had the kids, and he had all the earmarks of success, but his favorite thing to do was to hang out with his buddies from college and drink."

Gwyneth would feel pulled between money and art in her career. Bruce provided a template for the former, while Blythe remained committed to the latter.

Blythe's passion drew her to one summer stock theater, where Gwyneth absorbed her mother's craft firsthand.

.   .   .

THE WILLIAMSTOWN THEATRE Festival started in 1954 as a way to make use of Williams College's main theater during the summer. When the students moved out, the warm weather and longer days brought in a raft of Hollywood stars like Christopher Reeve, Sigourney Weaver, Austin Pendleton, and Olympia Dukakis, all eager to escape the commercial pressures of New York and L.A. In this pocket of the Berkshires in the northwest corner of Massachusetts, they lived modestly and relatively anonymously. Between rehearsals, they could relax on the lawn under a tree's shade, knowing that locals wouldn't think twice about finding Superman himself in their midst, reading over a script. The actors created plays together under the mercurial direction of the Greek maestro Nikos Psacharopoulos, who said, in his accented English, "If I have to be a tyrant, I will be a tyrant." He was determined to keep show tickets affordable because he didn't want Williamstown to be "an elitist theater like Broadway."

But he did want celebrities, and he managed to convince them to come spend the summers with him. "He was a serious star fucker," said Deborah Lapidus, who worked on the productions in the eighties and went on to teach at Juilliard. The festival had always been considered a place you went to find stars, not make them.

Nearing his twentieth year as artistic director of the Williamstown Theatre Festival in 1974, Psacharopoulos had chosen to stage Chekhov's *The Seagull* and was in search of the perfect Nina, a notoriously difficult role. The final decision came down to Blythe and rising star Meryl Streep. His staff understood why he ultimately picked Blythe, whom they viewed as the best American actor onstage at that time.

While Blythe landed the role of Nina, she was terribly nervous about it. She and Bruce drove up to Williamstown for Blythe's first season at the festival, Gwyneth in her lap, beginning what became an annual tradition for the Paltrow-Danner family for roughly the next twenty years.

Blythe was early in her second pregnancy. Once settled in for the summer, she would carry Gwyneth or wheel her in a stroller around campus. Once again, everyone was drawn to this doll-like toddler with blond curls and chipmunk cheeks who had a funny first name, just like her mom. Even then the festival staff wondered if she was the next Blythe. Though not even two years old, Gwyneth was already a local celebrity. She was also a *sponge*. After sitting with her mother through hours of rehearsals, Gwyneth had somehow ingested Nina's lines. One hot, muggy day, the crew propped Blythe's little girl up on the stage naked, her blond curls flowing, and she lisped the lines: "Men and beasts. Lions, eagles, and partridges, antlered deer . . ." Gwyneth knew from around this age that she wanted to act. "My playground was the theater. I'd sit and watch my mother pretend for a living. As a young girl, that's pretty seductive," she said. "I always just knew that this was my thing."

Gwyneth would never have a formal acting education. But as far as many casting directors were concerned, her summers of theater immersion in Williamstown, among the best actors in the English-speaking world, were as good as a Juilliard degree. Starting at toddlerhood, Williamstown exposed Gwyneth to some of the best plays ever written, while acclimating her to the realm of Hollywood and celebrity. The people at Williamstown signaled to her that she was born for this— that she belonged in this world, among these stars, just like her mother.

Yet, as she watched her toddler, Blythe just thought, "Uh-oh, this is a bad sign."

GWYNETH'S EARLY EDUCATION in Santa Monica was, like her summers, unconventional. St. Augustine's was a small private kindergarten-through-sixth-grade Episcopal school that the church had opened in the mid-1900s, with fewer than two hundred students around the time private-school enrollment was exploding owing to some parents seeking to avoid a relatively new policy of busing children between districts in an attempt to desegregate them.

A *Vanity Fair* story published in 2000, not long after Gwyneth won her Oscar for *Shakespeare in Love*, reported that Gwyneth "learned to twist her body into a new shape with each bang of her 'movement' teacher's tambourine, but never did learn how to spell," though faculty from the time disagreed with her characterization of the school as academically unserious. The curriculum emphasized the arts and creativity. Students called teachers by their first names. Book reports might be performed as skits.

Gwyneth's drama teacher, Carol Rusoff, didn't force the students to memorize lines; she encouraged improvisation. Gwyneth was an eager student, often raising her hand when Rusoff asked who wanted to step up onto the small funky stage in the large all-purpose room underneath St. Augustine's church. Some students, Rusoff recalled, had "built-in shyness" or "things that restrained them from revealing themselves.

"Gwyneth didn't have anything that restrained her from revealing herself."

TOWARD THE END of 1977, midway through Gwyneth's first year at St. Augustine's, Blythe and Bruce moved the family to a place at the corner of Georgina Avenue and Twenty-First Street in Santa Monica. The 5,300-square-foot home was surrounded by a dense green privacy hedge, inside of which Gwyneth remembered "a pool and a garden and a guesthouse and a big old tree in the backyard with a tree house." Gwyneth and her best friend from school, Mary Wigmore, could walk out the front door and down Georgina Avenue to the Brentwood Country Mart shopping center consisting of red barnlike shops with white trim and a courtyard at the center, where local residents Mel Brooks or Anne Bancroft or William Hurt might be seen sitting at a table with a soda and a script. Gwyneth made the walk every weekend; the Country Mart was just the neighborhood candy store to her. Santa Monica wasn't as ritzy then as it would become (her childhood home sold for $11.85 million in 2021); in 1977 it still possessed the quiet, unpretentious atmosphere Blythe wanted for her children. Arnold Schwarzenegger bought a home down the block on Twenty-First Street in 1980, when Gwyneth was eight, and she'd sometimes see him jogging through the neighborhood in a red Speedo.

For Gwyneth and Wigmore, this grid of blocks south of San Vicente Boulevard was a sanctuary and a stomping ground. "I didn't fit in perfectly with other people; I didn't want to go to dancing school and wear the white gloves and all that. I was wanting to climb trees and be outside," Gwyneth said. She and Wigmore would throw stuffed animals into the chimney of the house next door, or ring a doorbell, then scamper off. Sometimes, with a larger group, they'd toilet-paper houses in the neighborhood. Schwarzenegger's place, a Spanish-style house in white stucco with a long lap pool in the back, was the ultimate prize.

Blythe did what she could to teach the kids about the larger world and the environment. She would bring them with her to the Santa Monica recycling center, where they'd sort cans. They had solar panels installed on the house. For a while, Gwyneth seemed to follow her lead. "In Los Angeles, Gwyneth used to hold up a sign at passing trucks from our car saying, 'You're polluting,'" Blythe remembered.

Around age seven, Gwyneth started asking to audition for roles. Though her parents decided when she was a baby not to interfere too much in her development (so long as she was, Blythe has said, "polite and well-behaved"), they drew the line at acting. "[T]hey said, 'No, you're a child and you have to have an education and we'll support you completely if that's your decision when you're 18, but for now you have to be a child,'" Gwyneth recalled.

In the fall of 1978, Blythe took Gwyneth to Beaufort, South Carolina, where she was filming *The Great Santini*. Gwyneth made a friend there, Hugh Patrick, with whom she'd pick pecans, play in a tree house, and run through the marshes. "Gwyneth was in a school with a majority of black children. She not only survived in this new situation, she swam along and had a fantastic experience," Blythe said. "I'm happy I haven't denied her that. Most of the kids she goes to school with in

Hollywood are self-complacent and indulged. I guess that goes against my Yankee blood. I think exposing them to new things can do nothing but help them grow."

On set, Blythe talked about Gwyneth all the time. When her kids were around, Blythe doted on them. When she was away from them, she seemed to feel guilty. One day Blythe had friends visit while she was filming. She introduced them to Lisa Jane Persky, who was playing one of her character's children. Persky's character was a tomboyish, sarcastic teenager. Blythe said to her friends, "She can't possibly be my daughter, can she?" Blythe seemed to view her real daughter as beautiful and perfect, an extension of herself and her good breeding—and Persky as something else.

Persky, in her early twenties and just starting her acting career, identified with her character's shortcomings and felt so shattered by this remark that she later cried. Though she got over it, it stayed with her. She saw how special Gwyneth was to Blythe, how advantageous it would be to have a mother with such pride and belief in her daughter. For actors, confidence is everything, the ultimate armor against relentless and often opaque rejection. For Gwyneth, it was a birthright.

CHAPTER 3

Curtain Call

There was a sense—and I don't think there was anything
malevolent about it—that where she wanted to be is where she
would end up.

—Bonnie Monte

Gwyneth spent most of her childhood in one rarefied atmosphere after another, surrounded by the beautiful, the fashionable, the creators, and the dealmakers, but Williamstown
was a particular pilgrimage. The family would spend around six weeks at
the festival each summer. Some summers while Blythe performed, Bruce
would travel back and forth to L.A. to work on the television series
he produced—*The White Shadow*, which ran for three seasons on CBS
beginning in 1978, and later *St. Elsewhere*. Bruce caught plays when he
was in town. When watching one he thought was bad, after a character
pulled a gun, Bruce called out, "Shoot him! Shoot someone! Shoot me!"

Blythe would bring Gwyneth and Jake to rehearsals, sometimes
with a babysitter, sometimes on their own, to sit in the wings and watch.
Other days they ran loose on the grounds of the Williams College
campus, abandoned for the season. Along with other top actors who
came back summer after summer, like Maria Tucci and Frank Langella,
Blythe was like royalty, and her status soon extended to Gwyneth.

In 1980, Blythe was starring in Chekhov's *The Cherry Orchard*, in a role Meryl Streep had played a few years earlier in New York. (During rehearsals, Blythe would say, "I can't do this. Meryl did it, Meryl's so good. I can't come up to that." By now the Williamstown crew was familiar with her anxiety and knew that, however fretful Blythe was in rehearsals, she would always be ready by curtain.) That summer, Gwyneth was asked to be in the play, along with Maria Tucci's daughter, Lizzie Gottlieb, in small parts that involved spinning around during a party scene. Psacharopoulos thought of the theater company as a family, and he liked to give parts to the children of his favorites, often without an audition.

The festival had an apprentice program whereby actors without family connections could work their way up to performing. Those who were accepted would pay for the privilege, including their board. In exchange, they got to take acting classes and practice scenes in the morning, then spend the afternoons building sets, hanging lights, sewing costumes, and posting flyers. When one of Gwyneth's peers, a young woman who did have family connections, decided to enter the apprentice program as a teenager, Gwyneth was mystified as to why she would choose to do that.

At the end of the season, the apprentices would put on a play, and the regular actors and stars would sit in the audience. Only a handful of, say, eighty apprentices were asked back the following summer to progress up the ranks to the Act 1 company, which would be followed, if they were lucky, by the nonunion company, and finally, the union company. In 2021, the *Los Angeles Times* published an investigation of the sixty-year-old apprentice program, saying it "expose[d] artists-in-training to repeated safety hazards and a toxic work culture under the guise of prestige." ("The safety and the emotional well-being of the entire WTF community is our top priority. And we take any claims to the contrary very seriously," Board Chair Jeffrey Johnson said in a 2021 statement.)

The nepotism undergirding the festival allowed Gwyneth to bypass all that. Instead, when she wasn't watching rehearsals or rehearsing, she would spend time with her friend Mary Wigmore, whom she would sometimes bring along for the summer, and who would come to occupy a uniquely secure position in Gwyneth's social circle. They'd take tennis lessons or have playdates or go swimming.

She also befriended Robert Nugent Jr., roughly three years older, the son of a Williams College custodian who worked at the festival. One summer, Psacharopoulos randomly asked Nugent if he wanted to be in a play. Nugent didn't think much of it. The famous actors at the festival were just people to him, not stars. Psacharopoulos cast Nugent in plays each summer for the next several years, eventually in small speaking parts alongside Gwyneth.

The two spent time together offstage as well. "As young kids, if you call it dating, we dated. So she must've been attracted to me and obviously vice versa, even though I was only nine, ten years old," Nugent said. While some actors stayed in dorms during the festival, the top actors like Blythe stayed in houses with their families. Nugent, who lived in town year-round, would go to see Gwyneth— a few times, the family stayed in one of the nicest houses in town, owned by doctors who were away for the summer—and she would direct him and Jake in plays she'd made up. But most of their time was spent wandering the festival grounds and exploring the woods. Though the theater had drawn them together, they never talked much about acting.

Nugent's circumstances were very different from Gwyneth's. "I was certainly poor," he said. "I had a rough upbringing, so maybe I was a lost soul for her." They talked a lot about his difficult home life. "It doesn't matter if you're affluent or not, you have moments where you feel the same . . . it transcends just your socioeconomic background. And they might not be exactly the same, but the raw emotion kind of is."

One summer day when she was around ten or eleven, Gwyneth turned to Nugent and said, "Will you marry me?" She made them fake rings and, with Jake as a witness, they held a ceremony.

Gwyneth's first "marriage" ended that August. She returned to

New York, where the family had moved by that time, and after a few blissful summers together, she and Nugent fell out of touch.

BLYTHE OFTEN TOOK Gwyneth to see the various festival productions. Most kids didn't understand how to process plays and might have found them loud or boring. But Gwyneth got to see them through her mother's eyes, with Blythe gesturing at the stage and whispering, "Watch that guy" or "Look what's happening on the left."

In a 1994 interview, Gwyneth said, "A lot of times when I read something, I know how she [Blythe] would sound doing it. It's the first thing that comes off the page . . . I can just hear her inflection. Her voice. How she would say it."

The year after *The Cherry Orchard*, Blythe was set to star in *The Greeks*, a compilation of ancient Greek dramas. On the first day of rehearsal, Blythe arrived with Bruce and the kids to the large black-box theater on campus—a big empty room with no stage and little more in it than actors and folding chairs. "Baby Blythe," as Psacharopoulos called her, was late. But he stopped the rehearsal to welcome her. Gwyneth ran right up and gave him a big, warm hug.

Gwyneth then dropped down into the folding chair next to the green director's chair that bore Psacharopoulos's initials. This seat happened to belong to his assistant, Bonnie Monte, who had been standing when they arrived. Monte was earning fifty dollars per week for what she estimated to be 110 hours of work. (He later raised it to seventy-five when she told him she couldn't live on so little.)

"Do you want to sit there?" he asked Gwyneth.

"Yes," she announced.

Psacharopoulos asked Monte to go sit in the back of the room.

Looking back on it, Monte said, "She sat there for the very first rehearsal and kind of took her rightful place as the young princess in the room. And I remember thinking, *Well, that's my chair. Why are you sitting there?* There was a sense—and I don't think there was anything malevolent about it—that where she wanted to be is where she would end up."

PSACHAROPOULOS NEEDED KIDS for *The Greeks*, which had a cast of sixty. The production included seven plays by Euripides, along with one each by Sophocles and Aeschylus, plus the story of Achilles from *The Iliad*. In its London run, the play went for nine hours over three nights. For Williamstown, Psacharopoulos cut it down to six hours over two. The actors had three weeks to rehearse. At eight years old, Gwyneth was cast as young Orestes and Polydorus. *The Greeks* was a grueling production for a summer theater festival, and Psacharopoulos needed his actors to be as committed as the army of apprentices supporting the show. He had no problem firing the children of famous actors if they got lazy or distracted.

When powerful actors like Maria Tucci unleashed onstage, the crew worried that some of the kids would get scared, but Gwyneth didn't flinch. While her parts were small, the material wasn't exactly light. As Polydorus, she played a boy who was murdered in front of his mother, Hecuba. Psacharopoulos wanted Gwyneth to convey stoicism, to face death calmly while other characters lost their minds around her. She could handle it, but she was still a young kid, and Psacharopoulos and his staff had to remind her, "Don't scratch your nose when you're dead."

During breaks in the performances, the kids would gather in a room to color and play. But Gwyneth was often just offstage, watching the show.

THE FESTIVAL WAS a protective environment, and Blythe let her daughter roam freely. Gwyneth popped into rehearsals for the Cabaret, a musical revue including skits that took place at different restaurants in town. Cabarets were the most exhilarating part of the festival for the kids, who got to stay up late and—if they were lucky—perform themselves.

Starting at eleven thirty p.m., Cabarets were casual, though performers were cast and rehearsals were held. The venues were always packed. One night when Gwyneth was a tween, she was chosen to perform on the Cabaret stage at the '6 House Pub in town alongside her mother. Together, they grabbed the mics and took their spot in front of a curtain in the cleared-out area of the restaurant that served as a stage, while spectators watched from tables in front. Gwyneth and Blythe sang "Anything You Can Do (I Can Do Better)" to live musical accompaniment, alternating verses. The crowd was impressed; Gwyneth had enough stage presence to hold attention alongside her Tony-winning mother.

"I'm sitting there watching it," recalled Robert Nugent Jr. "I was thirteen, and I'm like, *Yeah, the irony of those two singing together, that song.* I mean, everybody got it."

Blythe would later remember Gwyneth performing that same number in New York at a Williamstown Theatre Festival Gala, an annual re-creation of the summer Cabarets, alongside child actor Christian Slater, to "thunderous applause."

"I saw her eyes look to the left and right, and I said to Bruce, 'She's got it. She knows.'"

CHAPTER 4

Spence and Sensibility

Not one person had a doubt that she was going to be famous.

—Former Spence classmate

When Gwyneth was around ten years old, Blythe was filming a television movie in London. The whole family joined her. Bruce decided to take Gwyneth to Paris for a father-daughter weekend. They stayed in a beautiful hotel, where he let her order french fries and a Coke for breakfast. They visited sites like the Centre Pompidou and the Louvre. On the way back, Bruce said to Gwyneth, "Do you know why I took you, and it was a special trip for you and I?" Gwyneth said no. He said, "I wanted you to see Paris for the first time with a man who will always love you, no matter what." This story would make Gwyneth emotional when she told it many years later—a testament to the love between father and daughter. But it also perhaps showed young Gwyneth that a grand gesture could be a substitute for real connection. By the time she became a public figure, Bruce's college friend Paul Glaser recognized the same emotional distance in her that he had seen in her father.

•   •   •

BRUCE'S BIGGEST HIT, *St. Elsewhere*, a television drama about doctors teaching interns at a run-down Boston hospital, premiered October 1982. As the show took off, Blythe decided that her kids needed the kind of education that she felt they could get only on the East Coast, and the family moved to New York City. Bruce commuted to Los Angeles when necessary during the week to work on the show.

In the fall of 1984, after passing a required entrance exam, Gwyneth arrived at Spence, a small private all-girls school on Manhattan's Upper East Side, at East Ninety-First Street between Fifth and Madison Avenues. Wealthy, high-strung parents stressed over getting their kids into Spence for kindergarten, believing it a pathway to Ivy League college admission. But Spence was more than an Ivy League funnel. An old saying of these private schools went, "Chapin girls date doctors and lawyers, Spence girls marry doctors and lawyers, and Brearley girls become doctors and lawyers." Spence was, one Brearley student said, "like the thoroughbred horse of girls' schools."

The school tucked itself into a narrow ten-story building and an adjacent squat one with playgrounds on the roofs. Between classes, all the girls converged in orderly chaos on the central staircase to get to their next period, some in leotards for dance class, others in the mandatory uniform, a white top with sleeves and a gray skirt or gray pants.

Gwyneth arrived at Spence at the beginning of seventh grade, a skinny eleven-year-old with braces. She had a short "bad haircut," which she later talked up in interviews. Boys from other schools started calling her "E.T.," because they said her eyes were far apart. Yet Gwyneth was always considered very pretty. Her classmates couldn't understand her name, and someone started calling her "Gwen." Over the years, she would appear in yearbooks as Gwyn, Gwen, Gwyneth, and Gwynnie.

Many of the roughly fifty girls in her class had been there since kindergarten, and cliques were well established. On her first day, Gwyneth wore penny loafers, a blue-and-white-striped Breton shirt, and a white skirt, but the preppy look flopped (the uniform wasn't required the first day of school). After school, she went home and changed into pink parachute Guess pants and a coordinating pink top and went back to the playground. "The girls who were not really into me in the preppy look were now so into me when I was in the pink Guess outfit. This one girl was like, 'You're totally going to be in our group' because they were the cool girls," she said. Gwyneth asked if any other girls had made the cut to join the cool group. "Well, maybe this one from this morning who had that striped shirt on."

Gwyneth's arrival unsettled the social dynamic in her grade, though the precise origin of the chaos spawned by her arrival was difficult to pinpoint. She had strangely potent charisma, and other Spence girls—even seniors—wanted to invest in knowing this new middle schooler. "She established herself as an interesting person—someone people wanted to hang out with," recalled the head of the middle school at the time, Kate Turley. "It was easy for her to make her way." But other students seemed to feel threatened. One classmate recalled, "Not one person had a doubt that she was going to be famous." After all, she might spend a weekend with someone like Steven Spielberg. But she was also polarizing.

Alison Cayne, whose father ran Bear Stearns and who lived on Park Avenue, was one of the Spence cool girls. "There are A girls and B girls, and A girls are popular," Cayne declared. At first she and Gwyneth were best friends. But they were both alphas and eventually became archrivals, creating a toxicity that affected the rest of the class. Gwyneth could be cruel—like when she wrote down a list of names of classmates she hated—but a lot of students could be savage. The difference with Gwyneth was that she was more clever and remarkably adept at reading people—she knew what would hurt other girls, and deployed much more devastating comebacks.

By eighth grade, the dynamic settled, and Gwyneth eased into the background somewhat. She and her friends would go to a nearby deli for lunch, then come back and happily sit on the floor, skirts splayed out around them. She found her crew with whom she would remain friends long after graduation, among them Julia Cuddihy, Betsey Kittenplan, Hilary Weekes, and Caroline Doyle.

In L.A., Gwyneth had a familiar pedigree and a sense of the culture; at Spence, where there weren't many Hollywood families, she was more conspicuous. Her parents had a five-story brownstone on East Ninety-Second Street between Fifth and Madison Avenues, steps from Central Park. They kept the Santa Monica home so Bruce could go back and forth to work on *St. Elsewhere*. But the girls at Spence didn't just have brownstone money—their parents worked on Wall Street or in corporate law and appeared in the business pages of *The Wall Street Journal* and *The New York Times*. They lived in apartments overlooking Central Park or Park Avenue with a Picasso or a Miró on the dining room wall. They were ferried by limousines to weekend homes in the Hamptons. They came from old-money families with last names like Astor and Vanderbilt. When they went to summer camp, they brought Evian water to spritz on their faces. Students who didn't come from that exclusive world of the five-block radius around the school said they felt like they were different—even Gwyneth. Within the walls of Spence, though, discretion was a practiced art. Gwyneth's peers knew her parents were famous but didn't make a thing of it. Mick Jagger's daughter Jade passed through during Gwyneth's early years, along with Princesses Alexandra and Olga of Greece—their last name just "of Greece."

When Gwyneth crossed lines or hurt feelings, her feigned obliviousness could be more alienating than the transgression itself. One day in the locker room, Gwyneth was changing into her green bathing suit—a uniform her teammates dreaded wearing—for swim practice. Gwyneth had always been naturally skinny, and possessed disdain for fat people that was apparent to her fellow students. She turned to the girl next to her, a classmate who was not as thin or nearly as confident, and said, "Isn't it interesting how different people's bodies are?" That girl's reaction was one of shame and embarrassment as she stood next to willowy Gwyneth. Years later, when she saw Gwyneth making similarly oblivious comments publicly, she thought back to that moment.

Whatever Gwyneth's motivation for the remark, she didn't seem to care that her words might have come across as hurtful, and to this student, that almost made it worse.

THAT INITIAL YEAR at Spence, Gwyneth smoked her first cigarette. Students would sneak past the two older ladies who guarded the front door, around the corner to a place known to private-school kids in the neighborhood as the Stoop, where they'd smoke and meet up with boys. The Stoop belonged to the building on Ninetieth Street between Fifth and Madison Avenues that happened to be the home of Robert Chambers (who became known as the "Preppy Killer" after he was charged with strangling eighteen-year-old Jennifer Levin to death in Central Park in 1986; he pleaded guilty to first-degree manslaughter).

"I was immediately drawn to [smoking]—probably because my dad smoked around my mom when she was pregnant with me and when I was little, and it just gets in there, I guess," Gwyneth said. When she wasn't smoking on the Stoop, she'd smoke at the pizza parlor on Madison and Ninety-First Street. After Bruce found out that was her spot, he would sometimes stop by to see if she was smoking. Desperate to get her to quit, he asked his friend Leo Penn, who directed episodes of *St. Elsewhere*, for help. Could he possibly get his son Sean's new wife, Madonna, to write a note to Gwyneth to discourage her from smoking?

"Dear Gwyneth, Just to jot down my average day . . . I wake up, I don't smoke . . ." the note said. "And I go home a happy healthy me. Love, Me, Madonna. P.S.: Good girls live longer." Gwyneth brought the letter to school, where a teacher gave her the floor to share it during class, then framed it to display on the mantel in her bedroom. But she continued to smoke. "I smoked a pack a day probably until I was 25 years old," she said. "Like wake up and light a cigarette, I really was into it—I loved it."

Gwyneth maintained an attitude of invincibility and not giving a damn, both at school and at home. Students weren't supposed to chew gum, but Gwyneth did anyway. In a famous photo from her senior yearbook, she's grinning and blowing a bubble, a charming fuck-you to the Spence establishment.

With exceptions including Fridays and the first day of school, Spence girls had to wear their uniform. All the girls hiked up their skirts, but only Gwyneth would show up wearing cowboy boots or sneakers and a leather jacket. She'd wear a white top with embroidery or an off-the-shoulder neckline instead of a plain blouse. She'd get into one look, wear it till she tired of it, then show up with some new twist on the uniform.

Gwyneth credited her school uniform with later informing her famously minimalist, casual idea of glamour. "I realized it's one of the things that influenced my style because you'd have to wear this very posh, clean outfit every day—your white shirt and little gray kilt, and put it with too much black eyeliner or whatever. It's a great look," she later told *Vogue*, after the magazine had christened her a "fashion icon."

By high school, Gwyneth had grown her hair long, lost the braces, and blossomed into someone even more gorgeous. "Suddenly, I was, like, a babe," she said. She was popular and cool, and some students, privileged though they were, showed their jealousy. "I never wished I had another girl's life," Gwyneth said. "The other [Spence] girls were mean to me at points. It was like, 'Wow, she has too much.'"

In ninth grade, biology teacher and head of the upper school James Dawson became Gwyneth's adviser. The two had a unique connection: she seemed to trust him, and he wanted to protect her, particularly since her parents were so famous.

Spence was a demanding college preparatory school, and most students took the academics seriously. Gwyneth had arrived unprepared. "She hadn't been trained to study. And Spence was a rigorous, no-nonsense academic institution," said Edes Gilbert, the head of the school during Gwyneth's time there. A former classmate recalled not wanting to miss a single day, even if she was sick, for fear she would fall behind. "The girls there were so advanced," Gwyneth said. "You cannot believe the classes—law and physics in the seventh grade! I was at sea. I mean, I would have had an easier time trying to translate Hebrew. I'm not kidding. It was hard." But by all accounts, the struggle didn't shake her confidence.

She made it clear to her teachers when she was disinterested in a class. She could look obviously bored in math. Shakespeare got more of her attention. The course involved reading just a couple of scenes each night, and Gwyneth and her class would discuss them in great detail the next day with their instructor, Patricia Ranard. Her peers didn't seem to think she was studying that hard, but she would complete the reading and say something astute about it during class. Two former faculty members remembered her as either a C-plus or B student. Some teachers remembered her as not particularly intelligent, while others thought she was smart, just disinterested in the obligation of attending school. She projected such an air of confidence that getting low grades seemed somehow like a choice—and maybe it was. Why work at school when her Hollywood-inflected life was so exciting? Her close friends believed she was smart, but that school wasn't for her. If she encountered a challenge or a bit of friction, Gwyneth could fall back on her belief that her fate was sealed, and whatever motions her classmates had to go through to achieve success, she could skip. As her parents and their world had always taught her, she was just that special.

WHILE GWYNETH WAS at Spence, Bruce called home from L.A. often to talk to Gwyneth and Jake. Mark Tinker, an executive producer on *St. Elsewhere*, remembered how Bruce spoke about his daughter. "She walked on water. Bruce would say these things about her that were so glowing. You would think she was the female version of Jesus Christ."

Bruce was intense, commanding, and charismatic. People bought what he was selling, or else they got out of the way. "He's such an entertaining guy. His enthusiasm's totally infectious, and you just couldn't help but get on board with him," said Tinker. In those days, Bruce seemed driven mostly by a desire for financial security and comfort for his family.

"Bruce loved a fight," said Channing Gibson, who worked his way up from story editor to producer on *St. Elsewhere*. "He had a healthy ego, and he was fearless. He was not afraid of anybody or any institution. He believed in what he believed in, in terms of art and in terms of a business, and he wasn't going to let anybody"—particularly network executives who gave him notes—"shove him around." He was never deliberately insulting, but he wasn't careful with his words, either. He trusted his own judgment so deeply, he sometimes lost sight of his effect on other people.

On *The White Shadow*, a second assistant cameraman came to him looking for a promotion. Bruce respected his work, but didn't like his teeth. "Listen, I can't look at you if you're going to be an operator," he said. "Get your teeth fixed and we will work you up to camera operator." Bruce helped pay for the dental work, and the guy became a camera operator.

Bruce had a way of creating his own reality. He liked to ski in Aspen with his family and his buddies during the winter, and, unsatisfied with the dining options, convinced Gordon Naccarato, a chef at Michael's in Los Angeles, to move there and open a restaurant, writing him a $125,000 check. When he was out for dinner and ordered a dish he didn't like, Bruce would call the server over and ask, "How can we make this better?" In New York, he frequented the Quilted Giraffe restaurant, and became friends with the owner, Barry Wine, who would send a complimentary bottle of Dom Pérignon to his table whenever he showed up. He liked oysters and Stoli vodka, French Burgundies and Bordeaux. Where Blythe was careful about her diet, Bruce was indulgent.

The same was true of his personal effects. His briefcase was Bottega Veneta, his stationery was Tiffany. He loved the luxury brands Asprey and Zegna. His socks were cashmere. He dressed in soft colors and soft fabrics, and clothes hung beautifully on him. In Los Angeles, he drove a black Mercedes with tan interior that he had bought one summer in Europe and decided to import, even though few gas stations pumped the leaded fuel it required. "It was a little like Bruce," said Tinker, "with classic lines and a bit elegant, but with some attitude."

As parents, too, Bruce was the indulger, Blythe the moderating influence. He showed Gwyneth and Jake a world that would bend to your will if you knew how to ask, whereas Blythe was attuned to fragility, mortality, and the importance of manners. When Bruce flew with the kids, he booked first-class seats. He would joke that Gwyneth didn't know how to turn right on an airplane (toward the coach seats). Blythe tended to book coach. "You mean—we're not flying first-class?" Gwyneth would protest. "We're flying *no* class?"

Gwyneth would mimic Bruce in so many ways—her taste in high-end clothing and food, her assertiveness, and, ultimately, her apparent pursuit of money over art. Quite unlike her mother, who was content to do summer stock theater year after year purely for artistic fulfillment.

CHAPTER 5

Acting Up

She's not trying to be a standout, she just is.

—Edes Gilbert

When Gwyneth was younger, when any of her parents' friends asked if she wanted to grow up to be an actress, she'd said no. But not anymore. At a reception at Bruce and Blythe's house following Nikos Psacharopoulos's memorial service, Ed Herrmann asked her, "Do you want to be an actress like your mom when you grow up?"

Gwyneth replied, "No. I want to be a movie star like Meryl Streep."

By that time, she had been back in New York only a few months following her tenth-grade spring abroad in Spain. Spence didn't run study abroad programs but gave the small number of students who participated in them credit. Gwyneth had stayed on an estate near Talavera de la Reina an hour from Toledo as part of a cultural exchange with the twin daughters of her host mother, Julia Ruiz, who owned a gas station with her husband. Gwyneth became so close with the family that she stayed in touch with them for decades, referring to them as her Spanish parents and siblings. In addition to savoring Ruiz's *morcilla* (she didn't know at first it was pig's blood sausage), she learned to speak Spanish perfectly. She also adapted very well to the late nights. Back home, she entered her rebellious phase and sneaked out of her town house at night to go to bars. Her bedroom was on the fifth floor, her parents' on the fourth. As she made her way out, she'd jangle the collars of their two golden retrievers so that if her mom woke up and heard the stairs creak, she would think it was the dogs. Or, if she was feeling particularly brazen, she'd leave a note on her pillow: "I snuck out. I'm at Dorrian's [an Upper East Side bar]. You can punish me in the morning." Often she would go with four friends from Spence who called themselves "the Posse."

There were also parties in hotel rooms and parties that Gwyneth would throw when her parents were away. Spence's start time was 8:15 a.m. Sometimes the day began with assembly, sometimes with advisory, and Gwyneth didn't always make it. "Gwyneth would just decide what she could miss," said Edes Gilbert, Spence's headmaster. She started showing up late to school so often—more than any other student—that adviser James Dawson was calling her house regularly to get her to show up. Once, he called the house, where Gwyneth was often alone given her parents' busy schedules, and she answered.

"Hello?"

"Gwyneth," he said.

"Yes?"

"Dr. Dawson."

"Oh no, it's Blythe."

Dawson wasn't that easily outwitted.

"You're not Blythe. Get to school," he said.

Other times when he would call, she'd try other outlandish responses, like, "Is today Tuesday?" She gave her parents, who might have been easier to fool, similarly fantastical excuses. Dawson sometimes called Bruce and Blythe, and they'd say, "Oh, she told us this class didn't start until ten."

But there was something about Gwyneth—he was never too mad at her. She was almost a relief in the stuffy institution of Spence.

Around this time she began discovering her sexuality, which wasn't something she could discuss with her mother. Gwyneth was well aware of Blythe's WASPy reserve. "She's just traditional," said Gwyneth. "We didn't talk about stuff like that."

When Gwyneth was in tenth grade, she went to Florida to visit Blythe on the set of *Judgment*, a television movie she was filming. Sheryl Berkoff was the makeup artist for the production. Gwyneth already thought Berkoff was cool for dating her celebrity crush, Keanu Reeves. She became even cooler in Gwyneth's eyes when she joined her to smoke behind a trailer, where Berkoff, Gwyneth recalled, gave her "blowjob lessons."

"I'm sure that I implemented it in the first chance I got," Gwyneth later said. "It was so cool to have someone treat me like an adult and see me as, like, a young woman and someone who was sexual."

Though she had her mom's WASPy look, Gwyneth had acquired her dad's bawdy sensibility. One day, Spence's rather humorless librarian approached Dawson outraged that a student had drawn, on the partition of a study cubicle, an erect penis. She sent all four girls—Gwyneth among them—who had been in the library at the time to Dawson.

Dawson made an ominous threat: "All right, folks, this is completely uncalled for and obnoxious, so I'm going to suspend you all and put it on your college record."

"I didn't do it," said one girl, who left. The second girl said she didn't have anything to do with it either. Down to the third girl and Gwyneth, Dawson doubled down on his ultimatum, prompting the other girl to insist she wasn't responsible and leave. Dawson now faced just Gwyneth.

"Gwyneth, you drew the erect penis in the library," he said.

"I'm not really sure what you're talking about," she said.

He presented a picture the library had given him of the masterpiece.

"Oh, that penis," Gwyneth said. "I wasn't sure what we were talking about."

Dawson pointed out that the other students had had to suffer through the confrontation with her.

"Come on, where's your sense of humor?"

He often found her amusing, but replied, "In the library, are you kidding me?" Gwyneth became annoyed when she had to clean it up.

DURING HER TEENAGE years, Gwyneth dated a lot, a friend recalled, and talked openly about sex. She fell for a gorgeous six-foot-three blond surfer who lived in California and said, "How's it goin'?" enough to turn Bruce against him, which perhaps worked in his favor with Gwyneth. But when he cheated on her, she moved on. At one point, she dated her cousin's college friend. She later admitted, "I kissed somebody's boyfriend when I was 15."

By all accounts, the Danner-Paltrow household was centered around Gwyneth in these years. Bonnie Monte, who worked for Blythe during a period, remarked, "She was a handful. She was beginning to be very much her own boss, and the household, to some extent, revolved around her."

One of Gwyneth's friends from the time remembered Bruce being home more than Blythe, who would leave for stretches to film movies or TV shows. Gwyneth behaved like an adult in her mother's absence—she made restaurant reservations at the Italian restaurant Elio's; her dad once gave her lace underwear as a gift—and seemed annoyed when Blythe returned, as though giving up a wifelike role in the household. (In a joint interview many years later, Bruce remembered taking Gwyneth to dinner at Elio's, where other patrons seemed to think they were dating: "The women were staring daggers at me at the tables and the guys are going, 'Way to go.'")

Gwyneth, however, didn't see the household as revolving around her—certainly not in the way hers did when she had kids. She found traveling with her mother during shoots "destabilizing." She said, "I think there were also really high standards prescribed to me in my house. I don't even know if my parents were conscious they were doing it, but I always felt like I had to prove on some level that I was worth something, that I was lovable. And not only from my parents, but I think just from the culture that I was growing up in."

Blythe could be almost checked out from Gwyneth's antics. Not knowing what to do with her, she'd sometimes just send her back to Dawson for another talk. Bruce, however, made his high expectations of Gwyneth known and his disappointment in her apparent, which seemed to acutely affect her. When she ended up in his office again and again, Dawson—who became something of a father figure to her—would say, "Stop doing this, your father's going to get annoyed."

Sometime in her junior year, to discipline her for all the tardies, Gwyneth was placed on in-house suspension, which involved sitting alone in the library during lunch.

One afternoon during that period, Gilbert, a warm but no-nonsense woman with short hair who favored smart jackets and large pearl earrings, was sitting in a leather chair at the desk in her office when the phone rang.

"Mrs. Gilbert, did you order a pizza?" the school receptionist asked. She had not. "Well, the delivery guy is here, and he says he has a pizza."

"Are you sure it's for me?"

The receptionist paused to check. "Oh, no—it's for Gwyneth Paltrow."

Gilbert went downstairs to pick up the order and tip the delivery-man. She brought the pizza back up to the library on the fourth floor.

"You know, Gwyneth," Gilbert said, "you're on in-house suspension."

Gwyneth looked up at her with the same memorable smile that had charmed Gilbert many times before, and said, "Well, I was hungry."

"Somebody in the kitchen was going to bring you your lunch."

"But I was hungry, and I just thought a pizza would be good."

Gilbert didn't lecture Gwyneth—which Gilbert recalled Gwyneth later thanking her for—she just said, "You know what? The pizza will be very much appreciated by the people in the kitchen."

"That does not mean she was a bad person," Gilbert said, looking back on it. "But she was always very creative about meeting her own needs."

• • •

LIKE DAWSON, GILBERT found it hard to be too angry with Gwyneth, who was completely comfortable with adults, including her teachers: "There was just something about her. She had a little extra personality, an extra ingredient. She's not trying to be a standout, she just is."

Acting opportunities started coming Gwyneth's way during her Spence years. When she was seventeen, in a coffee shop on East Ninety-First Street and Madison Avenue, a casting scout approached her and asked if she wanted to audition for a film called *Reversal of Fortune*, starring Jeremy Irons. Gwyneth agreed but didn't tell her parents. The casting team saw her name and figured out who she was and called her mother's agent, which didn't thrill Blythe. Gwyneth got a callback but didn't get the part.

STARTING IN THE ninth grade, students could join Spence's a cappella group, Triple Trio, consisting of three altos, three sopranos, and three melodies. Everyone wanted to be in it—it was sort of Spence's equivalent of being on the cheer squad—but only nine girls could join. The group was run by seniors, and ninth-grade Gwyneth, who had a beautiful singing voice, made it in, along with Alison Cayne, her nemesis, and Julia Cuddihy, a close friend. Victoria Strouse, whose father, Charles, had written the music for *Annie*, also made it in. She and Gwyneth used to bicker over whose parents were more famous.

Though she wasn't known as a drama nerd, Gwyneth was cast in several Spence plays. During rehearsals, she would often sneak out for a cigarette, and classmates would be dispatched by the director to go find her. According to Gilbert, she declined lead roles because she was already performing in Williamstown and wanted to let her classmates have a turn. Drama teacher Jennifer Fell Hayes, who directed Gwyneth in at least two student productions, didn't remember such a gracious motivation.

Spence put on a Shakespeare production every year. In later interviews, Gwyneth would recall playing Titania in *A Midsummer Night's Dream* (actress Kerry Washington played one of the fairies). But according to Fell Hayes (and an original printed program), she played Hippolyta—a smaller role. "She would've been a natural Titania," Fell Hayes said, but "she was a teenager, and some teenagers can get a bit flaky, and I was concerned that she wouldn't be there to rehearse enough. Or wouldn't learn the lines in time because she was distracted with boys." Even so, "You could see she was very talented . . . charismatic, had a presence, spoke beautifully, and was very beautiful. And all those things came out when she was performing."

By her senior year, Gwyneth often went to rehearsals in her leather jacket, or in faded, ill-fitting black leggings and a matching turtleneck—the kind of clothes no one really wore at the time. Students from neighboring private schools appeared in Spence plays, and Jessica Leader, who attended Brearley and played an attendant, remembered Gwyneth standing out to them the same way she had when she first moved to New York and everyone wanted to invest in getting to know her. A friend told Leader, "She looks more beautiful in those worn-out clothes than I'm probably going to look on my wedding day."

"Everybody from the lowliest spear-carrier to the few boys to the upperclassmen were all simultaneously terrified of her and in awe of her and wanted to be with her," Leader said.

The play ran a handful of times. One night, before act four, Gwyneth looked tearful, with a makeshift bandage on her hand. She had decided to go home during acts two and three where she was smoking out the window when it fell closed onto her fingers.

Gwyneth's peers thought of her as having a charmed life, someone who would succeed effortlessly no matter what she tried. Spence required students to complete a senior project, and Gwyneth's was recording a cover of a Bonnie Raitt song with Donald Fagen, the lead singer of the band Steely Dan. But she was hardly the only Spence student to have unique access. Other girls interviewed high-ranking government or U.N. officials. Princess Olga came back from Easter break saying she had had a great conversation with her aunt Elizabeth—the Queen of England.

When Gwyneth floated out of Spence and right into a speaking part in a Steven Spielberg movie, classmates thought, *Of course she did.* When she had to learn a British accent for a film and executed it flawlessly, they thought, *Of course she did.* When she won her Oscar, again they thought, *Well, it's Gwyneth—of course she did.*

THE SPRING OF 1990, Debra Michals from *Harper's Bazaar* called the Paltrow-Danner house in New York to interview Blythe and Gwyneth for a story called "Beauty Heritage," about how six famous women's daughters had "not only inherited their mothers' great looks, but also their approach to staying beautiful." Michals talked to Blythe; when it was Gwyneth's turn, Michals heard her race upstairs to take the call in her bedroom. Blythe waited on the other end until, in the background, Michals heard teen Gwyneth yelling to her famous mother, "Mom, get off the phone!" Gwyneth made sure to spell her name for Michals; people were always getting it wrong, she said. The write-up was short, and Michals didn't end up quoting Gwyneth, who'd been excited to be interviewed. Mother and daughter wore brown Ralph Lauren outfits with near-identical cashmere turtlenecks. Gwyneth's arms were wrapped around her mother, and she smiled so widely that her eyes nearly closed. Michals wrote, "Where mother is traditional, daughter is trendy; where mother is a bit reserved, daughter is fearless. They can talk endlessly about what sets them apart. But underneath all the words about mother's conservative values and daughter's fierce independence there is an unspoken symmetry, with each not only respecting but also relying on the other's strengths."

What the article missed, and what those who knew her witnessed, was that Gwyneth was a daddy's girl, determined to avoid relying on her mother for anything.

. . .

DURING GWYNETH'S SENIOR year, Bruce and Blythe met several times with Edes Gilbert about their daughter's academic performance. "We have to get her through high school," Bruce said, "because we know she is not going to college. We'll try, but we don't think she's going to."

Gilbert and her colleagues just assumed Gwyneth would end up with a career like Blythe's, but both she and Bruce had finished college, and they wanted the same for their oldest child, even if she insisted on acting after that. Gwyneth told friends that Dawson, her adviser, had agreed to pass her in a class in which she was struggling so she could graduate. That said, Dawson felt particularly protective of her, and it would have been highly unusual for Spence not to let someone graduate.

"You're going to win the Academy Award," Dawson told her.

"I'm going to thank you when it happens," she said. (She didn't.)

While her friends received college acceptance letters, Gwyneth was getting rejections. This stung, so she lashed out. When a friend got into Barnard, Gwyneth—who would feel inadequate in the face of her friends' college degrees throughout her life—hurt her by saying, "That's a backdoor way to a second-rate Ivy."

When Gwyneth got rejected from Vassar (Meryl Streep's alma mater, considered a midrange school for Spence graduates), her parents decided to call in a favor. Their friend, actor Michael Douglas, put in a word at his alma mater, the University of California, Santa Barbara, and Gwyneth was admitted for a January 1991 start.

Before she finished high school, Bruce relented and cast her in a pilot he was producing. She was going to act whether they wanted her to or not.

CHAPTER 6

Major: Hollywood

I was looking at her in the rearview mirror, and she was talking about the film [*The Silence of the Lambs*] and she had this really frightened look on her face, and it suddenly clicked . . . So, I turned around and said, "Do you want to make a movie?"

—Steven Spielberg

John Tinker joined Bruce again for the teen sitcom *High*, which was filming in nearby New Jersey. He had a theory about why her parents finally agreed to let her act in it. "Gwyneth has a mind of her own, always did," he said. "And I think Bruce felt, 'All right, she's going to get out of the barn one way or the other, so I might as well open this door and try and help guide her.' Lord knows he's got incredible respect for Blythe, and I think he felt it was in the genes and it was inevitable."

So by May 1990, a few weeks before Gwyneth's graduation from Spence, she was testing her range playing a popular high school cheerleader and homecoming queen, one of *High*'s lead roles. The show was like a black-comedy version of *Beverly Hills, 90210*, which would premiere that fall. In the pilot, Gwyneth's character dates a jock, played by Tyagi Schwartz, who's recovering from a surgery to correct, at long last, the effects of a botched circumcision. Because of the stitches, he must avoid erections at all costs. In one ambitious gag, Gwyneth and

Schwartz climb into what he remembered as a two-person donkey suit (Zach Braff, who was also in the cast, remembered it as an alligator suit) to masquerade as the school's mascot at a basketball game. Running out onto the court, Gwyneth is in the front of the suit and Schwartz in the rear, his face against her backside—an arrangement that endangers his stitches. He panics, breaks out of the suit, and dashes to the bathroom.

As Schwartz remembered it, Bruce didn't think much of the director and was unhappy with how he handled that scene. So Bruce fired him and took over directing himself. At that point, Schwartz said, Gwyneth thought Bruce was still hoping she'd give up on acting; but he clearly wasn't fighting it that hard. Another member of the cast overheard seventeen-year-old Gwyneth talking about her true ambition at the time: "I really wanted to go into modeling. But my father said not to, because if I become a very famous actress, then I can do modeling and photo shoots along with acting. So that's what I'm going to do."

The *High* cast and crew watched a screening of the pilot together, and Gwyneth told Schwartz, "This is a guarantee." But the network passed.

Gwyneth graduated that June, and in her senior yearbook, she borrowed her parting words to the class of 1990 from the 1989 movie *Bill & Ted's Excellent Adventure*: "Be excellent to each other and party on, dudes." The yearbook editors listed Cheech Marin of Cheech & Chong as her "Counterpart." (Her "Food Counterpart" was iced coffee.) Other students' "Dream[s]" included things like "Work at the U.N.," "*The New Yorker*," "Prince Charming," and "Debating on *Nightline*," while the yearbook editors decided Gwyneth's was "Loyalty." In the "Nightmare" column, other students got things like "A limit on her credit card," "Westchester," "Breaking a nail," and "AP Spanish Lang." Gwyneth's was "Obesity."

PEOPLE WHO WORKED with Gwyneth in those early years, or who saw her audition, were divided on the question of nepotism, of how much her parents' connections sped her rise from high school thespian to Oscar winner. Most of them, though, remember something exceptional if hard to define about her—radiance, precocious talent, natural poise, supernatural confidence. However, Gwyneth's famous parents helped her considerably. In addition to their connections, her childhood exposure to their world was a singular privilege. The entertainment business didn't faze or wow her, and she knew how productions worked, which was appealing to veterans of the business who'd later hire her.

Kevin Kelley directed her in Williamstown that summer, a few weeks after her high school graduation, in an adaptation of *The Adventures of Huckleberry Finn*, starring Chad Lowe in the title role. Her part was small, but Kelley saw "star quality," someone who could "attract your attention and hold it. Some people are just born with that quality. It's inevitable. I don't think you can fake it."

Bruce and Blythe were there that summer, too. Still ambivalent about his daughter's ambitions, Bruce pulled Kelley aside. "Don't cut her any slack," he said.

Kelley didn't. Gwyneth had been well cast in the role, he believed, and he didn't think she needed much direction. So he didn't bother giving it.

In the audience was Joanne Horowitz, a young, ambitious talent manager and friend of Lowe's who had, in 1984, signed a little-known actor named Kevin Spacey. Horowitz saw a star in Gwyneth and found her backstage after curtain. "You were amazing in the show," she told her. "I'd love to represent you."

Gwyneth was ecstatic—no other agents, Horowitz recalled, were pursuing her then. She said yes.

Horowitz got right to work. She took Gwyneth for headshots and began planning meetings with casting agents at Creative Artists Agency. Bruce was furious. She was supposed to start at UCSB in a few months. But Horowitz followed through and started working to get her an agent at CAA, which also represented Bruce.

·   ·   ·

ONE AFTERNOON THAT summer around lunchtime, casting director Glenn Daniels was sitting at his desk in his cramped office on the
Upper East Side. He was working on casting the film *What About Bob?*
With no appointments scheduled, he was surprised when Boaty Boatwright showed up at his office unannounced.

Boatwright was a legend. Her career began when she cast the 1962
Oscar-winning film *To Kill a Mockingbird*, having never cast anything before.
She became a talent agent at William Morris Agency, with a client list that
included Joan Didion, Sidney Lumet, and Blythe Danner. As she bustled
into the office and began making her pitch in her Southern drawl, Daniels could see a teenage girl Boatwright had deposited in the waiting room,
with a frightened—perhaps slightly mortified—expression on her face, like
she didn't know what she or Boatwright were doing just showing up like
this. Horowitz figured that Boatwright taking Gwyneth to the audition was
another effort by Bruce and Blythe to separate her from their daughter.

Boatwright explained that she'd brought Blythe Danner's daughter, and she told Daniels he just had to read her for the part of Richard
Dreyfuss's daughter in *What About Bob?*

As Boatwright remembered it, Gwyneth was around her office regularly, and she was just helping her out. "It wasn't that hard in those days. If
you came out of an acting school and your parents were well known, then
people wanted to sign the daughters or the sons." Boatwright also knew
the two stars of the film, Bill Murray and Richard Dreyfuss, so she was
well positioned to help Gwyneth. "I probably called up Billy and Richard,
too, because in those days I was more brazen than I am now," she said.
"[Gwyneth] was a star from the minute she came on the scene. Literally."

As Boatwright talked, Daniels thought, *Auditions don't just happen like this.* Only Boaty Boatwright would arrive unannounced at a
casting director's office with an unknown actress and insist she get a
tryout. But Boatwright was so charming that people tended to oblige
her, knowing she usually returned the favor.

"She's read the script and everything," Boatwright pressed.

"Okay," Daniels relented. "I'll read her."

Gwyneth came into his office, and by the time she started reading, she seemed totally at ease. Daniels figured she'd been more nervous about arriving unannounced than the audition itself. In any case, he wasn't impressed. She didn't bomb, but she didn't strike him as someone with potential star power. He said, "The most important thing was it was a comedy, and she wasn't funny."

Daniels cast Kathryn Erbe instead.

WILLIAMSTOWN'S 1990 SEASON was in full swing. The apprentices had been toiling all summer, building all the sets as always and laboring behind the scenes to make the festival run smoothly. Then Gwyneth swanned in. Known more around the festival as Blythe's daughter than Gwyneth Paltrow, she immediately got a song in the Cabaret, which did not go unnoticed by those who had been working intensely all summer in hopes of landing such an opportunity. As her mother had years earlier, she sang "Peel Me a Grape" by Blossom Dearie, her performance fine if not outstanding.

The festival also staged a play, written by the dramaturg, in a field instead of on one of the main stages, for which apprentices and nonunion actors were cast. Despite not being part of the company, Gwyneth got a prominent part. "Everyone was so pissed off," remembered Christine Lemme, who worked the festival that year as a production management intern. The apprentices and nonunion actors had been hoping all summer to land a part like that.

The actors and crew later attended an end-of-season party at a bar in town. Gwyneth, and Lemme's fling for the summer, who was in his twenties, both attended. He later told Lemme, "Gwyneth just felt me up." But he'd walked away.

ORIGIN STORIES CAN be murky in Hollywood, where people are eager to lay claim to their discoveries. As Nancy Nayor remembered it, she saw the pictures of Gwyneth in the *Harper's Bazaar* feature she had done with her mother and tried to track her down; as Joanne Horowitz remembered it, she introduced Gwyneth to Nayor, who was a friend.

Whatever happened, as a casting director, Nayor believed there was something to be said for genes, and for growing up in the industry. "You don't have to worry about a nervousness or an awkwardness. You're already comfortable in that world," she explained. Nayor wanted Gwyneth to audition for the female lead in the film she was casting, *Shout*, about a rock-and-roll music teacher who shakes up a conservative boys' home in Texas. It was supposed to be a vehicle to relaunch John Travolta's career.

Nayor had watched countless auditions for the role, but when she saw Gwyneth's tape, she got chills. In the scene, the character, Sara, remembers her mother, who died when she was eight. The girl thinks of her nose as her "kiss button": When she touched her nose, her mom would kiss her. Unlike the *What About Bob?* scene, this wasn't comedic. "She was so vulnerable. She was so moving," said Nayor, who believed Gwyneth's scant Williamstown experience gave her the foundation to make the jump to feature films.

Yet the studio executives wanted to give the lead role to Heather Graham, who'd just received an Independent Spirit Award nomination for a role in Gus Van Sant's *Drugstore Cowboy*. Nayor decided to fly Gwyneth out to Los Angeles, and when she walked into the office, everyone looked up. Talented actors lose out on jobs all the time simply because they don't know how to bring their whole self into a room—their auditions are weighed down by tentativeness, self-consciousness, something effortful in their reading. But Gwyneth had none of that. From the first introduction, she was warm, professional, a little bubbly. The casting director in the office across the hallway even noticed her and asked the *Shout* assistant for her information. It seemed everyone loved the idea of launching Bruce Paltrow's daughter in her first feature film.

The studio agreed. "The tape really stopped them in their tracks, and they realized this actress is so incredibly talented, so they were considering her in a way that they normally wouldn't consider a newcomer for a lead in a film opposite Travolta," Nayor said. Studios like known quantities, and—unlike Gwyneth—Graham had a résumé. Besides, to book Graham, Nayor would have to negotiate with her agent, Rick Kurtzman at CAA. If they chose Gwyneth, the negotiation would go away. Though Graham ended up getting cast, Nayor used Gwyneth as leverage. "We have someone amazing," she told Kurtzman. "If we need to move on, we'll move on."

"Sometimes you say it and you're bluffing. But in this case, it was very true," Nayor recalled.

This gambit worked out well for Gwyneth. Knowing she was their backup, Kurtzman decided to take a chance on her. He later said that he first decided to "hip-pocket" her, or represent her without an official agreement. "She was 17, she was kind of a kid still," Kurtzman told *Vanity Fair* for a 2000 profile of Gwyneth. "But there was also something very adult about her." The story about Heather Graham being in competition with unknown Gwyneth for the role didn't come out in *Vanity Fair*, but writer Michael Shnayerson asked Kurtzman if nepotism had anything to do with Gwyneth's early success. "It wasn't about her mother," Kurtzman said. About representing her, he added, "Unless you feel it passionately, you can't do it."

However, Gwyneth's success is inextricable from that of her parents, who commanded the respect of their industry. It was Bruce and Blythe who ushered Gwyneth into Williamstown productions and brought her to film sets, showing her and her brother from infancy that success in this business was possible. While Gwyneth had to be able to perform up to a certain standard, casting directors like Nayor were understandably drawn to the idea of breaking out the next Blythe Danner.

Nayor cast Gwyneth in the film anyway, in the part of Rebecca, whose sole line is "Rebecca." "She did it so beautifully every time she came on-screen," Nayor said. "I was like, *Oh my gosh, she's clearly a star, clearly destined for greatness.*"

The movie flopped. *The New York Times* called it "unintentionally silly" and "a period piece that doesn't seem to be for anyone at all," but Gwyneth's part was so small she wasn't mentioned, so the failure did nothing to hold her back.

BY THIS TIME Gwyneth had moved to Los Angeles. Before she headed to college, she stayed in the guest bedroom in Rob Lowe's spaceship-like bachelor pad, tucked into a hillside, where he was living with soon-to-be-wife Sheryl Berkoff, the makeup artist who had given Gwyneth blowjob lessons over a cigarette some years back. Gwyneth was seduced by Lowe's world, including the other young celebrities she was encountering in Hollywood, who were more dynamic than her parents' older celebrity friends.

Gwyneth was ostensibly on the West Coast to study at UCSB, where she declared a major in art history. After a lifetime as the center of attention and six years at Spence, where classes could be as small as eight students, she was now often one face among hundreds in a lecture hall. Rather than try to adjust to the new environment, she rejected academics. She wasn't there to work, she was there to party. Blythe had dropped her daughter off hoping she could be the next Margaret Mead, but Gwyneth was focused on "having a good time." And she was still intent on an acting career.

On Valentine's Day 1991, not two months into school, *The Silence of the Lambs* came out in theaters. Gwyneth went to see it at the Century City cineplex with her dad; Steven Spielberg, whom she called "Uncle Morty" (he called her "Gwynnie the Pooh"); and Kate Capshaw, who would become Spielberg's wife. Spielberg was working on *Hook*, a reimagining of *Peter Pan* starring Robin Williams and Dustin Hoffman, which would start filming the following week. But one small part hadn't yet been cast. "We were driving back from the movie theater," Spielberg recalled in a 2011 interview, "and I was going back to work the next day. I was looking at [Gwyneth] in the rearview mirror, and she was talking about the film [*The Silence of the Lambs*] and she had this really frightened look on her face, and it suddenly clicked, and I said, 'Hey, you could be the young Wendy! You could be the young Maggie Smith!' So, I turned around and said, 'Do you want to make a movie?'

"She got a SAG card because of it."

Gwyneth remembered the moment differently: "I was petrified."

Spielberg asked his casting director, Jane Jenkins, to audition Gwyneth for the part. Jenkins recalled, "We did, she was, and the rest is history."

Carla McCloskey worked as second assistant director on the film, and she had hoped to get her niece in for the part of young Wendy—then Gwyneth arrived. "Because she came from a showbiz family, we knew that she wasn't just Susie Smith off the street. Her mom was well known, [as was] her dad. So, we were like, *Oh, Bruce Paltrow's child's Steven's goddaughter.*" Clearly, no one else had a shot.

On her first day at work, Gwyneth struck the crew as beautiful, sweet, and unaffected. If she was scared, it didn't show, though she seemed to believe that her part would be larger than it was. In the end, she was on the screen for less than a minute. Someone on the publicity team who was visiting the set described the vibe as *Look who our Wendy is. Is this not the perfect Wendy?*

BY THE END of her first semester in 1991, Gwyneth was barely showing up for class, driving back and forth to Los Angeles to reshoot the ending for *Shout.* Her heart wasn't in her studies, and she wasn't doing any work. "I sort of gave up," she said.

In late spring, she traveled to New York to audition for the Williamstown play *Picnic.* Blythe had already signed on for a part. "I think Mom was trying to make sure I didn't get into any trouble that summer," Gwyneth said.

Casting director Pat McCorkle knew Gwyneth was Blythe's daughter, but she still had to prove herself in that audition room. "If you grow up in the business," McCorkle said, "a door might open early, but it doesn't stay open if you're not strong." She'd auditioned hundreds of actresses already. She chose Gwyneth, whom she remembered as "this tall, beautiful, thin girl—a lot of arms and legs."

When Gwyneth became a major film actress, McCorkle wasn't surprised. "Most of the kids, when they come out of school or training, don't understand the business," she said. She had seen young actors make mistakes with things as fundamental as choosing representation. But Gwyneth "had somebody who could explain all that to her."

Once Gwyneth arrived in Williamstown that summer, plenty of people assumed she'd gotten this great part in the play because of her mother. "Everybody was like, 'She can't act,'" recalled Grayson McCouch, who later became a soap star and who had worked his way up from the apprentice program to the nonequity company.

This was a setting where little-known actors like McCouch could take the stage in front of the most powerful agents and casting directors in New York, and this pretty blond nepo-baby was claiming a spot alongside her famous mom.

During a rehearsal, when Blythe leaned over and coached her daughter in front of other actors, Gwyneth bristled. "The director was explaining how he wanted me to get something across in a line," she said in a joint interview with Blythe. "And then my mother says, 'He means say it like this.' I felt chided, like a child."

"I guess I gave her some direction in public," Blythe said, "which I never did again." Gwyneth remained closer to her father but also wanted to distinguish herself from her famous mother and let her talent speak for itself.

On July 10, 1991, *Picnic* premiered on the festival's main stage. Gwyneth played Millie Owen, the younger sister to Madge (played by Jane Krakowski), whose plans to marry a respectable, well-off young man in her small Kansas town are thrown off by the arrival of a handsome grifter (played by Tony Goldwyn).

Gwyneth played the role with the same lightness and effortlessness her mother was known for. "She really did shine in that production," said Greg Naughton, who, like Gwyneth, had spent summers at Williamstown with his dad, actor James Naughton. "It was, I think, a big moment for her, and kind of a coming-out event in the business."

Blythe watched Gwyneth from backstage, and Bruce came to join them after the show. He finally told Gwyneth what she had been waiting to hear from her worried parents regarding college: "I don't think you should go back."

GWYNETH CELEBRATED HER success at the Cabaret. The venue was packed, as usual, with locals, festival people, and industry professionals. One year Amy Irving performed on the main stage and her then-husband, Steven Spielberg, went to watch the Cabaret. The festival hired young actors and singers just to perform in the Cabaret, since the celebrities sometimes didn't show up, which meant they'd end up getting to perform for the likes of Spielberg.

Rob Lowe showed up sometimes. James Naughton once performed in a band with Paul Giamatti and started snorting like a pig into the microphone when the cops came to break up the party. Gwyneth sang with Greg Naughton. When they hung out socially, they sang for fun, often sitting together in his car. He had a mixtape of Motown songs, and they would harmonize duets in the front seat. One of her favorites was "Cruisin'," the 1979 Smokey Robinson single. Gwyneth ended up taking the cassette from Naughton, and he would joke with her later that he was still waiting to get his mixtape back.

"People would just get smashed and go," remembered Grayson McCouch, who encountered Gwyneth one late-summer night in 1991 near the Cabaret stage following his rendition of Elvis's "Blue Suede Shoes," delivered with as much authenticity as he could muster. He'd gone outside for a break after the show; when he came back in, the crowd had thinned out, and the few remaining partiers were mostly wilting or passed out. But there was the young blonde from *Picnic*, bright-eyed and waiting for him.

"Grayson," she called. "Hey, I'm Gwyneth."

He recognized her, but they'd never met. He believed she was flirting. "Oh my God," she said, "you were so good. What are you up to? We should hang out."

McCouch was already seeing someone, and Gwyneth soon took an interest in McCouch's friend who wasn't involved in the festival but lived in town.

Years later, Gwyneth recommended McCouch to her father for a role. When McCouch arrived for the audition, Bruce said Gwyneth had said such good things about him, though he didn't get the part. He wouldn't see her again for years, until he had a part in *Armageddon* and she came to the set to see her then-boyfriend, Ben Affleck, and they were one of the most famous couples in the world.

AFTER *PICNIC*, RICK Kurtzman got Gwyneth an audition for Woody Allen's film *Husbands and Wives*. She got five callbacks, but the part went to Juliette Lewis. Kurtzman decided to sign her officially, and she returned to the West Coast a college dropout and a professional actress.

Bruce honored the occasion by declaring that she was cut off financially. "I'm not gonna help you," he said.

"Yeah, right."

"No," he insisted, "I'm not."

Gwyneth later said she "would scrounge quarters to buy Starbucks—and walk there to save gas." When she really needed money, she came to him again: "Please, I'm really stuck. Can you help?"

Bruce said no again, but he did offer, "You're more than welcome to come over for dinner."

She often did, and one day she and Bruce decided they were tired of the spaghetti and meatballs that Blythe had left in the freezer for them while she was working in New York. They embarked upon learning how to cook for themselves, and would call each other to exchange tips and tricks.

Gwyneth and her *High* costar Tyagi Schwartz had stayed friends, and after she'd left school and was living in Venice Beach, she invited him over to the apartment she shared with a roommate. Over a roast chicken—her favorite dish to serve friends—Gwyneth told Schwartz that her father had been pushing her to finish school so that she'd have a backup plan, but she didn't see why she needed to go to college to attain the career that had been right at her fingertips her whole life. She had taken a film class at UCSB, and her godfather—Steven Spielberg—was on the syllabus. "I'm sitting here learning about people I know who are family," she told Schwartz. "I want to do this."

Gwyneth has put a happy spin on this period in the years since, but Schwartz said it was a hard transition when Bruce cut her off. "He made her get a job. I remember she was so mad about it." While those close to Gwyneth and Bruce at the time had difficulty imagining him letting her manage on her own, another friend confirmed that he had. And Gwyneth worked hard to support herself while she pursued acting. She picked up a couple of restaurant gigs, including one at DC3 at the Santa Monica Airport, where her parents had connections. Bruce and Blythe were among the Hollywood crowd who made the place a hot destination in the late eighties. The co-owner August Spier had the impression that Bruce and Blythe were doing their best, or trying more than most Hollywood families, to give their children a normal upbringing. Answering phones at an airport restaurant where diners often arrived by private jet was a step in that direction. Before Gwyneth began her job there, Spier warned the staff, "Nobody touches her."

Around this time, Gwyneth was offered a part opposite Vanilla Ice in the 1991 film *Cool as Ice*. Gwyneth wanted to take it, but her parents dissuaded her. They wanted her to be practical—but not trashy.

"You have your whole life ahead of you. You don't want to do something because of the money or because it'll put you somewhere. You don't want to sell out to get to that place," they told her. Her parents' advice may not have made sense to a nineteen-year-old scrounging to pay for coffee and eager for stardom, but it served her well. Soon, a much better film opportunity would present itself.

CHAPTER 7

Flesh and Bone

There is the perception that I grew up very wealthy . . . and raised
with a silver spoon in my mouth . . . I didn't have a trust fund.
So it's not accurate, but I can see how someone would have that
perception.

—Gwyneth Paltrow

In 1991, Esprit sent out a mailer to customers asking them to
respond to a question: "If you could change the world, what
would you do?" The fashion retailer had a new leadership team
and an almost $10 million advertising budget for a rebrand that one
new executive dubbed "retail activism." While the campaign was
meant to focus on "real" people, the team decided to sprinkle in a few
chosen ones.

Gwyneth was on the audition circuit, and she was one of the pretty
people whose photo ended up on the casting board, even though she
had never done commercial work. The brand's image director Neil
Kraft knew who her father was, though that didn't influence his decision to choose her. Her looks were enough.

They also included her idea about changing the world. The text
ran alongside a black-and-white image of Gwyneth in her own jeans,
white T-shirt, and cardigan. She looks musingly off to the side, her hair

cascading undone over her shoulders: "i would distribute condoms in every high school in america."

Esprit later said her comment was specifically about preventing the spread of HIV and AIDS.

SUSAN BAERWALD WAS producing the TV miniseries *Cruel Doubt*, a psychological thriller. Baerwald and Blythe had gone to high school together and remained friendly. Gwyneth ended up auditioning, and Baerwald was inclined to cast her. "I think Gwynnie's got it," Bruce told her. Gwyneth hadn't done a lot of on-screen work at that point, but Baerwald trusted Bruce.

Her director, Yves Simoneau, was skeptical. "I didn't like the principle of that," he said of Gwyneth's preferential treatment. But when she came in and read for the part, she was so good that Simoneau forgot all about Bruce and Blythe. "There was no question in our minds she was the best," he said. He then decided he'd like to have a mother-daughter pairing on the show and cast Blythe, too.

Her family was opening doors for her all over, but Gwyneth wanted to feel she'd earned the role. "You just cast me because of my mother," she later told Baerwald.

"[W]e were having this weird family thing of our own," Gwyneth said, "where I was trying to be my own person. I think I was sort of resentful because I had gotten the offer for the miniseries before she did, and I felt, this is mine. I want to have my own career. I thought maybe it was cramping my style for my mother to be in the show, even though in the end I enjoyed working with her."

In a different interview, Blythe massaged the story from her side. "The only cruel thing about *Cruel Doubt* is that my daughter was cast in the miniseries several weeks before I was," she told a reporter, laughing. "I can only assume that she put in a good word for me with the producers." Blythe's modesty was studied but also genuine. She was content to return to Williamstown summer after summer and eschew movie stardom in favor of roles that truly interested her. Gwyneth, on the other hand, was already aligning herself with her father's unbridled ambition.

She got her first big paycheck for the role, an amount that was reported differently in early profiles as $48,000 or $30,000. "[O]f course, after paying agents, lawyers—I didn't know any of this stuff at the time—business managers, and taxes, [it] turned out to be about $3,000. But, I mean, I thought I was set for life. I was so psyched."

She was still smoking a pack of cigarettes a day, but this was the nineties, so Gwyneth probably wasn't thinking much about what would later be called "wellness." Though she did carry a gallon bottle of water around the set. The big jug struck Baerwald more as a talisman than a health choice. "It was a very young, teenagey, 'I'm going to be different' thing," she said. But a friend of Gwyneth's remembered her being the first person in her social circle to start carrying around a big jug of water in pursuit of better health, an interest she seemed to have inherited from Blythe.

Whether culinary craze or health fad, Gwyneth was an early adopter when it came to any trend. That same year, she also took her first yoga class. "I don't really know what drew me to it," she said. "I just went to a class in Santa Monica. Right away, I felt like I had found a missing piece in my life. You know, the yogis say that those who do yoga in this life did it in another life, and that's why they're drawn to it. I don't know if that's true, but there was definitely a sense of, 'This feels really right for me.'"

Gwyneth arrived every day on the set of *Cruel Doubt* with her lines memorized, fully prepared. She never seemed to Simoneau like a novice. The other actors had more experience, but she outshone them all, including, Simoneau thought, her own mother. And the more difficult a scene was, the more she seemed to enjoy performing it. He normally did a little rehearsal on set, but "I realized that it was interesting to capture her first take." The show was based on Joe McGinniss's book about the 1988 murder of Lieth Von Stein. Blythe played Von Stein's wife, Bonnie, who barely survived the stabbing that occurred in the middle of the night in their bedroom. Gwyneth played Bonnie's daughter,

Angela, who was asleep down the hall on the night of the murder, but who police think may know more about the crime than she lets on.

After one take, Simoneau got up from behind the camera and walked over to Gwyneth. In the scene, she was being interrogated by the police, but the audience wouldn't have known she was lying, and he said, "Give me a little more lie." Then, "Give me a little less lie." He had her do it more distracted, then more afraid of telling the lie. "All the shades of possible lies or ways of lying, she was able to deliver. There was no anxiety, no 'I cannot do that.' Things that you see often with actors or actresses who are a little less comfortable or a little more insecure—that was not there."

Blythe remembered watching one of Gwyneth's close-ups and being so entranced that she forgot this was her daughter. She and Gwyneth kept their distance on set. "It's rather ambiguous in the script, but there are indications that the mother-daughter relationship is somewhat estranged. And that was the key for Gwyneth and me to play the roles," she said.

Though polished in her scene work, Gwyneth was less so in an interview to promote the miniseries on CNN. She clumsily forayed into social commentary. "I think that everyone has that morbid curiosity," she said when asked about true crime. "And I think that—but I just think, it's getting sicker, you know. I think that a—this is sort of a sordid, really horrible story—I mean, the story of it. And it's going to be—it's really fun to make, and I think it's going to be entertaining, but I think, you know, maybe now we need shows and things that are a little bit more uplifting and enlightening."

By the time the family headed to Williamstown that summer, Gwyneth had been praised for "a really chilling performance" in the *Houston Chronicle*. Memphis's *The Commercial Appeal* called her—not Blythe—"a particular standout."

JUST SHY OF her twentieth birthday in 1992, Gwyneth drove around the Williamstown Festival in a white Jeep Bruce had given her, sometimes with her parents and sometimes with her manager Joanne Horowitz, all of whom still seemed protective of her. Blythe liked the idea of mother-daughter roles and agreed to star in the new play *The Sweet By 'n' By* with Gwyneth.

While Gwyneth had relative success in *Cruel Doubt*, she struck director David Dorwart as very much the novice. "She didn't know about preparing. You don't come onstage and start acting, you have to prepare. You enter the scene onstage at a certain level or a certain mental process. Where I could turn to a Juilliard or an NYU graduate and say, 'You know your offstage beat—you're not working on it, you're not preparing well enough,' they would know exactly what I meant," he explained. But Gwyneth didn't know what an offstage beat was.

She was tall and lanky, and Dorwart thought she hadn't grown into her body yet. "That's one of the things we do in training with all these young actors," he said. "We have a physical being. We have an emotional being, spiritual. All of them don't sort of coordinate at the same time." One of his solutions that summer was to give her props so she had something to do with her hands.

During rehearsals, Gwyneth flew to Los Angeles to pursue a supporting role in the film *Flesh and Bone*. As she remembered years later, she had to choose between the movie and another part that might have taken her career more in the direction of Blythe's. "One day I was thrilled because I got a call to say that I had been cast for a great role in a Broadway play. Later that evening, I got another call from the casting agent for *Flesh and Bone*, the Meg Ryan film, and that they wanted me to fly to Los Angeles to test for it. I didn't want to go because it meant I had to take the red-eye flight to the West Coast. But I spoke to my agent, and he told me that I absolutely had to go."

But all Dorwart could think of was the irony that the least experienced person in the Williamstown production was missing rehearsal to audition for a movie. Not that he blamed her. "You get the breaks, you're very lucky."

•   •   •

IN *FLESH AND BONE*, the role of Ginnie, a grifter in a small Texas town, required nudity, which had scared off a few actresses. The film was scheduled to shoot in the next few months, so time was running out.

Gwyneth arrived at the audition dressed casually. She sat down, the afternoon sunlight shining through the window, opposite director Steve Kloves, casting director Risa Bramon Garcia, and producers Paula Weinstein and Mark Rosenberg. She turned toward the VHS camera, and they were entranced. "I was looking for a young girl who had to convey a world-weariness, a certain dark wisdom beyond her years," Kloves said. "She came in all sunshine, then the minute she started reading, she transforms into this dark, white-trash girl." The part required a particular Texas accent. Many actresses had come in hamming up the dialect, but Gwyneth found her own, believable version of a drawl, mellow and subtle. Whatever was gangly and off-time on Dorwart's stage somehow showed up haunting and natural on camera.

"She just had this ease about her," remembered Bramon Garcia, who viewed her as "Hollywood royalty" as Bruce and Blythe's daughter. "And there was so much going on. There was such a combination of earthiness and depth and intelligence, which is really rare for an actor and especially a nineteen-year-old."

The group agreed she was the one, but first they had to address the nudity. Second, Kloves had to change his image of Ginnie after losing his first choice for the role—a television actress with dark hair who was nearly ten years older than Gwyneth.

When they told her about the nudity, Gwyneth didn't flinch. She said it wasn't about her, it was about the character, and she would do what was necessary to play the role effectively. In the end, the nudity was cut.

SOON AFTER THE audition, Gwyneth was back in Massachusetts, sitting with her mother again for a joint interview about *The Sweet By 'n' By*. The reporter noted that Gwyneth's career was picking up, with a small part in *Malice* alongside Alec Baldwin and Nicole Kidman, and a bigger one in *Flesh and Bone*.

Blythe stepped gracefully into her supporting role: "My movie star."

The Sweet By 'n' By received decent reviews, but the *Boston Herald* called Gwyneth's performance "ingenious." Gwyneth went up to Dorwart when the run ended, Horowitz at her side, and said, "Thank you. I learned a lot working with you." It struck Dorwart more as professionalism than as genuine feeling.

But Horowitz's work as Gwyneth's manager came to an end shortly thereafter. Bruce, whom Horowitz never met, ultimately got his way. "He was a bully," she said. She wondered if he had threatened to leave CAA if they didn't remove her from Gwyneth's account, led by Kurtzman as her agent.

While Gwyneth's fate as an actor seemed sealed, Horowitz still played a part in her early success. Yet Gwyneth didn't mention her by name in interviews, and her role in Gwyneth's career has been largely unknown.

IN THE FALL of 1992 when Gwyneth turned twenty, she traveled to Austin, Texas, to shoot *Flesh and Bone*, her first time on location for a film that neither parent was involved in. The film tells the story of Arlis, played by Dennis Quaid, who falls in love with Kay, played by Meg Ryan, whose family, the audience comes to learn, was murdered by Arlis's father, Roy, played by James Caan. Gwyneth played Ginnie, a petty thief who gets tied up with Roy before they both realize Kay is the only survivor of Roy's murders.

Many of Gwyneth's roles, particularly the ones that made her a star of the nineties, were refined, upper-class types whose sophistication she traced to her mother, her classmates, the denizens of Santa Monica and the Upper East Side. This was not that sort of character. The *Flesh and Bone* hairstylist thinned her hair at the ends with a razor blade. Gwyneth Paltrow needed to look poor.

Gwyneth's part was small, but the crew felt she took her work seriously. She was casual and friendly and spent her downtime doing the *People* magazine crossword puzzle. When one of the clues was "Marlon Brando's character in *The Godfather*," she didn't know the answer, so she called her costar "Jimmy." It was four letters ending with *O*, and Caan said he didn't know, then called her back five minutes later with "Vito."

Gwyneth said, "I couldn't believe that ... I called James Caan, who I was doing a *movie* with, to get the answer."

AFTER FILMING *FLESH and Bone*, Gwyneth returned to Los Angeles and got a job waiting tables at Enterprise Fish Co. in Santa Monica, beginning what would be her last few months of anonymity. Tyagi Schwartz and his wife visited her there.

"Listen, can you guys do me a favor?" she asked. "My dad's being, really, a pain in the ass. He's making me work, and he's not giving me money. Can I just borrow a few dollars?"

Schwartz was making money at the time. "Sure, no problem." He gave Gwyneth a twenty. "I always tell people that Gwyneth Paltrow owes me twenty dollars," he said. "I'm like, *What's the interest on that?*"

In 2015, Gwyneth reflected on this period, saying her father "was so hardcore about me making my own way." She concluded, "I've earned everything myself, and I've never taken any money from anyone, my father really pounded that into me, so I got the message." Gwyneth doubled down on this point in 2016. "There is the perception that I grew up very wealthy ... and raised with a silver spoon in my mouth." She noted again that her dad stopped giving her money once she quit school. "I didn't have a trust fund. So it's not accurate, but I can see how someone would have that perception."

ED ZWICK HAD dreamed of making the novella *Legends of the Fall* into a movie practically since he'd graduated from film school in 1979. After he'd waited seven years to acquire the rights, and another seven to start filming owing to various Hollywood delays, his dream was becoming reality in early 1993. He'd had to convince his producing partner to let him cast the handsome, affable newcomer Brad Pitt in the leading role, his second such part after *A River Runs Through It*. Zwick, also the director, was convinced Pitt was the one not only because of his unquestionable good looks but also, he later recalled, "the unnameable thing behind [the] eyes suggesting a fascinating inner life, whether they have one or not, that somehow emanates."

Four weeks out from filming, Zwick still didn't have a female lead. He didn't need to fill the role of Susannah with a known name, but he was struggling to find someone who could pull off the manic depression that leads her to kill herself. Zwick felt like he was seeing nearly every actress in Hollywood who could pass for late twenties to play the part. One day he brought about twenty actresses into his nondescript Santa Monica office, which he had outfitted with Native American blankets like on the *Legends of the Fall* set.

Gwyneth was one of the young women in that day's lineup. Zwick hadn't seen her in anything—*Flesh and Bone*'s release was six months off. When it was her turn to read, she came in and sat next to Pitt. The two of them seemed to be acting in the same imagined universe, and even in that short reading, Zwick saw the chemistry between them. At twenty-one, though, Gwyneth looked too young to play a character who's in her thirties by the end of the movie. Zwick also didn't view her as a convincing manic depressive. He gave the part to twenty-eight-year-old Julia Ormond.

To be successful, actors have to walk into the right room at the right time. Gwyneth had luck on her side, and the industry believed in her talent, but she had to somehow divine herself into castings where she was trying for parts that seemed written just for her. She didn't lose *Legends of the Fall* because she wasn't good; she lost it because she wasn't right for it. Blythe had told her, "If you don't get a part, that means it's just not your part. There'll be other parts that are yours, and you'll get those." But Gwyneth didn't seem content to sit back and wait for that to happen.

CHAPTER 8

Big Break

She could access her emotional life as fast as I've ever seen.

—Reg Rogers

Larry Moss taught his acting classes from six p.m. to midnight at the Santa Monica mall. At the beginning of each session, he would guide students in releasing muscle tension from their eyes, then jaws, throats, chests, hips, all the way into their feet on the floor. Sometimes students trembled; others broke into tears. Moss would see that someone's shoulders were hunched, and he would instruct them to take a breath, release that tension, and a laugh would erupt out of them, or a sob, or they'd find themselves suddenly terrified. Moss wanted his students to develop "a free emotional instrument that can go anywhere without any fear, but [also] without shame or judgment from themselves."

Gwyneth had missed out on several roles just before *Legends*. (She would lose out to Ormond again for the remake of *Sabrina*.) She was doubting herself, determined to be better, and finally willing to accept some formal training. So she found her way to Moss's class, where he had used his rigorous method to coach Oscar winners, including Hilary Swank and Leonardo DiCaprio.

While Gwyneth had learned acting from watching her mother,

and from being on sets her whole life, she had always resisted her mother's direct advice. "I was young, and she was my mom, and I didn't want to hear it from her. 'Let me make my mistakes myself,' you know."

When Gwyneth performed these exercises, Moss said, "I just had a flash of her light within . . . that certain people have. It's an electric energy that comes from need, desire, creativity." He recalled, "In the class, there was a very free exchange of ideas and emotion, and working through not being ashamed of your pain or your joy or your sensuality or your anger. I said, 'Let it go. Let it become part of your tools to be able to access that and release the tension in your body. Get in touch with your breath.'"

After relaxation exercises, they practiced scenes. If Moss thought his students were doing well, he'd let them go on. If not, he'd stop them: "You didn't do the script analysis. You don't know why you're saying that line." Students were to read scripts three times—once to themselves, once lip-reading silently, and then once saying every single line aloud. "You've got to know when the play took place, what the history of that time is, if the character has a dialect," he said. Actors had to know what their character was doing right before entering the scene. Were they walking in from the cold? From a fight? Had they just woken up?

"Could you play the part with no dialogue? Could we understand it just from your behavior—how you pick up a cup, how you wash your hands, how you eat, how you kiss?" Gwyneth would listen with a notable stillness. "I think that she knew that there was something that she needed to learn. And that energy—everybody in my classes who've gone on to have big careers had that quality and intense concentration," Moss said. "I think it had to do with the fact that she really, really passionately wanted to break through into a successful career."

.　　　.　　　.

FLESH AND BONE premiered on November 5, 1993. The reviews were mixed, but even the most Gwyneth-skeptical observer would notice a trend.

The *Chicago Sun-Times* called her an "impressive newcomer"; *The Boston Globe* said she "holds the screen impressively"; the *Chicago Tribune* wrote that she "plays Ginnie with a lusterless sullen callousness that's almost as terrifying as Caan's full-bore, kill-crazy rants"; the *Los Angeles Times* noted her "striking performance"; and *The New York Times*'s Janet Maslin offered, "Ginnie is played with startling aplomb by the scene-stealing Gwyneth Paltrow, who is Blythe Danner's daughter and has her mother's way of making a camera fall in love with her."

At last Gwyneth was being recognized mostly on her own merits. To promote the movie, she made her first talk show appearance, on *Late Night with Conan O'Brien*. Toward the end of her four-and-a-half-minute segment, O'Brien said, "You've made a few movies now . . . Are you starting to have some of the celebrity trappings—people seeing you, recognizing you?"

"Not yet," Gwyneth said, "but I did use it to my advantage in the video store the other night. I wanted to rent videos and I didn't belong to the store, so they said, 'You need a picture ID and a credit card.' I had a credit card, but I didn't have a picture ID. And I looked over and I noticed that they were selling an issue of *Premiere* which I'm in, so I said, 'Well, how about this?'"

Within a few weeks, *Flesh and Bone* had changed Gwyneth's life. "It was great, and it was terrible. I became a commodity. And a lot of people reappeared in my life. I remember getting seventeen phone calls in two hours in one day. I got Christmas cards from famous people whom I never met. I have this limo waiting for me, which is the size of Manchuria. And I just got scared and freaked out. For years when you go to premieres and stuff, you're always on the fringe, on the outside. Then all of a sudden, all the young famous people were treating me like I was one of them. And I sort of thought, *Well, I was me before this movie came out.*"

In early 1994, Gwyneth presented an award at the National Board of Review Motion Picture Award ceremony in New York, where Leonardo DiCaprio won Best Supporting Actor for *What's Eating Gilbert Grape*. Gwyneth had moved back to New York and gotten an apartment in SoHo, and she and Leo hung out. She has said he tried to make out with her (one friend recalled that they did), but Gwyneth didn't think he'd be a good boyfriend. "He was very loose with the goods from when he was nineteen," she later revealed. But DiCaprio, a vegan and environmentalist, did teach her something. "He was vegetarian," she recalled in a 2013 interview, "and he'd talk about how dirty meat is and how bad factory farming is. I haven't eaten red meat in twenty years, and although Leo's not totally responsible, he definitely planted a seed."

Now officially a bold-faced name, and more than her parents' daughter, Gwyneth hired publicist Stephen Huvane to represent her. (One of Huvane's brothers, Kevin, was an agent at CAA.) Dimpled and sharply dressed, he was on his way to becoming a powerhouse himself, with a client list that would include Jennifer Aniston and Julianne Moore. He could be cutting with the press and deeply protective of his clients, whom he'd shadow on red carpets, monitoring their interviews. Gwyneth's career was at the point that she needed someone to manage and massage her press coverage.

Vogue bookings editor Maggie Buckley's job was to find talent that editor in chief Anna Wintour would deem worthy of featuring in the magazine. Buckley saw *Flesh and Bone* at an early screening for media; she got goose bumps watching the funeral scene, where, in a closeup, Gwyneth's character wipes a finger across her heavily balmed lips, using the salve to pry a ring off a dead man in an open casket. Tall, willowy, and blond, with a breakout role in an artsy movie, she was a perfect match for Wintour's sensibility. Buckley called Huvane to book a photo shoot. Wintour was not impressed: "The regrettable 'trailer trash' look was at its peak," she recalled later, "and the pictures made [Gwyneth] look like someone in the late stages of drug addiction." Buckley hated to tell Huvane that the photos had been killed, and she asked Anna to write him a letter explaining the situation. But Buckley also had to call him personally—something that was rarely pleasant—and argue that *Vogue* didn't think Gwyneth would like the photos, either. Gwyneth Paltrow seemed like a star who would stick around, and *Vogue* needed to preserve the relationship with both her and Huvane.

In another photo shoot, Gwyneth was meant to be part of a portfolio of women wearing white, styled by legendary *Vogue* creative director Grace Coddington. And Coddington, who preferred working with models to celebrities, refused to rush her process. She insisted that actresses come in for a fitting before the shoot day, which wasn't typical for fashion magazines at the time. Plus, Wintour was early in her editorship, and she and the magazine weren't as powerful as they would become.

Once they get to the shoot, a stylist's and photographer's inclination is to take pictures with their subjects all day. For one of her *Vogue* shoots, Gwyneth brought a friend to hang out with her. At another, she seemed over it after about four hours.

Huvane asked why it was taking so long, then urged the team to wrap it up, saying that Gwyneth had a doctor's appointment. The *Vogue* team knew that a lot of actresses, whose time got booked up with all sorts of promotional work, viewed photo shoots as a drag. Plus, Gwyneth sat for *Vogue*'s cameras three times before they published any of the images. But still, they wondered, *Who schedules a doctor's appointment in the middle of an all-day* Vogue *photo shoot?*

IN JANUARY, AS the media awaited the list of 1993 Oscar nominations, Gwyneth's name was floated in the *Los Angeles Times* as a Best Supporting Actress candidate for *Flesh and Bone*. *Newsweek* profiled her as a "new face for the new year."

When the nominations were announced in February, Gwyneth's

name wasn't on the list. *The New York Times* and *Rolling Stone* suggested that it should have been. When the movie came out on VHS in April, the New York *Daily News* called her performance "Oscar-caliber." Gwyneth did get nominated for Best Supporting Actress by the National Society of Film Critics but lost by one vote to Madeleine Stowe for *Short Cuts*.

Meanwhile, an upper echelon of tastemakers was starting to anoint Gwyneth as one of their own. Calvin Klein decided he wanted to dress her after she came into the office with Donovan Leitch Jr., son of Donovan, the Scottish folk singer known for "Mellow Yellow." Gwyneth was dating Leitch, a face of the genderless fragrance (then a revolutionary concept) CK One along with Kate Moss. Klein was designing a lot of slinky slip dresses, and Gwyneth had the thin body type that he wanted to see wearing the style. She also embodied the understated, minimalist beauty ideal that his brand projected. Later explaining Gwyneth's appeal to *Vogue*, he said, "Real glamour is having the confidence to keep it simple." He happily gave Gwyneth clothes for everything from red carpets to her everyday life, and he loved having her at events as the ultimate representation of his brand.

Though Gwyneth had believed from a young age that she would be famous, she told a reporter she couldn't believe *Flesh and Bone* turned out "like *this*, for God's sake." Sounding very much like her mother, she added, "I'm on the upswing . . . but I'm well aware that everything that goes up must come down."

THANKS IN PART to Blythe's connections to producer-director duo Ismail Merchant and James Ivory, known for *A Room with a View* and *The Remains of the Day*, Gwyneth got a part in their next film, *Jefferson in Paris*, about Thomas Jefferson's time in Paris as U.S. ambassador in the late 1780s. Merchant and Ivory films were known for their obsessive attention to historical accuracy. Actors depicted in the eighteenth century, for instance, would have their hair cut with eighteenth-century implements. Meanwhile, James Ivory, who didn't give actors much direction, had no problem cutting their scenes down if he didn't like their work. So to play Jefferson's daughter Patsy to their standards, Gwyneth had to get to work.

Every Tuesday at eleven a.m., she arrived at the Juilliard campus in New York City, blending in with the other students as she made her way to the fourth-floor practice rooms. Her destination was little more than a dismal little cell containing a harpsichord and an ungenerous window looking out on Broadway. Linda Kobler had two months to teach Gwyneth part of "La Lugeac" by the French composer Claude-Bénigne Balbastre, an upbeat, challenging piece Patsy Jefferson plays when her new harpsichord is delivered. All the actors who played instruments in their scenes would be dubbed over in the final film, but Ivory wanted it to look real, so Gwyneth had to learn.

During her first lesson, Kobler told Gwyneth that she needed to learn how to read music, and Merchant Ivory had a harpsichord sent to her apartment so she could practice in her corset. Gwyneth was eager but soon overwhelmed by the task. She was also spending around eight hours a day near Wall Street, taking French immersion classes. On top of all this, she had to perfect her character's Virginian accent.

"I don't have time to learn how to read music," Gwyneth told Kobler. Kobler could see that she was organized and hardworking. "You can do it," she insisted.

By her second lesson, Gwyneth had decided there was no way. Kobler relented and taught her to play using the Suzuki method, in which students learn by listening and imitating. Fortunately, Gwyneth needed only to learn the first (and easiest) page of the Balbastre piece.

Gwyneth occasionally showed up to her lessons with tears in her eyes from all the exhaustion and pressure of preparing for the role. She hadn't eaten anything one day, so Kobler gave her the yogurt from her own lunch, causing Gwyneth to break down. Between bites, she said, "My mother's going to call you and thank you for this."

By April, Gwyneth had relocated to France for the shoot. The day she filmed her harpsichord scene, she had her hair styled into a period updo. She wore a corseted floral dress with a white scarf around her neck. She had been practicing in New York on a French harpsichord, which had keys so light they engaged practically from a gust of wind. On set, she faced an English-style harpsichord, true to what Jefferson had ordered for his daughter, and a completely different feel from what Gwyneth was used to. She improvised a line that made it into the final cut of the film: "My French harpsichord is easier." Despite the difference, Gwyneth played it so well that one of the cameramen remarked, "Wow. Where did they find a harpsichordist who could act?"

Merchant had a reputation for pulling off the impossible, like getting permission to film at Versailles, but he was also notoriously frugal. This made the already ambitious shoot especially strenuous. Some scenes included hundreds of extras, all in period costume, hair, and makeup that required three hours per person to apply.

While some actors struggled with the lack of direction and the intensity of the shoots, Gwyneth seemed bored. Off set, she said, "We were always having ridiculous dinners, throwing food and telling jokes." Still a kid, she seemed to have a lot of pent-up energy that she didn't know what to do with after sitting in her dressing room all day with a friend she had brought along. "We were like children, but it was really fun. It was the other side of all day in the corset, no one smiling or showing any emotions. In between takes, we'd all go into other rooms and start throwing our clothes at each other." The exhausted, overworked crew were working sixteen-hour days, but someone had to pick up after them.

Gwyneth's family traveled to Paris to keep her company during the shoot. Her brother, Jake, stayed for a while, and some friends who were graduating from college also came to visit. Gwyneth had two Labrador retrievers, Anca and Holden, the latter whom Bruce brought to the set when he visited. (As Gwyneth's circumstances improved, so did her dogs': For one film shoot when he traveled to be with her, Holden got to take a private flight on a Columbia jet that happened to be going to the same place.) After their stay in Paris, Anca started responding only to French. "Say 'come' or 'sit' in English and she ignores you," Gwyneth said. "It's so pretentious."

After a while, Gwyneth found her way to the kitchen supply store E. Dehillerin, in the first arrondissement, where she bought cookware to better outfit her apartment. It was here in Paris where she would later say she got into "asking the crew and any cool people on set where to go, what to see, and where to eat."

After all her work preparing for the film, Gwyneth had minutes of screen time. But it was just as well: Critics panned the movie when it came out in 1995. Yet *The Boston Globe*'s Jay Carr wrote, "Gwyneth Paltrow, whom I unhesitatingly declare one of America's best young actresses, is the film's strongest personality as Jefferson's possessive daughter, who cows him."

Her next role wouldn't go over nearly so well.

WITH ANOTHER FILM completed, Gwyneth returned to the Berkshires to star in a production of Chekhov's *The Seagull*, playing Nina, the ingenue, whom her mother had played in Williamstown when Gwyneth was a toddler. Blythe would play Arkadina, mother of Treplev. While Treplev falls deeply in love with Nina, she embarks on a doomed affair with Arkadina's lover, Trigorin, with whom she has a child who dies soon after birth, leaving both Nina and Treplev devastated.

The cast rehearsed in the linoleum-floored basement of a stone church with no air-conditioning. Humidity seeped into the building. The room had windows and a door to the outside where actors would take breaks. Leading into the basement was a dingy hallway where Blythe would pull Gwyneth aside from the other actors, including Christopher Walken, who may have been the most relaxed of anyone in the production, carrying around four or five translations so he could pick his favorite version of each line. But the hot, stuffy room had a way of bringing the actors' emotions to the surface.

Blythe, whose turn as Nina at Williamstown became a legendary PBS special, would try to quietly dispense actorly advice to her daughter. Once again, Gwyneth wasn't interested. "There was a lot of, 'Mom, quit telling me how to be Nina.' So it was funny," Gwyneth's costar Reg Rogers remembered.

The role of Nina is regarded as one of the most difficult parts ever written for an actress, never mind one with limited life experience. "The first three acts came easier to her because she was that kind of bright light," said director Michael Greif (whose smash hit *Rent* would premiere on Broadway two years later). "The Nina you first meet is exuberant and full of life and wants to take on the world and has extraordinary optimism. And the second Nina you meet in the fourth act is a broken, broken woman, all of whose dreams have been dashed. All of the hopes she had have been not only unfulfilled but they've been poisoned. She's been hurt by this man, by the world, by her own ambitions enormously."

It was the most complex role Gwyneth had played, made all the more complicated by performing it alongside her mother, a legendary Nina. Gwyneth "had the play on her shoulders," Greif recalled, "and she was very young, and she handled it all really, really admirably." She needed a lot of direction, however, and Blythe—who, when she played the role, had been a full decade older than Gwyneth and a mother— stepped in to shield her. She didn't want people telling Gwyneth what to do.

"She gets so panicked about me doing well that I don't feel judged by her, unless I'm doing something she thinks I could do better," Gwyneth said. "I was a bit nervous about doing it, but she really helped me. When I was bad, she told me I was bad. And when I was good, she told me I was good."

Gwyneth's life had little overlap with Nina's, but her acting talent was clear. "She could access her emotional life as fast as I've ever seen,"

Rogers said. "There are people who've got to work to get there, they've got to think about their dog or their mother. She could just turn it on. And that is a talent. I don't believe it's a skill. I think it's a talent that is just innate in her."

AT NIGHT, THE cast would gather to decompress at the college bar on the sloping three-block main street of Williamstown. Rogers would order a vodka tonic, Gwyneth a beer, and the two would talk about the day's rehearsal. Gwyneth's friend Matthew Perry, who was also supposed to perform that summer in the festival, showed up one night, but he left before *The Seagull* started, to work on the television sitcom *Friends*.*

The Seagull ran from August 3 to 14 on the festival's main stage. Reviews were brutal. While Rogers received scathing critiques, Gwyneth didn't fare much better; both got low marks for failing to capture the heaviness of the ending. A distinction had emerged between mother and daughter: Gwyneth was a film performer, whereas Blythe—whose reviews were significantly stronger—was a natural on the stage.

Ben Brantley wrote in *The New York Times*, "Actually, the real tragedy of the play's conclusion is that its director has steered two relatively untried actors, Mr. Rogers and Ms. Paltrow, into laugh-milking, cartoon performances and then abandoned them when those interpretations no longer make sense. In the devastating final encounter between Nina and Treplev, neither seems to have a clue as to what to do. I'm unfamiliar with Mr. Rogers's previous work, but Ms. Paltrow has demonstrated a sly, magnetic bravura on screen. She's a luminous presence and, physically, an ideal Nina; someday, she may be able to complete the portrait."

---

* After Perry died in 2023, Gwyneth remembered, in an Instagram post, hanging out with him that summer. They swam in creeks, drank beer at the local bar, and "kissed in a field of long grass." Perry had filmed the pilot for *Friends* but it hadn't aired yet, and he was hoping it would be his big break.

It was hardly the last time her projects would be poorly reviewed. One producer she worked with around this time said Gwyneth read some of the critiques of her work during this period. If they bothered her, she didn't show it.

RIGHT AFTER *THE Seagull* closed, Gwyneth packed up and headed to Canada to join the cast of *Moonlight and Valentino*, a film that had everything going for it: a great script; director David Anspaugh, an old friend of her father who was coming off two successful movies, *Hoosiers* and *Rudy*; and a cast that included Oscar nominee Kathleen Turner and Oscar winner Whoopi Goldberg.

Anspaugh had worked for Bruce in the eighties. When the network was threatening to push him out (Anspaugh believed this was owing to jealousy over him winning an award), Bruce had pushed back and hired him to direct nine episodes of *St. Elsewhere*. Anspaugh never forgot it. He had known Gwyneth since she was a kid on the set, and he cast her to play the sister of his main character, played by Turner, a young woman seeking comfort from her closest friends after her husband dies suddenly.

Anspaugh wanted Bruce to know that he'd take care of his daughter the same way Bruce had taken care of him. "Look, I'm hands off, David. You go dance with her. She'll do it," he told Anspaugh, adding what he'd previously told Susan Baerwald when she was casting *Cruel Doubt*: "She's got it."

When *Moonlight and Valentino* came out on September 29, 1995, the reviews were blistering. Roger Ebert called it "slow, plotless, and relentless—one of those deals where you find yourself tapping your watch, to be sure it hasn't stopped." *The Boston Globe* wrote, "Even Paltrow, that most promising of young actors, is stymied by the inane screenplay . . ." And the *Los Angeles Times* declared it "a lazy dramatic comedy where everything is implied and nothing revealed," conceding, "Paltrow gives Lucy a combination of flakiness and innocence that makes her the most interesting of the quartet." It earned only $2.5 million at the box office in the U.S. and Canada. Gwyneth never spoke to Anspaugh again and later damned the film with the faintest praise. "I kind of—how shall I put this?—ran out of money at one point," she said. "I just don't think *Moonlight and Valentino* has a specific appeal. [But] it's not an offensive movie." It was the beginning of a long pattern of distancing herself from projects that ended up poorly reviewed or box office flops.

The bad reviews in that period of her career, however, didn't seem to hurt Gwyneth's acting reputation. Many writers and critics have sought to explain her unstoppable ascendance, all the more notable given a résumé with so many forgettable movies. Though her parents were fading into the background of her biography by this point, a string of celebrity boyfriends would soon make her a media personality in an entirely new way.

But those critics may have changed—if temporarily—her attitude toward fame. Within a year, she claimed she had stopped reading about herself in the press. "There's a part of us that's so tender and a part of us that's our ego. Both of those parts get so hurt when people don't like us or they say, 'I hate what you're doing. I hate what you stand for.'"

CHAPTER 9

Brad Romance

I don't think she was in awe of his fame. I think she just liked him.

—Michael Kaplan

Around six months before a life-altering romance, twenty-one-year-old Gwyneth, wearing a white bikini and a gold Cartier Panthère watch, lounged in a chaise on her hotel room's patio in Cabo San Lucas, Mexico. Though she'd been in mostly middling movies, her trajectory was clear. The kind of mega-fame that befalls few Hollywood stars was nearing her reach. The same wasn't true for her twenty-seven-year-old actor/model boyfriend, Donovan Leitch Jr., who was lying in bed with food poisoning. He and Gwyneth had flown in from New York for a getaway with Leitch's sister, actress Ione Skye and her then-boyfriend, Adam Horovitz of the Beastie Boys. Horovitz had gone for a swim in the sea when Skye came out of her adjoining suite and reclined next to Gwyneth.

Gwyneth tossed the script she'd been reading onto the ground beside her. "Well, that one didn't make sense."

Skye had appeared in a few films, including the eighties classic *Say Anything*, but she was struggling to find her next role. She had switched agents but seldom heard from the new one. Gwyneth was having the opposite problem. She had brought a stack of scripts to Cabo, Skye recalled in her memoir, *Say Everything*, "so tall it could have *been* a coffee table."

The question of why Gwyneth, whose body of work was fine but not stellar, was so often the chosen one while careers of successful actors like Skye stalled is hard to answer. While Gwyneth wanted to be famous, one close friend from the time said she never gave the impression that she would do *anything* to achieve such status. People in the entertainment industry had a hard time explaining why Gwyneth became such a star. They often talked about of course wanting to audition Blythe Danner and Bruce Paltrow's daughter. Or how Gwyneth had a star's indescribable quality that alters the energy of a room. Or her professionalism. Or the ease with which she handled auditions and shoots. But they tend to come back to her famous boyfriends. "If you think about it," said a close friend from this period, "she's kind of famous by who she dated."

Leitch, who never seemed like a serious boyfriend to Gwyneth's friends, was much less known than her future partners. Though Skye found Gwyneth "intimidating," they had also had fun together. Not long before the trip, Gwyneth had attended a party at Skye and Horovitz's empty new house, where everyone there that night took hallucinogenic mushrooms, Skye later wrote in *Say Everything*. She alleged Gwyneth partook and claimed she curled up in a dog bed before they went on to play truth or dare.

However, Skye felt concerned about how Gwyneth treated her brother. Once, when he took Gwyneth to the movies and they showed up after the trailers had started, she refused to stay, her experience tainted. Then there was the casually cruel way she felt Gwyneth talked to him.

In Cabo, Leitch poked his head out onto the patio to ask what time it was. Gwyneth said, "It's half past four, darling."

"I've slept the day away," he said. "I'm sorry."

"If you say 'sorry' one more time . . . !"

When Skye confronted her brother about how Gwyneth spoke

to him, he said it happened only occasionally. "But I'm annoying," he added. "I don't mind."

One of the scripts Gwyneth received around then was for a shadowy thriller that would have her character lying in bed with the lead, played by the sexy hitchhiker from *Thelma & Louise*, the two of them cuddling and kissing. Leitch didn't like the idea of it, but Gwyneth laughed off his concern.

Not long after the trip, she was one of ten actresses—including Sarah Jessica Parker and Nicole Kidman—christened "the Class of 2000" by *Vanity Fair* for its first Hollywood issue, published in 1995. All ten women posed for a foldout cover.*

At the photo shoot, she told *Vanity Fair*'s Krista Smith that Leitch was still anxious about her upcoming role alongside Pitt. But again, Smith recalled, "She just laughed it off."

BRAD PITT HADN'T forgotten about his chemistry with Gwyneth from her audition for *Legends of the Fall*. As one producer remembered it, he had been interested in her since then, and when the team for David Fincher's *Se7en* was looking for someone to play his wife, Brad suggested Gwyneth. "This is the feel-bad movie of '95," Pitt said. "We needed someone who could take those little seconds she gets and fill them with soul, and that's what I'd always seen in her performances—soul."

Husband-and-wife producing partners Arnold and Anne Kopelson had hired Fincher despite his recent flop, *Alien 3*. The script, by Andrew Kevin Walker, told the story of a serial killer, played by Kevin Spacey, whose murders illustrate, in gruesome detail, the seven deadly sins. Gwyneth had tea at the Chateau Marmont in Los Angeles to dis-

---

* The magazine was slammed as sexist since the actresses were styled in lingerie and stilettos—except Sandra Bullock and Gwyneth. Unwilling to wear anything more revealing, Gwyneth appeared in a floor-length silver ball gown.

cuss the part with casting director Billy Hopkins, who had known her socially after casting Blythe in a 1990 Lincoln Center production of *Six Degrees of Separation* (though Blythe ultimately had to bow out of the role). Many actresses had been wary of the part, given the violence in the film. Gwyneth went home, read the script, and told Hopkins she liked it. She then went in to read with Fincher and Pitt and landed the part.

However, she received another offer around the same time to appear with Keanu Reeves in *Feeling Minnesota*. Unsure which one to take, she consulted with a friend, who said, "Well, who do you want to date, Brad Pitt or Keanu Reeves?" Gwyneth chose *Se7en* and Pitt, and Cameron Diaz took the *Feeling Minnesota* part.

The Kopelsons had worked with Morgan Freeman on *Outbreak*, and with their help, Fincher cast him to play the older, wiser detective opposite Pitt, the new hotheaded cop in town.

Gwyneth's part was small, so she wasn't on set that long. On one of those days, costume designer Michael Kaplan was finishing up a fitting with Pitt when Fincher called.

"Gwyneth is with me," Fincher said. "When Brad's done with his fitting, would you walk him over?" When Kaplan did, and Gwyneth and Brad entered the same airspace for the first time on the shoot, something sparked between them. "I think it was kind of love at first sight," Kaplan said.

Gwyneth hadn't given Brad much consideration before then. "I thought he was very handsome from movies—you know, the way people are. But I also thought, *Oh, he'll just be one of those young Movie Star Boys*. But he's not. He's a really good person. And I knew it that first day on the set. And then I got nervous."

Around that time, Gwyneth asked Leitch if they could take a break. Her rep at the time said the breakup "had nothing to do with Brad Pitt." But as Ione Skye put it, Gwyneth "wasn't ready for anything too serious."

•   •   •

BY THE TIME *Se7en* filmed, Pitt was a bona fide movie star who had a habit of falling in love with his costars—among them Juliette Lewis in *Too Young to Die?* and Geena Davis in *Thelma & Louise*. All the privileges that had defined Gwyneth's childhood—wealth, famous parents, private schools, Hollywood connections—were foreign to Pitt. He had grown up in Missouri and was raised as a Southern Baptist by a father who owned a trucking company and a mother who worked as a school counselor. Two weeks shy of earning a journalism degree at the University of Missouri, Pitt headed to Los Angeles to pursue acting. Once there, he took odd jobs, including dressing up as a chicken for the chain restaurant El Pollo Loco. He booked small roles on shows like *Dallas* and *Growing Pains* before landing his big break in *Thelma & Louise*. While *Se7en* filmed, *People* released the all-important issue crowning him the "Sexiest Man Alive." And yet Gwyneth, still a newcomer, seemed like a natural on set. After a take, she would approach Fincher to suggest changes, and often he would agree. Her taste also stood out. She would arrive wearing a tank top, but it was never just *any* tank top, but rather something specific and intentional. For one scene, she had her heart set on wearing the kind of long skirt that was fashionable at the time, and she talked to Kaplan about it. He wasn't sure it worked for her character—the wife of a police officer—but "Gwyneth used her feminine wiles to just get me to say okay." He continued, "She had this quality with men where she could kind of just put her hand on your shoulder, and there was something very seductive about her." Somehow, as she had when entering Spence as a seventh grader, she already seemed like a star. "She was just so self-possessed and sure of herself and graceful and articulate. She had arrived already before she arrived."

Gwyneth had always been like this. She wasn't wowed by what she was doing, she didn't worship at the altars of certain directors, and she had always been oddly comfortable around adults. Gwyneth was always on her own level, not anyone else's. "She's not like Nicole Kidman," said one very successful producer who worked with Gwyneth. "Nicole was very ambitious, and she sought out filmmakers to work with whose work she respected. I think that Gwyneth is much more confident in herself."

THE PITT-PALTROW ROMANCE came to fruition pretty quickly and didn't stay hidden for long. The two would walk around the set holding hands and leaning on each other, and smoked cigarettes together outside their trailers, Gwyneth holding hers like a thirties movie star. "I don't think she was in awe of his fame. I think she just liked him," Kaplan said. "If they didn't get together, it would've been a surprise."

Bruce, however, was in awe. After visiting the set, he said to his friend Aspen chef Gordon Naccarato, "Can you believe my daughter? Oh my God. It's fucking Brad Pitt!"

GWYNETH HAD JUST begun to emerge into her own spotlight. Now, as the tabloids caught on to her new relationship, she was frustrated to be pulled into the orbit of a brighter star, as she had been when her mother was so often mentioned as her modifier.

By late February 1995, about a month into filming, the romance was all over gossip columns, though their reps initially denied it. Gwyneth would learn quickly what it meant to be truly famous, the badgering scrutiny she had never imagined when she was fantasizing about this life as a little girl, the side effect of Hollywood success that her mother had avoided and always hoped to protect her from. Paparazzi started showing up to the *Se7en* soundstage, trying to photograph Gwyneth and Pitt together. The studio tried to hide them from photographers, not only to protect glimpses of Fincher's movie from leaking but also because they annoyed Pitt and Gwyneth. The paparazzi were the primary aspect of her public life that seemed consistently to bother her. On the set, security guards would tell them not to go out certain doors where paparazzi were waiting.

In April, just before the London premiere of *Legends of the Fall*,

Gwyneth and Pitt took a ten-day trip to St. Barts, where they rented a private villa at the Le Toiny hotel. Here, they didn't have the same protection they did on set, and paparazzi photographed them completely nude in broad daylight outside their rental. The villa was "in full view of a well-used footpath to the nearby beach," according to *The People*, the British publication that printed the photos on April 30. The images ran again a week and a half later in *The National Enquirer*, this time with strategic blurring.

After the trip, Pitt found out about the photos through his manager, who called one morning before Bruce was about to arrive for breakfast. Pitt knew he had to tell Bruce what happened.

Bruce buried his head in his palms and then, after a long silence, looked up and said, "Was anybody hurt? Anybody get sick? Well, then, okay." Bruce, who had high standards for his daughter, had been unimpressed by Gwyneth's past boyfriends. But he really liked Brad. "He's a really nice boy," he told friends.

Pitt said he wasn't worried about being exposed himself and was concerned only for Gwyneth, who found it annoying but didn't seem particularly rattled by it (the photos at the time were confined to print publications, not splashed widely across the internet the way they would be in later years). However, back on the *Se7en* set, Pitt didn't brush it off so easily. Kaplan told him, "I don't know why you're so upset. You have nothing to hide."

Pitt just said, "That's your opinion."

AFTER THE PHOTOS came out, Madonna, who had gifted Bruce years before with a personal note telling Gwyneth to stop smoking, stepped up once again. "She's experiencing the upsides and the downsides of being famous for the first time," she said. "That's a lot for someone to take . . . So I'm happy to help her." The two developed a friendship.

The week the photos were released, Gwyneth was already at work on her next project, a film then called *Sydney*, directed by Paul Thomas

Anderson. Word had come down to the crew from department heads not to mention the nude photos on set.

Anderson had offered Gwyneth the role of Clementine without an audition—a first for her—and she would be paid basically "pennies," one producer remembered. Anderson, who was only a few years older than Gwyneth, had achieved critical success with his previous short film, *Cigarettes & Coffee*. Producer Robert Jones had brought the project to the production company and distributor Rysher Entertainment with a budget of not more than $3 million. Gwyneth would act alongside John C. Reilly, Philip Baker Hall, and Samuel L. Jackson, who'd just finished *Pulp Fiction*. Rysher figured the movie was a safe enough bet, since at least two of the cast members were guaranteed late-night talk show segments. So they let Jones, Anderson, and their crew flit off to Reno to film without any supervision.

The plot revolved around Sydney, played by Baker Hall, a career gambler who teaches his tricks to John, played by Reilly, who was down on his luck and needed money. When John gets back on his feet, he starts dating Clementine, a cocktail waitress/prostitute played by Gwyneth.

With no producers hovering over them, the crew got along well and had a good time despite the punishing schedule. Gwyneth's brother, Jake, then an aspiring director, was hired as a production assistant. Professionally, Jake was taking after Bruce. "He and I were very close, so in so many ways, I wanted to be him," he said.

His fellow PAs thought Jake looked like his sister and would tease him about what a "beautiful boy" he was. Occasionally, Jake and Gwyneth would chitchat, but she was a star, and he was mostly running errands. Gwyneth and John C. Reilly would joke around on set, sometimes cracking up over a blown line, but as soon as they were called back to their places, Gwyneth could summon Clementine effortlessly.

Despite being a budding tabloid star and girlfriend of the "Sexiest Man Alive," Gwyneth enjoyed mingling with the crew. They filmed mostly at night, in a casino, where a makeshift greenroom was set up in one of the meeting rooms and outfitted with snacks and couches. When the crew had to reset lights, leaving many of them with down-time, Gwyneth would hang out in the greenroom with the rest of them, drinking tea. She disarmed them, sitting there once in her black waitress costume talking about a story printed in *Star* magazine about her and Brad that she said was untrue. "Sometimes these magazines just pick things up and run with them," she said.

Behind the closed door of her trailer, Gwyneth could be indis-creet. Alyson Murphy, the key hairstylist, hadn't heard of Gwyn-eth Paltrow and kept mispronouncing her name. Once settled into her chair, Gwyneth mostly wanted to talk about being Brad Pitt's girlfriend. "There were some things, I'm like, *Okay, I really prob-ably didn't need to know that about Brad Pitt*," Murphy said. Gwyn-eth would ask the hair and makeup team for advice about things like bikini waxing and how to handle being in a relationship. She seemed to Murphy like a tomboy who was trying to figure out how to be more feminine.

In these conversations, Gwyneth would call herself the media's "flavor of the month," invoking Blythe's strategic modesty, and predicting—perhaps sincerely—that her time in the spotlight would be over soon enough.

Asked later how she felt about the idea that losing her privacy was the price of fame, she said, "I resent it right now, because most of it is happening because of who I go out with. I hope that my work will speak for itself, and that people won't judge me based on things that go on in my personal life, whether it's to do with my parents or my friends or whoever."

AFTER A GRUELING twenty-eight days of filming in Reno, Anderson and his team went into the editing room. Anderson was headstrong about getting the final cut of the film (the ultimate say on the version released to the public after editing).

When a cut was completed, an audience test screening took place at a theater in Santa Monica for about a hundred people. One long scene involving Clementine and John holding an injured man hostage in a motel room because he didn't pay her for sex was disturbing enough that around a third of the audience walked out of the movie.

Unwilling to implement edits that producers thought would make the film more palatable, Anderson bought the movie back from Rysher. He told the *Los Angeles Times* that he, Gwyneth, and Reilly collectively chipped in $250,000 to finish the film, later renamed *Hard Eight*, which Gwyneth thought sounded like "a porno movie." It made $224,000 at the worldwide box office on its roughly $3 million budget.

While *Hard Eight* would be more appreciated in retrospect, critics gave it mixed reviews. The New York *Daily News* called Gwyneth "studiously vacant." The *Boston Herald* was even harsher: "In one scene, Paltrow is curled up in a fetal position on a motel room floor, hair stuck to her face, mascara running down her cheeks. You half expect Jon Lovitz's Master Thespian to appear and remind us that what we are seeing is great 'ACTING.'" Yet, the *Los Angeles Times* called it "her best role yet."

Gwyneth repeatedly denied being ambitious in interviews. In a specifically Hollywood sense, she lacked the desperation that certain actors had to make it. But those who worked with her saw her as ambitious, since she was driving toward a specific kind of acting career. She threw her support publicly behind designated people and projects while distancing as much as she could from the potential humiliation of others, which helped mold her image as a high-class, Oscar-destined actress.

To win that award, she would need to work with the right people. And she would find them at Miramax.

CHAPTER 10

Period Piece, Power Play

I have to say to Brad, "This is beluga and this is osetra."
—Gwyneth Paltrow

Gwyneth's transition from working actress and new tabloid fodder to A-lister coincided with her entrée to Miramax Films, at the behest of Harvey Weinstein. Weinstein, who cofounded Miramax with his brother, Bob, in 1979 (they named it after their parents, Miriam and Max), had a reputation for making quality movies. He was also known as a mercurial bully. Mark Gill, Miramax's head of marketing in the mid-to-late nineties believed that Weinstein was "clinically diagnosed bipolar." "You could get, within the span of ten minutes, 'Sweetie, baby, cookie, honey,' followed by 'You're the dumbest person who ever lived.'"

Miramax staff had a saying: "If Bob was driving the bus, he would run you over and keep going. If Harvey was driving the bus, he would run you over, but he would come back and take you to the hospital."

Gwyneth would later recall meeting Weinstein in 1994 or 1995 near an elevator at the Toronto Film Festival, when he stopped her to praise her work. She said she felt "legitimized by his opinion."

"He was at the Toronto film festival doing business, or whatever he does at film festivals—run around and yell at people," she said. "I guess he'd seen *Flesh and Bone* and wanted me to work with Miramax. I thought, *Yeah, right.*"

Weinstein said in an email that he had seen her "in a small part in a movie" (likely *Flesh and Bone*, but he didn't fully remember), and recalled "something outstanding about her." He said that her agent and his team asked him to meet with her, and he did, finding her "bright and very smart."

On the face of it, Miramax was a perfect home for a star like Gwyneth. The scripts were generally good, the films smart but accessible, and Weinstein relentlessly focused on winning Oscars for himself and his talent. Though he had a darker side, he was a champion for his darlings, often masquerading as their protector.

"He was a bully and an egotistical monster with the temperament of a child of five," said Jack Lechner, a former Miramax development executive. "It's like, well, how did this monster survive and succeed year after year? Because he was also really fucking smart."

As for filmmaking, Weinstein had a million ideas, and needed grown-ups around to tell him which ones had a shot. "At the same time that it was hellish in some aspects, it was fantastic in other aspects," said Lechner, who was part of that crowd. "You're working at great movies with great talent, you're going all over the world, and feeling like you're actually making entertainment that is reaching an audience."

Since Weinstein chain-smoked, he almost always flew private, on a plane the staff referred to as the "flying ashtray." Few wanted to be trapped in the smoky cabin with Weinstein. "We used to bring along what we called internally 'shiny rocks,'" said Lechner. That could be a new script or a new cut of a movie—but the best shiny rock of all was a movie star. Weinstein loved stars, and he behaved better when one was around.

Gwyneth also encountered Weinstein when she was auditioning for *Prince of Jutland*, which was released in 1994 as *Royal Deceit*, in which a Viking prince avenges his father's murder. She sat down with Weinstein in a room at the Peninsula Hotel in Beverly Hills, along with top

Miramax producer Meryl Poster. Gwyneth had already met with Poster about the movie; Weinstein had seen Polaroids of her from that session and decided to see her in person. However, as recalled by someone with knowledge of the encounter, Weinstein decided he didn't want to cast her because the part required nudity, and he didn't want to subject Bruce Paltrow's daughter to that when she seemed like "a nice girl."

DOUGLAS MCGRATH, A former *Saturday Night Live* writer who had cowritten the Woody Allen film *Bullets over Broadway*, was determined to make a film of Jane Austen's 1816 novel about a young woman who thinks too well of her own matchmaking abilities. His friend and producer Steven Haft agreed to support the movie with McGrath as director. Haft, who had produced *Dead Poets Society*, knew Weinstein and passed him the script.

Weinstein said no. Haft figured that whoever at Miramax had told Weinstein to pass wasn't appreciating the wry, mannered humor, which hadn't been done before in Jane Austen remakes.

"Harvey, I think you're not getting it," Haft told him. "By now I think I know what a good project looks like. Give me five thousand dollars, and I'm going to hire a casting guy, who I think is the best, to stage a reading in your theater."

Weinstein agreed, so Haft enlisted Billy Hopkins to cast about fifteen actors for the reading of McGrath's entire *Emma* screenplay. Having cast *Se7en*, Hopkins picked Gwyneth as the lead.

McGrath came from Midland, Texas, and he figured that if Gwyneth could do such a credible central Texas accent for *Flesh and Bone*, she could do the same thing with an upper-class southern English one. "I have never heard an actor or actress not from Texas sound remotely like a real Texan . . . We had many actresses, big and small, who wanted to play this part. The minute she started the read-through, the very first line, I thought, *Everything is going to be fine; she's going to be brilliant*," he said.

Weinstein, along with other executives, watched from the back of the screening room with Haft one row behind him. Weinstein knew the screenplay was good: McGrath's talents weren't in question. Weinstein and his team were watching specifically to see if McGrath's take on nineteenth-century humor would land with a young audience.

The reading had been populated with well-known actors, including Peter Gallagher and Stephen Collins; Gwyneth may have been one of the least known people on the stage. She was wearing casual street clothes, but Weinstein, who was paying rapt attention, knew that Gwyneth had an unusually luminous presence and delightfully embodied Emma's unique mix of cleverness and naïveté as the audience laughed along. By ten minutes in, the audience *knew* Emma, a character Austen described as "handsome, clever, and rich" with "a disposition to think a little too well of herself." No one in that room doubted, as they watched Gwyneth lift the character off the page so enchantingly, that the humor would work.

Making *Emma* with Gwyneth in the lead was Weinstein's opportunity both to hitch her to Miramax and to develop his own relationship with her. He turned around in his seat and said to Haft, "Let's make this movie." Then he turned back and watched the rest of the reading. *Emma* was, to Weinstein, all about Gwyneth.

Emma would be Gwyneth's first leading role—the movie that would make her a star.

McGrath said, "No other studio would have let me cast Gwyneth Paltrow in the lead at that point. Harvey takes risks in a business practically devoid of it—and turns out movies you know won't degrade you."

WITH *EMMA* UNDERWAY, Weinstein decided he wanted something from Gwyneth in return for giving her the part.

Matt Reeves had also attended the *Emma* reading. Miramax had hired him to direct *The Pallbearer*, starring Weinstein's pick to be the next Tom Hanks: David Schwimmer, then known only as Ross from *Friends*. Reeves wanted Gwyneth in his film, too. Not long after the reading, Weinstein claimed to Gwyneth that he'd cooled a little bit on *Emma*, but he was willing to make her a deal. "If you do *The Pallbearer*, we'll make *Emma*," he told her.

Gwyneth found the script for *The Pallbearer* weak and felt like Weinstein was bribing her. Gwyneth's original deal for *Emma* paid her six figures, remembered one person who worked on the film, but Miramax redid her contract before *Emma* came out to cover that and *The Pallbearer*, which meant she would earn more.

She later described feeling protective of her "artistic integrity" but agreed to risk compromising it (which she did, given that *The Pallbearer* was a flop) because she believed Emma Woodhouse was "the best part ever written for a young girl." It was the kind of movie her parents would approve of, as well as one that could cement her position among the A-list. Meryl Poster, then senior vice president of production at Miramax, said, "I think that in his unique way he was saying, 'Do *The Pallbearer* and I'm going to make *Emma* and that will make you a star.'"

Gwyneth saw Weinstein initially as a mentor. She had been charmed and flattered by their encounter in Toronto. Now here he was, giving her the lead part in a movie specifically to make her as famous as she'd always known she'd be. She loved his team at Miramax, who thought of themselves as a repertory theater company, like the group she'd grown up with at Williamstown. The appeal of working for Weinstein seemed obvious to her friends: He made good movies, he gave her good roles, and from what they could tell, he really liked her. Gwyneth was always wise beyond her years, good at managing older people like Weinstein (around twenty years her senior) without seeming intimidated.

But Weinstein soon revealed his true nature to her.

.　.　.

AFTER BOOKING *EMMA* but before filming started, Gwyneth, who was living in New York, took a trip to Los Angeles. Her agents at CAA had sent a fax to her hotel, telling her to meet with Weinstein in his room at the Peninsula Beverly Hills. Gwyneth thought nothing of it—she was happy to see Weinstein, who had begun acting as a father figure, building her up and nurturing her.

Gwyneth went to his suite, understanding the location to be for privacy. "I bounced up there, I'm sort of like a golden retriever, all happy to see Harvey," she recalled in Jodi Kantor and Megan Twohey's book *She Said: Breaking the Sexual Harassment Story That Helped Ignite a Movement*. Toward the end of an otherwise fine, business-oriented conversation, the dynamic changed. Weinstein, then around forty-three, put his hands on her, and suggested they move to the bedroom to give each other massages.

"I was a kid, I was signed up, I was petrified," she later told *The New York Times*. She was stunned and sickened to learn that Weinstein was sexually interested in her. He asked again to go to the bedroom.

Gwyneth found a way to excuse herself without offending her new boss. As she drove away, she kept thinking, *I thought you were my uncle Harvey*. She told her agent and a handful of close friends and family, including Pitt.

Back in New York on May 2, 1995, a few months before *Emma* started filming, Pitt and Gwyneth attended the opening night of *Hamlet*, starring Ralph Fiennes. Gwyneth wore little makeup, with her shoulder-length hair in a half-ponytail, and a pale satin gown under a black leather blazer. Pitt, with the same goatee he'd worn for *Se7en*, wore a white shirt, unbuttoned with no tie, and an oversize topcoat.

Pitt knew how terrified Gwyneth had been after her encounter with Weinstein at the Peninsula. He also knew she had signed on to do two movies for him. He decided to approach Weinstein, also a guest at the premiere. "At that moment, I was just a boy from the Ozarks on the playground . . . and that's how we confronted with things," he later recalled. He told Weinstein something to the effect of "If you ever make her feel uncomfortable again, I'll kill you." Pitt returned to Gwyneth's side and told her what he had said. She would later describe it as Pitt "energetically" throwing Weinstein against the wall.

"He leveraged his fame and power to protect me at a time when I didn't have fame or power yet," she said.

She and Pitt walked out of the theater, exchanging concerned looks as cameras flashed at them from the other side of a police barricade. With a protective hand on Gwyneth's lower back, Pitt escorted her through the crowd.

AFTER THAT CONFRONTATION, Weinstein called Gwyneth to unleash on her for talking about what had happened at the Peninsula. He screamed at her for what she would later remember as "a long time," threatening to ruin her career. She later told *The New York Times* that she feared she would lose the part in *Emma* and asked that their relationship remain professional.

Weinstein disputed her version of events. In an email, Weinstein admitted to asking Gwyneth for a massage, and said that he apologized to her. He also claimed that he never threatened her after Pitt confronted him, and that he apologized to Pitt. He believed Gwyneth forgave him for "making a pass at her," explaining, "we could never have had the working relationship and friendship we had if she hadn't forgiven me." Finally, he claimed he was respectful of her from then on, stating, "as far as my working relationship went with her, I never put my arm around her without her expressed consent, but she hugged me many, many times over the years."

Another Miramax source remembered that Gwyneth didn't want to do *Emma*, mainly because she didn't want to be away from Pitt and had received an offer for a Woody Allen movie (this person didn't know about the Weinstein incident but did not think it had impacted her decision about the film). Miramax insisted she keep her commitment.

Though Gwyneth seemed, to one friend who observed their relationship, easily able to manage him, Weinstein wasn't always capable of true professionalism. From then on, "he was alternately generous and supportive and championing, and punitive and bullying," Gwyneth told *The New York Times*. After the incident, she told the friend about another actress she'd heard of who'd performed a sexual favor for Weinstein for a part. While Gwyneth would say, "Harvey—he's gross," she didn't act intimidated by him or other powerful people.

THAT SUMMER, GWYNETH went ahead as planned with filming *The Pallbearer*, in which Schwimmer serves as an aimless pallbearer for a childhood friend he doesn't remember and falls for his high school crush, played by Gwyneth. Weinstein mostly left the crew alone during filming. Yet producer Paul Webster acknowledged, "He was in love with Gwyneth, thought of her as his next protégé, and was in his star-making mode."

Weinstein had to have known that if he and Miramax didn't launch her, some other producer or studio would. "For all his faults—and there are many that we're all too aware of—Harvey was very good at managing careers and massaging success in the way that he does," said Webster. "Harvey made it his job to be Gwyneth's best friend."

The Pallbearer was Schwimmer's movie, but Gwyneth, as the supporting star, also promoted it. At a press junket in New York, she was tasked with speaking to sixty-four reporters spread among eight hotel suites. She had twenty-five minutes in each suite, and the reporters mostly wanted to ask her about Pitt. Gwyneth handled it gracefully, confirming that Brad did indeed grow up eating mac and cheese in Missouri, and laughed off questions about the nude photos, saying, "I think they could have used a bit of airbrushing."

Gwyneth was chosen again to appear in *Vanity Fair*'s 1996 Hollywood portfolio that came out shortly before *The Pallbearer*, this time alongside her mother. Perched on the back of a couch above Blythe, the photo perfectly symbolized Gwyneth's star ascendant.

The Pallbearer came out on May 3, 1996, a few months before *Emma*, and bombed. Once again, since Gwyneth was not the star, it wasn't held against her.

The Pallbearer wouldn't be the last unfortunate movie Weinstein would talk Gwyneth into. "She ended up in some kind of horrendous films with him," Webster said. "He would pressure people immensely. And she clearly wasn't immune to that kind of pressure. Once he had your number . . . he'd bypass everybody and come straight to you and just ignore the system."

IN THE SUMMER of 1995, Gwyneth met Brad at the airport and boarded a British Airways flight to London to film *Emma*. He had a backpack, and she had around five suitcases. Had she come alone, the studio would have given her the same modest accommodations as the rest of the cast and crew. But Brad and Gwyneth together needed cover. For part of the shoot, Haft booked them a suite with a balcony at the five-star Berkeley Hotel, which had security to make coming and going easier for a major star like Pitt. Haft ensured that the hotel would make special accommodations for Pitt, allowing him to dine in a T-shirt despite the requirement that gentlemen wear jackets. But there was one condition: They had to vacate the suite for one night in the middle of their stay, and Haft couldn't tell them why. When the day came, Pitt and Gwyneth didn't feel like relocating, but Haft rallied his team to move all their belongings to another hotel room. "You just have to trust me that the reason is an overwhelming one," he told them.

That night, Haft escorted them to a spot near the side entrance of the hotel. "Just watch," he said. Within minutes, three Rolls-Royces pulled up, and out of one stepped Queen Elizabeth and the queen mother, who made their way inside to the balcony suite, where, Haft had been told, they planned to dine.

After Their Royal Highnesses cleared out, the production crew moved Gwyneth and Pitt back in.

. . .

GWYNETH RECEIVED LEADING-LADY treatment. The movie's budget wasn't huge, but she had a car and driver, a personal assistant, and first-class plane tickets in addition to the luxury accommodations. The filming took place in various Austen-esque estates and abbeys within a few hours' drive from London.

Harvey Weinstein didn't spend that much time on location for *Emma*. But when he showed up, entourage in tow, it was like the king had come to town. Everyone was on edge, and no one dared intervene when he lit up a cigar in the historic, stately home where they were filming.

One day when he was on the set, he visited Gwyneth in her trailer. Afterward, she expressed to Haft and Miramax producer Donna Gigliotti that Weinstein had made her uncomfortable. Gwyneth performed beautifully as always. But as one person familiar with the incident recalled, it made for an awkward day of shooting.

HAFT HAD BEEN told that British English had dozens of regional accents, each of which could identify where the speaker grew up or what kind of school they attended. If British audiences were going to accept an American in the title role of a story by one of their most beloved novelists, Gwyneth would have to get it right. Haft took a gamble and hired the relatively unknown accent coach Barbara Berkery, whose work made a tremendous difference in how Gwyneth played the role.

"It turns out that to actually do [the accent] properly, you have to relearn how to speak. So the English accent is so different, and the muscles are so different. Like, where you place the tongue on the teeth and the mouth is so different," Gwyneth said later. "Certain muscles are more relaxed and certain [muscles] are more tense."

Again, she made it look easy. It seemed to drive her costar Jeremy Northam crazy. Northam played Emma's love interest, Mr. Knightley. He had studied acting at the Bristol Old Vic Theatre School and played Hamlet at the Royal National Theatre and worked intensely to prepare for his role in *Emma*. Meanwhile, the prop department would put a bow and arrow in Gwyneth's hand to train for an archery scene, and she'd near the bull's-eye on her first try. Deliberate and studied, Northam worked for days to learn the gavotte dance between Emma and Knightley, but Gwyneth seemed to pick up all the steps before lunch. Gwyneth grew to dislike Northam and, according to someone with knowledge of her feelings, called one of *Emma*'s producers to complain about him. This person was seeing their chemistry in the dailies and told her, "I really don't care. Finish the movie and you'll never have to see him again."

Gwyneth arrived to shoot days with her script tucked under her arm, and she had meaningful suggestions for her character and the film overall, which surprised and impressed the crew. This kind of feedback from a twenty-three-year-old might have offended many directors, but McGrath, directing his first film, seemed to welcome it.

Others were less appreciative. Gwyneth appeared in a few scenes with Ruth Jones, who played a maid. This was Jones's first film role, and she had two lines: "Miss Woodhouse is here" and "Goodbye, Miss Woodhouse."

"Does she really need to say that?" Gwyneth asked one day during filming. "Can I just come in?" McGrath agreed, and Jones's two lines were cut down to one. Jones said later, "Imagine this for people who are starting out. You've got two lines, and someone cuts fifty percent of your script, it's heartbreaking."

DURING *EMMA*'S FILMING, Gwyneth expressed doubts to one crew member that Pitt was right for her, and admitted that she had a crush on Hugh Grant. Though she had finished less college than Pitt had, she perceived herself as an Upper East Side girl with a fancy private-school education who'd grown up around Wall Street families, while he was a boy from Missouri born to religious, conservative Southern Baptist parents. Pitt had attended church each week as a kid, and been baptized at around nine.

"Brad and I had very different upbringings," she told an interviewer. "So when we go to restaurants and order caviar, I have to say to Brad, 'This is beluga and this is osetra.'" When Nancy Jo Sales profiled her the next year for *New York* magazine, Gwyneth said, "*Emma* is funny . . . It made me laugh so many times. Brad was laughing when he watched it—and he wouldn't go and see it in the theater, you know what I mean? He went to see *The Rock*, okay?" (referring to the Michael Bay boom-fest about an escape from Alcatraz, released the same year).

Some of Gwyneth's closest friends also didn't think she and Pitt were right for each other. Pitt had spent his high school years going to Christian revivals where he'd "be moved by the Holy Spirit," he later said, while rock concerts were frowned upon. Though her brother, Jake, had been bar mitzvahed, Gwyneth didn't seem religious as a Spence student. Pitt started questioning his faith in college and later declared himself an atheist, but Gwyneth could not relate to his family's Christian devotion and poked fun at it with her friends. The main thing she seemed to have in common with Pitt was fame, which didn't seem to those close to her like enough to hold a relationship together.

That said, Pitt was a welcome presence on the set of *Emma*. He was kind to the crew, he remembered everyone's names and the drivers' names, he played with everyone's kids, and he was refreshingly unpretentious.

The shoots were taxing—hot and uncomfortable, with corsets and elaborate period updos, with four or five a.m. call times and little sleep in between. Her first time carrying a film, this tedium and the long hours wore on her.

"I have such a battle with the fact that I never feel I'm controlling my own destiny when I'm working," she said that year. "I feel trapped when someone is telling me when to get up and what to put on and which city I'll be in from week to week. I didn't used to think about it. Now, it's starting to drive me crazy."

SE7EN, GWYNETH'S MOVIE with Pitt, came out in theaters on September 22, 1995, while *Emma* was still in production. It debuted at number one and ended up earning $327 million worldwide, making it Gwyneth's biggest film to date. Though she claimed to have stopped reading reviews, she took issue with one critic's assessment of the final scene, in which her severed head is presented to Pitt's character. "I got a bit of heat for doing [*Se7en*] . . . I think it was Janet Maslin in *The New York Times* who said the film treats my character in ways you wouldn't treat a dog. She asked why I wanted to do it. First of all, I'm not in the scene in which I'm decapitated. I know it was disturbing for some people but I thought the script was brilliant, and if she's not played right and she's not a soulful person, the end would be less effective." Around the release of that film, Gwyneth leaned hard into the Blythe Danner media strategy, disavowing any ambition to be a Hollywood star or even to remain an actress for much longer.

"I mean, I would much rather be Robin Wright or Jennifer Jason Leigh than—no offense—Sandra Bullock." In another interview, she said, "I don't really understand the concept of having a career, or what agents mean when they say they're building one for you. I just do things I think will be interesting and that have integrity. I hate those tacky, pointless, big, fluffy, unimportant movies." In ten years' time, she said, "Hopefully I'll be married, with three or four children."

IN THE MEANTIME, when her boyfriend took the stage a few months later to accept a Golden Globe for his supporting role in *12 Monkeys* (*Se7en* had not received any nominations), millions of eyes were on Gwyneth's response from the audience. Brad confessed charmingly to his nervousness, thanking the makers of Kaopectate. He then ran through a long list of other recipients of his gratitude, ending with "especially the love o' my life, my angel, Gwyneth Paltrow." The broadcast cut to Gwyneth, wearing a black-and-white Calvin Klein sheath dress, who, in a dramatic moment, put her hand over her heart and looked down at the table before raising her gaze to Pitt and applauding.

BACK AT MIRAMAX, preparations were underway to release *Emma* and to launch Gwyneth as a bona fide movie star. The dailies were promising, but the studio still worried that viewers wouldn't get the tone. Jane Austen adaptations tended to be serious and sentimental. Once Miramax started testing the movie with audiences and screening it for critics, they saw that the humor was working, and so was Gwyneth—including with British viewers.

Weinstein started talking publicly about an Oscar nomination. "We hope she'll figure in our Oscar plans for next March," he told *USA Today*. Since he said that sort of thing all the time, many staffers at Miramax brushed it off. But Weinstein had something to prove. He believed his indies could outperform films by the major studios, which might invest $70 million in television advertising in hopes of earning $170 million at the box office. Instead of paid marketing, Weinstein relied on publicity. Miramax's publicity team at the time, led by Marcy Granata, felt like press for Gwyneth was in the bag, and their job was to ensure she got the *right* exposure—the kind that touted her acting talent versus just her glamour.

After those earlier failed attempts, Gwyneth finally got her *Vogue* moment in the August 1996 issue. As a tasteful period film, *Emma* appealed to Anna Wintour. *Vogue* sent famed photographer Steven Meisel to Charlottesville, Virginia, where Gwyneth was filming what would be one of her worst reviewed films, *Hush*, with Jessica Lange. Looking WASPy and barely made up, Gwyneth appeared on the cover wearing a tan Ralph Lauren coat over a white silk shirt and matching moleskin pants by Gucci, her hair down and slightly frizzed, behind the coverline "The Nineties It Girl Lets Loose." In the inside photos, she wore dresses by Marc Jacobs and Chanel, a tweed coat by Marni, and Prada tights. *Vogue* included Pitt in the shoot, which was unusual; publicists usually discouraged clients from doing this in case the couple broke up before the issue hit newsstands. Wintour noted in that month's editor's letter that while "*Vogue* is not a celebrity magazine . . . Gwyneth is well-known as the actress every designer wants to dress. She's also the daughter of celebrated actress Blythe Danner, and the girlfriend, you may have heard, of Brad Pitt."

The story, by Charles Gandee, was headlined "The Luckiest Girl Alive." In it, Tom Ford compared Gwyneth to Grace Kelly and Audrey Hepburn, and Calvin Klein referred to her "slightly removed elegance, a chic quality that we haven't seen in a long time."

Gwyneth also appeared on the cover of *New York* magazine around the same time. Editor in chief Kurt Andersen personally knew Doug McGrath and wanted to do what he could to support his film. Top makeup artist Kevyn Aucoin was hired to make Gwyneth up for the photo shoot, and they became friends. Like Weinstein and Wintour, Aucoin saw that she was about to tip over into full-fledged stardom, and he wanted to play a role. The two became close enough that, someone close to Aucoin believed, Gwyneth's publicist Stephen Huvane may have felt a bit threatened by the relationship.

Huvane's impressive list of clients included top actresses like Helen Hunt, who won an Oscar for Best Actress in 1998 for *As Good as It Gets*, and Elisabeth Shue, who was nominated for Best Actress in 1996 for *Leaving Las Vegas*. Huvane saw his job as not only landing major and exclusive media opportunities for his clients, but also protecting them from unflattering coverage. He worked closely with Gwyneth, and seemed to feel they shared a distinct loyalty. Yet Gwyneth developed loyalty to Aucoin, too, who believed Huvane was jealous of their bond. Huvane ran interference between Miramax and Aucoin's agent, which created further friction.

Aucoin's roughly five-thousand-dollar day rate became an issue at Miramax. Meryl Poster, who had become a friend of Gwyneth's, decided it was too costly but didn't want to insert herself into a potentially contentious situation. It fell to Huvane to call Aucoin's office and say that Miramax didn't want to pay their invoices. He may have wanted to fend off a story leaking about her being a diva with a massive makeup budget. The story leaked anyway.

The *New York* cover story ran under the headline "A Star Is Bred." Writer Nancy Jo Sales focused on Gwyneth's New York City roots, comparing the college dropout to her peers from Spence and similar private schools who had gone on to earn Ivy League degrees and ended up with, say, low-level publishing jobs. "People are jealous of her. *I'm* jealous of her," one told Sales. "Gwyneth makes us feel extremely lame."

Emma was released on nine screens on August 2, 1996, pulling in $230,000. On August 9, it opened on around a hundred more screens, earning $1.4 million and coming in twelfth at the box office. (*A Time to Kill*, starring Matthew McConaughey, Sandra Bullock, and Samuel L. Jackson, was number one for the second week in a row.) *Emma* went on to gross $22.2 million on its $7 million budget, which was pretty good for a Miramax film.

Reviewers agreed that Miramax had found their star. "Paltrow, one of the canniest young actresses today, uses her body in subtle ways to help convey her character's internal commotion," the New York *Daily News* wrote. Gwyneth's neck attracted special notice: "The wistful mouth, unguarded neck and a range of postures from defeated to defiant make Emma as lovable as a kitten." *The New York Times* called her "resplendent Emma gliding through the film with an elegance and patrician wit that bring the young Katharine Hepburn to mind."

Weinstein had given Gwyneth her star vehicle. However, like many of his employees, she found him tough. "He was a very difficult boss," she later said. "It was a fraught relationship. We would get in knockdown, drag-out fights." In one instance, Blythe walked in while she was yelling at him on the phone. When Gwyneth told her who she had been talking to, Blythe said, "Oh, my goodness, good for you. Stand up for yourself." Gwyneth also alleged Weinstein withheld money he owed her that was tied to *Emma*'s box office performance. But, as Miramax's hot new star, she was in a stronger position now. She kept pushing, and eventually received a check in the mail with a letter that she later remembered saying something like, "This is not an acknowledgment that we owe you this money, but here's a check."

Mark Gill, Miramax's then–marketing head, said a movie studio not paying someone what they owed was "pretty common," and that with Miramax "it was an issue a lot." Another Miramax employee from the time said, "That's the way he is with everyone."

While Gwyneth gave close friends the impression that she had the upper hand with Weinstein, he treated her in the same manipulative hot-and-cold way he did the rest of his staff. Gwyneth later revealed his bullying behavior: "I never had a problem standing up to him. I wasn't scared of him. I also felt for a period of time, I was the consumer face of Miramax, and I felt it was my duty to push back against him. We had a lot of fights."

Many at Miramax were not privy to Weinstein's harassment of Gwyneth. Reflecting on their relationship in 2018, she said, "[H]e was [always] a bully about work things, he was shaming, he was really hard on me and then was incredibly generous and would send me a private plane somewhere. It was a kind of typical abusive relationship, and I hadn't processed it, because so much of my acting career and so many of the incredible highs and lows, as well, were associated with him and Miramax."

Responding to this characterization of their relationship, Weinstein stated, "I would say that the word *abusive* has nothing to do with my relationship with Gwyneth. I treated her like a princess because I thought she was super talented. She was nice to the people around her and nice to my staff, so I resent the word *abusive*. As far as reprimanding her, usually I was there to patch things up, not reprimand her." He added, "The relationship was fantastic for all the years she worked as an actress for me."

•   •   •

AROUND THE TIME of *Emma*'s opening, Gwyneth and Weinstein were invited to screen the movie at the White House. They flew down on Miramax's jet, along with Marcy Granata. Gwyneth and Pitt sat in their own area, Weinstein in his, and Granata in hers. Hillary and Chelsea Clinton had been scheduled to join, but they ended up touring colleges that day, which left Gwyneth, Pitt, Weinstein, and Granata in a tiny screening room along with President Clinton. Gwyneth occasionally laughed about screening the movie for the president in interviews. "He was snoring right in front of me," she said. "I was like, wow I guess this is going to be a real hit movie."

ON SEPTEMBER 4, 1996, MTV was holding its annual Video Music Awards, and Weinstein wanted Gwyneth to attend. He told Granata, "She has to look like the VMAs." Specifically, he wanted her to wear something sexy by Tom Ford, who was then transforming Gucci into one of the most provocative fashion brands of the nineties. Granata liked the idea of the VMAs. Their hip adaptation of *Emma* was aimed largely at teenage girls and their mothers, and what could be a better way to reach them than the VMAs?

In the run-up to the show, MTV pushed for Gwyneth to walk the red carpet with Pitt, but Miramax resisted—they wanted the focus on *Emma*, not "Brad Pitt's girlfriend." She would go alone—provided they could convince her to attend. So Granata called Stephen Huvane and explained the situation.

"She's not going to go to the VMAs, let alone wear something that looks like the VMAs," said Huvane. "But I'll talk to her."

As Granata understood it, Blythe was opposed to her daughter going to the event, believing a future Oscar nominee wouldn't present at the VMAs.

Gwyneth had just been on the cover of *Vogue*, and the VMAs were comparatively lowbrow. But Granata knew that if Gwyneth had her sights set on winning an Oscar, she had to be a star. And to be a star, her movie had to open big. And to do that, this movie needed teen enthusiasm. Gwyneth agreed to go.

"Just do it your way," Granata said, "and Tom Ford will figure it out."

Gwyneth and Ford's solution would become one of the most iconic celebrity fashion moments of the nineties: a seventies-inspired tailored red velvet pantsuit, fitted to skim rather than cling to her figure, with a pale blue shirt underneath, unbuttoned just enough to be feminine but not enough to show cleavage. "Gwyneth Paltrow's cherry velvet Gucci pantsuit was the sanitized, designer version of a look Steve Tyler and Joe Perry of Aerosmith have been touring in since she was a baby. Onstage, their shirts were unbuttoned only a notch lower than hers," noted the *Los Angeles Times*.

Weinstein was furious. "Look what she's wearing," he said.

Granata saw what Weinstein struggled to understand—that Gwyneth had created a major fashion moment without showing a whole lot of skin. "Yeah, look what she's wearing," Granata said, pleased. "This is *it*."

Reflecting on the appearance, Granata said, "It wasn't just an It outfit on an It girl, it was an It moment."

NOW THAT SHE was famous, Gwyneth's life was becoming a series of perks. Shipments of free designer handbags and clothes started arriving, what seemed like daily, to the town house she had recently moved into with Pitt. She got free tickets for friends to ride the Concorde, a free stay at the Bristol hotel's presidential suite in Paris. When she went out to dinner, someone in the room would pick up the check.

She started getting recognized most places she went, so running errands and going out to eat became more of an issue. The need for bodyguards became more frequent.

Her friendships were changing, too. Though her kindergarten friend Mary Wigmore retained a special status, her Spence friends, who were starting white-collar careers and settling into long-term relationships, found the dynamic with Gwyneth beginning to change. Gwyneth, who seemed to struggle to continue trusting them, particularly those who worked in media, was leaning more on her friendship with Aucoin. He would do her makeup for her many promotional events that year. He spent his career talking to famous women about their lives and felt like he understood their problems.

After photo shoots at the Industria studios in the West Village, they would walk together back to the Chelsea duplex he shared with his boyfriend. They'd listen to music, have a glass of wine, and talk about the shoots. Just as Gwyneth could drop instantly into character on set, tapping into whatever persona and emotion the scene required, she could walk out of a professional situation and relax on Aucoin's couch and start cursing a lot, which was how she always spoke with close friends. The high-altitude, untouchable figure she cut in the press was replaced with her raunchy, irreverent self.

But now more than a year and a half into her relationship with Brad Pitt, strain was starting to show—though Gwyneth only revealed as much to select people. After *Emma* came out, Gwyneth went over to Aucoin's place and cried about Pitt multiple times, tucked into the couch in the cavernous living room. What she described seemed to Aucoin, according to someone with knowledge of his thinking, like Pitt might be verbally and emotionally abusive. He wanted to be with her but seemed to feel threatened by her success and all the attention she received. Aucoin sensed that she was afraid to lose the leverage and security that came with being Pitt's partner, and the public power of their relationship was muddled in her mind with the private experience of it.

His advice to Gwyneth was always frank, said someone close to him at the time: "You really need to end this."

IN EARLY 1997, when Miramax wanted to send her to Paris to promote *Emma*, Gwyneth asked for a private plane for herself and an entourage of around ten people (the flight there and back alone cost Miramax around $100,000—roughly $200,000 in 2025). She wanted the penthouse suite at the Ritz and requested no other guests on the floor but her friends, along with Mercedes vehicles to chauffer them around.

Miramax obliged, said a staffer who fielded the request. To friends who observed their relationship, this seemed like proof that Gwyneth had Weinstein wrapped around her finger. As far as they could tell, she was Miramax's Grace Kelly—a business asset he couldn't afford to lose. While studios indulged movie stars all the time, one Miramax person remembered Gwyneth being more demanding than many. Other Miramax sources said that all stars were demanding and that requesting a plane for herself and a few guests was typical movie-star stuff.

Weinstein had access to private planes and was willing to use them to splash out on certain stars because he wasn't making big blockbuster movies and couldn't pay as much as bigger studios. "One of the ways that you could curry favor with these people and get them to do more movies for you is spend a little bit on planes. And when you consider thirty, fifty, a hundred thousand dollars for a plane, as opposed to tens of millions of dollars for a movie or a fee, it's pretty smart," said Mark Gill.

Flying private to Paris with her friends, Gwyneth may well have felt a certain freedom—she was a leading lady, a fashion-world muse, and the partner of one of the world's most desired men. But every expression of her entitlement was now backed by a system deeply invested in her stardom, overseen by a difficult mentor, and held aloft by a viewing public that could turn on her in an instant.

AROUND THIS TIME, Gwyneth's appeal was measured by newsstand sales of magazines featuring her on the cover. Anna Wintour told *Women's Wear Daily* in December 1996 that the sales of her *Vogue* cover had been "disappointing"; *Us* magazine editor Barbara O'Dair added, "Gwyneth was soft for us." Wintour blamed the low sales on Gwyneth appearing on other magazine covers, like *New York*, at the same time. (*Vogue* had planned to run Gwyneth on the July cover, but since Wintour had killed those photos, they had to push it back.) It would be a lesson for *Vogue* but also for Gwyneth.

CHAPTER 11

"It" Happens

Gwyneth Paltrow got robbed.

—Harvey Weinstein

By the start of 1997, Gwyneth was very much an It girl. There were others around at that time—Liv Tyler, Alicia Silverstone, Winona Ryder—but Gwyneth was uniquely suited to the title: She was smart and discerning enough to exert some control over her image, to collaborate with high-caliber people and brands who wanted to associate with her, and privileged enough to think she could preserve some influence over the final outcome of those alliances. But that privilege had insulated her too well, and Gwyneth seemed to have no sense of what she didn't know. Having succeeded and been adored her entire life gave her an expansive confidence; exposure to creative and wealthy people gave her a natural instinct for style and self-creation; but the one thing no one taught her, and what did not occur to her, was how to build an identity apart from all these insatiable, adoring influences.

GWYNETH BRUSHED OFF her It girl status.

Kevyn Aucoin would joke with her, "You're the big It girl."

"Isn't it a fucking joke?" she'd answer.

In these years, if she won any type of award, she'd come back to her table and wink at her friends, as though it were all so silly—the same way she'd laugh at the trivialities of the fashion world, even as she evolved into one of its icons and most sought-after spokesmodels.

Director Alfonso Cuarón wanted Gwyneth as the female lead in a modern adaptation of *Great Expectations*. When he took the idea to the studio, Fox executive Tom Rothman worried she wasn't a big enough name and insisted that he needed a star. Producer Art Linson suggested they get Robert De Niro to play the convict in an extended cameo. De Niro signed on, and Cuarón got Gwyneth.

In the movie, Gwyneth's ice-princess character, Estella, is the ever elusive love interest of Finnegan Bell, played by Ethan Hawke, who had starred in 1994's *Reality Bites* after his breakout in 1989's *Dead Poets Society*. While Hawke would mingle with the crew, only a select few seemed able to get close to Gwyneth. She and De Niro were getting similar star treatment. "She hung out with us," hairstylist Angel DeAngelis said. "She would have a cup of coffee with us, because she knew we were there to help her and protect her, in a way."

Along with her Spence friends, Harvey Weinstein showed up on the New York set. Weinstein had a habit of showing up to other people's sets to get face time with actors and avoid going through their agents, who would ignore scripts he wanted their clients to read (he taught his team to take the same approach with talent). On set, actors were isolated from fans and the people who wanted something from them all the time. Gwyneth would roll her eyes and say, "I've got to go talk to him."

ESTELLA WAS GWYNETH'S most erotic role to date, with several nude scenes with Hawke, whom she knew a little bit from the New York theater scene. She expressed her discomfort to the hair and makeup team. The sets were closed, with only essential people there during filming, and Gwyneth had a body double for the most exposed shots, but films didn't employ intimacy coaches then, and the room was mostly men.

Around this time, Gwyneth and Hawke took a walk together and started trading notes. "Are they talking to you about *Titanic?*" he asked.

"Yeah," she said. "Are they talking to you about *Titanic?* What do you think?"

Gwyneth met with director James Cameron about the film, but she later told a reporter she was glad to have declined. "Are you insane? I couldn't have imagined going through what they did and working with Cameron all that time." She said in another interview, "I'm so glad that I have opinions . . . If I didn't, I'd feel completely lost. I'd be thinking, *Oh, maybe I should have done that movie or that one.* But I'm led so strongly by the way I react to things when I read them, and it makes me really sane. I can't be talked into stuff or cajoled into thinking that something is a smart move if I don't like it."

Only, these instincts would prove to be pretty fallible.

AFTER WRAPPING *GREAT Expectations,* Gwyneth flew on a private plane to Argentina, where Pitt was filming *Seven Years in Tibet.* He was staying in a house on a walled-in property in Mendoza with a small soccer field and swimming pool. Fans from as far as Buenos Aires, more than six hundred miles away, would cluster outside the gates and wait to see him. Gwyneth would help Pitt run lines and talk to the crew about her recent work when she hung around on set. She spoke Spanish with local crew, including the woman who escorted her to the grocery store to buy a chicken to cook for their dinner.

One day, one of the young women in the throng outside Pitt's house managed to scale the wall and break into the home. She found her way to the bedroom, where Gwyneth and Pitt were in bed. Security swooped in within seconds, terrifying the girl, who appeared to be a teenager. She started crying, and Gwyneth tried to comfort her, shielding her from the guard.

During one of those visits, Pitt surprised her on the balcony of the house with a marriage proposal and a diamond engagement ring he had designed himself. They had been dating for two years. Gwyneth was twenty-four and Pitt thirty-three.

Gwyneth's friends for the most part thought Pitt was a really good guy, and viewed her as a really good girlfriend to him. But they were still surprised that she said yes. While the relationship had momentum in the press, the two still seemed to have little in common. By late January, they were reported to be in talks to appear together in a karaoke film called *Duets*, which Bruce would direct. Columbia green-lit the project, and Kevin Jones, an executive there, left his job to work full-time on it. After his departure from Columbia, one of his old colleagues said to him, "What's the worst that could happen? They could break up."

ON FEBRUARY 11, 1997, Harvey Weinstein was working out of his brother Bob's cramped, windowless office at Miramax. The 1996 Academy Award nominations had just been announced. Harvey's assistant interrupted him to say that Gwyneth was on the line. Weinstein took the call.

"Gwyneth Paltrow got robbed," he ranted into the phone to Gwyneth, repeating it over and over: "Gwyneth Paltrow got robbed."

Miramax staff who overheard the conversation didn't know what he was talking about. They had been focused on promoting *The English Patient*, nominated for twelve awards, and *Sling Blade*. They hadn't thought of Gwyneth as much of a contender for *Emma*. But the conversation made it seem like Weinstein had promised Gwyneth a nomination, and now he'd failed her.

Gwyneth was disappointed that she hadn't been nominated for *Emma* and told friends she believed she was too new to contend for Best Actress, and that if she'd been in a supporting role, she might have had a shot for Best Supporting Actress.

Miramax producer Paul Webster, who worked on *The Pallbearer*, said Weinstein was "incredibly manipulative, and knew exactly what pushed your buttons and what made you happy, so he could get inside a star's ego and manipulate it in many ways . . . I don't think Gwyneth was immune to that. I think we all weren't, to an extent."

IN MID-MARCH, GWYNETH'S Spence classmate Caroline Doyle, the editor in chief of Russian *Marie Claire*, convinced her to attend a launch event for the magazine in Moscow. In a huge publicity coup for the magazine, Pitt joined her. Pitt was well known in Russia; Gwyneth was not.

They played the happy couple for onlookers. Gwyneth seemed "domesticated" with Pitt, one friend said. She would cook dinners at home and make plans for them to do things as a couple. But she would also go to designer showrooms to pick out clothes, and Pitt would say things like "Do you really think you should wear that? Don't you think that's too sheer?"

Also, Pitt and Gwyneth's Spence friend Julia Cuddihy didn't seem to get along very well. Then there was Pitt's habitual tardiness, which drove Gwyneth—who was always punctual—crazy. They visited the Kremlin during their Moscow tour, which required arriving at a specific time, and Gwyneth was furious when Pitt was late. "He's always late," she said. She could be dismissive of him the same way she had been with Donovan Leitch Jr.

On the day of the launch event, twelve hundred guests gathered in the Radisson Slavyanskaya Hotel, and organizers showed a clip from *Se7en*. Gwyneth made a few remarks before ceding the stage to the star: "A true *Marie Claire* girl chooses a *Marie Claire* man, so let me welcome onstage my fiancé, Brad Pitt." The crowd went crazy. Other media executives in attendance were terribly impressed with Gwyneth, including American *Marie Claire* editor in chief Glenda Bailey, who invited Gwyneth to guest-edit an upcoming issue of the magazine. Gwyneth accepted with one condition: She wanted to write an article herself—about spending time on a desert island.

. . .

BRITISH TELEVISION ACTOR Peter Howitt had been working on a script called *Sliding Doors* for four or five years, and the financing had just fallen apart. So he passed the script to his actor friend John Hannah, who was on his way to Los Angeles. Hannah's agent got him a meeting with director Sydney Pollack, who had been expecting a script to come in that never arrived. With a couple of hours now freed up, Pollack read the latest draft of *Sliding Doors* right there.

That night in London, Howitt was drowning his sorrows in alcohol when the phone rang. "Hi, is that Peter Howitt?"

"Yes," Howitt said.

"This is Sydney Pollack. I just wanted to talk to you about your script."

"Fuck off," Howitt said, thinking it was a joke, and hung up.

The phone rang again. "I'm sorry, I think we got cut off. This is Sydney Pollack," he said. "I've just read your script. John Hannah gave it to me. I love it, and we should make this movie."

Pollack, who had executive-produced *Flesh and Bone*, liked working with first-time directors. He helped Howitt hone the script and pulled together the financing and cast.

Jill Taylor, who had signed on to do costumes and knew the financing had collapsed, got a call from Howitt one day.

"Guess where I am?" he said.

"I couldn't begin to guess where you are."

"I'm in Sydney Pollack's beach house," he said, eager to report that Pollack had helped lock in the female lead. "We've got Gwyneth Paltrow."

Gwyneth would play Helen, a young London dweller who gets fired from her job at a public relations firm before the film's arc divides into two separate narratives: one in which she catches the next train, and one in which she misses it. In both plotlines, Helen ends up with Hannah's character, James.

Taylor traveled to New York to meet with Gwyneth about wardrobe before filming. Taylor didn't have much of a budget, and Gwyneth said she had arranged for an appointment at Calvin Klein, where she had become a regular presence at the office. One of the publicists on the brand's small team who helped Gwyneth was Carolyn Bessette (who would go on to become Carolyn Bessette-Kennedy). According to one person familiar with her thinking, Gwyneth irked her. When there were pictures of Gwyneth in the papers, Bessette, who viewed her as "little miss perfect," would make cutting remarks about her. This was before the days when Hollywood stylists were household names and celebrities were commonly paid to wear certain brands on red carpets. Relationships between designers and muses were less formal, but brands were happy to oblige a certain A-list group of actresses, Gwyneth among them. In those years, Gwyneth could call on designers like Klein or Donna Karan when she wanted to pick clothes directly from the showroom. Klein was wary of working with celebrities and refused to pay them to wear his clothes or attend his shows. But Gwyneth understood how to manage this kind of symbiosis. In early 1997, in a show of solidarity with Klein, she had her name taken off the invitation list for an Armani party.

So when she asked the brand to dress her for *Sliding Doors*, the team agreed.

When Gwyneth and Taylor arrived at the Calvin Klein showroom, the team had lined the walls with "rails and rails and rails of clothes," Taylor said. They spent several hours trying things on Gwyneth and pulling pieces for the two different storylines and ended up finding nearly everything she would wear in the film. Taylor was delighted, but she had two small problems. One, nearly all the Calvin Klein clothes were too fabulous for the storyline in which Gwyneth gets a job at a sandwich shop. Second, Taylor had already purchased some pieces for the film from Prada, and now it appeared Gwyneth's loyalties would not allow her to wear them. To fix the first issue, Taylor lent Gwyneth her own blue cardigan from midlevel department store Marks &

Spencer for a scene where she delivered sandwiches. (Calvin Klein had a casual line that included jeans, which Gwyneth wore as well.) For the second, Taylor cut the Prada clothes from the film, which meant Gwyneth got to keep them.

SLIDING DOORS OPENS with Gwyneth's character, Helen, getting fired in a conference room full of men. In response, she delivers a short, punchy monologue that ends, "I was getting a bit choked up with all the testosterone flying about the place, it's best I get out before I start growing a penis."

The moment she finished that speech, first assistant director Richard Whelan looked at Howitt and said, "Oh my God, no wonder she's a star." Throughout the production, Gwyneth "just took complete command over all of these male actors who were all excellent and very, very confident," he said. She did all this in an entirely different British accent than she employed in *Emma*, this time a more neutral one associated with the London professional class, working again with dialogue coach Barbara Berkery. Whelan remembered "her going mad with Barbara to try and figure out how to say 'wanker' convincingly in an English accent," along with "bollocks."

The young crew scrambled to get the most out of a $6 million budget. Gwyneth and Hannah's big embrace was filmed on London's Albert Bridge that was already well lit at night, enabling them to save on lighting. They then brought in machines to create pouring rain, and started filming on a cold spring night at three a.m. The crew had rented a warm tub so that, between takes shot over a few hours, Gwyneth and Hannah could jump in fully clothed. (She went through several versions of her Calvin Klein outfit that night.) They filmed until the sun came up.

Part of Taylor's job was to ensure continuity—that Gwyneth's bag was on the same shoulder in each take, for instance, or that her shirt was tucked in the same way in every shot. "She didn't like being fiddled with," said Taylor, who wouldn't go on set and adjust her unless absolutely necessary. "I'd look at her and she'd look at me and I'd go, 'Just tie your belt.' And she'd do it herself. She liked to be right." Between scenes, Gwyneth, Taylor, and Taylor's assistant, Charlotte Sewell, would hang out in their trailer along with her makeup artist Tina Earnshaw and drink prosecco. Gwyneth had turned her Miramax friends on to turkey burgers from Tribeca's Cornerstone near their office, and here, she introduced the crew to her alternative burger of the moment— a McDonald's cheeseburger with "everything but the meat," remembered Taylor.

Gwyneth threw a party for the crew and left them with parting gifts, including Tiffany heart bracelets for Taylor and Sewell. With the help of her assistant, she gifted other crew members black sweatshirts that said "Love GP" on the arm.

TOWARD THE SUMMER of 1997, Gwyneth's relationship with Pitt was fracturing.

Her tearful sessions in Aucoin's apartment had been dragging on for months by the time Kevin Jones flew to New York with Bruce and Blythe to work on casting *Duets*. On their way to the hotel, they stopped in a bodega to buy something and found themselves looking at a huge stack of *New York Post*s blaring the headline "It's the Pitts."

The public story of the breakup focused on Pitt's happiness: According to one report, he resented that Gwyneth was reining in his partying; another claimed that he was "burnt out"; and yet another alleged that Gwyneth had called off the wedding because Pitt was "nervous about such a serious commitment." What went mostly unacknowledged was that Gwyneth had valid reservations, but not about Pitt's partying. Gwyneth and Pitt never publicly gave a concrete reason for their breakup, though two people recalled a rumor about it stemming from Gwyneth cheating on Pitt while she was filming *Sliding Doors*. In her 2018 profile of Gwyneth for *The New*

York Times Magazine, Taffy Brodesser-Akner claimed, "I heard that she had an affair with her *Sliding Doors* costar John Hannah when she was with Brad Pitt."

Asked about it the next year in *Vanity Fair*, Pitt dodged, "Isn't it true of a lot of people? Since you started dating, there's always been that period until you find the one you want to go the distance with?"

"But you thought you had found the one," writer Cathy Horyn said. Pitt then looked away: "But I was wrong. You figure it out."

In later interviews, Gwyneth blamed herself. In 2017, she said "I fucked that up, Brad!" "I definitely fell in love with him," she told Howard Stern in 2015. "He was so gorgeous and sweet. I mean, he was Brad Pitt! . . . My father was devastated [when we broke up]. My father loved him like a son . . . I was such a kid, I was twenty-two when we met. It's taken me until forty to get my head out of my ass. You can't make that decision when you're twenty-two years old . . . I wasn't ready, and he was too good for me."

Kevin Jones was blindsided by the news, which Bruce and Blythe had kept from him. Pitt's representatives told the studio he would honor his *Duets* commitment, but he wasn't happy about it.

Bruce called Pitt from his office, and he emerged from the conversation with a downcast look. "Brad was willing," he told Jones. "But I told him he didn't have to do it."

Jones was understanding, but the studio was not. As soon as they heard Bruce had released Pitt from the movie, they ordered him and Jones to be out of their offices within twenty-four hours.

A FEW MONTHS later, when Princess Diana was chased by paparazzi and killed in a car crash, Gwyneth was one of many celebrities called upon by the media for comment. Not for the last time, she ended up mixing her own personal experience as a celebrity—"I've been chased by those same exact motorcycle paparazzi in Paris . . . where I was harassed and followed and where they were not lose-able"—with an overconfident pronouncement on the nature of a complex problem. "I honestly knew something like this would happen . . . People should stop buying tabloids and then there would be less of a market for it." Though she would spend the next couple of decades being skewered in the media, like many major celebrities, being chased by paparazzi always seemed to be her least favorite aspect of fame. And the chase only picked up after she and Pitt broke up.

A few weeks later, Gwyneth got a break from photographers. As requested, in September 1997, *Marie Claire* sent her to a deserted island off the coast of Belize, measuring 250 by 75 feet, for three days, to write about it as part of her guest-editor role for their January issue. The sailboat that dropped her off moored five miles away, and the Belize coast guard knew she was there. With the magazine's help, she brought little more than a flashlight, a lantern, a pound of rice, three oranges, two carrots, an onion, waterproof matches, a camera, a tarp, a two-way radio in case of emergency, and a machete. And, of course, a sincere hope that this very controlled experiment in solitude and renunciation might offer her some clarity—which could then be shared with thousands of readers.

Before the trip, a doctor had told her to keep a record of how many cigarettes she was smoking each day. She estimated nineteen. The doctor told her to cut down significantly. In the days before her departure, she weaned herself down to seven, then five, then three, and smoked her last one the morning before she arrived on the island.

Once she arrived, the girl to whom everything seemed to come so easily used her machete to whack palm fronds off a tree, which she propped up in the sand to create a shelter. She draped her tarp over the fronds, creating a makeshift tent to sleep under. She found a grate washed up on the beach that she placed on top of rocks to make a grill. Since she hadn't brought water, she smashed open coconuts to use the liquid to boil rice, which "took like three hours and tasted really bad," she said. Catching fish with her limited supplies—a fishing hook and line but no pole or bait—was even harder.

She kept a diary of her time there. "I'm positive there are no paparazzi out there, not that I wouldn't put it past them." She slept on sand so hard it gave her a bruise. She saw a shark from the shore but "just knew" she wouldn't die in an attack, so she waded into the tropical blue sea and began swimming. "The shark appeared right next to me," she remembered. "I was like, *Well, okay!* Then I got out of the water and took a picture of it and I put it in the magazine."

She lit a fire one night and cried on the lonely beach, then went to sleep on the sand. When it was all over, she wrote, "I have learned that I am stronger than I thought. I am braver than I thought." The *Miami Herald* picked up her story under the headline "I Am Loopier Than I Thought."

WHILE GWYNETH WAS reported to have met twenty-six-year-old Ben Affleck in late 1998, at a dinner hosted by Harvey Weinstein, she in fact met him alongside Miramax's head of production, Meryl Poster, during a *Good Will Hunting* press day. Miramax had released *Good Will Hunting*, which Affleck cowrote and starred in with Matt Damon, on December 5, 1997, and the two childhood friends won the Oscar for Best Original Screenplay. Gwyneth liked to hang out with Poster. Sometimes she would sit in Poster's office at Miramax and just listen to her make deals on the phone. That day, Gwyneth wanted to go to Fendi to look at furs. Poster went with her, then they met up with Damon and Affleck for dinner.

Affleck's background was much more similar to Gwyneth's than Brad Pitt's. Raised in Cambridge, Massachusetts, Affleck's mother, Christopher Anne "Chris" Boldt, had attended the Nightingale-Bamford School on the Upper East Side, not far from Spence, and then Harvard. Affleck had started acting as a child and learned to speak Spanish after traveling through Mexico with his mom and brother. His father was a playwright and alcoholic who moved out when he was young. Affleck himself was struggling with alcoholism and a gambling habit around the time he met Gwyneth, who was attracted to his intellect. She admired that he was also a writer—not just an actor reading lines.

Affleck said Gwyneth was "the smartest woman [he'd] ever met." While he was a better match for Gwyneth intellectually than Pitt, her friends had reservations about him, largely because of his addiction issues but also because he didn't always reciprocate her affection. He was figuring out how to manage his newfound fame and had a group of guys he liked to hang out with whom Gwyneth would later call his real-life version of *Entourage*. He at times seemed more interested in playing video games with the guys at his house than being with Gwyneth. He had the same exasperated demeanor that would be memed widely on the internet more than twenty years later. One of Gwyneth's friends from the time thought he "always looked kind of miserable."

Though Affleck was not able to give Gwyneth the same commitment and attentiveness she showed him, she might have had a hard time giving up their physical chemistry. She spoke openly about how much she enjoyed their sex life—it was the ribald side of her that her friends knew well but that the public didn't see. She told Kevyn Aucoin in his London hotel room one day after lunch that she loved when Affleck "tea-bagged" her. "I'm a very sexual person," she told *Harper's Bazaar* in 2001. In 2024, she went on the *Call Her Daddy* podcast and told host Alex Cooper that Ben was a "technically excellent" lover.

Gwyneth wanted to keep her relationship with Affleck out of the press. Calling the paparazzi an intrusive presence in her life when she was with Pitt, she told *USA Today* after news of their dating broke that she and Affleck were just "very good friends . . . [I]f there's one thing I've learned, it's that I'm not going to talk about relationships anymore. I did it in the past, because I didn't think about it. But it's just not a good idea. I think it's private. You dilute it, and you really mess with it when you start to let other people in—let alone the whole world in."

After breaking up with Pitt, Gwyneth stayed for a short period with her friend Winona Ryder, though it's unclear precisely why. By the end of 1997, Gwyneth had helped set Ryder up with Matt Damon, who was single after breaking up with Minnie Driver, whom he'd met on the set of *Good Will Hunting*. Driver would later say that she found out Damon was leaving her after he went on *Oprah* and said he was single. However, Gwyneth told her friends that Driver's version of events was untrue. Gwyneth understandably wanted to take her boyfriend's friend's side, but she also seemed to sour on Driver. Once, when she was staying in a rented house in Los Angeles for a shoot, she pulled together a last-minute birthday party for Driver (one person thought it had come about at the urging of Stephen Huvane). Driver was an air-kiss friend—Gwyneth didn't like what she perceived as her air of faux British aristocracy. When Driver wasn't looking, Gwyneth rolled her eyes to friends, one recalled, and mimed vomiting by putting her finger in her mouth.

Gwyneth's relationship with Ryder eventually soured, too. She told friends that after Ryder and Damon had gotten in a fight, Ryder left and returned to say that she had been robbed around Gramercy Park; she went out again and said she had been robbed again. Damon consoled her, but Gwyneth and Affleck believed Ryder had fabricated the robberies as a ploy for attention (there's no proof of this). Gwyneth was annoyed that Damon couldn't see it. Though Damon was kind to her friends, Gwyneth didn't seem to like him after that.

Her friendship with Ryder would only deteriorate further, and Gwyneth gave her the nickname, one friend said, "Vagina Ryder."

DESPITE SAYING SHE wanted to keep her relationship with Affleck private, on the set of *A Perfect Murder* in late 1997, Gwyneth talked about it openly with the crew. When Affleck visited the set, where he'd stand behind the camera watching Gwyneth with the director, they acted like a couple. In the film, a remake of Alfred Hitchcock's *Dial M for Murder*, Gwyneth's family friend Michael Douglas plays a Wall Street guy who hires his wife's lover to kill her. Director Andy Davis originally wanted to cast Russell Crowe in the part of the lover, and even had him read with Douglas, but Gwyneth said no. "I think they had had an affair, and she didn't want to have him in the movie," Davis said (though this hasn't been substantiated). Instead, he cast Viggo Mortensen. Davis needed a "trophy wife," and he decided on Gwyneth in part because she had grown up in the same rarefied New York City world as her character.

Gwyneth was paid $3 million for *A Perfect Murder*, which had a $60 million budget—the kind of big Hollywood movie she hadn't done yet. She told Harvey Weinstein, who was eager to cast her but also hadn't paid her nearly that much for anything, "Listen . . . I've got to buy an apartment here! If I keep doing movies for you, I'll be begging on the street! I'll be at, like, Covenant House, trying to keep the rain off! I've got to do this movie."

For twenty-five-year-old Gwyneth, playing the wife of her parents' fifty-three-year-old friend was awkward. "Michael was constantly kidding my father about playing my husband and lover and how we were going to do a nude scene," she said, "but Michael was just joking and trying to get a reaction from my father. They've been friends for twenty years and it was one of those guy things, I guess."

Gwyneth was starting to lose confidence in her appearance. After the movie's release, she revealed that producers Arnold and Anne Kopelson, whom she had previously worked with on *Se7en*, had become concerned that she had gained weight and developed a rash since quitting smoking and had hired a personal trainer for her. "I started to feel really fat and ugly—based on the way they were treating me," she said. "They made a point to sit me down and tell me that I couldn't gain another pound. They sent me off to a dermatologist to clear up my skin. It was this big deal. And I felt really terrible about myself."

A Perfect Murder's ending was a matter of great debate on the set. Gwyneth discussed it with Douglas and Davis, resulting in an hours-long filming delay. Since the movie was a remake, they wanted it to have a twist. Davis decided to film an alternate ending in which Gwyneth's character makes up her mind to kill Douglas. By this point, Gwyneth had traveled to London to film *Shakespeare in Love* with Miramax. Davis wanted her to come to California, where the sets were, to film the new ending, but word got back that Harvey Weinstein would not let her leave London, which infuriated Douglas. Now, Davis's crew had to pack their sets into a 747 and fly them and the cast and crew off to London's Pinewood Studios.

"I think Michael [Douglas] was sort of saying, 'Who is this prima donna that she won't come back to L.A.? It's going to cost us millions of dollars to rebuild this set in London,'" said Davis, who recalled that Douglas seemed to think Gwyneth could have demanded Weinstein let her go back, but didn't bother.

However, someone who worked closely with Gwyneth at Miramax believed that Gwyneth had asked Weinstein to tell them she couldn't leave as a power move. This person's understanding was that she had hated working with Douglas on the movie and found the whole experience creepy. She could have flown to L.A. for the reshoot—but didn't want to.

By the time they shot in London, Gwyneth looked "really thin," which created a continuity issue. Davis felt like his director of photography successfully obscured the difference in her appearance with lighting. But the new ending, with Gwyneth killing her husband, unsettled test audiences, so after the huge expense and headache of filming in London, they stuck to the original, using just a slice of the new footage.

Gwyneth's profile had clearly risen, along with her demands.

CHAPTER 12

Shakespeare in Love, Gwyneth in Overdrive

[T]he first lady of Miramax.

—Harvey Weinstein

At the beginning of 1998, Gwyneth had four films scheduled for release within the year: *Great Expectations*, which had been delayed to avoid competing with *Titanic*, the big Christmas movie of 1997; *Sliding Doors*; *A Perfect Murder*, and *Hush*. Before the year ended, she would add a fifth: *Shakespeare in Love*.

"I just hope that people aren't mad at me if I don't deliver," she said that year. "I hope they don't come to resent me. I can just be me, and if I fulfill something for you, that's great. And if I don't, don't think that I was supposed to and then hate me for it."

The release schedule meant that every few months Gwyneth would undertake a promotional tour. The It girl would be everywhere.

First came *Great Expectations*, with a poster featuring Gwyneth naked and lying on her front, head turned, gazing seductively at the camera with Hawke and De Niro in the background. In late January, she attended the Los Angeles premiere with Blythe and her grandmother (Ben Affleck went with a friend of Gwyneth's meant to be a decoy), but she asked her father to stay home; Bruce reportedly felt like she was being exploited. "I feel fine about the movie, but I'd better keep my father out of this," she told a reporter.

When reviews came out, the film's raciness ended up working against it. The New York *Daily News* called it "sleazy." *The New York Times*'s Janet Maslin noted that Gwyneth did a lot with an "underwritten" part, adding, "Incidentally, this is one more film in which the heroine's posing nude for an artist is supposed to make her more fully defined." (Cuarón himself may have agreed, later calling it "a complete failed film.")

Gwyneth's deluge of films in 1998 made it easier for her to distance from *Hush*, a psychological thriller starring Jessica Lange as pregnant Gwyneth's hyper-controlling mother-in-law. Though Gwyneth was developing a reputation as a performer who could often make something of mediocre material, *Hush* wasn't just mediocre—it was a disaster. She had decided to do it, she later said, for the chance to work with Lange, "which is the wrong reason to do a movie."

"Unfortunately," *Variety* wrote, "almost everything about the film is so unbelievable and misjudged that only the most gullible audiences will feel any transporting thrill at the end other than from the movie finally being over." The *Los Angeles Times* asked Gwyneth about it in late April, for a story pegged to *Sliding Doors*. "I don't know what you're talking about!" she said, grinning disingenuously. "I've never even heard of that!"

Though it went on to become a cult classic, *Sliding Doors* didn't fare that well in the reviews that spring. Critics pointed out many weaknesses, none of them directed at Gwyneth. *The New York Times* called it "her most winsome star turn since 'Emma.'"

To celebrate *Sliding Doors*, Calvin Klein threw a party for Gwyneth in its New York store. She came with Affleck but—presumably in the interest of trying to keep her relationship out of the press—made sure they weren't photographed together. "I'm sorry, but she said no," Affleck told a New York *Daily News* reporter who asked why they weren't posing with each other.

Her relationship with Affleck would only deteriorate as the year wore on. Her friends worried when she would prepare elaborate dinners for him, and he would then just decide to go out with the guys. Her friends were glad to see her with someone intelligent, but his issues doomed the relationship.

When Affleck was in Savannah, Georgia, to film *Forces of Nature* alongside Sandra Bullock, the New York *Daily News* reported, "[S]pies say that while the couple is apart, Affleck has acquainted himself with one of the local beauties. 'Tis said that the woman regularly stops by Affleck's house and that the duo has been using his back-yard pool and not just for swimming."

One of his friends denied anything was amiss with Gwyneth.

NOVELIST AND SCREENWRITER Marc Norman had written the original script for the period romantic comedy *Shakespeare in Love* and brought on his friend Ed Zwick to direct and produce. Julia Roberts signed on to play Viola de Lesseps, the young aspiring actress who falls in love with Shakespeare. Zwick felt like the script about a young William Shakespeare, broke and suffering from writer's block when he meets and falls in love with Viola, who inspires him to write *Romeo and Juliet*, wasn't quite where it needed to be. He hired acclaimed playwright and screenwriter Tom Stoppard to rewrite it. Universal started preproduction, but then Roberts—who got approval over who would play Shakespeare—dropped out after Daniel Day Lewis declined the role. Production halted, but Zwick kept trying to get another studio to take it on, for the high turnaround price that Weinstein later remembered as $4.5 million. He had various actors attached at different moments, including Winona Ryder. Kate Winslet, who was gaining major recognition for *Titanic*, ultimately turned down the part as well.

Harvey Weinstein cozied up to Zwick, who had been in demand after *Legends of the Fall*, and told him he would make *Shakespeare in Love* and keep Zwick on as director. But he then froze out Zwick, who retained a producer credit, and hired Miramax favorite John Madden to direct. Madden had directed *Mrs. Brown*, starring Judi Dench in her first major film role, which Miramax had bought. Madden then signed a deal to work with Miramax on two more projects, not fully understanding what being signed with Miramax meant. He was surprised when he went into a meeting about the *Shakespeare in Love* script, which he'd been asked to read, and Weinstein asked him if he wanted to direct it. Though not fully developed, Madden recalled, it was "the best script at that moment that I'd read in my life."

"Who would you want to see in it?" Weinstein asked.

Madden knew Gwyneth had a relationship with Miramax. But also, he had wanted to work with her since he'd auditioned her for his 1994 movie *Golden Gate*. At that time, Madden had done a lot of theater in the U.S. and run into Blythe here and there, though he didn't know Gwyneth. "She was a knockout" in the audition, he said. She hadn't been able to do the film, but here was another chance for him to cast her.

He told Weinstein the choice was clear: "Well, obviously it has to be Gwyneth, doesn't it?"

The choice for Gwyneth, however, was not so obvious.

GWYNETH WAS BURNED out by her four-film year when she received the *Shakespeare in Love* script. Not inclined to do another British period film just a year or two after *Emma*, she turned it down without bothering to fully read it, leaving Madden to embark on a long, tedious process of trying to find someone else.

Different people tell different stories of how she changed her mind. Two Miramax people remembered that Gwyneth, after turning down the part, then bumped into producer Paul Webster on the street one day. "I can't believe you don't like *Shakespeare in Love*," he told her. "It's such a great script."

Gwyneth seemed not to know what he meant.

"It's this incredible script that Tom Stoppard was involved in, and John Madden's directing, and it's an amazing part. I just don't know why you wouldn't do it," he pressed.

"I haven't read it," she said. "I don't know what you're talking about."

Webster then ensured she got a copy of the script, and she decided to take the part.

According to someone else who was close to her, Gwyneth turned down the movie without reading the script. Winona Ryder's name had also been bandied about for the role. Supposedly, Gwyneth picked up the script from Ryder's coffee table, read it (perhaps after the encouragement from Webster), and decided to do the movie.

"It was never sent to Winona as an offer, but Winona wanted to do the part and Gwyneth had recommended her for the part," said Weinstein. "Even though I thought Winona was great I just had my mind on Gwyneth and said I wouldn't make the movie without her."

Miramax sources didn't ever recall seriously considering Ryder for the role. Certainly John Madden never did. Suddenly he heard that Gwyneth had changed her mind. He met with her in Tribeca, and she seemed excited about the part, though she didn't know who would play her love interest, Will Shakespeare. Weinstein was intent on having a handful of Americans in the film, an approach Madden didn't necessarily agree with, but said fine so long as he could audition them.

Madden had read with Joseph Fiennes, who was an experienced Shakespearean actor, but it hadn't gone all that well. As the search for Shakespeare dragged on, Madden couldn't ignore his instinct that Fiennes was perfect for it. He insisted he come in and read again without preparing and nailed it. Weinstein gave the okay, then Gwyneth read with him. She seemed relieved that Madden had found Fiennes. Gwyneth hadn't done Shakespeare outside of Spence, really. Madden said she seemed to feel like Fiennes "would have her back, because she was both bold about wanting to do it, but at the same time, very nervous."

One Miramax producer was uncertain about Fiennes. She called Gwyneth. "He doesn't turn me on at all, but tell me if he does for you, because that's what's important."

Gwyneth gave Fiennes the green light.

After a story about Gwyneth allegedly stealing the script from Winona's coffee table reached the media, Gwyneth told friends that Ryder had started the rumor, and insisted she'd received the script through her agent. (Gwyneth's spokesperson called the story "totally untrue" in the *Daily News*.) The relationship now untenable, the two actresses parted ways that summer, and in September, after reportedly looking at fifty places, Gwyneth bought a three-bedroom, three-and-a-half-bath, three-story town house in Greenwich Village on West Fourth Street for $1.6 million (more than $3 million in 2025) and set about figuring how to renovate it.

AT SOME POINT DURING *Shakespeare in Love*'s London filming in the spring of 1998, word went around the set that this was going to be Miramax's big Oscar movie and that Gwyneth could contend for Best Actress. Madden said Miramax expected another film to be their Oscar frontrunner but it wasn't coming out that well, so they turned to *Shakespeare in Love*, increasing the pressure on Madden. He had been avoiding sending Miramax any footage, fearing they wouldn't understand the material in bits and pieces. But after he relented and cut together fifteen minutes, Miramax saw the film's potential. The budget increased to accommodate for a longer shooting schedule and additional expensive period costumes. Once again, Gwyneth would play a dual role: an aristocratic young woman forbidden to act on the stage (reserved only for men at that time) and that same young woman disguised as a boy to act in a production of *Romeo and Juliet*. Gwyneth would practice walking like a man on set, closely observing the men around her.

The crew re-created the Globe, a theater first built in London in 1599 where many of Shakespeare's productions were first performed, and filled it with hundreds of extras in costume. The first day of that breathtaking setup, after five to six hours of preparation, Gwyneth showed up last, as befitting a leading lady. One person who worked on the film recalled her chewing gum, looking like she didn't want to be there, and overheard her saying, "I'm so over this," meaning either the country or the film, no one was sure. The crew, recalled one observer, reacted with stunned, awkward silence. Affleck—who, at Weinstein's suggestion, had accepted a small role as the

Shakespearean actor Ned Alleyn—arrived at her side. (Gwyneth later said that she had to talk Weinstein out of casting Affleck as Shakespeare, telling him he needed a Brit in the role. Weinstein then denied he had ever considered Affleck for the part, which a Miramax source confirmed.)

When *The Sunday Times Magazine* sent writer Dylan Jones to the set to interview her, Gwyneth "could not have been less interested in talking to me or *The Sunday Times Magazine*," he wrote. When he walked into her trailer, she stayed seated with her arms crossed and didn't say hello: "She uttered nothing but monosyllabic answers and gave a good impression of someone who'd rather be picking skewers out of her eyeballs than talking to me."

After around thirty minutes, he gave up. She had given curt answers to every question while Affleck looked on, leaving Jones with no usable quotes. He then started asking the crew what she was like. One of the drivers said, "Couldn't tell you, mate. Walks around with her nose in the air. Looks like a snotty so-and-so to me."

On set, Gwyneth was receiving star treatment. An assistant brought her healthy food, which she had requested so she didn't have to eat what was available for the rest of the crew, described by one member as "very meat and two veg." ("I think she had a bit of a problem with English food," the person added, noting that it didn't seem unreasonable for the leading lady to want the best food, and that London wouldn't undergo its cuisine revolution until later.) She also had the star's dressing room (which was more like a suite of rooms) in Shepperton Studios. When supporting artists photographed her getting out of her car in costume to go to set, they got a talking-to from one of the assistant directors; the team didn't want her to feel like she was facing the paparazzi at work, but also, they didn't want stills leaking from the set that the publicity department could later release to drive valuable buzz.

Weinstein dropped by the production offices adjacent to the set around half a dozen times during filming. He was paying Gwyneth $2.5 million for the film, half a million less than she'd earned on *A Perfect Murder*, plus a small percentage of the gross. When Weinstein knew an actor really wanted to do a certain movie, he took advantage of that in negotiations. The crew later wondered if his hanging around had something to do with her apparent unhappiness during the shoot.

Madden suggested another reason for Gwyneth's perceived aloofness (though he himself didn't notice it): she could get nervous. "She's an incredibly instinctive actress," he said. "She just somehow knows where to go. She sees and senses it immediately, and if she gets offbeam or feels she has to do it multiple more times—not that she did very often—she would find that very difficult." This was why Gwyneth (like Blythe and many other actors) didn't enjoy watching her work—Gwyneth feared if she didn't like her performance it would shake her confidence completely. Thus, she developed a habit—useful when she became a mega-celebrity—of insulating herself from potentially debilitating feedback.

One scene Gwyneth struggled with took place early in the film, when Viola's nurse helps her get ready for bed while a distracted Viola can't stop thinking about the Shakespeare play she's just seen. She describes the love she wants in her future— ". . . not the artful postures of love, but love that overthrows life. Unbiddable, ungovernable, like a riot in the heart, and nothing to be done, come ruin or rapture."

The night before filming, Gwyneth had watched herself in *Emma* and decided she wasn't very good. Madden could tell watching her that she had been thrown off. He suggested they shoot it again a few weeks later. "She completely found it by then," he said.

But this was the side of Gwyneth that Madden believed others rarely saw. "They think of her as being supremely confident and so on, but actually there's a decided vulnerability there, which obviously manifested itself when she was finally rewarded with the Oscar."

ONE SCENE DEPICTED Viola's first meeting at court with Queen Elizabeth, played by the acclaimed Dame Judi Dench. "She was an icon in the British theater by that point," said Madden. "I'm sure Gwyneth was nervous as hell." In one of their three scenes in the film, we see Gwyneth say a line, then cut to Dench saying hers. The crew had been told Gwyneth had to wrap by a certain time that Friday so she could catch the Concorde back to New York for the weekend, as likely stipulated in her contract, meaning she wouldn't be able to film the scene alongside Dench. After Gwyneth finished her lines, she left for her flight, leaving some on the crew pretty surprised by her priorities—not that Dench, who was starring in a play when she wasn't filming, got visibly upset by it. Then again, Gwyneth had made her boundaries clear.

On set, Gwyneth and Affleck were openly affectionate and occasionally indiscreet. One day a crew member went to fetch Gwyneth from her dressing room. The door was ajar, and the runner knocked and entered without waiting for a response, at which point he glimpsed Gwyneth in an intimate moment with Ben, who heard the runner and said, "Not now." Panicked that he'd get fired for walking in on them, the runner asked the assistant directors what he should do. He was assured he'd be fine, but the story quickly spread among the crew. It's unclear if Gwyneth was aware of the gossip, but it's hard to imagine that incident making the set feel like a happy place to her.

Meanwhile in public, Gwyneth and Affleck refrained from speaking about their relationship. When a reporter asked Affleck about what it was like to work with her, he said, "Let's not get into personal territory. I have to stay away from that, or I'll take a beating." One person close to Gwyneth at this time speculated that her misery during filming stemmed from trouble with their relationship, which their physical affection concealed.

Also, fame was beginning to make Gwyneth question herself. She told *The Daily Telegraph* that celebrity was "such an empty pursuit." She added, "If you're not smart, you start hanging around with people on your payroll, people who won't disagree with you. When you're famous, no one disagrees with you. You get paranoid, you get isolated and everyone wants a piece of you.

"It really messes you up to have to actively pursue normalcy. But if you don't, you end up in another stratosphere behaving like an [ass] hole. Fame can really suck."

AFTER BRUCE RELEASED Brad Pitt from *Duets*, putting the film back together became "an odyssey," Kevin Jones said. Gwyneth was the only name attached. The budget was around $15 million, but every studio that expressed interest wanted it for less.

Ten weeks out from filming, the movie officially entered preproduction, which was when the studio had to start paying people. So around eleven or twelve weeks from a planned shoot date, Bruce and Jones would get a call saying the movie wasn't going to happen. This happened three times. They had a deal that they could take the project back, rework the script and budget, and try again with another studio. *Duets* finally landed at Disney's Buena Vista. As the ten-week deadline approached, Bruce was bracing for the call, but it never came. *Duets* was on.

Bruce was ecstatic. He had been struggling for a hit for years. He had cleared the way for his daughter's early success, and now her fame was giving his career a lift.

Around a week after *Duets* was green-lit, he got a throat cancer diagnosis.

Bruce went into denial about his illness. He would need radical neck surgery and radiation, but his plan was to have the operation, then go straight to the *Duets* shoot in Vancouver, wearing turtlenecks to hide his scar, and sneak away for radiation treatments when necessary. Bruce got sick as Gwyneth's fame was cresting—as the It girl was at her most adored, her most confident, her most profitable.

Jones tried to slow down preproduction, but Bruce didn't want him to tell the studio because it might jeopardize moving forward with making the film. Plus, the news would likely lead to press about his illness, then his parents would find out, which he wanted to delay as long as possible since his dad, Buster, had been diagnosed with liver cancer six weeks earlier. But the silence started to feel untenable, and Jones called Bruce's lawyer for advice. As it turned out, Bruce's lawyer didn't know, either.

The lawyer then called Bruce at home. Gwyneth picked up the phone. "My dad's been avoiding you," she said, then put Bruce on the line.

"Guess what?" Bruce told the lawyer. "I got cancer."

Jones and Bruce tried to suss out how the studio might respond to the news. They reasoned that if they could get a doctor to say that Bruce wouldn't die during the filming—and the diagnosis wasn't terminal—that Buena Vista would go ahead. So Bruce's doctor and another doctor testified the cancer wasn't likely to kill Bruce during the making of *Duets*. That was enough for the studio, and the film moved forward.

GWYNETH WAS ON Ischia, a craggy Italian island with narrow old winding roads and patches of sandy beach set idyllically in the Mediterranean, as the worst events of her life unfolded. She later told *Vanity Fair* that she was on location in Italy filming *The Talented Mr. Ripley* when she found out about her father's illness. One Miramax producer remembered that she hadn't wanted to take the *Ripley* part because she didn't want to be away for so long, and hadn't felt all that compelled by the material. She felt deep despair and guilt over not being able to be with her family during those weeks as she was stuck on set.

Gwyneth had joined the cast of *Ripley*, based on the 1955 Patricia Highsmith novel, after Weinstein decided to pour money into it, determined to be involved in whatever Anthony Minghella worked on after writing and directing *The English Patient*. (Gwyneth, however, wasn't enamored with Minghella, or any director, really.) Weinstein also brought on Matt Damon to join Cate Blanchett and Jude Law in rounding out the cast.

Ischia had no airport, so coming and going weren't quick or easy. Gwyneth's scenes were spread across the schedule, and she asked repeatedly to leave the production. "I'm not in much here," she told first director Steve Andrews. "I've got things I want to do in Milan, I want to go to a fashion show."

"You can't go anywhere," he said, "because don't you realize? Every day we change the call sheet." The one time the crew reluctantly allowed her to leave was for her father's cancer surgery. In his hospital bed, Bruce was preoccupied with work. Paul Giamatti and Forest Whitaker had joined the *Duets* cast. After the procedure, Bruce was with his family, but he insisted on seeing Jones right away: He wanted to know if the movie was still happening. Jones got the distinct impression that Bruce felt making this movie was going to power him through his illness.

Gwyneth returned to Ischia, where filming was unpredictable, each day's shoot depending on the whims of the forecast. They had to film the scene where Gwyneth, who played Jude Law's girlfriend Marge, meets Matt Damon's character on the beach, on a sunny day, but they didn't have that many sunny days. Several scenes were filmed on the water, using a sailboat so the camera wouldn't pick up the sound of a motor, which meant the wind had to be just right. All the actors had to be ready to film any of their scenes at the last minute, and Gwyneth was frustrated that hers were so spread out.

When telling the history of Goop, Gwyneth says that she started collecting recommendations during either the *Jefferson in Paris* shoot in Paris or the *Ripley* shoot in Ischia, sometimes asking the crew, many of whom were locals, for the best hotels, food, and shopping on location. She gathered enough information during *Ripley* to fill "dozens of notebooks," she claimed later, as she was "unconsciously" laying the groundwork for the business.

Andrews recalled Gwyneth at the top of her game in everything she filmed, he said, even in the face of her father's illness. Matt Damon was on a special diet to slim down for his role and isolated himself during the shoot, which was just as well for Gwyneth, since she didn't seem to care for him after the Ryder debacle. (Damon and Ryder wouldn't break up until early 2000.) Filming winter scenes, with heavy coats, in 95-degree heat in Rome, Minghella had to pause the cameras every few minutes so the crew could dab the sweat from the actors' faces. Gwyneth's fifties costumes, many of them custom-made, consisted of tied-up shirts, sweet A-line skirts, vintage bikinis, and hair scarves that would become "iconic" in some corners of the internet. Ann Roth, the legendary costume designer, saw the clothes as nondescript, the kinds of things she'd observed young women wearing in the fifties. Roth commanded tremendous respect from the actors and took no input from Gwyneth or anyone else on set. She coached Gwyneth, Damon, and Law on how to move in their clothes, how to smoke, how to sit.

Roth's team borrowed pieces from Gucci, like a scarf and leather bag for Gwyneth. The filmmakers included a scene of Tom Ripley buying a wallet in the Gucci store as an homage, since the brand loaned them so many wardrobe pieces. After filming wrapped, some of it ended up with Gwyneth and other actors.

Ben Affleck—who wouldn't be Gwyneth's boyfriend for much longer—visited her for a short time during filming. Her assistant was her Spence friend Julia Cuddihy, who lived with her on Ischia. Cuddihy seemed to guard this special status vigilantly and feel threatened by others who got close to Gwyneth. But even with Affleck and a childhood friend on the set, the *Ripley* shoot was a strain on Gwyneth.

"The actual work was cathartic," Gwyneth said. "But you didn't get to do it for very many minutes during the day. There was a lot of sitting around, and that part was very hard for me.

"We all got homesick," she added. "Everybody has this image of going to Italy for six months being so great. But meanwhile, that's a long time to be away from the people you love. You're mostly in a hotel room, having room service and going, 'This is my life?' It's just not what people think."

AS *RIPLEY* FILMED, Miramax was finishing up the edit of *Shakespeare in Love*. The audience in one test screening liked it but not as much as Miramax had wanted them to. Afterward, Weinstein debated the film's prospects with a group including Marcy Granata, Meryl Poster, Donna

Gigliotti, Mark Gill, Miramax's international head Rick Sands, and consultant Arthur Manson. Miramax had spent $25 million on the film, which was high for them as a boutique studio, and Weinstein was determined to get it right. A gender divide seemed to emerge in the discussion, said someone privy to it: the men seemed to fear the film had Oscar potential, but was too brainy and esoteric to also possess commercial appeal. But Weinstein and most of the women disagreed.* (The whole point of winning Oscars, aside from scratching Weinstein's competitive itch, was to get a wider audience to see the movie and make more money.)

The ending was a particular issue. Test audiences had taken it hard when Viola left Will behind to marry the cold Lord Wessex, played by Colin Firth, and move across the ocean to America. Weinstein wanted Viola and Will to end up together. Madden remembered people at Miramax telling him, "It's a romantic comedy but the guy doesn't get the girl."

"But that's the point," he told them. "It's not a romantic comedy— it's a piece of its own." He and Tom Stoppard had to think of an ending that would satisfy Weinstein, and came up with the idea to connect it to *Twelfth Night*, which opens with a shipwrecked protagonist named Viola. Madden re-shot the scene where Viola says goodbye to Will inside the theater after the queen sends her in to ask him to write a comedy next time, with a slightly different inflection, to indicate that each had gotten what they needed from the relationship—bittersweet but less devastating.

Viewers also hadn't understood why Gwyneth had to marry Firth, so they looped lines repeatedly throughout the film about Gwyneth needing to marry him because the queen had ordered it. In the closing shot, Gwyneth walks on the shore in America in a dress, suggesting that Shakespeare channels his heartbreak into writing his next masterpiece, Viola his muse eternal.

---

* John Madden recalled that having "Shakespeare" in the title had freaked out previous people who had thought about making the movie, and one suggested instead *Romeo and Juliet, Viola and Will.*

At the second preview, audience scores went up. Miramax had a hit.

DETERMINED TO ENSURE that the media held space for coverage of the film, given that it was coming together last-minute, Miramax made the unusual move of holding the very first press screening of *Shakespeare in Love* the night before Thanksgiving. Teri Kane, who worked for Marcy Granata, called her from the screening after it ended. "Marcy, Marcy, Marcy, you don't know—they were going nuts," Kane said. Weinstein's strategy was working, and Granata started getting excited calls from the film press and studio executives, who were all of a sudden worried about what sort of competition their films might face that Christmas.

On December 3, Miramax held a red-carpet premiere in New York. Gwyneth attended wearing a sheer ice-blue embellished column gown by Giorgio Armani, her blond hair straight and her eyes more kohl-rimmed than usual. Hillary Clinton showed up this time, having just appeared on the cover of *Vogue* following the revelation of her husband's affair. In a *New York Times* story about Clinton's attendance, Weinstein told the paper that Gwyneth was "the First Lady of Miramax." (Clinton left, as she had planned, before the movie ended.) Five days later, Miramax held a premiere in Los Angeles at the roughly one-thousand-seat Motion Picture Academy theater and invited lots of academy members. Mark Gill remembered the movie receiving one of the top five best responses out of the hundreds of movies he's worked on: "Everybody who walked out was our new best friend."

Shakespeare in Love opened in select theaters on December 11 to ravishing reviews. *Variety* called Gwyneth "irresistible." ABC's entertainment editor Joel Siegel reported Gwyneth was "exquisite," adding, "It is one of the best films of the year, the cleverest comedy of the year and one of the best love stories of the year." The *New York Post* said, "If you want to see Audrey Hepburn live again, buy a ticket for 'Shakespeare in Love.'" Janet Maslin, who had praised Gwyneth's talent while denigrating many of her films, noted in *The New York Times*, "Gwyneth Paltrow, in her first great, fully realized starring performance, makes a heroine so breathtaking that she seems utterly plausible as the playwright's guiding light."

In an interview with Matt Lauer on the *Today* show, Gwyneth framed the movie as unpretentious and accessible, emphasizing, "[T]he language isn't Shakespearean. It's English that we can all understand."

The audience seemed to agree. *Shakespeare in Love* would ride its Oscars buzz to become a box office hit.

GWYNETH AND AFFLECK broke up the next month, after a little over a year of dating. Her friends weren't surprised. They viewed her as a great girlfriend to her boyfriends—and hadn't seen that reciprocated by Affleck, who seemed plagued by his personal struggles. Gwyneth had been drawn to his intellect, but even that attraction and their physical chemistry couldn't overcome his self-destructive impulses, which may have even included cheating on her, according to one friend from the time. After they broke up, Gwyneth said, "I love men, even though they're lying, cheating scumbags."

GWYNETH HAD A busy few months ahead of her. On January 26, 1999, she attended the Golden Globes as a Best Actress nominee, wearing a gray iridescent skirt and black tube top by Calvin Klein, her long straight hair pulled half up. She won and, in her acceptance speech, said, "I would like to thank Miramax, especially the bomber Weinstein, my godfather." Weinstein noted, "I like to think that was her being honest and that it was reflective of the way she thought about me." She also thanked "my father, Bruce Paltrow, who's had a tough year."

Not only did Gwyneth win that night for Best Actress, *Shakespeare in Love* won for Best Film in the comedy category. *Saving Private Ryan*, directed by Gwyneth's godfather, Steven Spielberg, won for Best Picture in the drama category, setting the two up for an Oscars rivalry.

In the press, Gwyneth was circumspect. "I'm human, so of course the idea [of an award] appeals to me," she said. "It would be a tremendous honor and a lot of fun. But I try not to focus on end results and 'gravy' like that. I just try to do my work the best I can. Awards are the wrong place to put my energy."

According to several people at Miramax, Gwyneth very much wanted the Oscar, especially since she had failed to earn a nomination for *Emma*. And if she was going to win one, she knew she would have to work for it.

WEINSTEIN WAS NERVOUS about *Shakespeare*'s Oscar chances. After the Globes, he had his team join him at the last minute at the Sundance Film Festival for a meeting where he went around the table and asked each one if they thought their film would beat *Saving Private Ryan*. For Weinstein, no expense was too great when it came to Oscars campaigns. He told his team they needed to do "hand-to-hand combat," meaning, marketing head Mark Gill said, "trotting out the stars to, just as they say in politics, do the retail part, shake hands and kiss hands." Weinstein had done this successfully with *The English Patient* and repeated the effort with *Shakespeare in Love*. He was probably the first person to put together a comprehensive list of the entire six-thousand-member academy who decided the awards, and where everyone was. He'd then hold screenings where they would be—Aspen, St. Barts, Los Angeles—and send talent along to schmooze at receptions, as when the *Shakespeare in Love* cast did sonnet readings for an A-list event.

"It was just relentless," said Miramax development executive Jack Lechner. "Everyone on the staff was expected to call anyone they knew who was an Oscar voter—and you couldn't lobby them because that was against the rules—but just to say, 'Did you get our screeners and will you be voting?'"

Weinstein was clear with his team: Gwyneth would win that Oscar. The Miramax team believed in her, but Cate Blanchett was strong competition as Queen Elizabeth in *Elizabeth*. Gwyneth knew it, too. But as one person who helped plan the events recalled, she was determined to win and turned on all her charm in the scheduled schmoozing sessions. The events Miramax planned were grueling—one person likened it to having your own wedding reception over and over again, all around the world. The talent was wrung dry by the end of it. Gwyneth called it "traumatic," adding, "It goes on for months, and it's so exhausting and draining. I mean, you think, *Is this some popularity contest?*" As Gill remembered it, Gwyneth didn't turn down that many of the events Miramax asked her to do: "She was a really, really hard worker."

Miramax wasn't working hard just for Gwyneth. The team also worked hard for Joseph Fiennes, who ultimately wasn't nominated, and Judi Dench and Geoffrey Rush, who were.

Miramax also bought ads and drove publicity and Weinstein would later be accused of, as *Vanity Fair* put it in 2018, "start[ing] negative whisper campaigns" about *Saving Private Ryan*. To distinguish her performance from Blanchett's, Miramax played up Gwyneth's dual role and designed print advertisements that showed her playing both Viola and her male alter ego. The *Saving Private Ryan* team was supposedly upset that Miramax bought *Shakespeare in Love* ads during Monica Lewinsky's Barbara Walters interview, which aired on March 4, 1999, and happened to be a big event for the film's target demographic.

During the media blitz, Weinstein learned Gwyneth was Jewish. In the interest of pursuing every possible publicity opportunity, he told Marcy Granata that Jewish publications should do a story with that angle. *The Jewish Chronicle* then ran one headlined "Meet Gwyneth Paltrowitch," which read, "She might look like a WASP" but was "descended from [a] line of rabbis, dating back to 16th-century Russia."

At one point, Stephen Huvane told Miramax that his client was feeling oversaturated. She wanted to promote the movie, but she also wanted to be able to ease up once it had been properly positioned.

Gwyneth's ambition was different from Weinstein's. The game of being of the moment, of courting fashion designers, of turning on the charm for a press event, was getting harder. Gwyneth pushed back at points, declining some interviews when she was exhausted, speaking frankly at times about the celebrity machine churning around her. But she was losing ground to fame.

Not long after the Oscar campaign wound down, she told an interviewer, "It's not like I go out there and say, 'Will you please put me on the cover of the tabloids?' or 'Will you please mention me in every article about lipstick?' People just do that and it's beyond my control. I'm sick to death of it, I'm sick of this Gwyneth Paltrow person I see everywhere. I hate her and I wish she would go away. But there's nothing I can do about it."

But her omnipresence in the media dragged on, and her instincts were proved correct. There was such a thing as overexposure.

CHAPTER 13

A Family Affair

[T]hey're all in the room watching [Bruce]. They can't take it. Forget the movie.

—Kevin Jones

As Gwyneth's fame grew, her relationships became more transactional. Valentino Garavani and his partner, Giancarlo Giammetti, saw actresses like her as vital for promoting their brand. The Valentino label had earned renown by dressing Jackie Kennedy after her husband's assassination, along with other society women. But as those women aged, the brand needed fresh faces. One close observer likened Valentino to a spider waiting to catch a fly, Gwyneth being the fly. Valentino and Giammetti knew how to seduce people like Gwyneth. They'd invite their muses to vacation on their yacht or at their French castle, where they'd be served by white-gloved waiters, their every possible need attended to. While Gwyneth might have known the difference between beluga and osetra caviar, these Italians lived with even greater grandeur.

Gwyneth was always particularly savvy when it came to managing relationships. That she became a fashion-world muse seemed as inevitable as her becoming a movie star. She liked the status but wasn't blown away by it, considering it simply the next step in her career.

Valentino and Giammetti were capable of friendship, but never seemed to lose sight of the status trade. Gwyneth was expected to show up to big red-carpet events wearing Valentino, perhaps on the arm of Valentino, or to present him with an award that, in theory, would boost his visibility and help him sell more dresses. What Gwyneth was missing in true, honest connection, she was gaining in market power.

DUETS FILMING WAS delayed six weeks for Bruce's cancer treatment. Radiation was so taxing that he was unable to focus on the script or much of anything else. Since he couldn't swallow, he was being fed through a tube in his stomach.

Right before they left to scout locations in Las Vegas, Blythe called Jones. "Bruce is really sick," she said.

Jones told her that if they didn't go scout locations, they wouldn't make their deadlines, but he also understood Blythe's concerns. Bruce, always headstrong, wanted to go.

More than anything else, Bruce wanted to work with his daughter. Gwyneth was being paid scale, along with all the other actors; she was there to be with her father. Blythe and Jake joined them on the Vancouver set, and they were all together on the first day of filming, February 9, 1999, when the Oscar nominations came out. *Shakespeare in Love* had earned thirteen, including one for Gwyneth for Best Actress. *It's five thirty a.m.*, she remembered thinking, *and I have to report to work at eight thirty a.m. I better just try to keep it together and not ruin my first day of work.*

Gwyneth and Bruce had an intuitive connection on set. He would come to her after a shot, give her a note, and she would appear to shrug it off. Moments later, she had transformed, according to his direction, and played it back to him just as he wanted. Other times, Gwyneth would give Bruce a look, like that of a mischievous teenager, and he would say, "Oh, I know what that look means." When filming a scene where Gwyneth had to storm off, Bruce and Blythe looked at each other and thought, *Oh yeah, I recognize that walk.* The set was like a post–empty nest family vacation. Gwyneth called it "the opposite" of the isolation she'd felt while filming *Ripley* in Italy.

The crew filmed the strongest material in the beginning of the shoot, before Bruce started struggling. Toward the end of filming Andre Braugher (who had replaced Whitaker) and Paul Giamatti's scenes, Bruce had to get through an overnight shoot. "It was a bad night," Jones recalled. Jones decided to wrap it when the sun came up. He said goodbye to Bruce, and they both went off to their hotel rooms. Jones drifted off around seven a.m. and woke six hours later to his phone ringing. Gwyneth's agent, Rick Kurtzman, was calling. "I hear you're pulling the plug," he said. Jones was confused.

"He's really sick," Kurtzman said.

"I just saw him and said good night," Jones said.

Jones hung up and called Bruce's room, where his family was watching him. Jones learned that Blythe, Gwyneth, and Jake had been worried enough to start talking about flying him home and ending the production. Jones figured that one of them had put in a panicked call to Kurtzman. He asked to speak to Bruce, who sounded like death.

"Are you going to work tomorrow?" Jones asked.

"Yeah," Bruce said.

Jones, who described himself as "chickenshit" in these situations, just said, "See you on set."

"The whole family's there, so they're all in the room watching him. They can't take it. Forget the movie," said Jones. Bruce's family seemed to fear that continuing to work on this movie might kill him. "Obviously, he didn't agree, and he pulled it together and he showed up on time the next day."

Bruce finished filming *Duets* with just a couple of weeks to rest before he planned to escort Gwyneth to the Oscars.

CHAPTER 14

The Oscar—and the Curse?

*I felt like people were making fun of it and thought, Oh, God, I
didn't deserve this.*

—Gwyneth Paltrow

In the weeks leading up to the Academy Awards, Gwyneth's win
for *Shakespeare in Love* was declared "inevitable"; she "would
seem to be the shoo-in." The *New York Post* ran a whole article
about what dress the It girl would wear to collect her prize, while the
Los Angeles Times noted "the body to dress" was Gwyneth's. Meanwhile,
her grandfather Buster continued to deteriorate, while Bruce's health
was more or less the same as it had been in Vancouver.

In private, Gwyneth shrugged off the hype or rolled her eyes, carrying out the subtle dance of reluctant celebrity: bestowing on fans
and patrons the glamour they expect of her, while trying to preempt
everyone's envy with demonstrations of humility and normalcy. After
all, she wanted to be taken seriously as an actress, like her mother. But
she also wanted the win to advance her career.

Just before the Oscars, Gwyneth said, "I feel a kind of pressure that
I've never felt before. Pressure to make all my friends and everybody
around me comfortable with it. When you're going through something
like this, you want to rely on everyone you know and love to say, 'Hey,

we're all normal. You're still normal. This isn't a big deal.' But everyone's going, 'Oh, my God! It's such a big deal! What are you going to wear?' And I'm just going, 'Oh, no!'"

INSIDE THE POLO Lounge the Saturday night before the Oscars, Miramax held its annual pre-ceremony party, where Weinstein had nominees stage *Saturday Night Live*–style skits of one another's films. The actors didn't rehearse but got a heads-up about the concepts and a chance to give input in advance. The party had become a hot ticket and was a way for Miramax to celebrate its hard work now that the campaigning had ended. Gwyneth brought the house down when she came out wearing a Groucho Marx mask to impersonate Roberto Benigni, who would win Best Actor for *Life Is Beautiful*, and shouted in an Italian accent, "I want to make love to you over and over." Tom Stoppard wrote a skit called "Tina Brown and Two Gentlemen from Queens," in which Geoffrey Rush played Weinstein, Matt Damon played Bob, and Gwyneth played Tina Brown, the former *Vanity Fair* and *New Yorker* editor with whom Miramax had just launched the glossy magazine *Talk* for $75 million. The big laugh line came from Rush as Weinstein: "What do you care? It's Eisner's money." (Michael Eisner was the chairman of Disney, which owned Miramax.)

It was Harvey's dream: Miramax as a close-knit repertory theater company, gathered to celebrate their hard-won nominations and pay tribute to their powerful benefactor.

ON OSCAR NIGHT, March 21, 1999, Gwyneth got ready in a suite at the Shutters hotel that included two bedrooms connected by a living area. She and Ben Affleck, even though they weren't together, shared one of the two bedrooms that night, while two of her Spence friends shared the other. Kevyn Aucoin did Gwyneth's and Blythe's makeup. Bruce came along, and they attended the award ceremony as a family, along with Mary Wigmore and two siblings from the family she'd stayed with in Spain during her time at Spence. They sometimes visited Gwyneth in New York, and she regarded them like close relatives.

Instead of the sleek Calvin Klein dresses the media had been predicting, she opted for something unexpected. Various designers had been sending her sketches to consider when she was filming *Duets* in Vancouver. "It was so funny, because I really found most of their ideas had nothing to do with what I think I look like. It wasn't what I was going for, I just didn't want to look like I feel I always do. I had a hard time because some designers actually made dresses and sent them to me," she said. Gwyneth didn't have a stylist—the whole celebrity-fashion industrial complex didn't exist yet—so Stephen Huvane approached Ralph Lauren directly to ask about a gown.

However, Lauren wasn't about to just send over a dress. If he was going to create a red-carpet look as a designer who didn't participate in celebrity dressing, he wanted it to be special. He insisted on speaking with Gwyneth directly, and the two went back and forth a bit about what her dress might look like. She had a vision of looking like Grace Kelly, and wanted a certain pink, but Lauren wanted a softer pink, so they compromised. Leading up to the awards, she hadn't been eating much and kept losing weight, necessitating extra fittings, where Gwyneth asked the Ralph Lauren team in New York to bring the neckline lower and lower. Lauren became so frustrated by the process that he didn't want to send the dress back to Los Angeles. But his team convinced him to let them send it anyway, and found a skilled seamstress to fit the pieces of the dress onto Gwyneth there.

A night or two before the awards, Gwyneth was trying on different gowns—including options by Michael Kors and Versace—and didn't even let Lauren's seamstress into the room. Lauren's team had no idea she would wear his dress, a spaghetti strap, full-skirted confection in that distinctive carnation pink, until she stepped out of the limousine on the night of the Oscars. She accessorized with a diamond choker on loan from Harry Winston, which had made her another necklace called the "Shakespeare"—though she chose the "Princess" instead. She swept her hair back into a tight, simple chignon. The look felt like a throwback to fifties Hollywood glamour—a classic choice that was pretty but purposefully not sexy.

The designers at Ralph Lauren noticed that something looked off when she wore it that night. The fabric was puckering, a little wrinkly, loose around her torso—as if she had instantly lost ten pounds. They realized she hadn't worn the inner detachable corset that came with the gown, which would have made it look smooth and fit more snugly. Lauren himself was not happy about the fit.

Gwyneth walked into the Oscars more excited than nervous, as far as her friends could tell. Though she was favored to win in the press, Weinstein and his Miramax team weren't so sure. (Weinstein was sure about Dench, however, telling Madden, "Judi's a lock.") Weinstein walked in like a gambler entering a casino. The Miramax team also was not convinced that *Shakespeare in Love* would win. Comedies didn't usually win Best Picture, never mind sweeping the awards.

Early in the ceremony, Bruce, sitting next to Gwyneth and still hiding his illness, looked over at his daughter in her pink gown and borrowed diamonds and thought she looked so, so beautiful. Spontaneously, he decided to buy her the necklace.

Shakespeare in Love started winning right away. Judi Dench took the award for Best Supporting Actress, a triumph even for a talent like her, given that she had been on-screen only around eight minutes. The movie also won for Art Direction, Costume Design, and Original Screenplay. Spielberg won Best Director for *Saving Private Ryan*, beating out John Madden. When Jack Nicholson walked onstage to present Best Actress, the Miramax team was on edge.

After Nicholson opened the envelope and called Gwyneth's name, making her an Oscar winner at age twenty-six, Weinstein rubbed his hands together. Gwyneth later would say she drew a "holy blank" at that moment. Her face crumpled and her head fell momentarily into her hands, then she turned and embraced each of her parents. She later described the feeling as "like when you have a dream and you're trying to run but you can't." Madden was seated a few seats away from Blythe. Right after her name was called, Madden and Blythe noticed Gwyneth losing her composure, and shared a moment. "I remember Blythe and I kind of locking eyes, and our eyes rolling because she was already in tears before she even got up from the seat," he said. Blythe "was just nervous for her." Worrying that her legs wouldn't carry her, she ascended to the stage, heisting aloft the hem of her dress and slightly shaking her head. When she got to the microphone, she put her hand to her chest and spoke through frantic breathing.

In her speech, she acknowledged each of her fellow nominees, Fernanda Montenegro, Emily Watson, Cate Blanchett, and "the greatest one who ever was, Meryl Streep—I don't feel very deserving of this in your presence." She thanked Weinstein and Miramax and her costar Joseph Fiennes and "my friend Ben Affleck," with whom she had broken up three months earlier. When she thanked Rick Kurtzman, she called him "a beautiful man and a wonderful agent—and in his case that is not an oxymoron."

"I would not have been able to play this role had I not understood love of a tremendous magnitude, and for that I thank my family—my mother, Blythe Danner, who I love more than anything." At this point, her face contorted into a sob. She continued, "And my, my brother, Jake Paltrow, who is just the dearest person in the whole world. My earthly guardian angel Mary Wigmore. And especially to my father, Bruce Paltrow, who has surmounted insurmountable obstacles this year. I love you more than anything in the world. And to my grandpa Buster, who almost made it here tonight but couldn't quite get here." (He had flown out to Los Angeles but felt too weak to attend.) In Gwyneth at that moment, Madden saw genuine emotion. "That's a person who was standing there thinking, *I don't know how I did this. I don't know if I deserve this,*" he recalled.

Shakespeare in Love then won Best Picture, one of the only comedies to do so since *Annie Hall* in 1977. With seven awards, it beat out *Saving Private Ryan* for the most of the night.

Bruce, who considered himself "a weeper," was determined not to fall apart in front of the cameras, knowing his tears would become a part of Oscars history—as his daughter's did. He kept it together until they finally got outside.

After the ceremony, Gwyneth met up with her friends Julia Cuddihy and Caroline Doyle and went to the *Vanity Fair* party at Morton's, still wearing her pink dress, where she danced while Buster, who had joined the family there, held her statue. She continued on to the Miramax party at the Beverly Hills Hotel's Polo Lounge. Before she arrived, Weinstein had pulled his team into a bungalow to tell them about DreamWorks's executives' ire that *Saving Private Ryan* had lost. For many years, the industry would wonder how Miramax and *Shakespeare in Love* had managed to beat *Saving Private Ryan* for Best Picture, and how Gwyneth won for Best Actress over Cate Blanchett. And quite often, their explanation came back to Weinstein's campaign.

Gwyneth attended the Miramax party with actor Scott Speedman, who had ended up in Brad Pitt's role in *Duets*. (Amid rumors that they were dating, Huvane told reporters he was "a good friend" and "like a little brother to her," though according to one of Gwyneth's friends from the time, they did actually date briefly.)

That night, Gwyneth reveled until the wee hours of the morning. The Miramax party went so late that Weinstein ordered an impromptu breakfast buffet. By this time, he was referring to Gwyneth as "our muse" and "our little sister." "Anything she wants to do, we'll do," he crowed.

The next morning, Gwyneth headed to the bank. She had bet CAA agents Patrick Whitesell and Kevin Huvane ten thousand dollars that she wouldn't win. She met them both in the lobby of the CAA offices and happily made good on the bet before going out to lunch.

Weinstein sent Meryl Poster to pick out a gift for him to give to

Gwyneth: she selected from Hammerman Brothers a roughly $7,000 pair of sapphire and diamond earrings.

THE FOLLOWING DAY, Gwyneth went to a health food store to pick up Evian water and freshly squeezed juice. She wore no makeup and responded warmly to the strangers who congratulated her. She probably knew about the Oscars curse, the Hollywood legend that women who win Best Actress or, even worse, Best Supporting Actress would struggle to find roles that compared. But true to his word, Weinstein sent her every part he subsequently came across that she could play.

Gwyneth wanted to branch out. "It's interesting because when I started, I did several character-y roles. *Flesh and Bone* was very against type. And *Hard Eight* was not a glamorous part: a prostitute. I feel like I've done a lot of different kinds of things, but . . . people don't associate me with those parts. After *Emma* and *Sliding Doors* and *Shakespeare in Love*, it would be nice to work back toward some things that people would, I guess, characterize as against type. I would like to be open to anything." She had plans to perform at Williamstown that summer. "I'm looking at comedies. I want to go up to the Berkshires and lie in the grass."

For a short period post-Oscar, the press adored her. The New York *Daily News* said she had "seemed destined for stardom." "Gwyneth Paltrow is incapable of looking bad," *The Philadelphia Inquirer* wrote. "She is magnificent, beyond supermodel, and perhaps not human." The *New York Post* called her "impossibly lovely and graceful." Now that she had won the Academy Award, she could reportedly command $10 to $12 million per movie. Weinstein said that whatever that figure was, "we'll pay it," adding grimly, "She already has a nice piece of action on the movie." *Shakespeare in Love* had earned $72 million before the awards. It went on to earn another $27 million in the U.S. and grossed $289 million worldwide.

Four days after the ceremony, *The New York Times* published an article about how Gwyneth's parents had decided to purchase the $160,000 choker she wore to the Oscars, made from forty carats of diamonds. Harry Winston official Carol Brodie told the paper she had seen Gwyneth at a party that night after she won. "She's holding her gold statue, she's beaming from ear to ear," Brodie said. "I go, 'Congratulations.' She looks up and goes, 'My daddy's buying me the necklace.'"

Gwyneth was excited, certainly, to have won, but she quickly experienced an existential crisis. What was she going to do now that she had won an Oscar at twenty-six years old? She described being sick in bed for ten days at her parents' house after winning. "I think I had adrenaline poisoning or post-traumatic stress syndrome," she said. "I didn't want to leave the house. I felt really exposed and embarrassed. I felt like people were making fun of it and thought, *Oh, God, I didn't deserve this*." She reached out to Madonna for her take on dealing with it all.

"It's your karma, where you are right now," she told Gwyneth. *She's right*, Gwyneth thought, *I have to accept this*.

The coverage of Gwyneth was so glowing that—particularly by the sexist press standards of the media in the late nineties and early aughts—it had nowhere to go but down.

CHAPTER 15

The Backlash Begins

[S]he would be easier to take if she couldn't act at all—then, at
least, there would be some rational excuse for the visceral hatred
she brings out in so many.

—Salon.com

Shortly after the Oscars, Buster died. Bruce continued his slow
recovery as he worked on finishing *Duets*. When Gwyneth
returned to New York, she started to renovate her town house.
Around the same time, the sparkling global adulation she had been
receiving began to curdle. Gwyneth became another example of the
press building a woman up seemingly only to tear her down. On April 1,
Salon.com called her the "current backlash queen," referring to Gwyneth's "riches-to-riches story" and citing the *Times* article about her new
diamond necklace: "It's an embarrassing story, to be sure; necklaces
costing this much money should be against the law." In another essay
the next day, Michelle Goldberg wrote on Salon.com, "The way the
fluff media, and now the academy, have anointed this pampered It girl
tells the rest of us one thing—that being skinny, blond, well-bred and
well-connected trumps everything in this culture, even talent . . . It's
not that she's not talented, it's just that she's not that talented, surely
not talented enough to deserve the accolades raining down upon her.

In fact, she would be easier to take if she couldn't act at all—then, at least, there would be some rational excuse for the visceral hatred she brings out in so many."

By October, British tabloid *The People* ran an item about how Gwyneth was afraid people would laugh at her after winning the Oscar. "Gwyneth, you're right. Your tearful speech was a perfect example of sheer, buttock-clenching embarrassment," it read. "You should have stayed in bed, Gwyneth, we haven't stopped laughing."

This hatred was something Gwyneth would never manage to outrun, the relentless public contempt that later would similarly trail actresses Anne Hathaway and Blake Lively. After a certain point, the public tires of hearing how amazing the world's most beautiful, privileged women are. This rarely happens to leading men. While the hatred was sexist, much of it seemed to stem from all the privilege that Gwyneth's Oscar win had highlighted: nepotism (which wasn't as big a flashpoint then); growing up rich only to become even richer; her parents buying her a six-figure necklace to congratulate her on winning an Oscar at the age of twenty-six.

However, friends never sensed that this press bothered Gwyneth. Only occasionally would a specific story—typically, one she participated in—upset her enough that she'd reveal as much to friends or the public.

THE MEDIA AND public backlash was so bad that one Miramax producer mentioned to coworkers that there had started to be doubts about Gwyneth on the casting circuit, but Weinstein—believing, he said, that the backlash "was an invention of the press"—remained eager to work with her. He offered her $8 million for a lead part in *Bounce*, a familiar, slightly high-concept romance starring opposite her ex, Ben Affleck. He and Gwyneth would earn the same fee. Gwyneth also successfully requested that Miramax producer Meryl Poster, whom she liked and trusted, live in L.A. and come to the set while she was filming the movie.

Yet the *Bounce* role wasn't the mold-breaking part Gwyneth had been looking for. After winning her Oscar, she told a friend, "I proved myself as a serious actress, and they just want to keep making me do romantic comedies. That's just not where I want to be." But for Weinstein's Oscar-winning "muse," it was difficult to say no.

TRUE TO HER word, Gwyneth returned to Williamstown in the summer of 1999. Before the Oscars, she had started talking to festival organizers about a homecoming of sorts and settled on playing Rosalind in Shakespeare's *As You Like It*. The play, in which Rosalind flees to the forest and disguises herself as a boy after being exiled from her uncle's court, is often produced in a haunting, ominous tone. But director Barry Edelstein wanted his version to celebrate joy and love and beauty. Gwyneth would be considered the heartbeat of the production and of the festival itself.

After Gwyneth approved Edelstein (her prerogative now that she was on a certain professional level), Alessandro Nivola was called in to audition for the part of Orlando. Nivola was one of several distinguished theater actors Edelstein was able to land now that Gwyneth was on board. Stifled by what Hollywood had to offer her, dazed by the attention, Gwyneth looked forward to returning to the stage and her acting roots. "But even though it was this sort of an escape to this little idyll up in the forest, which is not unlike the story of the play, she still had a shitload of pressure on her," Nivola said.

Now she had to prove to theater audiences and critics that she wasn't just a celebrity who had gotten lucky, or the beneficiary of Harvey Weinstein's powerful publicity machine, but a bona fide actress who could deliver in a single long take seen from many angles.

In early July, when it was time to head to Massachusetts to start rehearsing, Gwyneth rode up with Nivola and their costar Megan Dodds in her silver Mercedes SUV, playing "Steal My Sunshine" over and over again during the roughly three-hour drive to the Berkshires.

Wearing sunglasses, Gwyneth would dance in her seat to the music, throwing her arms above her head, momentarily abandoning the wheel. "It was totally infectious," Nivola remembered.

Gwyneth stayed in a rented house near the festival and focused mostly on work. Their timeline of a few weeks for rehearsals was tight, as usual, especially for Shakespeare. They rehearsed in a small gym on the Williams College campus, where they taped off an area on the floor the same dimensions of the stage. Gwyneth showed up in jeans and sweatshirts, still in a goofy mood, as if trying to shake her anxiety. "I think what it afforded her was just to keep loose and free and not tighten up and sort of feel like she had to have reverence for this language, because the technical side of doing Shakespeare is so extreme," Nivola said.

Edelstein thought that Gwyneth had a gift for language. Performing Shakespeare was the opposite of, say, a soap opera, where the sentences are short and characters' thoughts clear and compact. Gwyneth, coming off *Shakespeare in Love*, knew which words to stress, which to soften, and where to breathe. She could float easily into metaphor and make Shakespeare's allusive language accessible and immediate.

The show sold out quickly. "Unless you're Harvey Weinstein, you don't stand a chance of getting a ticket," wrote theater critic Michael Riedel in the *New York Post*. (After locals complained, the festival added seats for the public.)

The opening night crowd included Meryl Streep, Paul Newman, and Joanne Woodward. Gwyneth was nervous. Much as she'd hoped to avoid the media circus—she didn't give a single interview to plug the play—they found her anyway. All the top New York theater critics came. E! sent a camera crew.

In the first moments of the show, Gwyneth rose up from beneath the floor wearing a red ball gown, a red flower tucked into her upswept hair, a delicate choker around her neck. It was reminiscent of her Oscars look but in fiery red. Alternating between playfulness and irreverence in her performance, she had what Nivola recalled as a devilish look in her eye, like she knew she had been holding back her abilities in rehearsals and now was letting loose.

Critics adored it. *USA Today* praised her chemistry with Nivola, saying, "you forget it's Gwyneth Paltrow." *Newsday* and the *New York Post* lauded her as well, though both noted that she didn't project enough (such are the differences between film and theater acting). And *The New York Times*'s Ben Brantley wrote that Gwyneth "turns her entrance into a witty comment on her image as an elegant clothes hanger, while reminding us that there is a sharp and playful intelligence beneath the gloss."

If only her upcoming films came anywhere close to drawing such praise.

CHAPTER 16

A New Altitude

[S]he . . . made it quite clear there was no point in trying to get in touch again.

—Former Spence classmate

Bounce had started out with Universal, but Weinstein bought it away from them, delighting Don Roos, who wrote it. An executive on Weinstein's team had read the script, about an advertising executive named Buddy who gives his seat on a flight to a man trying to get home to his family for Christmas. After the plane crashes, Buddy guiltily seeks out the man's widow, Abby, and they end up falling in love. In the memo the executive wrote for Weinstein, he said the movie was brilliant and would be an automatic hit if he cast stars like George Clooney and Meg Ryan.

When he met with Roos in New York, Weinstein said, "I want to get Ben and Gwyneth." While an executive in Weinstein's office argued that Affleck, at twenty-seven years old, didn't have the life experience to play Buddy, Weinstein remained determined. He had put options in place with Affleck and Gwyneth, meaning he could cast them in two projects, but he had to do it within a year. Unlike Miramax's executives, Gwyneth believed that Affleck could be a Serious Actor, and this would be the film that did it. Though they'd broken up, they had remained friends. Affleck said Gwyneth called him and encouraged him to do the movie: "I'd be lying if I said it was easy, but the benefit was that if you work with somebody that good, you're in good shape and it just makes you better. She's too much of a professional to ever let any of her, like, whatever, personal issues, get in the way."

Gwyneth chose to dye her hair brown for the role. She thought it would help her look like, someone at Miramax recalled, a "real person." Weinstein wasn't happy about it—"I want a movie star," he said—but Gwyneth got her way. (The hair color became a problem when Gwyneth left the set to attend an event and bleached it blond but returned to work with the wrong shade of brown, causing the crew to lose a day of filming.)

Between breaking up with Affleck and *Bounce* wrapping in November 1999, Gwyneth dated around. She had a habit of taking on a certain persona based on whom she was seeing. When she was reportedly with Madonna's manager, Guy Oseary, she would wear a Star of David necklace. (Gwyneth's and Oseary's spokespeople wouldn't comment on their relationship at the time.) But their supposed romance was short-lived, and she got back together with Affleck after *Bounce* wrapped in November 1999.

THE TALENTED MR. *Ripley* could have been another *Shakespeare in Love*—a Miramax film with a glamorous and talented cast, a literary pedigree, and plenty of high-low appeal. But Weinstein was concerned about the ending, in which Matt Damon's character murders his lover, fearing he'll uncover his earlier crimes. Director Anthony Minghella was adamant that they keep it and let the film end with the killer's pained isolation, but Weinstein didn't think it would sell. First Director Steve Andrews believed he pulled back Miramax's support for the film after that.

Minghella was upset that the studio didn't push the movie harder for Oscar consideration, including Gwyneth for Best Supporting

Actress. However, others at Miramax said Weinstein's long illness that winter may have had something to do with what Minghella perceived as a lack of support.

The Miramax team knew a movie that invites an audience to somewhat sympathize with a gay serial killer would be a hard sell, and they tried to sniff out receptive writers. Frank Rich did a big feature for *The New York Times*. But generally, the reviews were unfavorable, and some suggested it was proof that Gwyneth didn't have the talent required to pull off the role. The New York *Daily News* called her character, Marge, "a blank slate without the imagination to steal someone else's personality."

After the lousy reviews, the film's Oscar chances died on the vine, as far as Miramax was concerned, and the studio put its promotional efforts behind *The Cider House Rules*, based on the bestselling novel by John Irving. *Ripley*, however, has aged well. *Vanity Fair*'s story celebrating its twenty-fifth anniversary called it "almost obsessively rewatchable."

DESPITE MIRAMAX LOSING faith in *Ripley*'s awards chances, Gwyneth and her castmates were obligated to undertake a promotional tour. She traveled around Europe to various events with an entourage that included her yoga instructor and four friends; the film's publicists were relegated to the back of the plane so her friends could sit with her up front. Gwyneth was happy when engaging with her people but cold and aloof to others.

Even within her entourage, however, there was tension. When Gwyneth was invited to movie premieres, she'd often receive four tickets for herself and three friends. One observer felt like she was dangling them like bait to play her friends off one another, knowing that one would be left out depending on who was in her good graces at the time. It seemed almost cruel. While she had reserved her coldness for those outside her inner circle at Spence, she now seemed to be turning on her oldest friends. Often she left out Betsey Kittenplan (never a full-fledged member of her entourage), who at the time was working for *People* magazine, apparently because she was part of the media.

When Gwyneth, Matt Damon, and Jude Law were to depart from the Berlin Film Festival, where they'd appeared on a private jet, producers of the film wanted a ride also. But the three actors insisted on those seats going to their friends, leaving the producers to fly commercial.

Yet Gwyneth had been generous with her Spence friends as her fame grew. She took them to trendy restaurants like Nobu, where she had become famous enough to get a reservation at a moment's notice. When Spence classmate Hilary Angle got married in Connecticut, Gwyneth brought a friend on the helicopter that Calvin Klein had chartered to fly her from the bridal shower to his fashion show and then back in time for the wedding. Warner Bros. loaned her a private plane to fly Julia Cuddihy and two others to St. Barts, where Gwyneth rented a house for Caroline Doyle's wedding shower. At Doyle's wedding in Ireland, Gwyneth served as a bridesmaid—and an excellent one. She did Doyle's makeup, sang the first song, and gave her a foot massage during the reception. But when Gwyneth found Kittenplan sitting in the front seat of the car that was to take the bride and her friends to the rehearsal, one person recalled her saying, "Get out of the front seat. I should be sitting in the front seat." It struck onlookers as awkward and humiliating.

Since seventh grade, Gwyneth had liked to be the center around which everything revolved. When Kittenplan got married in October 2000, Gwyneth had said she would attend but then didn't show up, likely knowing Kittenplan would be hurt. It was just as well, friends reasoned. If she had shown up, she would have found a way to receive all the attention. When she missed a friend's wedding, the bride was sometimes relieved. (Meanwhile, Gwyneth did make time to attend Madonna's wedding to Guy Ritchie at Skibo Castle in the Scottish Highlands on December 22, 2000—a tabloid frenzy preceded by weeks of speculation about Gwyneth being a bridesmaid. ABC reported that she attended as a guest while a friend from the time remembered her having a minor role.)

In late May 2000, around the time of Gwyneth's ten-year Spence reunion, her publicist placed a call to one of her classmates, who'd invited her to a reunion party. The friend was told that Gwyneth "wouldn't be showing up and made it quite clear there was no point in trying to get in touch again."

"Gwyn went totally Hollywood," she added. "She had a big falling-out with the closest friends she grew up with and went to school with—and now we don't speak at all."

Gwyneth did end up attending her ten-year Spence reunion at a bar in New York, where she encountered her former nemesis, Alison Cayne. Cayne said something like "Hey, Gwen, what have you been up to?" Gwyneth took it personally. "Why did she say it that way? I want to leave. She's so mean," she said.

Her friends were confused. Gwyneth had won an Oscar and been engaged to Brad Pitt, and she was upset about a seemingly innocuous remark from a former classmate who was married and having kids. But while she was praised and pampered on sets all day, the Spence crowd, which Gwyneth joined as a California-reared outsider all those years ago, never acted overly impressed that Gwyneth had ascended to the pinnacle of the entertainment business.

Gwyneth's Spence friends, who liked her before all this happened to her, may have felt like the rare people she could trust now that so many wanted something from her simply because she was a star. But they were also a bothersome reminder of how she had never earned a college degree, and of the world she entered as a seventh grader that valued a certain wealth and pedigree over tabloid fame. Plus, the challenges they faced in their twenties were not something that Gwyneth, now one of the most famous movie stars in the world, could relate to or learn from.

•   •   •

EVEN BRUCE, WHOSE daughter could seemingly do no wrong in his eyes, sat Gwyneth down for a talk around this time.

"You know," he told her, "you're getting a little weird . . . You're kind of an asshole." He had no problem calling his kids out if he believed they were mistreating people, endangering themselves, or behaving badly.

Gwyneth was ashamed, "devastated," she said. "But it turned out to be basically the best thing that ever happened to me. It's the difference between someone who loves you more than anything in the world giving you criticism and getting it from some bitter stranger on the internet. What my dad said to me was the kind of criticism where I was like, *Oh, my God, I'm on the wrong track*."

Gwyneth realized that she needed to work on herself. "When you achieve the kind of fame that I did by the time I was twenty-five or twenty-six, the world starts removing all your obstacles because you're now a 'special person.' You don't have to wait in line at a restaurant, and if a car doesn't show up, someone else gives you theirs. There is nothing worse for the growth of a human being than not having obstacles and disappointments."

ONE HOT JUNE day in New York City in 1999, Gwyneth met up with *Vogue* editor at large André Leon Talley. He was profiling her for the cover story of the September issue, the year's most important, and the piece would revolve around them shopping at Manolo Blahnik, Calvin Klein, and Gucci. Anna Wintour had decided to photograph Gwyneth wearing fashion that embodied different time periods from the century, ranging from "a fringed and flapper twenties look" to "the Ivana eighties," in honor of the coming new millennium.

Gwyneth had also agreed to do a photo shoot for the premier issue of *Talk* magazine, edited by Tina Brown, and which Miramax co-owned. In one image, she crawled across the floor in black lingerie; in another, she reclined in black thigh-high stockings with a leather whip. She was stunned when *Talk* published one on the cover, next to the headline "Gwyneth Goes Bad." The inside headline was "Gwyneth Paltrow Is a Bad Girl," and the images ran with an extended caption, but no article.

Gwyneth had agreed to do the photo shoot with the understanding that it wouldn't appear on the cover since *Vogue* demanded exclusivity from cover talent. Plus, Wintour had blamed Gwyneth's multiple covers the summer of 1996 for her August issue's low sales. Gwyneth was furious, taking her anger out in part on Miramax's Meryl Poster, who'd had nothing to do with the decision. *Vogue* ended up running their cover as planned—they would have Gwyneth back for several more—and Weinstein made it up to her with private plane rides.

That wasn't the last time Gwyneth would find herself angry with Miramax. The following July, Miramax subsidiary Dimension Films released *Scary Movie*, a comedic parody of horror films. It included a scene where characters Brandy and Ray go to see *Shakespeare in Love* in the theater and poke light fun at the movie, an example of "white people doing white things in white places." Gwyneth was angry that no one from Miramax, which she considered her home, had told her about it.

"There were certain favors that he [Weinstein] asked me to do," she told the *New York Post* in 2001, regarding the *Talk* cover, "that I felt were not exploitive, but not necessarily as great for me as they were for him. I brought this to his attention, and he said, 'I will never do that again.' And he's been true to his word."

ONE YEAR AFTER appearing on *Vogue* for the second time, Gwyneth landed another coveted September cover story, this time for *Vanity Fair*, which declared her "the Über-'It' Girl." She was living in New York but, in order to maintain some privacy, didn't give interviews in her home, so she showed up to writer Michael Shnayerson's family apartment on Riverside Drive in Manhattan, dressed in all white, with matching white bags full of food from the upscale grocery store Dean & DeLuca. Gwyneth had brought an immaculate spread—plates, cutlery, more lunch than necessary. She had found a new response to the exhausting fickleness of fame: On the one hand, her inner world was off-limits, even for a profile cover story that would purport to bring us the "real" Gwyneth. On the other hand, she would show up with maximum graciousness, a star with "authentic" warmth and a flair for domesticity.

The story was pegged to *Duets*, which ended up tanking. The release had been pushed back after the studio asked Bruce to change the ending. When the movie premiered at the Toronto Film Festival on September 9, 2000, Gwyneth joined her father for his big moment. The *Toronto Star* noted before she arrived that *New York* magazine had recently called her "wildly overexposed" after attending "every event party and every trendy nightclub and restaurant-to-be before their public openings." The story continued, "Maybe that's the real reason she's coming to Toronto, where twentysomething women who drool over Her Paltrowness as the icon of their generation likely don't read the grown-up *New York*—just the fluff mags that also worship her." A Disney publicist then canceled her interview with a reporter from that paper, saying Gwyneth was jet-lagged—but pointed out that Bruce was available. But the media hadn't shown up for Bruce.

The reporter found Gwyneth at the after-party that night, where she was determined to talk up Bruce, noting that the audience "burst into applause five times. I was so happy for my father."

The mood turned when the reporter asked about Affleck. Gwyneth remarked that the interview was "very gossipy." The reporter then asked how she felt about Brad Pitt marrying Jennifer Aniston the previous month. "Are you really asking me this question?" Gwyneth replied, her eyes now "daggers." "I can't comment on this kind of thing." In reality, Gwyneth confided to friends that she'd felt sad when she learned they were getting married. (She was also fond of telling them that Brad "has terrible taste in women.")

Duets would pull in $2 million its first weekend, coming in tenth place. The ticket sales led the *Los Angeles Times* to write, "The only aspect of *Duets* that is successful is its singing, which not only sounds good, but keeps all that other nonsense off the screen." And Salon.com's critic reported, "Leaving the theater, I heard one woman mutter, 'Why would she take this role after winning an Oscar?'"

AFFLECK'S ADDICTION ISSUES resurfaced, and he and Gwyneth broke up for good in October 2000. While he had been turning to alcohol, she was obsessing over her own health, practicing Ashtanga yoga six times a week, meditating daily, and watching her diet. "It doesn't take Freudian analysis to see that her grandfather's death made her decide to get even more healthy than she was," Affleck said. "She's not wheatgrass and kelp, but it's very clean, very lean. She's always telling me I'm going to get cancer from diet soda, not to mention cigarettes." In 2001, Gwyneth participated in an intervention for Affleck led by Charlie Sheen, who had been put in touch to help him get sober. Sheen helped arrange a room for Affleck at the Promises rehab clinic in Malibu, where he once was a patient. Gwyneth called Affleck "brave" for going.

Gwyneth briefly dated Chris Heinz, Teresa Heinz Kerry's son and John Kerry's stepson, and heir to the ketchup fortune, then a student at Harvard Business School. Dating him inspired her to wear a cross around her neck. ("I'm wearing a cross, I'm dating a Catholic!" she said.) But they were together only briefly, and Gwyneth was single as she moved into her next film role.

FOR HIS NEW movie about an eccentric New York family, director Wes Anderson hoped to cast Alec Baldwin and Jodie Foster as leads. He had envisioned Baldwin in the role of Chas, the entrepreneurial prodigy, and Foster in the role of his adopted sister, Margot, who grows up to become a depressed playwright.

Anderson's distinctive style of filmmaking—meticulously art-directed, symmetrical shots, stories that blended humor and melancholy—had established him as an auteur with *Bottle Rocket* and *Rushmore*, which both had cult followings, but he hadn't had a box office hit. When Foster couldn't do it, producer Will Sweeney told Anderson, "Why don't you get real New Yorkers?" (Baldwin ended up narrating the movie.)

Gwyneth's childhood as a wealthy private-school student enmeshed in the creative class was the perfect credential. "Wes had just moved to New York. He wanted to be a New Yorker. Also, Gwyneth is smart, funny, beautiful, sophisticated, stylish. I think Wes was totally charmed by her," said someone who worked closely with him on the film.

When Gwyneth joined the cast of *The Royal Tenenbaums*, Anderson's crew gave up on Brad Pitt for the role of Richie, the youngest brother and a tennis star, despite Pitt's interest. Owen Wilson had cowritten the screenplay with Anderson, and both he and his brother Luke were given parts in the film: Owen played a family friend, while Luke played Richie Tenenbaum, who wrestles with romantic feelings for his adopted sister, Margot. Gene Hackman signed on to play the patriarch and Anjelica Huston the matriarch; Ben Stiller took on the role of their eldest son, Chas; Bill Murray joined as Margot's husband; and Danny Glover played their longtime accountant. The eight lead actors were being paid scale, plus a percentage of home video sales, which would end up being millions if the movie was a hit; but that wasn't a guarantee—they wanted to work on a Wes Anderson film.

Anderson was the kind of director who saw the entire movie in his head before he shot a single frame. The Tenenbaum children were supposed to look like they had gotten stuck in time, so all their clothes were, as Anderson insisted, entirely custom and slightly shrunken (a style Anderson, whose personal tailor made the costumes, favored himself). Costume designer Karen Patch had the idea to dress Margot in a fur coat, because the thought of a ten-year-old girl wearing one was amusing. She called Fendi and asked them to make a fur coat—which they were happy to do because it was for Gwyneth Paltrow.

Patch thought the fur coat would look ridiculous unless the character also dressed in something classic, so she decided to put Margot in Lacoste dresses. Since everything had to be custom, she called Lacoste and told them she planned to essentially knock off their clothing for Gwyneth to wear in the movie and asked them to send fabrics, and they agreed. She dressed Gwyneth mainly in stripes, and added penny loafers and a Birkin bag, which she bought secondhand. "I had to bargain for it. But it helped that, obviously, it was Gwyneth Paltrow," said Patch. (Gwyneth wasn't allowed to keep the bag, but she did make off with the loafers.)

Patch had seamstresses working around the clock making the costumes, and when at last Gwyneth came in for her fitting, she was inspired—particularly by the footwear: "I couldn't figure out the character, but when you put me in these shoes, I knew who I was." Her look as Margot eventually became iconic, resurfacing regularly as inspiration for high-fashion runway collections by brands like Fendi and Miu Miu. As he watched her play Margot, Anderson gave Gwyneth one particularly trenchant note: "Do one more take like that, but make it more sad."

The atmosphere on set was mostly harmonious, and various stars came to visit—Moby, Will Ferrell—having heard that it was one of the coolest shoots in town. Gwyneth's entourage included an assistant, her friend Mary Wigmore, and her brother, Jake, who was still working on his writing and directing career, and who befriended Anderson. Blythe also came by to visit.

Anderson wanted the cast to feel like a theater troupe, and he developed an easy and friendly rapport with Gwyneth. She became one of his allies, a protector in his ongoing struggle with Hackman, who yelled homophobic slurs at him, would change lines in the script just to mess with him, and once walked off the set and refused to work. But Anderson stuck it out with Hackman because, another director who had endured Hackman's antics told him, when you start watching dailies and cutting the movie, "it's like butter—he's the best."

One day Anderson was on set looking for someone to play a guy with a Mohawk whom Margot kisses during a montage of past lovers.

He summoned one of the young grips. "The good news is we want you to do a little part in the movie, and the part involves basically making out with Gwyneth Paltrow," Anderson said. "But the bad news is that you have to shave the sides of your head and spike the rest of it into a Mohawk."

The young man did not pause: "I'll do it."

Luke Wilson, who had gotten his big break in *Bottle Rocket*, joined the cast and spent most of his screen time opposite one of the all-time great actors (Hackman) and a recent Best Actress winner (Gwyneth). "I have two goals for this movie," he declared. "Not to look like an asshole and figure out how to get a date with Gwyneth Paltrow." Bill Murray had been cast as Margot's husband, Raleigh St. Clair, and watching him, Wilson sensed a rival. "Son of a bitch Bill Murray—this guy's going to laugh his way right into Gwyneth's bedroom, isn't he?"

The crew member he was talking to shrugged, and Luke continued, "I'm telling you, man—comedy. Women have a soft spot for comedy." Luke found a way eventually, and he and Gwyneth became an item. They thought they were keeping it a secret, but everyone on the set knew.

"I hate dates," Gwyneth said around this time. "They make me sick and make me feel nauseous . . . No, it's just that I hate first dates. But I like dating and getting to know people. If you get past the first date, then your time is running out." Marriage, she added, was a long way off for her. "I'm lucky if I get past six weeks. The make-or-break is six weeks."

The Royal Tenenbaums premiered at the New York Film Festival in late 2001 as its "hottest ticket," per the *New York Post*. Reviews were generally good, for the film and for Gwyneth, whose character was described in *Variety* as "a woman who has everything—looks, talent and money, anyway—except a properly functioning heart."

CHAPTER 17

Fat Suit Fiasco

I got a real sense of what it would be like to be that overweight,
and every pretty girl should be forced to do that.

—Gwyneth Paltrow

I hope you don't have to do anything unladylike."
Blythe was worried about her daughter, who, after a few years playing chilly Anglophile princesses, had signed on to wear a fat suit in a film by the same guys who dangled a glob of semen from Cameron Diaz's ear in *There's Something About Mary*.

"Well," Gwyneth answered, "I think I'm okay."

Gwyneth had seen *Charlie's Angels* in the theater with a friend after it came out in November 2000. (Diaz, one of its stars, became a good friend around this time.) "God, I would have loved to do something like that," she admitted. "Something funny and girly"—and undeniably mainstream.

Gwyneth felt some part of her was lost in the wellborn, mannerly roles that had made her famous. "I sensed that people had no real understanding of who I am," she told her Spence friend Caroline Doyle, who interviewed her for a 2001 *Harper's Bazaar* story about *Shallow Hal*. "And in this day and age, if you sit up straight, chew with your mouth closed, and have good manners, you're a snob . . . But my friends wanted me to do something that was more closely connected to the side of me that they know. The side that is more guileless and funny."

The Farrelly brothers were dominating comedy after a run of films that included *Dumb and Dumber*, *There's Something About Mary*, and *Me, Myself & Irene*—all number one at the box office. Gwyneth was nervous about the role but not because of the raunchiness or the fat suit—which would make this part the most controversial of her career—but because this was her first major big-budget Hollywood movie. This was: Gwyneth Paltrow in *Shallow Hal*.

In her role as Rosemary, Gwyneth would play an obese woman who appears to one man—played by Jack Black—as thin and beautiful after he falls under a spell that forces him to see only "inner beauty." Gwyneth would play the role straight, but most of the film's gags would arise from the idea that this man would find a fat version of her attractive.

Before the filming started, Gwyneth's representatives asked that she be given lodgings a certain distance from everyone else working on the movie. (Black stayed in the same condo complex as the crew.) She also requested a car and driver on her days off and, since she was on a strict macrobiotic diet, a chef who could prepare her meals.

"I was helping him [Bruce] one day, you know, feeding him with a syringe and feeding tube. And it struck me, like, 'What is in this can that I'm injecting directly into his stomach?' And it was the first time I made a connection between food, wellness. I'll never forget that moment," she said. As Bruce's cancer grew worse, Gwyneth set about trying to cure him through her own commitment to health. "I felt I could heal him by proxy," she said. This marked the beginning of what would be her defining interest in wellness. She began searching for a solution, researching his illness and the potential causes. "I was trying to take control of his life because he wouldn't . . . I started looking at environmental toxins and how food affects our health." She hired a "macrobiotic counselor" who claimed she'd healed herself of cancer through diet. Calling the idea "perhaps naive," Gwyneth believed that her father could do the same thing and "heal himself with good foods and alternative medicine," even if he was resistant to the idea.

She recalled reading anything she could find "that linked processed foods, pesticides, growth hormones, preservatives, and the like to cancer and other diseases." (While there's scientific evidence that certain diets are more cancer prone than others, "once you have cancer, diet's not going to really change your prognosis much," said infectious disease expert Dr. Amesh Adalja.)

Gwyneth said that she didn't follow this diet "to keep thin." She explained, "It's about eating healthily and cleanly. When I reached my late twenties, I couldn't eat whatever I wanted to anymore. I was thinking, *What's happened to my metabolism?*" She said she only rarely enjoyed cheese or a slice of cake, not for her figure but for health reasons.

A macrobiotic diet and so-called clean eating were among the first health fads that seemed to stick to Gwyneth and her evolving persona. "That was the beginning of people thinking I was a crackpot. Like, *What do you mean food can affect your health, you f—ing psycho?*" she later said. By the time she was doing interviews to promote *Shallow Hal*, she was espousing the kinds of health theories that would define her next career. The media generally quoted her without any fact-checking: "I used to drink vodka tonics all the time . . . but I found that my kidneys got really hard because of it, and I noticed that my liver wouldn't drop down in my yoga backbends." ("I don't think you could say there's some physiological explanation for what she's talking about," said Adalja.) Gwyneth's Ashtanga yoga routine involved getting up at four a.m. six days a week for an hour and forty-five minutes of practice. "I never skip it unless I'm ill," she said. She'd bring two yoga instructors with her on location shoots. While all of this was going on, she was spending her working hours in a fat suit.

As a slapstick comedy, *Shallow Hal* was a long way from the quirky, urbane vibe of *The Royal Tenenbaums*. The Farrellys' crew had worked together before and felt like a family by the time Gwyneth showed up with her strange diet requests and intensive workout schedule. She was ready to cultivate the irreverent side of her personality, the fun-loving mischief maker, but the people around her were still seeing elitist Gwyneth.

.   .   .

BEFORE FILMING BEGAN, 120-pound Gwyneth slipped into a rubbery, twenty-five-pound fat suit. It came in six pieces—one that zipped over her torso, one that slipped over her legs like shorts, two calf pieces, and two gloves—plus a face that was essentially glued to hers, and was meant to make her look like she weighed 350 pounds. She planned to walk around downtown Charlotte, without an entourage or full camera crew, to experience what her high school yearbook had called her "worst fear"—obesity.

None of the pedestrians at the intersection of Trade and Tryon Streets knew that a major movie was about to start filming in town, or that the star was in their midst. They mostly ignored her, or skirted around her body like an obstacle dropped in their path. Barry Teague, a line producer, had been instructed to stay close, but to keep enough of a distance so that she felt like she was alone.

Teague, who weighed 325 pounds himself, felt pained as he watched the scene play out before him. She moved more slowly than everyone else and blocked most of the width of the sidewalk. Pedestrians couldn't step off the curb to pass by because cars were parked, so they had to squeeze around her single file on the other side. Teague watched two attractive, middle-aged men hurry around her like she was a trash can, without saying "excuse me" or regarding her at all. A pair of teenage girls gawked as she passed, then giggled to each other as she walked away.

She did the walk a few times. Teague watched her stop at a hot dog stand and noticed how impatient the crowd behind her got, seemingly for no other reason than her being fat.

After twenty minutes of walking around town this time, she called it quits. The exercise seemed too distressing for her to finish. Teague said, "It was difficult to watch."

Before Gwyneth got to Charlotte, she had done a test run in New York. The crew dressed her in the fat suit in a room at the Tribeca Grand hotel and sent her to the bar to see if anyone could recognize her.

"No one would even look at me," she recalled. "If I was walking by a table, you know how naturally you just glance up. But people would see that I was heavy in their peripheral vision and not look, because I think they assume that's the polite thing to do. It was incredibly isolating and really lonely and sad . . . I didn't expect it to feel so upsetting," she said. "I thought the whole thing would be funny, and then as soon as I put it on, I thought, well, you know, this isn't all funny."

GWYNETH HAD A sign made for her trailer that read "Kate," seemingly as a decoy, even though the only people coming near it were crew who knew she was inside. She wasn't chummy the way big stars had been on other Farrelly brothers sets. She didn't rush to make conversation, and she let her attention drift if the topic did not interest her. She seemed out of her element. One day the crew member driving her to set announced with excitement that Bret Michaels from the band Poison was visiting that day. Gwyneth groaned.

"Come on, how do you groan about Poison?" someone asked.

Gwyneth answered flatly, "I'm from the Upper East Side of New York."

Her costar Jack Black sometimes tried to draw her into his off-camera goofing around, but Gwyneth seemed embarrassed—not by his raunchy jokes but by being stuck in this production with these people. At one point, crew members observed her lifting her leg and resting her ankle on Black's shoulder, as though using his body for a yoga pose.

"Sometimes she felt like she was maybe more talented or more in-demand than other people, and you could see that," said Teague. "You could hear her eyes rolling sometimes." When she finished a scene with an actor she didn't like who had a bit part in the film, she walked away poking a finger in her mouth, miming throwing up.

During some scenes, Gwyneth wore a short skirt but chose not to wear anything underneath. One of the camera operators went over to her dresser, Cookie Lopez. "Cookie, she's flashing us. You might want to tell her to sit differently."

Lopez looked at him and said, "There's nothing I can do."

He said, "You don't want to tell her so she can change what she's doing?"

Lopez replied, "If she likes doing that, I can't get her to stop."

Another day, the crew watched her riding around set on one of the electric scooters they used to get around, wearing only the bikini that was her costume for an upcoming scene. Though she never liked her legs, she struck one crew member as "very, very comfortable in her own skin."

Compared to other Farrelly brothers film stars, Gwyneth was remote. Renée Zellweger joined the *Me, Myself & Irene* cast and crew at a skating party. Jim Carrey, who starred in *Me, Myself & Irene* and *Dumb and Dumber*, threw the *Irene* crew a dance party on a boat. Gwyneth ordered an ice cream cart for the set and had her assistant push it around saying, "It's from Gwyneth, it's from Gwyneth." The crew was surprised—not that the gesture was comparatively small but that Gwyneth had done anything at all. When a technician died suddenly during filming, cast and crew contributed to a fund for his widow and children. The person in charge of collecting the money was telling colleagues one day how much they had amassed; Gwyneth overheard and asked them what they were talking about. One crew member signaled another not to tell her, sensing that Gwyneth wasn't someone who should be requested to donate. Later, someone overheard Luke Wilson, who had visited the set, tell her, "The world doesn't revolve around you."

After *Shallow Hal* wrapped in June 2001, Gwyneth spent time in Martha's Vineyard with Peter Farrelly and his family, including a daughter named Apple. Gwyneth never mentioned this as inspiration when she chose the same name for her daughter nearly three years later, and Farrelly didn't seem to take offense. His wife, Melinda Kocsis, just said, "Maybe it'll make it easier for my Apple when she gets older."

EVEN BY THE relatively permissive standards of 2002, *Shallow Hal* generated controversy for using fatness as a punch line, in gags that included a massive splash when thin Gwyneth jumps into a pool, and Jack Black's shock when he sees the size of her underwear. Gwyneth told friends and some of the crew that she felt like the film could bring attention to what would later be widely termed fat-shaming, which she experienced for the first time in her life in the fat suit. But that's not exactly where the discourse landed.

"If you're overweight and you see this movie, you're going to be disturbed. To be honest, I was uncomfortable throughout the whole movie," singer and talk show host Carnie Wilson told *USA Today*, calling out scenes of chairs breaking under Rosemary's weight. "It made me feel like I was a big joke, and that crushes my heart."

Advocacy groups agreed. "Rosemary jumps into a pool cannonball-style, and a kid gets thrown up into a tree as a result of the splash that is made," said Miriam Berg, president of the nonprofit group Council on Size & Weight Discrimination. "It's making horrible fun of fat people, and that is still acceptable in our culture. Would it be acceptable to make the same kind of joke about a person in a wheelchair or a person of color? No."

Sandie Sabo, spokeswoman for the five-thousand-member National Association to Advance Fat Acceptance, told *The New York Times*, "If Gwyneth Paltrow had decided to make a movie about the African American experience, and she portrayed herself in blackface makeup, and yet her quote-unquote inner beauty was perceived as white, I don't think people would put up with that . . . Maybe that will help people understand."

Despite the backlash, the film fared fairly well in reviews and opened third at the box office, with first-weekend ticket sales of $23.3 million. It would go on to gross $141 million on a $40 million budget.

Gwyneth did her best to respond to the controversy, but her well-intentioned innocence sometimes floundered on the spot. Matt Lauer asked her on the *Today* show if the film made fun of fat people. "No. I wouldn't have done it if that was the intention. You know, and I, I was concerned, I thought, 'Well is this going to be—is this going to be making fun of, of heavier people?' But it really doesn't. I mean—and actually the film is really—it ends up being a love letter to, to people who are overweight. It's like finally a film for people who are overweight, and, and, and it's—it's really a love letter," she said. In an interview with *Entertainment Tonight*, she said, "I got a real sense of what it would be like to be that overweight, and every pretty girl should be forced to do that."

Gwyneth had never seen the movie as mocking fat people and was disappointed that it hadn't ended up being her *Charlie's Angels*, though it was commercially successful. (*Angels* earned around $120 million more on the same budget.) But the backlash didn't seem to bother her all that much. She simply moved on to her next project.

AS PART OF *Shallow Hal*'s promotion, Gwyneth appeared on the cover of Miramax-owned *Talk* magazine for the December/January 2002 issue.

Weinstein remained eager to see Gwyneth featured in *Talk* for any reason, including non-Miramax films like *Shallow Hal*, so the editorial team went about booking her through her publicist, Stephen Huvane. *Talk* editors were especially careful in their coverage of Gwyneth, fearing Weinstein wouldn't be happy with a profile that wasn't adequately fawning.

In the photo spread, Gwyneth appeared as a fat version of herself in some of the images, thin in others. The magazine explained that it achieved this effect by Photoshopping her head onto a larger woman's body. She was initially told that she would appear as her fat self on the cover. When the planes hit the towers on September 11, 2001, the magazine pivoted: They pushed the profile of Gwyneth back and decided, after considerable debate, to run one of the skinny images on the cover, featuring Gwyneth wearing a black blazer with no shirt underneath, her hands pressing her breasts together, which editors believed felt more tonally appropriate following the tragedy.

After the towers fell, and Manhattan was in lockdown, Gwyneth was able to get from there to Westchester County, just north of the city, and then charter a private plane to Texas. She was upset about the cover change and felt "lied to," according to the *New York Post*, even though the editors had explained to Huvane why they were pushing the story back and changing the cover image.

Yet she was developing a pattern of feeling unhappy with these profiles. When her friend Caroline Doyle's story came out in *Harper's Bazaar* pegged to *Shallow Hal*, Gwyneth was angry about how racy the photo spread by Patrick Demarchelier had turned out. She appeared fully nude in two black-and-white images, her butt obscured through artful lighting and shadows. Once again, she made sure her dissatisfaction went public. "He lied to me and said he wasn't going to put my whole bottom in the picture—and he did," Gwyneth told *Us Weekly*. (Demarchelier said, "I asked her to do some nudes and she said Yes." A *Bazaar* spokesperson said, "We are really surprised that she is saying this because she didn't raise any objection to posing nude then. . ."). She thought her boyfriend Luke Wilson's mom would react badly to the photos, and blamed Doyle—who wrote the story but didn't have control over every aspect of it—for failing to protect her. She stopped speaking to Doyle for a while after the issue came out.

GWYNETH REMAINED WEINSTEIN'S darling. When she signed on for a black comedy about flight attendants called *View from the Top*, Miramax agreed to pay her $10 million. "She was the highest-paid female actor in an independent film. Higher paid than all the men," Weinstein later said.

The original script was sharp and satirical, with Gwyneth playing what Miramax development executive Jack Lechner described as "this white-trash girl who is utterly ruthless and will stop at nothing to become a stewardess in international first class and is stabbing people in the back." Gwyneth was taking another big step away from gentility, but Weinstein stepped in to protect her image: "We can't have Gwyneth playing this bitch," he said, and ordered the writers to soften the script.

Five rewrites later, the film was basically a mess. Bruno Barreto, who never quite got the film's tone, signed on as director. As the movie spiraled toward certain doom, a new producer was brought in to make it funnier in the vein of *Legally Blonde*. Gwyneth's costar Mike Myers took a crack at rewriting scenes. Each time a page got revised, it would be printed in a new color. The script had so many revisions that it was a veritable rainbow. Along with Myers, who played a flight attendant trainer, the cast included Candice Bergen as a flight attendant mentor; Rob Lowe as a pilot and Gwyneth's love interest; Christina Applegate as her friend turned rival;

and Mark Ruffalo as an airport security guard (and other love interest). Everyone who worked on the movie or who saw the dailies, including Gwyneth, knew it wasn't funny. Gwyneth took to making mocking faces when Barreto wasn't looking, which the crew could see on the monitors.

Toward the end of the shoot, Barreto gathered everyone to watch a rough cut, hoping it would boost morale. But afterward, the crew members were staring uncomfortably into corners of the room.

Weinstein came to the set to visit and gathered Gwyneth, Applegate, and costar Kelly Preston for a photo. "It's Harvey's angels!" a crew member dutifully exclaimed. But the relationship between actress and studio head was coming apart. *View from the Top* bombed spectacularly, and critics wondered why Gwyneth was "squandering her talents" (*The New York Times*) on "the movie equivalent of airline food" (*New York Post*). Gwyneth's "relatable" roles had tanked with viewers, and Weinstein was on the hook for two flops.

Gwyneth later said that Weinstein started treating her differently around this time, and she distanced herself from him. "I wasn't the golden girl with the Midas touch," she said. "My worth had diminished in his eyes."

However, another Miramax source saw the coming apart as stemming more from Gwyneth and her anger over the first *Talk* cover and the *Shakespeare in Love* joke in *Scary Movie*.

Weinstein pinpointed the fracturing to another incident entirely. Around 2002, Miramax acquired the rights to Donna Tartt's bestselling 1992 novel *The Secret History*. Gwyneth asked Weinstein to hire her brother, Jake, to write the screenplay and direct, with her as a producer. Though Weinstein recalled paying Jake little or no money, he had forked over a large sum to Tartt for the rights to her book. "To check myself on a screenplay that I paid $800,000 for, I went to Donna Tartt and asked her what she thought, and she told me she didn't like it and that's why I decided to drop the project, which made Gwyneth upset with me," Weinstein remembered. "To renew the project would have cost another $2 million for rights and I just couldn't afford to do that on a script I did not like."

With so many disappointments piling up, Gwyneth decided to turn away from films.

CHAPTER 18

Losing Bruce

It's literally my worst nightmare, and it came true.

—Gwyneth Paltrow

Gwyneth's post-Oscar pivot into a comedic blockbuster that could show her raunchy, relatable side hadn't gone well. She was dissatisfied with many of her films these days and the press seemed to delight in her apparent flop era. For the 2002 Oscars, where she presented Best Original Song, she went noticeably braless in an Alexander McQueen dress with a full dark skirt and a sheer tank-top bodice. She thought it would be "a little bit punk at the Oscars," but the press ripped her apart, calling it an "unflattering, figure-flattening goth getup," a "fashion disaster," and "the worst dress ever."

"Hollywood is a completely male-dominated world," she reportedly told a German paper just before the awards. "I want to leave." She hadn't had a big role in a movie since wrapping *Shallow Hal* in the middle of 2001. "Frankly, I'm a little bit burned out on film, just the structure of them and how much of your life they take. And I haven't found anything that's shaken me out of that way of thinking about it," she said.

Four months earlier in New York, she had seen David Auburn's play *Proof* on Broadway, starring her friend Jennifer Jason Leigh. Her agent sent her a screenplay adaptation to consider the leading role for the film version. While she liked the material, she wasn't certain it would be as powerful on-screen. Then she found out that *Shakespeare in Love* director John Madden was directing *Proof* as a play in London, and she made up her mind. "I would do anything he was doing," she said.

Madden remembered that he and Gwyneth had talked about doing theater together during *Shakespeare in Love* and reached out to see if she was available. He was "flabbergasted" when she agreed. Gwyneth took the part for five hundred dollars a week. She flew over in the spring of 2002 to stay for a few days with Madonna, who was living in Westminster with her then-husband, British director Guy Ritchie, while experimenting with her British phase. Within a few days, Gwyneth found a place of her own: a two-bedroom, 1,250-square-foot flat off King's Road in Chelsea that she rented for $14,600 a month before buying it for $1.9 million (around $3.3 million in 2025). The ground floor opened to a private garden, though the place had access to another large communal one. Furnishings came in chrome and pine, the floors with a deep-pile cream carpet. A spiral staircase led to the second floor.

In addition to Madonna, Gwyneth had other famous friends in London, including fashion designer Stella McCartney. She told an interviewer that the city "feels very much like a second home."

Gwyneth's friends viewed her as too smart to spend her life reciting someone else's lines, but she had no ambition to write or direct. In *Proof*, she was hoping to find a reason to love acting again. "Every time I do a play, I think, *I remember why I wanted this job in the first place*. It puts you back in touch with everything that's fun about being an actor," she said.

Gwyneth would play Catherine, whose mathematician father dies after deteriorating mentally, causing her to wonder if she inherited both his mathematical genius and his mental illness. Playing her father was Ronald Pickup, who had a habit of going to "a completely dark place" during rehearsal, Madden said. This threw Gwyneth, who was understandably nervous about starring in a challenging play. He'd arrive fifteen minutes before the rest of the cast and pace and curse himself, saying, "Why would you cast me? I'm dreadful."

Madden had worked with Pickup before, and knew that that was just how he was. But he had to sit Gwyneth down with him and say, "Everybody needs everybody else's confidence in something like this."

"She was not used to any of this stuff," Madden recalled.

Before the play opened on London's West End—and although she had been uncertain about it working in film—Weinstein had signed her up to star in the movie, with Madden directing. Bruce and Blythe came to London to see Gwyneth's performance and stayed with her at her new place. She was terribly nervous about doing the play and climbed between them in bed, saying, "Protect me!" Though Gwyneth wasn't used to the dynamics of the theater, Madden felt like "she bowed down to it and unlocked the whole thing." He thought Gwyneth would feel validated by the reviews: *The Guardian* said she had "the theatrical gift," *The Independent* wrote that she "makes an arresting impression," and the *Telegraph* reported that she "thoroughly deserved her standing ovation."

"Are you aware of how good the reviews have been?" Madden asked her right after the play had opened.

"No," she said.

"They've been very, very, very good and admiring of your performance," he said.

Madden, astonished that Gwyneth hadn't read any of the reviews, recalled Gwyneth then looking innocently at him, as though to say, *How did that happen?*

Gwyneth claimed performing in the stage version of *Proof* made her feel "totally reinvigorated about being an actor, and I made a pact with myself that I was never going to do anything to compromise myself again."

The feeling wouldn't last.

BY THE TIME Gwyneth's thirtieth birthday approached, her closest Spence friends had all settled down with husbands and started to have kids. As they became less available to her, she escaped into the trappings of her celebrity persona, and into more transactional friendships like the one she had with Valentino Garavani.

After *Proof* ended, she attended Valentino's couture show. Valentino himself was generous with his muses, but he expected them to show up when he needed them to show off his work. "It's a kind of quid pro quo," Gwyneth said of her relationship with designers. "I get to wear something beautiful, and if it gives the person exposure, that's fine. It seems like a reasonable business transaction."

She enjoyed traveling with Valentino and his entourage, and they always put together a rack of clothes for her to choose from. If they sometimes leaked the photos afterward of her wearing their dresses, she figured it was worth it. After the couture show, she went to Valentino's Château de Wideville, less than an hour's drive from the center of Paris, for a party covered by *Vogue*. Described as a "houseguest," Gwyneth was shown petting one of his pugs in the opening photos. Valentino took her on their yacht in late August, and on the twenty-ninth, she attended the Venice Film Festival on his arm, wearing a dress she had grabbed off a rack of clothes just before the show, after doing her own makeup.

Though Gwyneth was comfortable in this kind of relationship with certain designers, the demands sometimes left her feeling exploited. In September 2002, Gwyneth happened to be in New York at the same time as Calvin Klein's show and agreed to go as a favor to the brand. The public relations team sent her some clothes to choose from, and she opted for sandblasted bootcut jeans and a black button-down shirt. She showed up and sat in a front-row seat. Sandra Bullock, whom she had publicly dismissed as a commercial actress in the past, was seated in a more prominent front-row seat, sandwiched between Anna Wintour and André Leon Talley from *Vogue*. The paparazzi who always photographed the front row were particularly aggressive: The Calvin Klein team had a hard time getting them off the runway, and Gwyneth seemed disgusted by all the cameras in her face.

That same month, when Gwyneth turned thirty, Valentino hosted a party for her in Rome. Blythe was filming a television show, but Bruce came, though his illness had weakened him. The surgery and radiation had compromised his breathing and swallowing, and he was on painkillers and antibiotics.

For her birthday, Bruce gave Gwyneth a letter, which she later described as saying that "everything up until that point had been a dress rehearsal, and that the life I had ahead of me was going to be so rich and full of amazing things."

After their time in Rome, Gwyneth and Bruce rented a car and embarked on a road trip through Italy, beginning in Umbria, with plans to head to Tuscany. They toured the Uffizi Gallery in Florence before it opened to the public, then went shopping in the afternoon. While Gwyneth was trying on clothes, Bruce reportedly fell asleep in a chair. At some point during the trip, he started coughing up blood. He tried, at first, to hide it from his daughter. One night in Cortona, known for its sweeping views of the Tuscan countryside, they went to dinner, and Bruce gave Gwyneth some advice about respecting herself and her ambition. He talked about how much he loved Blythe, and how their marriage had worked because they supported each other more than anyone else. He said his only regret in life was not having had more children, since his had brought him so much joy.

That was the last meal Gwyneth had with her father. Within a day, she realized just how sick he was. "We are going to the hospital," she told him. "We have got to get to the Splendido," a luxury hotel in Portofino, he countered. Gwyneth insisted, and Valentino and Giancarlo Giammetti arranged for a helicopter to take them to Rome. When they got to San Camillo hospital, thinking Bruce had pneumonia, they learned the cancer had returned in his bronchial tubes. He didn't make it through his first night there and died of complications from the cancer and pneumonia before dawn on October 3, 2002. Gwyneth's father, the love of her life, was now gone.

Blythe and Jake immediately flew to Italy to be with Gwyneth. But she reportedly felt that Blythe hadn't taken Bruce's illness seriously enough when his health started deteriorating on the trip, leaving Gwyneth to endure his dying alone, and she later described to someone she worked with holding on to the anger she felt toward her mother in her liver.

After the shock of her father's death, she relied on Valentino and Giammetti. (According to Weinstein, Gwyneth leaned on him, too: "The greatest compliment she gave me was when her father died, she said that Valentino and I were the two best, nonfamily members, that she could turn to.") They called the consulate and translated the autopsy report and helped her figure out how to get Bruce's body home. For a while, they became her surrogate family.

Wearing dark sunglasses, Gwyneth returned to the hospital on October 4—the paparazzi snapping her from a distance—and Bruce's body was transported back to the United States. Gwyneth then traveled to New York for a memorial service on October 6 at Michael's restaurant. Looking stunned, wearing uncharacteristic thick-framed eyeglasses, she clutched her cousin Rebekah Paltrow's hand as her teetering black stilettos carried her into the restaurant her father had loved so much. Caroline Doyle flew in to attend as well, and Gwyneth resumed their friendship after their falling-out less than a year earlier. At the service, Gwyneth addressed the crowd briefly to say a few words about her dad and to thank them for coming.

She had never felt pain like that before, like she had been split apart. She later recalled, "I was so traumatized by his death; one of the things that surprised me so much was how the world kept going in its complete flurry of events. I couldn't reconcile it, I was so devastated, and my heart was so broken."

AFTER THE FUNERAL, Gwyneth went back to London. In the middle of the night, she awoke with a pain in her chest, unable to breathe. She thought she was having a heart attack. She was due to start work on *Sylvia*, a biopic about the poet Sylvia Plath, filming a week later around London. The start of production had been delayed by one week to allow for her grieving. "I don't know how I got through it," she later said. "It was all sort of just right under the surface. It's literally my worst nightmare, and it came true. It's really horrible because he was the one person in your life that you always think, *I'm safe because they're there, and they're so smart, and they know everything, and I can always go to them.* And then they evaporate."

Within a few months, she had pulled out of two movies, *I Heart Huckabees* and *Happy Endings*.

AFTER HER FATHER'S death, Gwyneth started smoking cigarettes again, and experienced an important realization: that she wanted to start her own family. She had thought about having a baby with Luke Wilson, but according to one of Gwyneth's friends, he smoked a lot of pot and didn't seem ready to be a parent. She asked Mary Wigmore to come stay with her in London, where they planned to see a Coldplay concert.

Gwyneth had been a fan of Coldplay since seeing them perform on TV in 2000. She had predicted they would be huge, and had listened on repeat to their debut album, *Parachutes*. She and Wigmore had gone to see Coldplay perform at a small venue in New York, and the band's second album, *A Rush of Blood to the Head*, was part of her and her brother's grieving music.

Now, faced with the prospect of a night out in London, she told Wigmore she didn't want to go to the concert. Wigmore replied, "We need to get you out of the house and get some air. We've got to get you out of here." Gwyneth relented.

Coldplay lead singer Chris Martin's assistant Vicki found Gwyneth in the crowd that night. "You want to go meet your boyfriend after the show?" she joked. The tabloids had been writing—wrongly—that Gwyneth and Martin had been dating since she was spotted at their earlier show in New York, though they hadn't met yet.

Gwyneth agreed and met twenty-five-year-old blue-eyed Martin at the London concert for the first time. "He was like Tigger the tiger bouncing around," she recalled. Gwyneth thought Martin was "so sweet," his curly hair reminding her of Bruce, though she didn't expect to date him after that encounter. But then he called and asked her to come see his show in Ireland. She balked initially, then a friend pointed out that she was smiling for the first time since her father's death.

MARTIN CAME FROM a middle-class family in Devon; he met his best friend and Coldplay's future manager, Phil Harvey, at a nearby boarding school. He had graduated from University College London with a degree in ancient world studies and first-class honors in Greek and Latin. When Martin was twenty-three, Coldplay released *Parachutes*, which won a Grammy for Best Alternative Music Album and sold well over ten million copies.

As a couple, Gwyneth and Martin were two very famous people struggling to preserve a private, more mindful version of themselves. Gwyneth liked morning yoga; Martin liked a morning jog. Gwyneth rarely drank alcohol; Martin didn't drink or do drugs, once joking to a reporter, "I wear a habit." Both aspired to some kind of soulful, intellectual seriousness at a moment when their work was pulling them toward mass appeal and triviality. "Mainstream pop culture is so awful and so bland and so packaged," Martin said. "[Coldplay's] goal is to change the mainstream. We don't want to just keep ourselves a secret. We want to fight to have sincere music be the main thing again."

Martin's sobriety may have cast him, to Gwyneth, as an antidote to Ben Affleck and Luke Wilson. Yet her friends felt like something didn't quite click between them. While Gwyneth was extroverted and loved entertaining friends, Martin was an introvert who could be socially awkward. He seemed to always be writing music in his head, even when they had company over. But he was incredible onstage, and Gwyneth, who was ready to settle down, was seduced by his persona. What's not to like, a friend pointed out, about a rock star who adores you?

In 2005, Coldplay released the song "Fix You," with the lyrics "Tears stream down your face / When you lose something you cannot replace." Martin said it was inspired by "trying to empathize" with someone he loved who was grieving. That someone, Gwyneth later said, was her.

BEFORE *SYLVIA* CAME out, the *New York Post* reported that Gwyneth was depressed about it after seeing a first cut. (Stephen Huvane denied this, saying, "We are doing an Oscar push for the movie...."). Plath's daughter, Frieda Hughes, whose mother died when she was two, had come out against the film, blasting the producers for repeatedly soliciting her help. She withheld the rights to Plath's poetry. Gwyneth described being "completely sympathetic" to Frieda. "I mean, I'm a person who is fiercely protective of my private life, and I believe so much in people's right to privacy and not exposing things about people for commerce... But at the same time... it's an amazing story. I'm also an artist who wanted to tell the story of this woman who I think more people need to know about and hear about. You'd be surprised how many people don't know who Sylvia Plath is." The film failed at the box office and was generally panned by critics, despite a publicity campaign that included another *Vogue* cover.

Shortly before Gwyneth traveled to Chicago to film Miramax's film adaptation of *Proof*, Vicki Woods interviewed her for the *Vogue* story at Claridge's in London. Gwyneth ordered Parmesan crackers, then described them as "terribly unhealthy." It wasn't that Gwyneth feared getting fat herself—rather, she seemed to have a problem with what she viewed as others' lack of self-control. (After she became successful, she even allegedly paid for a Spence friend's tummy tuck.) Her diet was still extreme, but she was integrating other fads. "A mix of macrobiotic diet, blood-group diet, and Mediterranean diet," she told Woods. "The principles are everything being local, in season, organic. No dairy, sugar, eggs, or meat. Lots of fish and dark, leafy veggies. If

I'm out, I can't resist Parmesan. And hey—if you want a mouthful of key lime pie, why not?"

The diet would last only a few weeks more. By August 2003, she was pregnant and just wanted ice cream.

WHILE FILMING *PROOF*, Gwyneth was able to hide her pregnancy, as well as her morning sickness. The crew arrived in Chicago in early September, and by the middle of the month, the weather had turned unseasonably frosty. Gwyneth's feet were so cold that costume designer Jill Taylor put her in warm boots that wouldn't be seen in the frame. Though Gwyneth knew the part well and got along with director John Madden and her costar Anthony Hopkins, the dark subject matter took a toll. Gwyneth played Catherine, who reflected her own fear—which grew after she became a mother—that she would inherit her father's illness and leave her children early in their lives, forcing them to endure the same pain she had. The scenes were very long, and Gwyneth was in nearly all of them, sometimes delivering five-page monologues. "It was very intense," Taylor said. "It wasn't a romcom."

Martin made extended visits to the set to be with Gwyneth, where he played her music from his new album. Sitting under a tree, he asked her, "What do you think of this song?"—something that then became a giant hit. To the Miramax crew who had worked with her before, Gwyneth seemed crankier than usual. They later wondered, after they learned she had been pregnant, if her mood was partly a result of her not feeling well early in the pregnancy while having to take on this intense, emotionally draining role.

But one Miramax executive who had watched Gwyneth evolve from her first leading role in *Emma* to her current leading role in *Proof* got the distinct impression that she just wasn't happy with this career anymore. She had always seemed a little bit bored by performing, which came so easily to her. And as she delivered these monologues while hiding her morning sickness, she felt like she was "dying," she later said. Every movie she did these days seemed to be a flop. Asked in 2003 which projects since *Shakespeare in Love* she was proud of, she named *The Royal Tenenbaums* and *The Talented Mr. Ripley*, adding, "I'm trying to think if I left anything out. No, not really." She was starting to find things like makeup touch-ups and riding in a van to set unbearable. During *Proof*, she just thought, *I've had it. I can't do this anymore.*

Around this time, she was also dealing with the more troubling aspects of her fame. She testified in court against a stalker, Dante Soiu, who had sent her sexually explicit correspondence, toys, and magazines. "I thought if I'm in the same place with him, then he would rape me or that he would hurt me," Gwyneth testified in Los Angeles County Court. "He was expressing a lot of anger at my parents for keeping us apart." Soiu was found criminally insane, convicted of stalking Gwyneth, and sentenced to up to three years in prison—though that wouldn't be the end of him contacting her.

Gwyneth had also been nearly run off the road in Los Angeles by paparazzi, and she had to keep all the curtains closed at home in order to protect their privacy. "I sound like a complete jerk. I've been given this incredible life and now I'm complaining, but honestly, when people are stalking you to that extent, it's just really awful," she said. "I've made it abundantly clear in all my actions and in the way I lead my life, I don't want to be a tabloid person. I'm not putting myself out there in a celebrity way. I don't go to this premiere, that premiere, party, opening." Yet that same month, she was on the cover of *Vogue*; the last six months of the year, she attended a Valentino fashion show, a party for *AnOther* magazine, participated in a Shakespeare charity event, and headlined two *Sylvia* premieres.

At the end of filming *Proof* in Chicago, Gwyneth asked to meet with Harvey Weinstein and requested that one of the producers join them. Weinstein had always been more deferential to Gwyneth when other people were around. "You built this company," he would say. "We wouldn't have this company without you." According to someone familiar with the meeting, the producer figured that Gwyneth wanted her there because she and Weinstein were fighting. Gwyneth had witnessed

Weinstein's angry tirades, where he sometimes threw things. She knew his employees feared him and called him "the H-bomb." However, after Weinstein's sexual harassment of Gwyneth came out in 2016, the producer wondered if there was another reason she'd asked her to attend. Gwyneth revealed to Weinstein that she was pregnant. Then she turned to the producer and said, "It's fine, you can go. Everything's good."

This marked the beginning of Gwyneth leaving behind a career that had been so closely tied to Weinstein and Miramax. "I had a really rough boss for most of my movie career at Miramax," she later said. "So you're like, *I don't know if this is really my calling.*"

However, a friend from the time remembered it differently: "She wanted to make a lot of money." Gwyneth had transformed from a friendly and accessible newbie to a star who was highly transactional. She became "money, money, money-hungry. I think she was always kind of money-hungry. I think her father did instill that in her." Weinstein recalled that Miramax films had a budget cap of $25 million, and that "if we paid Gwyneth $10 million which she deserved, it limited what we could do on the film so in a way her success outpaced her from working on independent films."

The artistic aspect of her work no longer seemed like her main concern.

ON DECEMBER 1, 2003, in New York City, Gwyneth hosted the Music Has Power Awards, a fundraiser to benefit the Institute for Music and Neurologic Function, which raised money for music therapy. Wearing a black silk and chiffon Stella McCartney flapper dress, she looked pregnant enough that reporters started asking questions. By December 4, major outlets were confirming the news. Gwyneth went on *The Tonight Show with Jay Leno* that evening. "It's been a secret for a while. We thought: *Well, we'll tell everybody and just make a nice clean statement.* There are all these strangers who are like, 'Congratulations.' It's a little bit weird, but it's lovely that people care."

Likely aware that her pregnancy would lead to heightened interest in her relationship, and perhaps in an effort to control the narrative, "sources" told the New York *Daily News* that Gwyneth staged a photo shoot two days later of her and Martin leaving an ob-gyn office in Manhattan. In the images, she wears jeans, stiletto boots, and a trench coat, her hair in a ponytail, and they smile at each other in the doorway of the brick building, doctors' signs clearly visible. In one photo, she and Martin appear to be cooing at her stomach. The *Daily News* reported the photos were taken by Jake's girlfriend, Taryn Simon. *People* paid around $50,000 for the U.S. rights, and the photos earned $150,000 worldwide.

Within two days, Gwyneth and Martin, their relationship a little over a year old, retreated to San Ysidro Ranch in Montecito, part of Santa Barbara, a five-star hotel with private luxury bungalows. They hung a "Do Not Disturb" sign on their door and kept the shades closed. After an early breakfast was delivered to their room, they drove into Santa Barbara around nine a.m. and waited in line at the courthouse for a marriage license, paying an extra two dollars to designate it "confidential" instead of becoming public record. A judge later reportedly came to their bungalow, where they were married in secret, with no guests, not even their parents. Gwyneth, then around four months pregnant, wanted the wedding to be for her and Martin, not the public, though a courthouse witness immediately leaked the news to a local radio station. The county clerk confirmed the marriage to media on December 10, though Stephen Huvane said Gwyneth and Martin refused to confirm the report.

Once the wedding leaked, Gwyneth started wearing her engagement ring, a substantial diamond on a thin band. Two photographers jostled to get a shot of it when she and Martin were heading to board a plane in California. As they snapped away, Gwyneth apparently tried to hide her ring, and Martin shouted expletives at them while he scraped his key down the side of one of their cars. He hit the other in the face, giving him a black eye. This wasn't out of character for Martin— he'd angrily damaged a photographer's windshield in July in Australia, though charges were dropped. In 2009, he told *60 Minutes* that he did what he could to avoid that kind of public exposure: "If you talk about your family life, then the amount of people who hang around outside your house trebles the next week. Because then you become a necessary story in those magazines. So the aim is to make yourself not necessary."

He and Gwyneth seemed to sincerely believe that a normal life was possible. Gwyneth dutifully acknowledged that their lives were extraordinary, while also sounding indignant at the intrusions of fame. "You look at celebrity couples who go out on the red carpet together and all of a sudden their relationship becomes the main thing," she told *Vanity Fair* for a cover story around the time of their elopement. "I'm still able to have my career be at the forefront. I do not go around saying, 'Let me tell you what I ate for dinner, and we'll hold hands and kiss on the red carpet and invite you into our world.'"

AS GWYNETH PULLED back from acting, she became even more focused on optimizing her health. Still grieving her father and unsure where to direct her ambition, she was starting to form attachments to certain gurus. She recalled her acupuncturist at the time telling her "that we kind of live in fear. And if you insist on living your life in a circle of fear—which we all do, because it feels comfortable—that life has these built-in things to knock you back, in hopes that you will rebuild yourself and break this pattern. And that the wake-up calls keep getting louder and louder. I really understand what he means. The only way to achieve real growth is to suffer and stare it in the face. It's beautiful, in a way. Then, when you can learn to detach yourself from all of that personal suffering, you start to understand what it means to be a person in the whole universe."

In the spring of 2004, Gwyneth drove out to the English countryside to visit Stella McCartney at her weekend place, a classic Georgian house situated in a wide valley surrounded by low hills. Gwyneth thought she was there for a weekend away, but when she opened the door, she saw friends from high school and college. McCartney had arranged a surprise baby shower. Elated, exhausted, and hormonal, Gwyneth burst into tears.

In addition to Gwyneth's friends, McCartney had brought in nail technicians for manicures and pedicures. Included in that weekend's pampering were sessions with an osteopath, Vicky Vlachonis, who was blond and Greek and reminded Gwyneth of the goddess Hera. When it was Gwyneth's turn for a treatment, Vlachonis led her to a room. "After weeks of suffering from unrelenting back pain and anxiety about the birth, her hands lifted it all away, leaving me feeling light and at peace. I felt ready for the baby," Gwyneth later wrote in the foreword to Vlachonis's book, *The Body Doesn't Lie*. "As an osteopath, she understands that a pain in the back is rarely just a pain in the back—it may also be a dysfunction in the ovary or the gut, the thyroid or the liver. And, perhaps more important, she understands that the pain almost always connects to the heart."

Gwyneth's approach to her own healing and health was taking shape. No one seemed to have taught her what to do with grief, doubt, self-reproach. She had no vocabulary for it in her own experience, and neither her mother's decorum nor her father's bravado was enough to sustain her, especially now that Bruce was gone. Her pain was an attractive project to any number of experts, and Gwyneth didn't want to be alone with it. She opened herself up to others' explanations and latched on to endless possibilities of healing that didn't necessarily answer to science. She also increasingly tried to connect to her fans in a new way, by sharing these stories of self-improvement in interviews. Whenever she believed something was wrong with her, she could always find an expert who would agree and offer an explanation, be it scientifically sound or designed to generate profit.

GWYNETH'S FIRST BIRTH was a harrowing ordeal. After her water broke, doctors at the private St John & St Elizabeth Hospital in London didn't induce her, which posed an infection risk. One friend from the time believed the birth was not handled well by the hospital, which was known for offering homeopathic remedies and birthing pools. After around hour sixty-two of her seventy-hour labor, her doctor suggested an epidural, and she agreed. With the indecipherable murmurings of Icelandic trio Sigur Rós playing in the background, Apple Blythe Alison Martin was born on May 14, 2004, weighing nine pounds, eleven ounces, after an emergency C-section. Gwyneth had avoided publicly stating her due date to thwart paparazzi, but photographers and reporters quickly gathered outside the hospital, where other A-list celebrities such as Kate Moss and Kate Winslet had given birth.

"Battered and raw, I knew I needed some care—but my first thoughts were for Apple, who had been through the same epic struggle," recalled Gwyneth, who summoned Vlachonis to perform "cranial osteopathy" on Apple's newly emerged head, which involved using a light touch to manipulate a baby's skull bones (according to a study in the journal *Pediatrics*, it's unclear that this does anything beneficial; the practice is not recommended by the American Academy of Pediatrics).

As Gwyneth later wrote, this "endeared me to her for life."

Gwyneth and Martin were "900 miles over the moon," he announced in a statement. About the name Apple, Gwyneth told Oprah, "When we were first pregnant, her daddy said, 'If it's a girl, I think her name should be Apple.' It sounded so sweet, and it conjured such a lovely picture for me, you know. Apples are so sweet, and they're wholesome, and it's biblical."

Around a week after the birth, in a scene that resembled the debut of royal British babies, Gwyneth put on jeans and a light blue top and went outside with the baby in a carriage to greet the paparazzi. Motherhood, she said, "is absolutely wonderful and I feel great. Apple is wonderful. I think she looks a bit like both me and Chris."

Though Apple herself was hidden, one of two bodyguards present told photographers, "This is your only chance to get a photograph of them for a very long time."

The baby was only days old, but mockery of her name was everywhere. Australia's *Daily Telegraph* wrote, "What the press release should have said is: 'Academy Award–winning actress Gwyneth Paltrow and Coldplay lead singer Chris Martin are proud to announce the arrival of a piece of fruit.' We can't wait to find out what sort of Apple she grows up to be—Granny Smith or Golden Delicious. But where do you go from there? Will Apple's siblings be Mango and Banana to make it one big fruit salad?" Promoting the mediocre sci-fi action movie *Sky Captain and the World of Tomorrow*, which she filmed after *Sylvia* and which costarred Jude Law and Angelina Jolie, Gwyneth was teased about the name on CBS's *The Early Show*. "I don't know if it's a scandal," host Harry Smith said, "but it leads to—is she a McIntosh? Is she a Granny Smith? Is she a Rome? Is she a Golden Delicious?"

Gwyneth replied, "I think she's either—I think she's a Golden Delicious." For many years, Apple Martin would be known as an exemplar in the trend of, as the *New York Post* put it, "wacky celebrity baby names."

Five weeks after Apple's birth, Gwyneth left her daughter at night for one of the first times to attend the Women in Film Crystal and Lucy Awards in Los Angeles. The media noted how slender she looked and asked her how she did it. "Two girdles! It's a great trick. That's how all the Hollywood girls do it. There are these great things called Spanx, which are like bike shorts, and they just squeeze you in. It's terrific," she said, which earned the nascent brand a waterfall of publicity. Three weeks later, Gwyneth went to a party for the premiere of the Will Ferrell comedy *Anchorman* with red marks on her back from "cupping," in which heated suction cups are applied to the skin and then removed in the hope of helping with a variety of ailments like stress and pain relief. (Though cupping is generally considered safe, scientific studies have failed to offer convincing support of its effectiveness.) Like Spanx, cupping hadn't yet entered the mainstream. But Gwyneth's radiant image made her a natural for these incidental endorsements. Both CNN and CBS's *The Early Show* aired segments about it, and a *New York Post* writer tried it, concluding that it "sucked."

JOHN DEMSEY WAS looking for a new face for Estée Lauder's Pleasures fragrance in early 2005. Estée's global president, Demsey was known for his transformative work at MAC Cosmetics. His decisions that were considered revolutionary for the time—like hiring drag queen personality RuPaul as a face of MAC—helped grow the brand into a juggernaut and made Demsey one of the beauty industry's most respected executives.

The Pleasures fragrance had long been fronted by model and actress Elizabeth Hurley. When Demsey decided it was time to hire someone new, he asked *Vogue* editor in chief Anna Wintour for advice. *Vogue* had just photographed Gwyneth for its October cover (pegged to *Proof*) when Wintour called Demsey in February to suggest he hire Gwyneth.

If Gwyneth was looking to get out of movies, it was just as well. The *Chicago Sun-Times* included Gwyneth in a story about "Oscar winners who lost their golden touch," noting that just one of her last four films (*Shallow Hal*) had earned at least $35 million at the box office. In the spring of 2005, Gwyneth filmed *Running with Scissors*, adapted from Augusten Burroughs's bestselling memoir, another money-losing flop. Gwyneth seemed to have fallen victim to the Oscars curse.

Gwyneth had already been top of mind for Demsey. He had wanted to hire her a year or so earlier, but the Lauder family, who owned a controlling stake in the $3.3 billion company, had said no. Gwyneth had the unique distinctions of growing up on the Upper East Side and attending one of its elite private schools, which put her in the same social scene as 1988 Chapin graduate Aerin Lauder. Yet she didn't seem to put Aerin entirely at ease. Gwyneth's aloofness wasn't the only complicating factor—she was also known as the "cover killer" after her *Vogue* cover hadn't sold that well in 1996, even though her magazine sales had since improved. Plus, her Q Score, which measured a star's appeal for marketers, was about average, not as high as Lauder executives would have liked. They feared she came across as someone who would steal your boyfriend and not let you into her club; that ultimately, she wasn't relatable.

But the Lauders trusted Demsey when he told them that Gwyneth was a star who would elevate the brand. Plus, she had more appeal with women than Hurley, according to Q Scores. Her multimillion-dollar deal required a few photo shoots a year and a couple of press days—"it was not a heavy lift," remembered someone familiar with the terms. Gwyneth seemed to enjoy working with Estée models like Carolyn Murphy and Liya Kebede, who were *Vogue* girls just like her. But she turned up her nose at the brand's association with Hurley, whom she didn't view as being on her level.

When the ads launched, with Gwyneth outdoors surrounded by pink flowers, sales of the fragrance increased significantly. The company had made the right decision.

Aerin Lauder and Gwyneth had cordial relations throughout the process. At one dinner, the two were talking about Brad Pitt. According to someone who heard the discussion, Gwyneth allegedly told her, "He's dumber than a sack of shit."

THE LAUDER CAMPAIGN was one of Gwyneth's cushiest endorsement deals to date, though not her first. She had fronted a Dior handbag campaign in 1999 and been the face of Damiani jewelry. Not long before Apple was born, she earned $3 million to appear in international commercials for Martini & Rossi vermouth (the ads didn't run in the U.S. or U.K.).

By that point, her wellness journey had led her to transcend drinking. "I think it's gross. I really don't like drunk women," she said. "I think it is such a bad look. I think it's very inappropriate and I don't like it." Asked if she felt boring at parties, she said, "No. I think they're the idiot people and I'm the normal person . . . My friends are kind of adult; they have a drink. But they hold their liquor. I think it's incredibly embarrassing when people are drunk . . . I think, *Ooh, you're really degrading yourself right now, to be this pissed out in public.*"

Instead of having to spend months on a movie set, Gwyneth spent just four days filming the vermouth ads in California. The advertising work "allows me to be with my daughter, which is what I want to do until some fantastic movie role comes along and makes me change my mind."

A decade or so later, actors would actively seek fashion and beauty sponsorships to offset payments like home video royalties lost to the streaming era. But around this time, endorsement deals were seen as riskier, potentially cheapening actors. To protect their well-managed images in the U.S., many of them participated in ads that ran only abroad and not domestically.

In 2006, *The Guardian* asked Gwyneth to justify taking the Estée campaign. "I'll tell you why . . . I basically stopped making money from acting in 2002. All the things I've done since then have been things I've really wanted to do, and I have not made money from them." She said the contract would finance her career the way Calvin Klein's checks enabled actress Scarlett Johansson to work with Woody Allen "and never have to do a movie where they put her in a bikini and give her a gun." Asked what happened to the millions she'd earned from movies, she said, "Good question . . . I spent it on shoes. No. Well, I had saved money, but I bought a house, and I never made Julia Roberts kind of money. I made really great money, but not that kind of money." Gwyneth also spent a lot on things like chartered private jets, personal security, real estate, and private chefs.

The summer after Apple was born, Gwyneth and Martin bought a five-bedroom town house in London's Belsize Park area from Kate Winslet and her then-husband, Sam Mendes, for £2.52 million ($5.8 million in 2025). The following spring, Gwyneth sold her New York town house for $6.9 million ($11.3 million in 2025) and bought a more than seven-thousand-square-foot Tribeca condo for nearly $8 million ($13 million in 2025). It came with four bedrooms, six bathrooms, two maids' rooms, a terrace, and cutting-edge security features.

Stephen Huvane said that she and Martin were looking for another place with a yard in nearby suburban Westchester County. The Tribeca apartment, he said, was "for when she has to be based in the city."

But Gwyneth never bought a place in Westchester. She set her sights instead on a ritzier spot that oozed wealth and good taste in the public imagination: the Hamptons.

CHAPTER 19

Mass Appeal

Don't you want to be in a movie that people see?
—Robert Downey Jr.

As her personal life became more demanding, and she felt more vulnerable as a new parent, Gwyneth began subtly altering the balance between her public and private selves. She was withdrawing from Hollywood, choosing work that would allow her more time at home, playing herself rather than a role, to make money and reach an audience.

Around 2005, to help mold her image, Gwyneth hired Anna Bingemann, a stylist whose clients would include Rachel Weisz, Claire Danes, and Uma Thurman. Bingemann, an Australian whose daily uniform included American Apparel T-shirts and Club Monaco sweaters worn under statement Yves Saint Laurent and Balenciaga jackets, had been hired initially to style Gwyneth at a photo shoot for *Variety* offshoot *VLife* magazine. She had just moved to New York from London, and she and Gwyneth seemed to understand each other immediately. Gwyneth asked Bingemann to come on board full-time.

Landing on best-dressed lists helped cement a celebrity's reputation as a tastemaker. And for Gwyneth, this brought her one step closer to building her own lucrative brand.

Bingemann described her client's taste as a "very cool New York,

London feel. It wasn't an L.A. feel." She now envisioned a look that was a little bit rock and roll but also feminine. Bingemann would also keep in mind how Gwyneth's dresses would appear in flash photography, how the clothes would read to her various audiences and critics, and how those choices would inform her public persona.

Gwyneth could wear any designer's clothes, since she wasn't being paid to wear a particular label. Valentino was shifting away from Gwyneth toward Claire Danes and Hugh Dancy, which freed Gwyneth from the unspoken pressures of her reciprocal friendship with him and Giancarlo Giammetti. As a mother to an infant, Gwyneth could no longer show up to their yacht for days-long adventures, but she could pop over to their London house for lunch on occasion.

When the film version of *Proof* opened in the U.S. in September 2005, scripts were still arriving at Gwyneth's home, getting buried under toys, but she hadn't found anything that inspired her. Martin was touring and she was at home with Apple, which meant, she said, "I couldn't be making a movie now even if I wanted to . . . But to be honest, I don't want to." She didn't want to travel as much as her parents had. "I think it was sometimes hard for my brother and me," she said.

Proof got another round of mixed reviews, as did her performance, which came across as either devastating or obtuse, depending on the reviewer. The *Los Angeles Times* wrote that Gwyneth delivered "an exceptional portrait of psychological fragility that is honest, direct and devastating," while Manohla Dargis wrote in *The New York Times* that her *Proof* character "demands our pity, our attention, our indulgence, our love, while giving little in return but her narcissism." She earned a Golden Globe nomination for the role, for Best Actress in a Drama.

As Gwyneth traveled around promoting the film (after not having a nanny for her first fourteen months as a mom, she hired someone), she kept talking in the press about her lack of ambition and fatigue with acting. But she was keeping a secret: She was pregnant with a second child. In an interview with *ET Online*, Blythe let it slip. "I hope there'll be more fruits and vegetables coming along, since we're all pretty much vegetarians," she joked about naming the next baby. In January, at a Screen Actors Guild screening of *Proof* two days before the Golden Globes, host Lou Diamond Phillips introduced Gwyneth as "a pregnant woman" and asked, "How far along are you?"

"Far enough along to feel very cumbersome."

By the night of the Golden Globes, Gwyneth was seven months pregnant and planning to premiere the bump she'd been hiding. No amount of middling-to-poor movie debuts seemed to downgrade her from the A-list. Meanwhile, other It girls of that era came and went. Gretchen Mol appeared on the cover of *Vanity Fair*'s September 1998 issue, pegged to her roles opposite Matt Damon in *Rounders* and Leonardo DiCaprio in Woody Allen's *Celebrity*, with the headline "Is She Hollywood's Next 'It' Girl?" Though Mol worked consistently, she never became as famous as Gwyneth (though one Miramax producer said Mol "wasn't a fraction of the actress that Gwyneth is"). The same was true for Leelee Sobieski, who crested as a teenager with roles in *Never Been Kissed* and *Eyes Wide Shut* in 1999 before fading. Yet Gwyneth, owing in part to her celebrity relationships but also to her becoming a lifestyle personality, remained one of the top famous women whom brands wanted to dress.

Bingemann had her pick of designers willing to custom-make Gwyneth's look. She thought primarily about color—what shade hadn't been worn recently on the red carpet? She also thought about how Gwyneth could make a new statement. For the Globes, Bingemann approached Balenciaga's Nicolas Ghesquière and told him what Gwyneth liked and left him to come up with designs. Gwyneth enjoyed being pregnant, and Bingemann wanted a look that could convey that joy. She went to Lanvin's Alber Elbaz as well but warned him that she couldn't promise Gwyneth would choose whatever he made.

"Oh, you don't have to promise me that. She's divine, I love her dearly," he said.

If Gwyneth chose to wear a designer's look in those days, they'd be guaranteed coverage that would impact their business more meaningfully than the fleeting social media impressions of later years. A great dress could end up on the cover of nearly every major tabloid the next day. Before big events, designers would create sketches and pair them with fabric swatches for Gwyneth and Bingemann to review. After going to around five designers, they settled on a romantic ivory pouf-sleeve gown by Ghesquière.

Bingemann always met with Gwyneth in person before a big appearance, and for the Golden Globes, she drove out to Amagansett in the ritzy East Hamptons on Long Island, where Gwyneth and Martin had recently bought a seven-thousand-square-foot home for $5.4 million ($8.7 million in 2025). Bingemann pulled up to the house in the middle of a storm that dropped a foot of snow on the ground. With five bedrooms, seven and a half bathrooms, nanny's quarters, a large pool, and ocean views, the house was large enough that guests sometimes couldn't tell which door was the official entrance. It would become a November 2007 *House & Garden* cover story, after senior style and beauty editor Kim Gieske helped Gwyneth secure decor for free with the understanding that it would be splashed gorgeously across the pages of the magazine.

Bingemann hustled inside and found Gwyneth waiting for her in casual clothes. The dress was loose but still had to fit perfectly. She would wear her hair wavy, swept into an updo, and simple makeup. There was no question that Gwyneth, despite being in her third trimester, would wear heels. This was not an occasion to consider comfort. Describing the ritual of preparing for a big public event, Bingemann said, "I don't think anyone gets used to it. I think that's why the hair, makeup, and dress are so important. Because you're putting on armor. You're making yourself safe."

GWYNETH LOST THE Golden Globe for Best Actress in a Drama for *Proof* to Felicity Huffman for *Transamerica*, and she wasn't nominated for an Oscar, which may have been just as well since she was in the final weeks of her pregnancy by that time. After her terrifying first birth, Gwyneth had no desire to deliver in London again and elected to have the baby in the U.S., following a shower in the backyard of her parents' Santa Monica home. On April 8, 2006, Moses Bruce Anthony Martin was born in New York City's Mount Sinai Hospital. The media again had a field day with the name. "Rather than drawing inspiration from the produce section this time, the couple apparently turned to the Bible," quipped the *Miami Herald*. In fact, Gwyneth later explained, Moses was her father's Hebrew name.

Moses made his public debut in *People* magazine, which bought pictures of him with Martin and Gwyneth from the famous parents for a reported $125,000 (nearly $200,000 in 2025). Describing having her second child in an interview, Gwyneth sought again to connect her experience to that of someone "normal" while stumbling to acknowledge her privilege in the same sentence. "I do not know how single mothers have more than one child with no help . . . It requires so much of my life, and I don't have to change sheets and clean toilets, you know. My hat—no, my clothes go off to the single mother with no help; I stand naked, kowtowing before her."

GWYNETH WAS HOME with her two kids, thinking that was where she would be for the foreseeable future, when Robert Downey Jr., who had appeared with her in 1994's *Mrs. Parker and the Vicious Circle*, about writer Dorothy Parker and her friends known as the Algonquin Round Table, called and posed a provocative question: "Don't you want to be in a movie that people see?"

Though she had no interest in returning to long days on some faraway set, Gwyneth had started to worry that people would forget about her. "What happens if, one day, I say, 'Okay, I'm ready to go back to work,' and people are like, 'So? We don't care. We don't want you,'" she said. Besides, it paid well. Gwyneth had privately admitted that she needed to pay for the Hamptons house she and Martin had purchased.

By January 2007, she had been cast. Though she'd desired more time at home after Apple was born, when Moses was six months old, the "fire came back to work," she said. And if the movie was a hit, Gwyneth and her costars were signed for two sequels.

Though she was told it would "feel like doing an indie film," perhaps because the studio didn't think it would be a hit, it ended up being the big commercial, box-office-blowout-type movie she had spent her early career avoiding. *Iron Man*, based on the Marvel comic book, would star Downey Jr. in the lead role, and Gwyneth would play Pepper Potts, his cheeky assistant.

Gwyneth credited director Jon Favreau with luring her back to work after a period of full-time parenting. "When I had Apple, I just couldn't bear the thought of leaving her. When I work, I leave the house before the kids are awake. And I come home and they're asleep. So that's why, ever since having them, I've never played a lead in a movie . . . but when Jon called me about *Iron Man*, I thought, this is the kind of cast I dream of working with, and I could go back to work and not work five days a week. It was the perfect, perfect, perfect job for me," she said.

Perfect was perhaps an exaggeration. Moses was around one and Apple was around three when the movie filmed, and shoots occurred at all times of the day and night. Sometimes Gwyneth could bring Moses to the set, but often she left both kids at home with a nanny.

IN EARLY 2007, fewer than two years after she bought it, Gwyneth listed her Tribeca apartment for $14 million ($22 million in 2025). She had bought a new 4,400-square-foot place in the River Lofts on nearby Washington Street for just over $5 million, and she was toying with the idea of a new kind of work. At a dinner party, her friend Mario Batali,*

---

* In 2017, Batali was accused of sexual misconduct as part of the #MeToo movement. He was later found not guilty in a criminal trial in Boston on charges of indecent assault and battery, and settled with two other women there. He and a former business partner also settled a case with the New York Attorney General's office that involved paying $600,000 to at least twenty former employees who had come forward to accuse them of sexual harassment. After the allegations surfaced in the press, Gwyneth distanced herself.

the celebrity chef, told her he was going to appear in a public television show about the cuisine of Spain. Gwyneth loved Spain, continued to be close with the family who had hosted her semester abroad, and saw an opening. "Can I go?"

Batali assumed she was joking.

"I'm deadly serious," she said. Batali texted Charlie Pinsky, who was producing the show and had come up with the idea for it. At the time, a mainstream celebrity like Gwyneth hosting a food show was a novel premise. But the Food Network was already turning chefs into mainstream celebrities. "Putting stars with food was sort of a sociological inevitability," said Pinsky. "It was a no-brainer."

Pinsky texted Batali back: "Are you fucking kidding me?"

"No, she really wants to do it." Gwyneth jumped into the text chat herself to prove she was serious.

The three met for lunch soon after at Batali's restaurant Otto in New York City. Gwyneth came across, to Pinsky, not like one of the world's most famous women, but a normal person, and seemed genuinely excited about the show. After around ten minutes, Martin joined them, having just come from yoga. (He and Gwyneth often practiced together.)

"How much are you going to be paid for this, honey?" Martin asked Gwyneth.

"Chris, this is, like, PBS."

Pinsky couldn't pay Gwyneth her usual rate, but he told her, "Whatever you're used to in terms of traveling, bodyguards, or anything like that, we will take care of it."

Their next meeting was a few weeks later in Los Angeles in the private room of Osteria Mozza, with Batali's other celebrity friends, including Joaquin Phoenix and members of REM. Everyone had had a couple of drinks, when, to Pinsky's surprise, Gwyneth pulled up her shirt to expose her belly and ordered, "Give me a shot, give me a shot." He gave her a soft punch. "Not bad for a mother of two," she said.

Gwyneth talked with Pinsky about how her priority was her kids. She arranged to travel to Spain to film *Spain . . . on the Road Again* each week on Monday, leaving Apple and Moses home in the care of a nanny, and then fly back home on Friday. She flew private with her bodyguard to the shoot, where she liked Pinsky to meet her on the tarmac. Each time she got off the plane, she'd be wearing around six-inch heels. She'd link arms with Pinsky, who was six feet tall, and say, "I think I'm taller than you, Charlie." (She was.)

After one arrival, she told Pinsky's assistant, "That was the best private I've ever had. We could all stand up, and we all had room. That was fabulous."

If Gwyneth Paltrow was impressed by a private jet, they were surely overspending. Pinsky told his assistant if he ever heard her say that again, the assistant would be fired.

At the start of production, in October 2007, Gwyneth's first order of business was a press conference at the Santo Mauro hotel in Madrid. Pinsky went into the hotel to change and saw Gwyneth standing in the doorway of her room. She pulled him aside and said, "Don't you think you got me here a little bit early?"

"The press conference is in an hour, and you still have to do hair and makeup. So we tried to time it right," he said.

Gwyneth smiled. "I think you got me here a little bit early, Charlie."

"Okay, I get it. I'm the person in charge, so I'm the one who's going to get your shit all the time."

"You got it exactly right, Charlie."

She wanted his full attention, to be able to talk to the boss at any time. Pinsky understood, and he saw, too, that Gwyneth was committed; he viewed it as a small price to pay for her professionalism and performance. She would give him shit, the same way she would Batali, and Pinsky and Gwyneth developed a brother-sister rapport. Pinsky had expected to see around fifty journalists in the hotel courtyard for the press conference, but there were hundreds. He introduced the cast of the show, which included *The New York Times* food journalist and cookbook author Mark Bittman and Spanish actress Claudia Bassols along with Batali, but he saved Gwyneth for last. She was the main attraction.

That first day filming, Gwyneth wanted to stop in a temple. Never religious, Gwyneth had gone back and forth between identifying with her father's religion and identifying with her mother's. Madonna, who was in her kabbalah phase, had convinced Gwyneth to learn Hebrew. Pinsky let Gwyneth check out the temple, but after fifteen minutes of waiting in the car, he got impatient and went inside. "Charlie, you really should learn Hebrew," she said before ducking into the gift shop. A nonpracticing Jew, Pinsky was surprised by her interest in Judaism. "The only way I got her out of it was telling her the paparazzi was coming."

The next morning, Gwyneth was set to film her first scene with Bassols, in which the two of them would dip churros into hot chocolate. Gwyneth remarked to Pinsky that she'd never played herself before, and she wasn't sure how to do it. As it turned out, she was "a complete pro," and he never had to shoot her twice. Indeed, Pinsky gave Gwyneth almost no direction. For the other talent, he would pipe in facts about the region and the culture through walkie-talkies. After a while, Gwyneth told him, "Nobody's interested in that fucking history."

Pinsky tried to make sure everyone had the best available accommodations, particularly Gwyneth. In most places they shot, those were easy to find, but that wasn't the case at the Alhambra palace in Granada, where fancy hotels were in short supply. Here, he reserved the top part of a château across the street. Gwyneth's room was large, painted gorgeously in Matisse blue, with windows set high in the walls. Sure she would love it, Pinsky showed Gwyneth up to the room, and when they walked in, she turned to him with a smirk. "Oh, thanks, Charlie. You booked me the Anne Frank suite."

During that shoot, when the cameras were off, Gwyneth was looking up at the mosaics on the walls of the palace, the sunlight flowing through one of its intricately carved windows, before turning to Bittman. "If I wrote a cookbook, would you read it?" she asked.

"Absolutely," he told her.

•   •   •

GWYNETH WAS CORDIAL with her costars and the crew, but no one had any illusions about her status. After all, she was the only one who needed to travel with a bodyguard, Terry, whom the crew would tease for carrying her purse. "I can say we had a nice time," Bittman said. "She didn't treat me like a second-rate citizen, she didn't insist on being treated like a goddess other than, the sort of, I guess, unquestioned star treatment . . . If you were going to do something with Ryan Gosling or with some star, you would expect them to be treated really, really well, whether that's fair or not. You felt like she expected that, but she wasn't a jerk about it."

Like most of her public appearances in those days, the show gave food people another reason to hate Gwyneth Paltrow. "I haven't eaten anything from a four-footed animal since I was about fifteen," she'd said at the press conference. Anthony Bourdain was on a panel with Batali around this time and asked him, "Why would you go to Spain with the one [expletive] who refuses to eat ham?" (Batali didn't answer.) During the filming, Gwyneth would eat poultry only if she knew it had been raised humanely. Her favorite dish in all their Spanish travels was a plate of vegetables that Bittman had grilled with olive oil and salt, along with, Pinsky said, "every fried potato dish we were offered." He teased her that he could do an hour-long special of her eating potatoes. Gwyneth retorted, "And I could get on the private jet and fly home."

DURING THE SECOND week of filming, near Camino de Santiago, a pathway in Basque Country that pilgrims began walking over a thousand years ago, Gwyneth walked over to Pinsky, who was lying in the sun on a chaise longue.

"Charlie," she said, "the movie business is becoming a dirty business. I love cooking and fixing up houses and stuff like that. What should I do?" Gwyneth was thirty-five years old, and, as far as Pinsky could tell, her priority at that point in her life was motherhood.

"You can't become the next Martha Stewart," Pinsky said. "Give me a week to think about it, and I'll come up with something for you."

The next week, when she touched down in Spain, Pinsky met her on the tarmac, as usual.

"Did you come up with an idea?" she asked.

"Yes."

"What is it?"

"Motherhood," he said. Imagining her as a Princess Diana–like figure, he suggested she travel around the world, making documentaries about mothers and children.

"I love it," she said, and joked. "I'll give you fifteen percent."

HAVING GWYNETH IN *Spain . . . on the Road Again* lent the show publicity opportunities it wouldn't have had otherwise. *People* almost gave the show a cover, but then Sarah Palin became John McCain's running mate, and that bumped it. *The Oprah Winfrey Show* offered Gwyneth and Batali an hour-long special to promote *Spain . . . on the Road Again*. Gwyneth and Batali made paella with Winfrey on air, which couldn't have been better exposure for the show, particularly since its budget wasn't big enough to pay for national print or broadcast ads. It was also terrific publicity for Gwyneth, who had found a way to show the public a different side of herself. She talked about her interest in cooking healthy food and said her favorite kitchen appliance was her Gaggenau steamer, which retailed for over four thousand dollars in 2025. "It's kind of an investment, but honestly, it's the best thing that's in my kitchen," she said. "You can make steamed veggies, fish, rice—it's incredible. We reheat food in it so you don't have to zap it in the microwave."

Gwyneth never took Pinsky's advice about aligning her brand primarily with motherhood. Instead, she had set herself up perfectly to go the Martha Stewart route.

CHAPTER 20

Goop Rising

I would rather die than let my kid eat Cup-a-Soup.

—Gwyneth Paltrow

Stepping onto the red carpet in Leicester Square for *Iron Man*'s London premiere in late April 2008, Gwyneth wore a slightly punk black Balmain dress so short that *Glamour* headlined a story, "Did Gwyneth Forget Her Pants?" Her hair was newly cropped, framing her face in undone waves, barely skimming the lapels of her tuxedo jacket. Her black platform pumps weren't just high—they were so tall they looked dangerous. Her bare, toned legs were a walking advertisement for her latest guru, fitness trainer Tracy Anderson, a petite blonde whose signature dance-cardio sessions had another fan in Madonna. In photographs of the event, Gwyneth served a confident smirk. The insecurity she had long felt about her legs seemed to be gone now that she had been working out with Anderson. She knew it was a blockbuster look to go with a blockbuster movie.

"The coverage [of the Balmain look] was extraordinary," Binge-mann said. "We had never seen Gwyneth like that."

ACCORDING TO ANDERSON, Gwyneth found out about her through a friend whose body she saw "changing and changing and changing." Gwyneth wanted to lose the weight she had gained with Moses and asked the friend what she was doing to become so fit; the friend referred her to Anderson. After their first session together, Gwyneth told Anderson, "That was the hardest thing I've ever done," and asked to train with her for *Iron Man*.

Anderson was not impressed. "I thought she'd have a supermodel body, because she was so tiny on top. But her butt was long and lifeless, and she held on to weight in her outer thighs."

Gwyneth introduced Anderson to Madonna, but then their friendship fell apart. Their relationship reached a breaking point when Madonna showed up to an island where Gwyneth and Martin were vacationing. Madonna seemed to know that Gwyneth would be there, which Gwyneth seemed to find strange, a friend remembered. Madonna then insisted Gwyneth and Martin join her for a big group dinner at a long table where Madonna went off on her daughter, Lourdes. Gwyneth and Martin were disgusted by the behavior. "I can't be around this woman anymore," Martin told Gwyneth. "She's awful." Gwyneth agreed that Madonna was toxic and ended the friendship. (Anderson later said that Madonna being demanding along with her lack of "consistency" was ultimately why she stopped training her.)

During the filming of *Iron Man*, Gwyneth moved her family to a rented house in Los Angeles and enrolled Apple in the same preschool she had attended. She set up a daily routine of ninety-minute sessions with Anderson and hired an assistant who ensured that the house was stocked with flats of precut coconuts (she drank the water). Ever the early adopter, she deepened her investment in the wellness fads then gaining traction among her ritzy Los Angeles friends, such as kabbalah and healthy meals prepared by a private chef. Everything in her that felt unmoored after her father's death, including the "asshole" behavior he had warned her about, found a corrective outlet in self-work.

But all this effort she put into herself would never vanquish her privileged persona, like when her staff failed to do something for her and she'd snap at them, or when her house was filled with extravagant gifts from brands and she'd say, "Just have the cleaning lady take it away."

Gwyneth fit in training sessions whenever she could during filming, day or night. She never missed a workout. Spending that time together every day, Gwyneth and Anderson became close. Gwyneth began sneaking the gospel of wellness into their conversations, pointing out what she perceived as poisons in Anderson's diet. "I was so good at designing bodies, including my own, that I could eat a pizza and a tub of ice cream every day and you wouldn't see it; it was like a free card to eat whatever I wanted," Anderson recalled.

Watching her trainer eat cookies dipped in frosting one day, Gwyneth couldn't help herself. "Do you know how toxic that is?" she said. Anderson kept eating. "And you're still eating it."

Anderson decided she agreed. "That was the last cookie dunked in frosting I ever had."

GWYNETH'S PRIVATE COMMITMENT to wellness was now informing her public stance. After spotting an instant soup packet on the set of a short film she was directing in New York, she said, "I would rather die than let my kid eat Cup-a-Soup." She told an Italian newspaper, "Cancer has been the curse of my family . . . I am challenging these evil genes by natural means. I am convinced that by eating biological foods it is possible to avoid the growth of tumors . . . Today in my home we are all vegetarians and we only use organic soap and cleaners. I want to protect my children from anything harmful."

The experts were up in arms. "Diet cannot prevent cancer," Ursula Arens, dietitian at the British Dietetic Association, told *The Guardian.* "It is reasonable that the risks of some of them can be reduced with certain diets, but some cancers, alas, show no link to dietary factors." In early 2008, Sense about Science called out Gwyneth in its report on celebrities who made bogus health claims. (Madonna, who'd claimed that kabbalah water had "gotten rid of my husband's verrucas [a type of wart]," was also an offender.) "It's interesting that many of the people who talk about toxins don't talk about things like Gardasil [the HPV vaccine] or the hepatitis B vaccine," said infectious disease expert Dr. Adalja. "They talk about this diet or that . . . You have a treatment that basically eliminates the risk for cervical cancer—they're never touting that."

IRON MAN, RELEASED around the world in April and May 2008, was a huge success. The reviews praised Downey Jr.'s clever performance, but Gwyneth's role was noted respectfully in most of the coverage. Britain's *Daily Mail* wrote that she had "never looked lovelier or had less to do," but the film seemed to please the masses, and Gwyneth rode its giant success to a new kind of stardom. With nearly $100 million in U.S. box office revenue its first weekend, it had the second-best premiere ever for a nonsequel (with another almost $100 million overseas) and ended up grossing nearly $600 million worldwide on a budget of $140 million. It would be Gwyneth's most financially successful film. With a guarantee of more *Iron Man* movies to come, and a huge payday to go with it, Gwyneth sat at her kitchen counter back in London and began typing out a pet project she'd been kicking around for the past few months—a newsletter filled with her own personal recommendations for restaurants, travel, and more.

A COUPLE OF weeks after *Iron Man* came out, Gwyneth headed to the Cannes Film Festival in the South of France to promote a small independent film called *Two Lovers*, in which she costarred with Joaquin Phoenix. The Sunday night before Gwyneth had to walk the red carpet, Bingemann got a call. Gwyneth was reassessing the Balmain dress she had chosen. "I'm not feeling it," she said.

Bingemann always had backups. "What about the other two?" she asked.

"No, I'm not feeling it, they're not working."

"Okay," Bingemann said, "I'll get something else to you," and she hung up the phone. At this point, she knew better than to argue with any star. The previous year, when she had dressed Gwyneth in a pink Gucci minidress with a giant satin neck bow for a UNICEF fundraiser hosted by Gucci and Madonna, Gwyneth felt like the look was wrong, and Bingemann could tell by her lackluster expression in the photos. She didn't want a repeat in Cannes.

Bingemann, who was in New York, needed to get Gwyneth a dress in under a day, and she needed something that would match the buzz of the punk-rock Balmain. Bingemann had attended Chanel's resort show in New York the previous evening and had a dress in mind when she called their press office that night.

Chanel agreed, though they couldn't just FedEx it; normally, a brand would send an assistant. But this was Gwyneth Paltrow. The head of Chanel's press department decided to get on a plane with the dress, a dark blue gown with a bow at the bust and cutout detail, and fly it personally to Cannes. Once there, she would deliver it to Gwyneth alongside a Chanel seamstress, who would get straight to work.

After many anxious hours, Bingemann's phone rang. It was Gwyneth.

"We've got it."

Gwyneth clearly felt fabulous in the dress as she stepped onto the red carpet for the horde of photographers, her hair swept into a loose updo, with the same relaxed confidence she'd had at the *Iron Man* premiere.

BY THE SUMMER of 2008, Gwyneth was earning the kind of money she had left Miramax to make, even if she wasn't appearing in films of the same artistic caliber. She debuted on the *Forbes* list of highest-paid entertainers. Gwyneth's representatives provided her earnings (before their cut came out) for the story, which reported her income as $25 million for the year, making her the fourth-highest-paid actress in the world. (She tied with Reese Witherspoon; the top three were Cameron Diaz with around $50 million, Keira Knightley with $32 million, and Jennifer Aniston with $27 million.) She was the sixty-seventh-highest-paid entertainer.

Gwyneth had "certainly prioritized being a mom," said friend and CAA co-chairman Richard Lovett. But she also wasn't interested in acting anymore, and felt ready to make a change. "She made a really giant choice." She was an in-demand movie star, attracting valuable endorsement deals that fed off her film work. "Now she's going to not do this thing, and it's being one of the biggest movie stars in the world who's just won the Oscar," continued Lovett. "That's just a hard thing for any human being to do, to leave the thing that is your ego and identity, but she did it."

As she turned further away from her acting career, she decided to write a cookbook. And she made plans to visit a New York branding agency to talk over an even bigger idea.

CHAPTER 21

Gwyneth, Inc.

My life is good because I am not passive about it.

—Gwyneth Paltrow

Peter Arnell had spent his career pairing brands with celebrities—in the nineties he put Tina Turner with Hanes and Ray-Ban with Will Smith for *Men in Black*. He had created campaigns for DKNY, Bergdorf Goodman, Chanel, and Banana Republic. Gwyneth went to him to explore what she could do with a brand of her own.

Arnell saw huge potential right away. "It was clear that, between her vision and her knowledge and experience, there were opportunities for massive areas of different categories, product development, which she could curate or design or lead," he said. "It was crystal-clear that she was a brand, and she had a vision. Her personal experiences, life experiences, and her taste levels allowed her to potentially step into a next-generation Martha Stewart type across many categories."

Arnell, who had worked with Stewart on advertising for her Kmart Everyday line, among other things, put together a presentation for Gwyneth about what her brand could be, focusing on how her desires and vision could fit into the marketplace. He thought her product lines should focus on the home. Furniture was on the list, but he believed her real strength was in other housewares, particularly for the kitchen.

The brand needed a name. The way Gwyneth tells the story in interviews, Arnell advised her that successful internet companies— such as Google and Yahoo!—had two *O*s in their names and there was something effective about it, so Arnell put *oo* between her initials and came up with a name she initially thought was "stupid and funny." In at least one interview since its inception, she has also said that Goop was "an old nickname," but she may have never publicly linked it to her father, who, Gwyneth told Arnell, used to call her "Goopie." (Two Miramax executives remembered Gwyneth using a Goop@aol.com email address back in the nineties.)

At the time, Arnell thought this link was essential to the origin of the brand. "It's personal and familiar, but at the same time, she could distance herself from it and look at it as a corporation," he said. In other words, Goop could be connected to Gwyneth if that connection was an asset to the brand, but it could also stand on its own as a typical nonsense brand name.

The narrative that Gwyneth was trying to become the next Martha Stewart stuck for years, despite Gwyneth's assertion that emulating her was "not what I set out to do." Few Hollywood celebrities were known at that time for selling their personal lifestyle. Movie stars were expected— and generally happy—to stay in their lane. By starting Goop, Arnell said, Gwyneth "initiated a new way to generate one's own brand."

She also initiated a new way to be a celebrity. Stars used to support their art with brand endorsements. But the attention Gwyneth got for Goop inspired so many imitators that, as streamers made it harder for actors to earn big royalty checks, the art became something that supported celebrities' own brands.

BEFORE GOOP WAS a Martha Stewart–like universe of product lines and editorial content, it was a humble website. Instagram was about two years off from launching, and the influencer economy was basically a zygote. But Gwyneth was about to tap into the biggest marketing revolution since television.

Around the time *Spain . . . on the Road Again* first aired in September 2008, Gwyneth launched Goop.com. It would soon serve as a repository for content she would publish in the Goop newsletter. Visitors to the site were greeted with the brand name and the tagline "Nourish the Inner Aspect." Rendered in tasteful, muted colors, the site was divided into sections labeled "Make," "Go," "Get," "Do," "Be," and "See." Initially, each section linked to the same introductory essay, in which Gwyneth wrote, "My life is good because I am not passive about it. I want to nourish what is real, and I want to do it without wasting time. I love to travel, to cook, to eat, to take care of my body and mind, to work hard. I love being a mother who has to overcome my bad qualities to be a good mother. I love being in spaces that are clean and nice . . . Whether you want a good place to eat in London, some advice on where to stay in Austin, the recipe I made up this week, or some thoughts from one of my sages, GOOP is a little bit of everything that makes up my life."

She advised readers, "Cook a meal for someone you love. Pause before reacting. Clean out your space. Read something beautiful. Treat yourself to something. Go to a city you've never been to. Learn something new. Don't be lazy. Workout and stick with it."

In those early days, the main purpose of the site was to get people to sign up for the free Goop newsletter, which became Gwyneth's primary medium for distributing new content. A weekly newsletter freed Gwyneth from uploading new stories every day, as popular blogs did at the time. "We're having an especially good and creative time in the kitchen right now. I'll send along some of the recipes I've been working on," she wrote. Subscribers would be privy to "some travel notes, some fashion buys, and some other surprises." Gwyneth was spending her own money on the venture with no apparent monetization strategy in place.

But as soon as the site went live, the critics went to town. Gwyneth had planted a big fuzzy UGG boot in their sandbox—an online publishing world that magazines and newspapers were still trying to understand and monetize themselves. The *Los Angeles Times* wrote that "the road ahead looks bumpy for this little operation! It's not just that apparently no one wants to take life direction from the girl who has it all," but the site has "so little content," and "It feels like something that won an award for Web design in 1998." Regarding the "See," "Go," "Do," etc. categories, New Jersey's *Star-Ledger* quipped, "May we recommend 'Retch'?" Lots of writers mocked "Nourish the Inner Aspect" for not making grammatical sense. And a *Daily Mail* correspondent joked that the phrase made them wonder "whether I'd accidentally logged on to a site for hemorrhoid cream, but, no I was in the right place."

Gwyneth was a celebrity who had consistently been everywhere for the better part of fifteen years—her privilege and occasional hardships practically their own beat—and now she was not only fueling that coverage but also telling those who happened to engage with it everything they were doing wrong or at least could be doing better. In the process, she often seemed to suggest that her charmed life was merely the product of her own hard work.

The Guardian captured the critics' tone most succinctly: "Gwyneth has, to her extraordinary credit, found a way to be even more annoying."

Goop was a window into a certain elitism. And people couldn't look away.

IN THE MIDST of the rollout, Gwyneth turned thirty-six. Two days later, on September 29, 2008, the stock market crashed, triggering a financial crisis and the loss of millions of jobs. Jezebel, a website founded in opposition to the kind of diet- and consumerism-driven women's media Gwyneth was now creating, wrote, "Lady, you should take your macrobiotic recipes with their expensive ingredients and shove them up your yogariffic ass. Talk about tone deaf! Debuting this website the week after a stock market crash shows that Paltrow is about as publicly savvy as Marie Antoinette."

But Gwyneth had been hated for one thing or another for the past eight years, and now she had a purpose—a mission that turned her most hateable qualities into a resource for others, giving her a forum to rewrite the story of her charmed life. She forged ahead. Sitting in the kitchen of her thirty-three-room mansion (an amalgamation of the house she bought from Kate Winslet plus two homes she bought on either side) that she shared with her mega-successful husband in North London, while the public's savings and homes fell out from under them during the Great Recession, she clicked send on her first Goop newsletter. Entirely oblivious to world events, the email included recipes for turkey ragu and banana-nut muffins, with photos of the dishes that Gwyneth had taken herself on her BlackBerry. For all the haters, there were admirers. People who cooked the recipes loved them.

Gwyneth's second newsletter, sent the following week, was about her favorite places in London, offering a view into her taste and upmarket lifestyle. She wrote, "The first installment of this three-part newsletter will include restaurants, hotels, and pubs. The hotels are on the pricey side, but my GOOP girls are doing some research into some more affordable places, which we will personally try before recommending." She included the five-star Berkeley Hotel, where, in 2025, rooms went for around a thousand dollars a night on the low end (and where she had stayed when she filmed *Emma*), and two expensive sushi restaurants.

While the hatred continued, Gwyneth's fans felt like she was showing them her authentic self: the Oscar-winning actress who happened to exist with confident oblivion at an altitude they would never understand. The recipes and recommendations were useful for some, sure, but the whole spectacle of Goop was just plain entertaining, like a very curated look into her life.

At its most personal—and Goop was very personal to Gwyneth—the company created a channel of dialogue between her and the masses, where she could theoretically humanize herself and provide a form of service going beyond the bounds of a glossy magazine interview. Explaining Goop's purpose later, Gwyneth said, "I've had this crazy, amazing life where, you know, when my friends are still in college, I was living in Paris, doing a film. Or, you know, I bought a house before they did, and I redid it so they would say, Oh, now I'm doing it. What should I, where should I buy this? Or where should I go, or I'm going to have, you know, is there a good pizza place in Paris? And so I started collecting all of this information, and cooking stuff. And anyway, I was getting, I was privy to such good information, that I thought, *Well, if my girlfriends want to know, you know, this information, surely other girls and guys may want to know, too.* So, if they do, I'll do it, I'll just put out a newsletter."

Early dispatches also included fashion advice. Gwyneth suggested readers choose a uniform, or a single item that made them feel the most comfortable. She offered that hers was a little black dress, noting one by Chanel would be a good investment, because you could pass it down to your daughter (she suggested a more affordable $70 Topshop option but paired it with $1,300 Christian Louboutin boots). She also recommended a $1,850 Hermès watch and a $1,350 Mulberry handbag. Her recipes went from the humble banana-nut muffins to "Fried Oysters with Curried Crème Fraîche," with the tip "Feel free to use any kind of caviar (salmon roe would be good), or none at all." She told readers the Ritz was the best place to stay in Paris, and shared tips on how to get reservations at two popular Momofuku restaurants that didn't take them (at least not for noncelebrities). And, because this version of the good life wasn't just acquisitive, but also spiritual, Gwyneth shared advice from a kabbalah leader on how to foster a harmonious family.

"I am who I am. I can't pretend to be somebody who makes $25,000 a year," she infamously said shortly after Goop launched.

Many people said that Gwyneth really did want to share her

recommendations—she was almost forceful about them, the way her father had been. But her ideal life went beyond the purely materialistic, since she tied it to health, too. In GoopLand, wellness was, like a Chanel dress, a status symbol: a hallmark of privilege, class, and wealth. In subsequent newsletters, Gwyneth wrote in more detail about her diet and health beliefs. "Recently I have found three doctors who have helped me tremendously," she reported in an October dispatch. ("The docs are in London, New York and L.A. Best of all, they have trained her to treat the rest of us!" cracked *The Philadelphia Inquirer*.) She went on, "Sleep eight hours for two weeks, then start eliminating 'white' foods. After two weeks of sleeping and eating better, you'll have the energy to exercise."

In November, Claudia Connell lived according to Goop newsletters for the *Daily Mail*. She cooked Gwyneth's recipes for buckwheat and banana pancakes, an Asian tuna sandwich, and caramelized black pepper chicken, and found that Gwyneth delivered: "My inner aspect feels well and truly nourished." However, she continued, "She wants me to eliminate white flour, sugar, dairy and caffeine from my diet and drink two liters of water every day. I should also try to eat only foods that can be dug out of the ground, cut from a tree or hunted or fished for. In addition, I am to power walk every day and do some yoga . . . I must also learn to 'police my thoughts,' so whenever anything negative, judgmental or disruptive comes into my head I should 'redirect' it."

Despite the critics' outrage to her tone-deaf comments and advice, Gwyneth's recommendations—expensive hotels and restaurants, outfits that cost upward of three thousand dollars—were in line with what women's fashion magazines had been plugging for decades. The main difference was the direct regular connection to someone who actually lived this way. Tallying up the cost of her seasonal wardrobes became a regular exercise for journalists. "The Gwyneth Paltrow guide to spring fashion (but be warned, it'll set you back nearly half-a-million dollars)," went a 2013 *Daily Mail* headline.

The divergence from legacy media was more striking in Goop's health coverage. In January 2009, Gwyneth published the first of what would become an annual media flashpoint: her "detox" diet. "I like to do fasts and cleanses a couple of times during the year," wrote Gwyneth, who had done the Master Cleanse in her twenties. She advised not eating solid food until one thirty p.m., at which point she suggested "salad with carrot and ginger dressing." She added, "There can be no dairy, grains with gluten, meat, shellfish, anything processed, fatty nuts, potatoes, tomatoes, peppers and eggplant, condiments, sugar and obviously no alcohol or soda."

Though Gwyneth didn't want to be Martha Stewart, she shared the tendency to publish a perfectionist's ideas on how to live well. However, while Stewart generally gave her audience the sense that her advice could be executed by anyone who wanted to try with whatever resources they had available, Gwyneth did not. Most Goop readers wouldn't be able to fry oysters at home or successfully eliminate all refined carbohydrates from their diets or undertake Gwyneth's detox regimen for all sorts of reasons. But, like Stewart, she offered a patina of aspirational relatability, through easy muffin recipes and occasional affordable picks, that made audiences think living like Gwyneth was possible.

That same month, Gwyneth gave her first interview about Goop to a mass, unpretentious outlet—*USA Today*. The public was struggling to understand why she would sideline movie stardom to, well, create lifestyle content for the internet. She talked again about how her friends had asked her for tips on restaurants and travel and home remodeling often enough that she'd decided to share her answers with the world.

"I never really knew where I wanted it to go when I was starting it. I just thought if I could affect one woman's life positively who was trying to do all the things I was doing, and I had one solution that worked for me that might work for her, it was worth it to try and share it."

Asked about the backlash, Gwyneth offered a signature move: a note of relatively valid social commentary delivered in a tone of entitlement. "I think part of the problem is people get a hit of energy when they are negative about something, and it is a very detrimental way for them to get that hit of energy. They do not understand why they do not have a happy life. That kind of stuff is just noise to me. I just feel sorry for them."

THE INTERNET WAS drowning in Goop mockery by early 2009. The effect of all the attention was clear: By February, around five months after launch, Goop claimed to have 150,000 newsletter subscribers— the kind of growth a legacy media outlet could only dream of. *Two Lovers* was coming out, but journalists just wanted to talk about Goop. A *New York Times* piece, ostensibly tied to the film, talked mostly about how Gwyneth had left behind movie stardom to do a public television show, share her workout on *Oprah*, partner with Tracy Anderson on a gym she planned to open in Tribeca, and launch a newsletter that the internet couldn't stop dragging.

James Gray, who had directed *Two Lovers*, told the *Times*, "I was concerned that she wouldn't be invested in the work, but she was wonderful . . . At a certain point I asked if she missed acting, and she said she wanted to come back to it and that it was important to her as an artist, but that there aren't that many roles and she doesn't get enough scripts."

Gwyneth didn't comment for the *New York Times* story. Huvane told the paper that discussing the Tracy Anderson gym or Goop would be "premature." She recalled the article in 2017: "I remember once I also had a movie coming out around the same time and there was a huge article in *The New York Times* about why am I doing this? And I thought, *This seems extreme, like I'm just writing banana-nut muffin recipes!*"

EVERY OPPORTUNITY GWYNETH seized seemed designed to lead to another. She had planted a flag in the publishing world but didn't need to limit herself to writing newsletters. Literary agent Luke Janklow had grown up in a social circle similar to Gwyneth's. His father, Morton Janklow, had started the agency Janklow & Nesbit with Lynn Nesbit in 1989 and now represented authors like Danielle Steel and Pope John Paul II. Luke's grandfather was Mervyn LeRoy, who had produced *The Wizard of Oz*. Like Gwyneth, Luke had attended an Upper East Side private school (Dalton).

Janklow had known Gwyneth socially, and when she decided to pitch a cookbook based on dishes she'd made with her father, he agreed to represent her to publishers. The world rights to the book sold at an auction to Grand Central Publishing in January 2009 for what *Forbes* later estimated to be a $1 million advance—a significant amount for someone who had no professional culinary training and only a burgeoning presence in the food space.

Like much of the general public, the publisher's sales force didn't totally understand why Gwyneth Paltrow was writing a cookbook. Giving a celebrity a big book advance was a risk. If the author decided not to promote it, the publisher would have no chance of recouping its investment. So Grand Central looked for stars who wanted to write for personal reasons, who had book ideas they were passionate about and eager to introduce to the world. Gwyneth's book was part of her process of polishing a personal struggle and turning it into a public offering. In the introduction, she wrote, "I always feel closest to my father, who was the love of my life until his death in 2002, when I am in the kitchen." To satisfy the sales team's concern about her lack of a food-world footprint, Gwyneth had her friend Mario Batali write the introduction.

Gwyneth hired Julia Turshen, a trained chef who had worked on *Spain . . . on the Road Again* and then cooked for Gwyneth's family, to help with recipe development and testing. Each dish in the book had some connection to Gwyneth's family, and Turshen worked with her in her kitchens in London and the Hamptons, figuring out the ingredients, proportions, and methods for turning food into recipes.

Gwyneth wrote the headnotes that introduced each dish. When her editor, Karen Murgolo, had editing queries, Gwyneth went to the Midtown publisher's office to review them, a task most authors managed by email. "Gwyneth, you really don't have to do this," Murgolo told her.

Murgolo had worked with celebrities and chefs who didn't write their own cookbooks (though the chefs usually developed and tested their own recipes). Gwyneth impressed her editor: She clearly knew how to cook, and she did the writing herself. When Murgolo gave her edits, such as a suggestion to write longer headnotes, Gwyneth responded capably. She also seemed to have an instinct for what people liked and loathed about her. Reading over page proofs, she spotted a line she had written about a rice steamer built into a counter, the sort of expensive cooking tool that might be normal to Gwyneth but to almost no one else. "Oh, take that out, I hate myself just reading that," she said.

These new projects, the newsletter and the cookbook, allowed Gwyneth far more control over her public persona and her work, and the way they reached the marketplace, than movies. She had drawn on the payout from her biggest Hollywood film to create a professional life and a personal brand that—however out of touch, however unattainably luxurious—was serving her new priorities.

ONE OF GWYNETH'S first targets of attack as a budding wellness authority was a broad category of invisible material known generally as "toxins"—where they came from, how to avoid them, and how to purge them from one's body. After her detox diet dispatch, she waded into the subject again with a newsletter about chemicals in personal care products.

"A couple of years ago I was asked to give a quote for a book concerning environmental toxins and their effects on our children. While reading up on the subject, I was seized with fear about what the research said," she wrote. "Fetuses, infants and toddlers are basically unable to metabolize toxins the way that adults are, and we are constantly filling our environments with chemicals that may or may not be safe."

She continued, "The research is troubling; the incidence of diseases in children such as asthma, cancer and autism have shot up exponentially and many children we all know and love have been diagnosed with developmental issues like ADHD."

Gwyneth quoted Mount Sinai pediatrician Philip Landrigan, who had focused his career on reducing children's exposure to harmful substances like lead and asbestos. He said children risked exposure to eighty thousand chemicals, "nearly all of these are new chemicals developed in the past 50 years. These chemicals are used widely in consumer and household goods, like personal care products, cleaning supplies, pesticides, paints, toys, home furnishings, carpeting and electronics." She also quoted entrepreneur and advocate for nontoxic living Christopher Gavigan: "Ever read the chemical ingredients list on your shampoo or lotion? Not an easy task. Sixty per cent of what goes on the skin is absorb [*sic*] into the body—so avoiding chemicals here is super important, especially for pregnant moms."

Gavigan would go on to found the Honest Company with Jessica Alba as its celebrity face, thereby turning a fear of toxins into a business that went public in 2021 at a valuation of $1.4 billion,* with a brand ethos similar to Goop's. However, unlike Goop, Honest sold its products, such as shampoo and diaper cream, at Walmart for under ten dollars.

Meanwhile, experts outside Gwyneth's sphere—the kind with medical degrees and positions at respected universities—saw not just silliness, but danger in Gwyneth's vigilante health journalism.

TIMOTHY CAULFIELD WORE thick-framed glasses, dressed casually in T-shirts and jeans, and kept his short dark hair a little longer on the top. He had been drawn to celebrity culture since before anyone thought of it as that. He grew up wanting to be a member of the Partridge Family

---

* However, Honest Company—like Goop around the same period—would struggle; its market cap in April 2025 was around $450 million.

and then a rock star; he became a fan of Gwyneth's after watching her in *Se7en*. In 1987, he enrolled at the University of Alberta and went on to earn a law degree and become a professor of health law and science policy there. His research would be published in more than four hundred papers, covering topics like stem cells, genetics, and research ethics. As stars like Gwyneth drew media coverage for their health ideas, Caulfield became fascinated by celebrity culture as a uniquely powerful vector for spreading health misinformation.

Caulfield decided to visit a slew of Gwyneth's favorite self-proclaimed wellness and medical experts when writing his 2015 book, *Is Gwyneth Paltrow Wrong About Everything?: When Celebrity Culture and Science Clash*. "None of them go, 'Oh, you're fine, you're good. Your energy's all aligned. You don't need to cleanse anything. You certainly don't need any supplements,'" said Caulfield. "No, you're always deficient. You always have some kind of energy problem. There's parasites all over your body that you need to rid yourself of, et cetera, et cetera. Because they're trying to sell a product. And they're also trying to instill fear, because we know that fear sells."

Years after Gwyneth published the newsletter on toxins in kids' products, PFAS, or "forever chemicals," became a topic of regular discussion and investigation in the media. While researchers acknowledged that these substances were concerning, experts like Caulfield cautioned, "This is a very important topic, especially for future generations, but the fearmongering is still there about the relevance to your day-to-day health." Regarding Goop appearing to be right occasionally, he invoked the old broken-clock analogy.

Goop didn't use fact-checkers the same way a more traditional media outlet would to review its content for accuracy. Gwyneth trusted her own good intentions to minimize any harm done. Her claim that cancer rates had increased "exponentially" as a result of unspecified chemicals was exaggerated. "There has been very little change in the number of childhood cancers detected during the past ten years," Dr. Lesley Walker, director of cancer information for Cancer Research

UK, told the *Daily Mail* at the time. Thomas Pennington, emeritus professor of bacteriology at the University of Aberdeen, added, "It's a load of nonsense. Shampoo is perfectly safe, unless you drink it in large quantities."

As a rule, Goop leaned on the assumption that "natural" things were good, and anything "not natural" was bad. "How can the sun be bad for you? It's natural," Gwyneth said in 2013, though sun exposure causes thousands of skin cancer deaths each year.

But critical readers in those days were more likely to laugh at Gwyneth's stories than rage at the inaccuracies. As Viv Groskop wrote in *The Observer* after Gwyneth published a newsletter about why the Bible leads people to think homosexuality is wrong, "These pronouncements are more entertaining than many of Paltrow's films. This is actor as ambassador for truth. And with these well-meaning but crazed posts she is really spoiling us." Gwyneth answered critics by saying that "journalists are terrified of celebrities having a journalistic voice," which may have been true, but it failed to address the question of accuracy. In addition to not spending money on fact-checking, Goop was a lean operation, which Gwyneth wasn't monetizing. She in fact refused to accept any advertising, and, she said, "I would never want to."

In May 2009, Gwyneth's work as a spokesmodel for Estée Lauder came to an end, freeing her to use her image to promote her brand and her brand alone. "I started questioning being hired as a face for companies to represent," she said. "I started to question . . . what would it be like if I were to channel the power of that into my own brand and to kind of—the equity be it . . . sweat equity that I put into the company, but also my actual equity. And wouldn't it possibly be more meaningful for me in the long run if it was a business that I owned a significant share of?"

But also, Estée Lauder—Aerin Lauder in particular, as one executive recalled—didn't want to renew her contract. The company had had its Gwyneth moment and was comfortable with letting her move on. But the work with Lauder had given Gwyneth a window into the beauty business, which she would soon enter herself as an entrepreneur.

The year after her contract ended, she encountered an Estée executive she had worked with at a dinner sponsored by one of the company's makeup brands. He sat down next to her to say hello. Before, when she wanted something that he could give her, she had made him feel important. But now she acted like she had never met him.

GWYNETH AND MARTIN had been together nearly eight years when they spent her thirty-eighth birthday in Italy, going for long walks in the Tuscan countryside, lazing around their rented cottage, holding hands, and drinking Barolo. The kitchen table overflowing with tomatoes from the vine, peaches, basil, and eggs from a local farm: all the trappings of a lifestyle influencer's getaway. And yet a revelation was asserting itself, amid the autumn hillsides and fragrant evenings: The uncoupling had begun.

Gwyneth tried to ignore the feeling, a sense that despite their friendship and their shared sense of humor and taste in music and yoga, they "had never fully settled into being a couple." As she put it later, "We just didn't quite fit together. There was always a bit of unease and unrest."

Her friends weren't all that surprised. Gwyneth and Martin's relationship seemed to grow from convenient timing more than anything else. After the honeymoon phase wore off, Gwyneth seemed to find him "dorky," one friend said. Plus, unlike his wife, Martin was an introvert whose mind always seemed to be on his music, which made for a household dynamic that guests found stilted and uncomfortable. The pair didn't seem to have real chemistry, and friends wondered if she was ever really in love with him, or if the romance stemmed from extraordinary circumstances—Gwyneth devastated after losing her father, Martin presenting himself to help her pick up the pieces, singing his heart out to her, among the tens of thousands in the stands.

Plus, being in a relationship with a touring musician was innately difficult. After Martin married Gwyneth, Coldplay went on three world tours between 2005 and 2012, performing a total of 381 shows. Martin was worshipped by fans night after night. One person who knew the couple speculated that a rock star like Martin—though a wonderful father—would have had little room in his life for much else, which must have made parenting challenging. Yet Gwyneth was, friends said, an incredible mother who loved her kids more than anything else and was happy to work less herself and take on a bigger share of the child-care. (Since she chose to keep her kids out of the spotlight when they were growing up, discussion of them in this book has been limited.)

Gwyneth would try for a few more years to make it work with her first husband. Soon she would meet her second one.

GWYNETH WAS CONFIRMED, in September 2010, to appear on two episodes of *Glee*, the Fox musical dramedy about a glee club at a fictional Ohio high school. A fan of the show, Gwyneth had worked on *Running with Scissors* with its creator, Ryan Murphy, who wrote the part just for her. Gwyneth would play the substitute teacher Holly Holliday, whose musical numbers included "Forget You" by CeeLo Green and Fleetwood Mac's "Landslide."

In 2010, Gwyneth traveled to Los Angeles to film her scenes. On Murphy's team was writer and co-producer Brad Falchuk, who had driven cross-country to L.A. after graduating Hobart and William Smith Colleges in 1993 to study at the American Film Institute. Half Venezuelan, with a muscular build, blue eyes, and brown hair just long enough to tuck behind his ears, he had a taste for V-necks and cardigans that hinted at his preppy East Coast roots. "It was a very curious family," he said of his upbringing. "We traveled a bunch. My parents were always like, 'What's out there? We're gonna check it out, we're gonna go on an adventure.' It was a kind of safety without caution. And there were always books around, and a great deal of humor." He'd attended private school as a kid but failed to earn good grades, only to find out in his sophomore year of college that he had severe dyslexia. In 2003, Falchuk had married television producer Suzanne Bukinik, with whom he had two children. Like Martin, Falchuk tended to be more introverted than Gwyneth. Murphy considered himself the "brain" and Falchuk "the heart" of *Glee*.

"She's stunning and she's charming and she's completely disarming," Falchuk later said of meeting Gwyneth on set for the first time. "We had similar enough backgrounds—a little bit Jewish, a little bit East Coast, her dad was a TV producer—and so we just sort of developed this really lovely friendship." (Unlike Gwyneth, both of Falchuk's parents were Jewish; his mother, Nancy, was the president of Hadassah Women's Zionist Organization of America from 2007 to 2011.)

Glee was the beginning of a music-making phase for Gwyneth. Prior to this, she had sung meaningfully only in *Duets*. In early 2010, Gwyneth began filming *Country Strong*, about an alcoholic country singer, the first leading part she had taken in seven years. The character demanded the kind of grit and recklessness that Gwyneth's work hadn't demanded since *Flesh and Bone*: "She's just off the rails a bit, and it's sad. [The addiction] was just bigger than her, and she just couldn't fight it off." The role led her to perform the movie's title track, "Country Strong," in November at the Country Music Awards. A few months later at the Grammys, she sang "Forget You" with CeeLo Green. Later that month, she performed *Country Strong*'s "Coming Home" at the Oscars. She talked repeatedly in interviews about advice she'd received from her friend Beyoncé, whom she got to know since Martin was close with her husband, Jay-Z. (Jay-Z would come by their Hamptons house, sometimes dropping off a nephew or other family member for the day, which Gwyneth found odd but was also fine with. "That's their culture," she'd tell friends.)

"This story always makes me cry . . . It's ten in the morning and Beyoncé schleps it all the way down to the Staples Center to watch [me rehearse]. I mean, she's Beyoncé! Beyoncé's like, 'Okay. The singing is great. But you're not having any fun.' She's like, 'Remember when we're at Jay's concert and Panjabi MC comes on and you do your crazy Indian dance? Do that. Be you!'" Gwyneth said. She added that Beyoncé and Jay-Z gave her more music advice than Martin when she was considering doing her own album: "Beyoncé and Jay—they think that I should just go do it by myself. That I should go . . . in a studio and see what happens. And if it's good, do it. And if it's not, don't. So that's probably what I'll do." An album never materialized, nor did a singing career.

In 2011, Goop reported reaching four hundred thousand subscribers. When it was around a year old, Gwyneth had hired Eliza Honey, a young editor with experience at *House & Garden* and *The New Yorker*, to work out of her London house and help her write stories and find contributors. But outsiders saw Goop's potential to expand in a much bigger way. Venture capitalist Juliet de Baubigny, who received the newsletter, told Gwyneth at a party in London that she should monetize it. Gwyneth later said that she had no idea what a venture capitalist was.

Through friends, Gwyneth met successful British entrepreneur Seb Bishop. He asked if she had thought about turning Goop into a for-profit business. In interviews, Gwyneth has downplayed her early ambitions to monetize Goop, despite having hired one of the world's foremost branding experts at the beginning of the whole experiment.

But she liked making money and was leaving it on the table when it came to Goop. Using her own money, she hired Bishop as CEO, along with a COO and a website editor. Goop was known primarily as the forum for Gwyneth's expensive recommendations and detox diets—and would soon become a powerful platform for spreading health misinformation. Instagram had launched on October 6, 2010, and influencing the public's purchases was starting to become a big industry. Goop and Gwyneth had been doing just that for years and were well positioned to capitalize on it.

·   ◦   •

GWYNETH'S FIRST COOKBOOK, *My Father's Daughter*, came out April 13, 2011. Gwyneth had the opportunity to promote it early with a *Vogue* cover story—practically unheard of for a cookbook author—for the August 2010 issue, by the magazine's food correspondent Jeffrey Steingarten. He met with her at her New York apartment and then her London home to cook recipes from the book. "Things had gone so smoothly between Gwyneth and me that I thought I had a journalistic obligation to shake things up, to peer behind what seemed to me an impossibly perfect life, and so, despite the strong affection I had developed for Gwyneth, I wanted to ask her some rude questions," he wrote. "Had she ever had plastic surgery? Would she rather have somebody else's body? Did she hate any part of her own, the way Nora Ephron had written about how much she hated her own neck?" Gwyneth said she'd have to think about it. Gwyneth was supposed to talk to Steingarten again at her photo shoot, but when he arrived, he was told the set was closed. (He figured that he'd offended her, though she told him over email that wasn't the case.)

Many critics admitted that they didn't want to like her cookbook, but they couldn't help themselves. "Once you get past your initial nausea of Gwyneth's clueless haute couture sensibility, the recipes themselves are relatively simple and easy to make," wrote Drew Grant for Salon.com. Grant noted that in addition to recipes for "bake stuffed lobster" and "duck cassoulet," the book included an easy, five-ingredient lemon pasta dish, describing it as useful for both college students and Hamptons hostesses—"but then she felt the need to GOOP it up with all this early, condescending text just to fill her quota of snobbishness. But skip the essays and go straight to the recipes, and you might be surprised how easy Gwyneth's healthy medicine goes down."

The book was an instant *New York Times* bestseller. Though she appeared on *Glee* around the same time, the cookbook was getting all the attention. Journalists continued to ask her about it when she was on the promotional circuit for *Iron Man 2*, which opened less than a month after publication. When she did an interview with BBC host Jonathan Ross at the iTunes Festival that summer, she kept the focus on her sensibilities around food, declaring, "I would rather smoke crack than eat cheese from a can." The cookbook went on to sell more than one hundred thousand copies.

Gwyneth's publisher eagerly signed her up for another one.

TITLED *IT'S ALL GOOD: Delicious, Easy Recipes That Will Make You Look Good and Feel Great*, that cookbook opened with one of the most confessional pieces of writing Gwyneth had ever published, about a health scare that contributed to her wellness philosophy and brought her closer to the kinds of gurus who would guide much of Goop's health content.

One warm Sunday afternoon in the spring of 2011, Gwyneth wrote, between the *Country Strong* promotion, *Glee*, and her award-show performances, she served lunch for a group of family and friends in the sunny garden of her London home. Midway through, she was sitting at the table when she started feeling like she was "going to die." She thought she might faint, and her thoughts got fuzzy. She didn't say anything during lunch but felt worried. "I stood up to clear the table and found that my right hand wasn't working as it should, and then everything went blurry." A sharp pain went through her head, and she lost her breath and couldn't speak. She worried she was having a stroke.

A girlfriend held her hand and talked to her until the symptoms subsided, but Gwyneth didn't feel right for hours. She tried to sleep but could hear her kids playing in the garden and experienced a burgeoning fear: that she could fall ill enough that she would be unable to be with them.

She went to see a host of doctors (she referred to them as "doctors," but not all of them were medical doctors who practiced traditional Western medicine) to get everything checked out. She was convinced something was wrong with her. She was told that she had a benign cyst on her ovary that needed immediate removal, a nodule on her parathyroid gland, improper thyroid function, and a hormone imbalance. But she hadn't had a stroke. They suggested it was a migraine headache coupled with a panic attack. Gwyneth presumed this was her body reacting to her busy schedule and the accompanying air travel, stress, and adrenaline. (Singing at the Oscars hadn't exactly been a relaxing proposition.) Plus, she had recently been drinking wine and eating french fries.

At this point, Gwyneth had been trying to optimize her life for years, overriding ordinary emotional pain—anxiety, grief, anger—through physical interventions like intense exercise and radical changes in diet. As her reliance on gurus and self-described wellness experts increased, so did her belief that every physical symptom in her body signified a disease state. She blamed herself for the episode. She had always tried to be healthy, she wrote, and put herself through regular "cleanses," but she "usually interspersed this clean living with hearty chunks of happy indulgence. And clearly I had gotten out of balance."

After her medical tests in London, she went to see another doctor, whom she considered a "good friend." Alejandro Junger was born in Uruguay, where he graduated from medical school, then trained at New York Downtown Hospital and Lenox Hill Hospital before heading to India where he was exposed to all kinds of Eastern medicine. Gwyneth had met him in 2007, when she was feeling exhausted and he had come to her Manhattan hotel room to administer an IV solution of nearly a dozen vitamins and minerals known as a "Myers' cocktail." He had also prescribed her a supplement regimen of pills and powders, and left Gwyneth a happy customer.

Now, on top of what Gwyneth's previous tests had revealed, Junger informed her that she was "severely anemic"; vitamin D–deficient; suffering from a "very congested" liver; very stressed out, as evidenced by her adrenal glands; and suffering from "a lot of inflammation in [her] system." The solution, he told her, was to undergo an "elimination diet" to "clear out" her "system," "heal" her gut, and "revive" her body.

Junger's plan forbade a long list of foods: coffee, alcohol, dairy, eggs, sugar, shellfish, deepwater fish, potatoes, tomatoes, bell pepper, eggplant, corn, wheat, meat, soy, and anything processed. Gwyneth built a diet out of whatever was left, and her subsequent blood work, she said, revealed "a different person."

Gwyneth asked Junger when she should stop the diet.

"Well, it's hard for me to tell you this, because I don't do it myself all the time," he told her. "But this is the way you should try to eat for the rest of your life." Gwyneth decided that she would try to make this diet her "baseline" and enjoy "the occasional cheat day." Gwyneth asked Julia Turshen to help her come up with recipes that eliminated these foods, which were ultimately published in Gwyneth's second cookbook, *It's All Good*.

ALONGSIDE THE AUTHOR'S note for *My Father's Daughter*, Gwyneth had included a photo of herself with Julia Turshen. "I literally could not have written this book without the tireless, artful assistance of Julia Turshen, who stood over my shoulder at the stove and chopping block for the better part of the year, bringing a method to my freestyling madness. She quantified, tested, and retested every recipe, oversaw the production of the photos, helped brainstorm in a crisis, and, above all, was my intellectual and emotional support through the whole process."

About a year after the book's publication, *The New York Times* ran a story about celebrity cookbooks written by ghostwriters. It led with a photo of *My Father's Daughter*, with the caption "Gwyneth Paltrow's ghostwriter is Julia Turshen," and noted that Turshen had also ghostwritten for Mario Batali. Veteran food journalist Julia Moskin reported the piece by cold-calling writers who were acknowledged on recent celebrity cookbooks. Turshen answered and chatted with Moskin about working with Gwyneth, a routine part of public-figure cookbook creation.

Moskin included stories about her own experience ghostwriting nine cookbooks: "Because cookbook ghostwriting brings low pay, nonexistent royalties (most writers are paid a flat fee, or a percentage of the advance doled out by the publisher) and only a few perks, most ghosts don't last long. When a ghosted book is successful, watching someone else get credit for your work is demoralizing." She explained that "many chefs do not pretend that they do their own writing." She quoted Bobby Flay: "I consider myself an 'author,' in quotes, but not a writer." And she included quotes from Turshen in the piece, explaining that "like many younger ghosts, [she] is generally thrilled to be paid for the combination of writing and cooking."

Gwyneth had developed a habit of publicly reacting to coverage she didn't like, which only amplified it. She didn't seem to mind trampling over people in the process. It was this callousness, observed by some members of her Goop staff, that made them terribly afraid of Gwyneth and her power to retaliate. "Love @nytimes dining section but this weeks [*sic*] facts need checking. No ghost writer on my cookbook, I wrote every word myself," she posted to her Facebook page and Twitter.

Moskin had also interviewed Wes Martin, who helped Rachael Ray with her cookbooks. This angered Ray, who also denied that she had a ghostwriter. Gwyneth went on Ray's show via video from her London home, where she sat in her pajamas drinking a glass of wine. "Every single recipe in the book I came up with and cooked on the spot," Gwyneth said. "I understand the word 'ghostwriter' to mean someone is writing your book. And I think *The New York Times* clearly says that someone who is writing the glossary or organizing pantry items, that that constitutes a ghostwriter as well. I wrote every single word of my book."

The reaction was a surprise at the *Times*, which hadn't been trying to produce a work of "gotcha" journalism. Stephen Huvane called Moskin and yelled at her, threatening to call people he said he knew who were high-level at the newspaper. But the *Times* stood by Moskin's work, telling ABC that the story "did not say that someone else wrote Rachael Ray's, Jamie Oliver's or Gwyneth Paltrow's cookbooks. It said that they, like many other chef-authors, had help." This was true for Gwyneth, who relied on Turshen's expertise to turn the dishes she wanted to feature into recipes, even if Turshen didn't write her headnotes.

Blythe and Gwyneth
at a Cabaret benefit for
Williamstown Theatre
Festival at Studio 54 in
New Yok City, 1985,
when Gwyneth was twelve.
RON GALELLA/GETTY IMAGES

Gwyneth performing in
A Midsummer Night's Dream,
circa 1990, as a senior at
Spence. JENNIFER FELL HAYES

Gwyneth's headshot, 1990.
BRIAN HAMILL/GETTY IMAGES

Gwyneth with Tyagi Schwartz,
filming the *High* pilot, 1990,
produced by her father for CBS.
CBS PHOTO ARCHIVE/GETTY IMAGES

Performing with Blythe in *Picnic* at Williamstown Theatre Festival, 1991.
RICHARD FELDMAN/WILLIAMSTOWN
THEATRE FESTIVAL

With Blythe, Bruce, and brother Jake at the December 1991 Los Angeles premiere for *The Prince of Tides*, in which Blythe played a supporting role. Around five months earlier, Bruce had told Gwyneth not to return to college and cut her off financially. JIM SMEAL/GETTY IMAGES

Gwyneth in costume as Thomas Jefferson's daughter Patsy for the *Jefferson in Paris* shoot in France, 1994.
MIKKI ANSIN/GETTY IMAGES

With Leonardo DiCaprio at the National Board of Review of Motion Pictures Awards in New York, 1994, where he won Best Supporting Actor for *What's Eating Gilbert Grape.*
VINNIE ZUFFANTE/GETTY IMAGES

Costume designer Michael Kaplan with Gwyneth and Brad Pitt on the set of *Se7en* in Los Angeles, in which they played husband and wife.
COURTESY OF MICHAEL KAPLAN

Attending the *Legends of the Fall* premiere in London, April 1994, with her new boyfriend, Brad Pitt, in one of their first public outings.
DAVE M. BENETT/GETTY IMAGES

Brad Pitt leading Gwyneth from the theater in New York where they saw *Hamlet*, 1995, and where he confronted Harvey Weinstein over his earlier harassment of Gwyneth in a room at the Peninsula Hotel in Los Angeles. RON GALELLA, LTD./GETTY IMAGES

At the Golden Globes, January 1996, with Brad Pitt, the night he won Best Supporting Actor for *12 Monkeys* and called Gwyneth "my angel" in his acceptance speech.
RON GALELLA/GETTY IMAGES

Gwyneth at the New York premiere of *Emma*, July 1996.
EVAN AGOSTINI/GETTY IMAGES

Attending the 1996 MTV Video Music Awards in a suit by Tom Ford for Gucci, after Harvey Weinstein suggested she dress sexy.
JEFF KRAVITZ/GETTY IMAGES

Gwyneth on her first *Vogue* cover, pegged to *Emma*, 1996, after editor in chief Anna Wintour killed her previous three photo shoots.

Filming *Great Expectations* in New York, 1996, wearing Donna Karan. LAWRENCE SCHWARTZWALD/GETTY IMAGES

Filming *A Perfect Murder* in New York, 1998.
RON GALELLA, LTD./GETTY IMAGES

At the New York premiere of *Shakespeare in Love,* attended by Hillary Clinton, December 1998.
DIANE FREED/GETTY IMAGES

With Ben Affleck at the premiere of *Armageddon* at the Kennedy Space Center in Florida, June 1998.
KEVIN MAZUR/GETTY IMAGES

At the Los Angeles airport with Ben Affleck, October 1998, a few months before they broke up the first time.
RON GALELLA/GETTY IMAGES

Officially a Best Actress
Oscar winner, March 1999.
JIM SMEAL/GETTY IMAGES

Gwyneth's Oscars dress appeared
to have fit issues after numerous
alternations and she decided to
wear it without the inner corset
provided by designer Ralph Lauren's
team. Lauren was seemingly so
frustrated by the process of making
the dress that he had to be talked
into sending it to Gwyneth for the
ceremony. BOB RIHA JR/GETTY IMAGES

Performing in *As You Like It* at Williamstown Theatre Festival in the summer of 1999, after winning her Oscar. RICHARD FELDMAN/ WILLIAMSTOWN THEATRE FESTIVAL

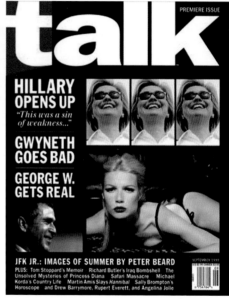

The debut 1999 cover of *Talk*. Gwyneth agreed to the photo shoot as a favor to Weinstein, and was upset to see one of the photos on the cover, fearing it would interfere with a *Vogue* cover exclusive. HULTON ARCHIVE/GETTY IMAGES

At a London gala with Harvey Weinstein, October 2002, just over two weeks after the death of her father. YUI MOK - PA IMAGES/GETTY IMAGES

Watching Coldplay perform in London, July 2005, when Apple was around fourteen months old. MJ KIM/GETTY IMAGES

Pregnant with Moses and wearing Balenciaga at the 2006 Golden Globes, where she was nominated for *Proof*. KMAZUR/ GETTY IMAGES

Arriving at the London *Iron Man* premiere wearing Balmain, 2008. FERDAUS SHAMIM/GETTY IMAGES

With Chris Martin at a Beverly Hills gala, January 2014, around three months before announcing their conscious uncoupling. KEVIN MAZUR/GETTY IMAGES

Chris Martin performing with Coldplay in Central Park, New York, September 2015, for fans including Apple and Moses, eleven and nine years old respectively. KEVIN MAZUR/GETTY IMAGES

Gwyneth
addressing acolytes
at a 2019 In Goop
Health summit
in Los Angeles.
NEILSON BARNARD/
GETTY IMAGES

At the September
2019 premiere of *The
Politician*, the Netflix
show she appeared in
at the behest of her
husband, Brad Falchuk,
who wrote the part
just for her. DIMITRIOS
KAMBOURIS/GETTY IMAGES

With Elise Loehnen, former chief content officer of Goop, at a January 2020 screening of the Netflix show *The Goop Lab*. RACHEL MURRAY/GETTY IMAGES

Entering the courtroom after a lunch break in Park City, Utah, 2023, after Terry Sanderson sued her over a skiing collision. Her courtroom wardrobe became a brief internet sensation, and *GQ* identified this suit as Brunello Cucinelli. GETTY IMAGES

Spain . . . on the Road Again producer Charles Pinsky was working with Turshen on a shoot with Thomas Keller in London when this unfolded. Turshen, he said, never represented herself as a ghostwriter to the *Times* and later asked them to clarify this in the story. They never did. Pinsky encouraged Turshen to tell Gwyneth that it was all a big misunderstanding. But he also reminded Turshen that she had nothing to apologize for.

The incident ruined what had been a close relationship. Gwyneth's second cookbook, *It's All Good*, had already been completed. Since it was a diet cookbook, which involved making brownies with ingredients like spelt flour and rice syrup, she'd leaned even more heavily on Turshen to come up with the recipes. Turshen was credited as a coauthor, her name in small print on the cover when it came out in 2013, despite their public falling-out over the *Times* story. But she wouldn't collaborate with Gwyneth again.

AROUND 2012, ALEJANDRO Junger introduced Gwyneth to Habib Sadeghi, a doctor of osteopathic medicine whom she described in *It's All Good* as "a conventionally trained physician who also practices other integrative healing methods," including "osteopathic manipulative medicine, techniques from the world of Ayurveda, Tibetan medicine, anthroposophical medicine, acupuncture and energy healing." Gwyneth called him "the kind of doctor I had been searching for." Sadeghi asked her "what unspoken emotions could be contributing to [her] stress," and put her through more tests, which revealed "high levels of metals and a blood parasite, among other things" that she believed often went "undiagnosed" and caused, she wrote in the book's introduction, "incredibly negative impacts on our well-being."

Friends and colleagues wondered about Gwyneth's susceptibility to wellness gurus like Junger and Sadeghi. She had rarely been challenged in her life, rarely told she was wrong. And no one close to her had the confidence now to say they believed she was being swindled.

Given her lifetime of privilege, perhaps things had come so easily for so long that, as Timothy Caulfield noted, "There's almost the narcissistic quality that she can figure out the truth [that others are missing].

"There's really interesting research about those people who believe misinformation, believe conspiracy theories," he continued. "They like the idea that they figured something out and they have special knowledge, a special ability to discern the truth, and I get the sense that's happening with Gwyneth." After a lifetime of being treated as more special than most everyone else, how could she not see herself that way?

Gwyneth was constantly searching for health problems now, and the gurus were always willing to tell her she had them. In a few years, once Goop had started hiring dozens of staffers, she would ask them about their medical issues, and they would find themselves sitting on the other side of her desk—in a surreal experience—telling their famous boss deeply personal information about their ailments and treatments.

Gwyneth had her whole family tested for "food sensitivities and allergies," which she said she "would highly recommend to anyone looking to feel better, shed weight, etc." She recalled in her cookbook that the tests showed "Everyone in my house is intolerant of gluten, dairy, and chicken eggs, among many other surprising foods I had always thought were healthy." She acknowledged that her new plan was not without challenges: "Sometimes when my family is not eating pasta, bread or processed grains like white rice, we're left with that specific hunger that comes with avoiding carbs."

Of all the inaccurate health claims Gwyneth promoted, Caulfield found her statements about gluten to be especially frustrating. "There's a large body of evidence that going gluten-free [is unnecessary] unless you have a clinical reason for doing it, like you're celiac, and there's some evidence around things like [the neurological disorder] POTS [Postural Orthostatic Tachycardia Syndrome]. But that's a really small percentage of the population."

Caulfield was far from the only expert with these sentiments. Marion Nestle, professor emerita of nutrition, public health, and food studies at New York University, said, "The body automatically detoxes through digestion and excretion. Some people might feel better not eating these things [that Junger recommended banning], but for most people it won't make much difference."

Andrea Love, a scientist and public health consultant with a PhD in microbiology and immunology who writes and speaks regularly about medical misinformation, called it "orthorexia [an unhealthy obsession with health food] under the guise of health," adding, "Food sensitivity is not a thing. You can have allergies, but a sensitivity is a wellness pseudoscience claim." She explained that food sensitivity tests are designed to respond to things someone recently ate—so if you just had, say, macaroni and cheese, it will tell you you're sensitive to gluten and dairy because you just ingested it. Plus, when people omit healthy food from their diet because someone tells them they're sensitive to it, that puts them at risk of not getting adequate nutrients.

The recipes for *It's All Good* mostly followed Junger's plan, along with a few meat recipes for those "cheat" days. The book included avocado toast on gluten-free bread; waffles and muffins made with gluten-free flour; Mexican chopped salad; teriyaki chicken; Middle Eastern turkey burgers served with yogurt sauce instead of a bun; lamb tagine; plain roasted sweet potato; plain brown rice; veggie dumplings; brownies made with maple syrup instead of sugar, with the option to add whey protein powder to make them "power" brownies; vegan "cheesecake"; and popcorn. When *It's All Good* landed at Grand Central Publishing with a recipe for popcorn—ingredients: corn kernels, olive oil, and salt—one executive wondered if Gwyneth was running out of ideas.

The book became a platform for Junger and Sadeghi. Junger's commentary appeared alongside the list of staple ingredients and included pronouncements unsupported by science, such as: "I have known many women to get pregnant soon after stopping all soy products." Junger would later found a business that sold twenty-one-day "reset" supplements for $475. Sadeghi wrote the book's introduction, in which he discussed "psychospiritual nutrition," seeming to suggest that dieting was a spiritual calling, particularly for women and mothers. His online "wellness store" would go on to sell a long list of supplements, including an "immune repair kit" ($125 for a mini, $275 for a large) that failed to list its ingredients on the website.

A couple of weeks before publication, on March 17, 2013, the *Daily Mail*—one of the most devoted chroniclers of Gwyneth-related controversy—published an excerpt from the book in its *YOU* magazine supplement. The text ran alongside an exclusive interview with Gwyneth, conducted fireside in her London home. Interviewer Jane Gordon confessed to falling for her subject completely, despite her skepticism.

"I am so charmed by her that I begin to harbor fantasies of becoming her new best friend," Gordon wrote. "And I do not believe that even her harshest critics—those envious cyber trolls who subscribe to, but mock, Gwyneth's weekly online blog Goop (in which she shares 'all life's positives,' offering helpful tips on everything from fashion to the fiscal cliff)—would be able to resist her either." Gwyneth delivered sound bites that she surely knew would drive a fresh round of coverage, along with the revelation that she'd had a miscarriage some time after Moses was born and "nearly died." "My children ask me to have a baby all the time and you never know—I could squeeze one more in. I am missing my third. I am thinking about it."

Gwyneth had become an expert at deploying anecdotes from her private life to heighten the appeal of her brand and tweak the distinct balance between the aspirational and the relatable. Toward the end of March, she wrote for Goop about something she had revealed in *Redbook* in January in a joint interview with Tracy Anderson, but that had failed to become a media flashpoint at the time: "[O]nce a week, on the way to school, we stop at the corner shop in London and I let them pick out whatever they want. They get a bag of crisps [British for chips] or candy and a soda. It's called the Coke of the Week. I don't want them growing up in a hippie vacuum." In the newsletter, she reported that Apple liked to get Cheetos at the airport, and that her kids adored their weekly junk food: "They love a brown rice stir-fry but they also love their 'Coke of the Week.'"

It's All Good landed in spring 2013, and Gwyneth's critics played directly into her hand. *The Atlantic* wrote that it took "laughable Hollywood neuroticism about eating to the next level." The *New York Post* said it "reads like the manifesto to some sort of creepy healthy-girl sorority." The lifestyle website Yahoo! Shine calculated that her eating plan would cost three hundred dollars per day.

As the backlash built, *The New York Times* wrote that the book was "taking heat for being an elitist farm-to-table guide sprinkled with duck eggs and $25-a-jar Manuka honey," adding that "at best it makes it seem like healthy eating is strictly for the wealthy; at worst, it's quack science for attempting to export Paltrow's wacky elimination diet (no bell peppers, eggplant or corn? Huh?) to a populace that's improperly nourished and financially struggling."

It's All Good was an early example of a lifestyle cookbook. Readers and home cooks were treated, along with the recipes, to a window into Gwyneth's extravagant and eccentric life—just as they were when they bought a cookbook by her much disavowed (and less eccentric, particularly when it came to matters of health) rival Martha Stewart. *It's All Good* was a monster hit—the *Iron Man* of cookbooks that year—selling more than two hundred thousand copies.

If Gwyneth took anything away from its success, it may have been that the more extreme her health advice, the bigger the audience she could attract.

CHAPTER 22

The Uncoupling

I really had the sense that I wasn't allowed to have needs.

—Gwyneth Paltrow

Gwyneth marked her fortieth birthday in 2012 with a series of international events—first a yacht trip around Italy with her family, then a party at London's swanky River Cafe attended by its former junior chef Jamie Oliver and *Shakespeare in Love* director John Madden. When she got to New York, two weeks after her actual birthday, she threw a party at Elio's, the upscale Italian spot on Second Avenue and Eighty-Fourth Street that she used to frequent as a teenager with her family. She arrived with her hair pulled into a tight ponytail, wearing black cigarette pants and stilettos. Among the guests were Cameron Diaz, Chelsea Handler, Christy Turlington, Steven "Uncle Morty" Spielberg, and some Spence friends. Then a big black van pulled up to the curb, and out into the dark early-fall night, with the help of a bodyguard, stepped Beyoncé, wearing sunglasses and stiletto boots. Though Gwyneth's friendship with Beyoncé was played up in the press, it was unclear to her old friends how close they actually were. They were also surprised when a number of people at the party started talking loudly about one of Gwyneth's earlier birthday celebrations, organized by Chris Martin and Julia Cuddihy, to which they hadn't received an invitation.

. . .

THOUGH GWYNETH'S PARTIES looked like rote celebrity-laden excess, she was terribly anxious about turning forty. Part of the problem was her deteriorating relationship with Martin and her desire to move back to the United States. By this time she had hinted in interviews—uncharacteristically, given her attempt to keep her relationship private—that things with Martin were strained. "Sometimes it's hard being with someone for a long time," she told *Elle*. "We go through periods that aren't all rosy. I always say, life is long and you never know what's going to happen. If, God forbid, we were ever not to be together, I respect him so much as the father of my children . . ." In a little aside that few people seemed to notice, she told the *Daily Mail*'s *YOU*, "Regardless of what happens in our marriage, I chose the best father."

Around a year before they announced their breakup, Gwyneth later told a friend, she and Martin decided to see other people.

Gwyneth planned her return to the States and was looking at Los Angeles houses for sale online from London when she saw one that made her feel "something more than my usual covetousness." The next time she was in L.A., she went to see the eight-thousand-square-foot, white-brick house set on two-thirds of an acre in the premium, postcard-perfect neighborhood Mandeville Canyon. The house had six bedrooms, a large kitchen featuring a rotisserie, soothing shades of gray, and a floor made of reclaimed stones from "an old church somewhere in Peru."

She and Martin bought it for around $10 million and hired Ryan Murphy's decorator, Windsor Smith, for a project that involved "many months of back and forth," including attempts to get brands, such as the high-end bathroom fixture company Waterworks, to sponsor her renovation.

Later, Rupert Murdoch's son Lachlan and his wife Sarah, Dr. Dre, and Tom Brady and Gisele Bündchen bought homes in the same neighborhood, but Gwyneth was credited by *The Hollywood Reporter* with turning it into "the newest—and arguably hottest—destination for L.A.'s power elite."

BY THE TIME Gwyneth and Goop CEO Seb Bishop had hired a staff of not quite twenty people, the company was large enough to move operations out of her home and into a light-filled office in London's Oxford Circus. The space was small, just two banks of eight or so desks each, and the staff shared a kitchen with other companies on the floor.

In 2011, Goop's revenue was nearly $130,000, but the company ended up with a loss of around $255,000. In 2012, revenue increased to nearly $1.9 million, but the site still lost nearly $40,000. That year's $1.5 million in administration expenses included Gwyneth's and Bishop's salaries, which totaled nearly $600,000 combined (other wages and salaries totaled just over $450,000). *Radar* wrote that the figures, which were publicly available in the UK's Companies House registry, showed Goop was in crisis. But the figures didn't necessarily illustrate a company in crisis, according to an outside analyst who reviewed the filing and a former employee familiar with the financials. Goop was more than $1.2 million in debt, and Gwyneth had received a company loan, but many companies take on debt and make loans to executives. Goop was paying its bills and maintaining its liabilities without problems.

When she went into the office, Gwyneth sat at a desk in the open floorplan space with the rest of her team. The staff tried to keep her comings and goings secret, since paparazzi would cluster outside and others in the building would sneak up to their floor to get a look at her.

By 2013, the five-year-old company was growing, but still not turning a profit, and the atmosphere was fevered. Bishop was scrambling to monetize Goop. He and Gwyneth considered selling beauty products directly from the site; collaborations like Stella McCartney x

Goop and Cynthia Rowley x Goop; personalization, where customers could get their own initials on a handbag; advertising (which Gwyneth had previously sworn off); subscriptions in the vein of ShoeDazzle, a site cofounded in 2009 by Kim Kardashian, that sent subscribers a new pair of shoes each month; and a wholesale business.

To test the site's selling power, they decided to offer one product per week, created in collaboration with another brand. The first was a white Kain Label T-shirt, embellished with grosgrain piping, priced at $90, and advertised as "one size fits all."

As usual, critics swarmed. *Gothamist* was one of many outlets to decry the shirts, noting they cost $90 plus $10 shipping: "The shirt is one size fits all, but in Gwyneth terms that means it 'fits US sizes 0-8.' FYI: the average American woman wears a size 12 to 14."

The shirts quickly sold out.

Once the newsletter touting a certain item went out, the staff was surprised to see how quickly it moved product. The collaborative products sold particularly well. Goop also hired a few buyers. Gwyneth's manager's niece Brittany Pattner reached out looking for a job, and moved to London from Los Angeles to serve as head of collaborations and special projects. (Pattner had also created the website iwannabegwyneth.com.)

Despite her non-Goop work obligations, Gwyneth remained engaged with day-to-day operations. And while matters of taste— design, editorial, and product—came naturally to Gwyneth, running a business did not, and Goop brought on its first in-house financial person, Preete Janda, in 2013.

"As we monetized and as we got into e-commerce, I didn't understand anything," Gwyneth said. "I didn't finish college. I didn't go to business school. I didn't go up through a corporate environment."

"I used to google the acronyms under the table, and I was like, *Everyone's gonna think I'm an idiot,*" she added. "And then I was like, *Fuck it. I'm actually really smart. I just haven't learned this yet.*"

GWYNETH TOPPED *STAR* magazine's list of the most hated celebrities in April 2013, eight spots above Anne Hathaway, whose unpopularity spawned its own epithet ("Hathahate"), and nineteen above Chris Brown, who had been arrested for beating up his girlfriend, Rihanna. "I remember being like: Really? More than, like, Chris Brown? Me? Really? Wow," Gwyneth said. Around the same time, *People* put her on its cover as the "World's Most Beautiful Woman!"

Was she the most hated celebrity—or the most beautiful—or the most hated because she was beautiful? It didn't matter, really. The press only helped draw attention to Goop. Regarding the *People* cover, she told Jay Leno, "I'm forty, I have two kids and that's pretty fucking awesome."

The *People* issue was timed to the release of *Iron Man 3*. With the Marvel Cinematic Universe in full swing (following *Iron Man*, *The Incredible Hulk*, *Thor*, and *Avengers* movies had all come out and been box office hits), the reviews hardly mattered. *The New York Times* described it as: "Stuff blows up, and then more stuff blows up, because that's what happens when diversions like this hit movie screens around this time of year: chaos reigns, and then some guy cleans it up." *Iron Man 3* made the second-biggest box office debut in U.S. history, with $175.3 million in ticket sales its first weekend (behind *The Avengers*).

The Monday after *Iron Man 3* was released, Gwyneth stopped by the Met Gala, Anna Wintour's annual fundraiser for the Metropolitan Museum of Art's Costume Institute and one of the most coveted fashion-world invitations of the year. Gwyneth arrived separately from Chris Martin, as she usually did. Afterward she said, "I'm never going again. It was so un-fun. It was boiling. It was too crowded. I did not enjoy it at all," remarks regarded as blasphemous given that stars generally feared and kowtowed to Wintour.

But Gwyneth had something else going on that she was trying to conceal in the press.

She and Martin were over.

. . .

VANITY FAIR EDITOR in chief Graydon Carter had seen the news about Gwyneth being the "most hated" in *Star* and the "most beautiful" in *People*, and he wanted a cover story on Gwyneth for the September style issue. September was the biggest issue of the year for glossy magazines, and Gwyneth—who had appeared on the *Vanity Fair* cover five times already—reliably sold copies. The magazine assigned the story to then–contributing editor Vanessa Grigoriadis, who had written the cover story on Gwyneth for *Talk* magazine pegged to *Shallow Hal*. Grigoriadis didn't usually do the cover profiles, which tended to be fluff pieces. She preferred to focus on more zeitgeisty features, but her editor told her that Carter had asked for her specifically. There was, however, a problem: Gwyneth wouldn't participate.

Gwyneth was tired from promoting *Iron Man 3*, Grigoriadis learned. Her editor suggested that she approach it like an essay, asking if Gwyneth was someone to love or hate—and finally concluding that she was someone to love. Grigoriadis was being asked to produce a seven-thousand-word profile without Gwyneth—what was the story if Gwyneth's friends wouldn't talk to her? "Shouldn't I call her rep?" Grigoriadis said, thinking Stephen Huvane would at least give her a list of people to interview.

"Go ahead, knock yourself out," her editor told her.

Grigoriadis called Huvane. He was not pleased.

"Well, who would photograph her?" he asked.

"I don't know," said Grigoriadis, who had no say about photos.

Huvane sounded outraged. "*Vanity Fair,*" he said. "This is why nobody wants to work with you guys anymore, because you guys are sneaky, sneaky, sneaky, sneaky, sneaky. And nobody wants to work with people who are sneaky, sneaky, sneaky, sneaky, sneaky." According to someone close to Gwyneth, she feared that the magazine was reporting on a rumored affair she'd allegedly had with wealthy hotelier Jeffrey Soffer—which had never happened. Huvane clearly didn't want Grigoriadis calling sources without Gwyneth agreeing to participate.

Grigoriadis protested. She was being the opposite of sneaky by calling him and telling him about the story. "Can you help me?"

"Absolutely not, we are not participating," Huvane said. "I know exactly the piece you're going to write. It's going to be: Gwyneth, love her, hate her, and then you're going to say, hate her."

She went back to her editor, who responded, "We told you not to call."

But she had to get to work, so she phoned a handful of people who she thought could share some stories about Gwyneth. One of them was Spence alum and *Odd Mom Out* creator Jill Kargman, who was initially forthcoming but then said, "Let me just call Gwyneth and see if it's okay for me to share this story."

Grigoriadis knew that Gwyneth would find out the story was proceeding anyway, so she told Kargman to go ahead, said someone familiar with their discussion. Besides, Gwyneth had said repeatedly that she didn't care what people said or thought about her.

A few minutes later, Kargman called back. "She said don't talk to you," she told Grigoriadis. "She just emailed everybody in her address book"—including friends like Cameron Diaz—"saying, 'Don't talk to her.'" The email, which leaked to the press, read, "*Vanity Fair* is threatening to put me on the cover of their magazine . . . If you are asked for quotes or comments, please decline. Also, I recommend you all never do this magazine again."

Everyone at *Vanity Fair* was mystified. The magazine had always been generous in its coverage of Gwyneth. But Gwyneth was very attuned to her public image, and some of the magazine staff later figured she might have been trying to control the story of her separation from Martin. Whatever it was, her reaction to the story was a rare example of her behavior—the flawed and vengeful kind that glossy magazine profiles tended to conceal—leaking to the press.

The Gwyneth versus *Vanity Fair* saga played out in the media over the course of months. Yet Grigoriadis still had no idea that Gwyneth was getting divorced; she turned in her story at the end of the summer, as planned. Carter sat on it, waiting for people to forget about the conflict (the magazine had received letters from readers who believed that *Vanity Fair* was afraid of publishing a Gwyneth takedown and threatened to cancel subscriptions if it didn't run). *Vanity Fair* finally published it in March 2014. A takedown it was not. In it, Grigoriadis concluded that the hatred toward Gwyneth got stirred up mainly when she started talking to an audience directly, and that it "show[ed] more than anything [that] she still needs a mediator to make her palatable."

IN RETROSPECT, GOOP emerged clearly around this time as a template for the celebrity brands that would flood the marketplace in the next decade. By late 2013, Jessica Alba's Honest Company was in full swing. *The Hills* star Lauren Conrad, *Pretty Little Liars* star Shay Mitchell, and *New Girl* star Zooey Deschanel all had launched lifestyle websites that shared things like fashion advice, recipes, and craft projects. *The New York Times* noted that Goop had "spawned a group of imitators: midlevel actresses and entertainers who want to grow their brand and become lifestyle gurus, just like Ms. Paltrow." Blake Lively was planning to launch a site of her own, which she said would be "about living a very one-of-a-kind, curated life and how to achieve that"—words that could just as well have come from Gwyneth herself. But most of those websites didn't last: Lively's site, Preserve, would launch in 2014 only to be shut down a little over a year later, after being plagued by accusations of racism for one fashion spread titled "Allure of Antebellum." Deschanel's HelloGiggles was the exception—she sold it to Time Inc. in 2015 for around $30 million. Celebrity product lines seemed to have more of a chance if they had a mass price point, like Reese Witherspoon's Draper James, which sold day dresses for under two hundred dollars. Mary-Kate and Ashley Olsen were quietly growing their high-end clothing brand the Row, but their success selling thousand-dollar sweaters was the exception.

Asked about the Goop copycats, Gwyneth took a broad interpretation. "I feel there's something slightly misogynistic" about pointing it out, she told *Time*, claiming that men weren't subjected to the same coverage.

WHEN GWYNETH MOVED to Los Angeles, so did Goop. She was uncoupling from her husband; Goop was uncoupling from London.

By 2013, Gwyneth had relocated Goop's operations to the pool house on her Mandeville Canyon property, which her staff referred to as "the barn." The fifteen employees who started their Goop careers in that three-hundred-square-foot space would be known internally as "barn people." The Goop team in London assisted with the transition, even though it meant they would be out of work. Bishop stated publicly that he had decided to stay in London rather than make the move. However, according to two people familiar with the situation, he tried hard to go to Los Angeles. Though Gwyneth no longer wanted him as CEO, it's unclear precisely why.

The transition to L.A. meant giving Goop a facelift. Gwyneth seemed unsure of what to do with it. Elise Loehnen, a veteran ghostwriter who had worked as deputy editor at Condé Nast's *Lucky* shopping magazine, had helped Tracy Anderson open a fitness studio in Los Angeles and had worked with her on a book. Anderson connected her to Gwyneth. Loehnen met with Gwyneth in L.A. around the fall of 2013 to offer some thoughts about possible next steps in growing Goop. Though the whole operation needed to be professionalized, Goop had clear potential. Gwyneth was having early success where legacy media was struggling: the newsletter email list was big (it would hit roughly 700,000 the following year) and the percentage of people who opened each newsletter (open rate) was high. By February 2014, Loehnen had joined as a part-time editorial lead, working out of the barn.

Within her first month, Loehnen had drafted what would become the most famous headline in the company's history for a story announcing Gwyneth's separation from Martin. Gwyneth and Martin had worked on the story together, and Gwyneth approved the piece with the headline, as she did all Goop content, and on March 25, 2014, Loehnen listened through the phone for her boss to tell her to hit send on a deeply personal story. On the other end, Gwyneth was trembling.

"We have been working hard for well over a year, some of it together, some of it separated, to see what might have been possible between us, and we have come to the conclusion that while we love each other very much we will remain separate. We are, however, and always will be a family, and in many ways, we are closer than we have ever been. We are parents first and foremost, to two incredibly wonderful children and we ask for their and our space and privacy to be respected at this difficult time. We have always conducted our relationship privately, and we hope that as we consciously uncouple and co-parent, we will be able to continue in the same manner." It ended "Love, Gwyneth & Chris." The story was headlined "Conscious Uncoupling."

Gwyneth said she saw her divorce as a failure. Her parents had stayed married in an industry where many couples got divorced. Her childhood friends had married the college boyfriends they'd met when she was dating Brad Pitt. While she privately struggled to generate optimism about the separation, she found a way to do it publicly, to turn this painful, confusing failure into a project that might inspire and illuminate—and maybe boost the brand.

Gwyneth had heard about conscious uncoupling from Sadeghi; he seemed to have heard of it from marriage and family therapist Katherine Woodward Thomas, who had coined the term in a 2004 book and was teaching a five-week online course on it. Gwyneth liked the idea that even if she and Martin were no longer a couple, they could remain a family.

"It was very challenging for me," she said later, "in terms of having to reassess what that said to me about me, these ideas that I had about that kind of failure and how, you know, I could process through it and, ultimately, really embed myself with myself. And my real self couldn't be married." Explaining the breakup the following year, she added, "There was nothing dramatic or anything. I had built my life on trying to be all things to all people, and I just couldn't do it anymore, and I really had the sense that I wasn't allowed to have needs, and I had to prove my specialness or self-worth by doing all this stuff and taking care of everybody else, and I just sort of hit a wall." Gwyneth recalled that something had clicked for her after her fortieth birthday. "When I turned forty, I felt like I got this free software upgrade that I wasn't expecting. It just happened," she told *InStyle*. "Suddenly I was like, 'Oh, this is fantastic: I don't care! I like myself, and I'm just going to live my life. I'm going to stop worrying and tearing myself down.'" While she'd repeatedly said this before, her actions—trying to shut down the *Vanity Fair* story, going on television to refute that her book was ghostwritten, even worrying about Alison Cayne at the Spence reunion—told a different story. She cared about what *certain* people thought, according to old friends. But she also liked control, particularly when it came to telling her story.

She also said that she stopped worrying about being alone, about disappointing people: "I chose myself."

While some of Gwyneth's old friends were shocked by her divorce, she told them she was fine, that they had separated a year earlier, and that she had come to terms with it.

Martin was a little more candid: "[I]t was a very difficult period for about a year or so of feeling completely worthless and nothing to anybody." He had approved the newsletter and had been with Gwyneth when it went out, describing himself as "a mess." After announcing their separation, Martin uncoupled himself to a house across the street.

Those two words, *conscious uncoupling*, drew a fresh round of coverage for Goop and a new level of indignation. "Tonight on *Nightline*: It seemed like a perfect romance which became a perfect marriage. Now Gwyneth Paltrow's trying to have herself the perfect divorce?" intoned ABC News anchor Dan Abrams.

"The Goop has hit the fan," said the *Philadelphia Daily News.* CNN quoted a Twitter user: "Gwyneth Paltrow and Chris Martin are getting divorced, citing 'insufferable similarities.'" Anne Perkins wrote in *The Guardian,* "The suspicion that there is a way of being from which ordinary people are excluded, by their sheer, well, ordinariness, is now confirmed by the revelation of Gwyneth Paltrow and Chris Martin's divorce, or rather their 'conscious uncoupling,' which turns out to be a holistic form of splitting up."

In the explainer companion story Goop published alongside the announcement, Habib Sadeghi and his wife, dentist Sherry Sami, expanded on the concept (though they didn't cite Woodward Thomas). "For our purposes, conscious uncoupling is the ability to understand that every irritation and argument within a relationship was a signal to look inside ourselves and identify a negative internal object that needed healing." In her *Guardian* story, Perkins called it "the most deluded 2,000 words of tosh ever to be associated with sentient adults," and Sadeghi and Sherry, "snake oil salesmen of the soul." Gwyneth's friends and former employees contended she was unfairly attacked over conscious uncoupling—that all she was doing was getting divorced and taking great effort to not have her kids negatively impacted. "Any child whose parents were kinder to one another as a result of that can be very grateful to Gwyneth for being an example of it," said Richard Lovett.

Goop.com received so much traffic, the site crashed.

ASKED ABOUT THE vitriol a few years later, Gwyneth managed once again to sound both reflective and naive. "What I didn't understand at the time was, I think there's a message in that, which is, 'If you don't do it this way, you're hurting your kids.' I think people take that as: 'She thinks she is better than me.'"

But that awareness rarely caused her to refrain from comment. That same year, Gwyneth talked to E! about taking the rest of 2014 off to spend more time with her kids. "It's much harder for me. I feel like I set it up in a way that makes it difficult because ... for me, like if I miss a school run, they are like, 'Where were you?'" she said. "I think it's different when you have an office job, because it's routine and, you know, you can do all the stuff in the morning and then you come home in the evening. When you're shooting a movie, they're like, 'We need you to go to Wisconsin for two weeks,' and then you work fourteen hours a day, and that part of it is very difficult. I think to have a regular job and be a mom is not as, of course there are challenges, but it's not like being on set."

The headlines wrote themselves. "Gwyneth Paltrow: Moms Who Work 9-to-5 Have It Easier," *USA Today* published. The *Today* show ran a segment in which reporter Kristen Dahlgren noted that Gwyneth was "taking some heat," adding, "Well, it's nothing new for Gwyneth Paltrow to be called out of touch with the common folk."

The *New York Post* published an open letter from one of its writers: "As a mother of a toddler, I couldn't agree more! 'Thank God I don't make millions filming one movie per year' is what I say to myself pretty much every morning as I wait on a windy Metro-North platform, about to begin my 45-minute commute into the city. Whenever things get rough, all I have to do is keep reminding myself of that fact. It is my mantra."

Gwyneth surveyed the coverage and decided to seek higher ground, from which she wrote a piece for Goop called "Ending the Mommy Wars," shifting the issue from an indictment of her entitlement to a call for peace among long-suffering women. "As the mommy wars rage on, I am constantly perplexed and amazed by how little slack we cut each other as women," she wrote. "Is it not hard enough to attempt to raise children thoughtfully, while contributing something, or bringing home some (or more) of the bacon? Why do we feel so entitled to opine, often so negatively, on the choices of other women?"

Appearing at the Re/Code conference in May of that year, Gwyneth almost seemed to be parodying herself. Asked how she handled mean online comments, she remarked, "You come across [comments] about yourself and about your friends, and it's a very dehumanizing thing. It's almost like how, in war, you go through this bloody, dehumanizing thing, and then something is defined out of it."

CNN.com just went with the headline "Gwyneth Paltrow Makes People Mad—Again."

UTAH'S AMANGIRI IS considered one of the world's most exclusive and stunning resorts, its signature understated luxury making it a natural fit for inclusion in Goop's travel guides (the cheap rooms cost around $4,000 per night). Built among the rock formations in the desert canyons, Gwyneth traveled there with *Glee* producer Brad Falchuk in July 2014, around four months after her conscious uncoupling announcement. The pair were seen having dinner together and sunbathing by the pool that swooped around a craggy rock.

Gwyneth had appeared in three episodes of the second season of *Glee* in 2011, which won her an Emmy for Outstanding Guest Actress in a Comedy Series. Though there was speculation that Gwyneth and Falchuk's romance began before Gwyneth and Martin consciously uncoupled, no one interviewed for this book said Falchuk caused the breakup. The two had a lot in common: They both loved traveling and fine dining and were compatible in a way that friends hadn't seen with Martin.

Early in Gwyneth's new relationship, Martin was around much more than Falchuk was. He would give the kids guitar lessons at the house, and Gwyneth would invite his parents over. As far as people could tell, she was really committed to consciously uncoupling. But they could also see that Martin, who got together with Jennifer Lawrence for two brief periods beginning around the time Gwyneth took up with Falchuk, was so absorbed with his music that he seemed unable to pay attention to much else.

GOOP'S RESPONSE TO controversy mirrored Gwyneth's own coping strategies—spiritual bypass writ large. Instead of ignoring conflict, anger, or criticism, the approach was to turn toward it, smile graciously, and pivot toward some nugget of personal growth. Goop had every reason to lean further into "woo." Articles about wacky stuff Goop was publishing seemed to drive so much traffic that the media couldn't resist publishing them. They pounced again when Gwyneth wrote about Masaru Emoto, author of books like *The Hidden Messages in Water*, who claimed that water reacted to positive and negative thoughts and words: "I am fascinated by the growing science behind the energy of consciousness and its effects on matter. I have long had Dr. Emoto's coffee table book on how negativity changes the structure of water, how the molecules behave differently depending on the words or music being expressed around it."

Shortly after this missive, Gwyneth pulled back from first-person introductions to Goop's newsletters in an effort to free the brand from her name and image and allow it to stand on its own. She told interviewers, "My dream is that one day no one would remember that I have anything to do with it." And while that may have been a sound strategy, the media still tied Gwyneth personally to some of its more fringe ideas. A July 2014 newsletter about Kelly Dorfman's book *Cure Your Child with Food* stated, "Chronic ear infections? There's a good chance it's dairy." The *Daily Mail* picked up the issue, writing, "It's Gwyneth Paltrow's latest far-out diet advice for optimum health—this time aimed at your children." Gwyneth's byline hadn't appeared on the article, but by now, non-scientifically backed ideas about health had become part of her personal brand.

WITH BISHOP OUT, Goop needed a new CEO. "I just didn't know what the fuck I was doing, and so I thought I just needed to outsource everything, and I thought I needed a grown-up around me to, you know, tell me what to do," Gwyneth said.

Lisa Gersh came to Goop from Martha Stewart by way of Tracy Anderson. As CEO and president of Martha Stewart Living Omnimedia, Gersh started to see the potential in using content to help sell product. Martha Stewart had a magazine that told readers what to buy, but the editorial team was reticent to recommend Stewart's own lines. Besides, those lines were licensed, so they would have had to buy them in order to sell them. Gersh felt like the company was leaving money on the table. Her ideal "contextual commerce" business included three pillars: content, monetized through advertising; proprietary product lines; and a wholesale business to sell items the company didn't make itself.

In Goop, Gersh saw an opportunity to build just that sort of business. She would be charged with expanding the staff, adding advertising, experimenting with brick-and-mortar pop-up shops, and figuring out how to launch proprietary product lines. Wellness was an obvious potential revenue stream for Goop, since it could be a high-margin business, and Gwyneth had become associated with health fads.

Goop had been partnering with brands, but not monetizing these partnerships to the full extent Gersh believed possible. As part of a partnership with J.Crew, for instance, Gwyneth modeled eight outfits from the fall collection in the newsletter, a photo shoot she would have been paid for personally. In the images, Gwyneth wore chinos with a jacket and cashmere sweater and skinny jeans with a silk printed blouse. A healthy 8 percent of the J.Crew website's total traffic the day it went out came from Goop. Brands and retailers struggled to lure consumers to their websites to shop. But Goop, thanks to its editorial content, didn't have that problem. People were constantly going to Goop.com because the newsletter had directed them there or because Gwyneth had published something that had been covered in the media. And when people visited the site to read an article, they might buy something.

The newsletter had nearly one million subscribers by the summer of 2015, Goop told *Fast Company*, a high open rate of around 40 percent, and an estimated 3.75 million page views per month, according to analytics firm Alexa. Goop was on the vanguard of affiliate marketing (where an influencer or publication receives a cut of sales of products they recommend) and, with Gwyneth as its face, online influencing in general. Gwyneth was one of the first entertainers to both embrace this status and use it to build a brand. Gersh had been attracted to Goop, someone familiar with her thinking said, because it wasn't called "Gwyneth Paltrow," but it was still all about Gwyneth. This was a strength—love her or hate her, people wanted to know what Gwyneth thought—but also a weakness. Gwyneth, like many founders, wanted control.

GERSH WOULD WORK out of a New York WeWork (Gwyneth's cousin Rebekah had married company founder Adam Neumann), but Gwyneth needed help with day-to-day management in L.A. The staff at that time was, in Loehnen's words, "reporting to no one."

Gersh's main project, however, was raising Series A funding. Goop needed to hire staff: writers, editors, buyers, ad salespeople. So far, Goop had run off Gwyneth's money and that of one other investor (the investing website PitchBook listed this seed funding as $3.5 million). Gwyneth didn't spend much time on the fundraising, which was as challenging a process for Goop as it was for other companies.

Many venture capitalists passed for the same reason that Hearst, the publisher of magazines such as *Elle* and *Cosmopolitan*, gave Gersh: "We just won't invest in a commerce business that takes on inventory." Plus, investors were looking for unicorn businesses (which achieved a valuation of at least $1 billion). Gersh thought Goop could be a great business that would make money—maybe it would be a $1 billion business—but she didn't think it would be a $10 billion business. That said, Goop had two things going for it: a unique idea in a commerce business supported by content, and Gwyneth.

Around the time Gwyneth moved back to Los Angeles, venture capitalists began looking to invest more money in companies founded by women, and she was a prime candidate. "I think there was an advantage to being a celebrity," said Anarghya Vardhana, a health-care-focused venture capitalist at Maveron, which did not invest in Goop. "That was before the proliferation of influencers, who are now mini-celebrities. They all want to have a company."

Gwyneth could be incredibly clever and charming in important meetings, but she remembered fundraising as "scary. I have a very weird thing as an entertainer because I come to it as a famous lady," she said. "So I would walk in and think I was prepared, especially in the early days, and have my [investor] deck and for the first ninety seconds of the meeting I was Gwyneth Paltrow and they would take a selfie for their wife. Then all of a sudden it was like I was dropped on the floor. I was drop-kicked into this other realm and just being grilled and [there were] really hard questions and it was like, 'Oh, my God.' It was an incredible lesson, especially when I think about that Series A and how hard it was to raise the money." That said, in her previous career as a movie star, her coworkers sought to remove all obstacles and problems from her existence and make her feel like a goddess so that she delivered the best possible performance. As a founder, the nature of work had to change. She had to confront problems and be able to fix them.

Gersh took first meetings with potential investors, who sometimes very much wanted to meet Gwyneth—but Gersh wouldn't bring her in unless they seemed serious about writing a check. She would tell Gwyneth what she wanted her to say, and, Oscar-winning actress that she was, she'd memorize the five or so points and deliver them perfectly.

As Goop professionalized, Gwyneth's lifestyle-brand rival took notice.

Martha Stewart told Bloomberg TV in 2013, "I haven't eaten at Gwyneth's house, and I've never seen how she lives. But if she is authentic, all the better. I mean, I certainly hope she is . . . She's a charming, pretty person who has a feeling for lifestyle. She wants to be a lifestyle arbiter. Fine. Good. I think I started this whole category of lifestyle."

Within a year, Stewart's tone changed. "She just needs to be quiet. She's a movie star. If she were confident in her acting, she wouldn't be trying to be Martha Stewart." After hiring Gersh in October 2014, Gwyneth responded, "If I'm really honest, I'm so psyched that she sees us as competition. I'm so psyched. I really am. At this point in my life I don't take it personally, I see it as a projection."

Of course, Stewart's bristly acknowledgment only lifted Goop. Leading up to Thanksgiving in 2014, *Martha Stewart Living* ran a story about pie fillings and titled it "Conscious Coupling." "Every Thanksgiving table should be blessed with the presence of a long-married pair who bring out the best in each other, are completely enamored despite their differences, and leave every other guest thinking, I'll have what they're having."

Gwyneth had been working with a Hollywood publicist, Stephen Huvane, but Goop needed a different approach. His strategy seemed to be to say "no" to most all press requests, but Goop needed to raise money, launch products, and mold Gwyneth's public image as a businessperson instead of a Hollywood icon. So Gersh and Gwyneth brought in crisis public relations specialist Matthew Hiltzik as a publicist for the business. Hiltzik wanted the public to see a new side to Gwyneth—more of her ability to laugh about herself and Goop, someone who was in on the joke. These efforts were more successful than her previous attempts to show the less serious side of herself via *Shallow Hal.* Gwyneth responded to Stewart's troll with a troll of her own on Goop.com: a recipe for "jailbird cake" (Stewart had spent five months in jail for charges relating to insider trading)—a classic icebox cake with white whipped cream and dark chocolate wafers making stripes. Hiltzik also encouraged her to go on Howard Stern in early 2015, where Gwyneth admitted, "I avoided you for twenty years . . . I was scared of you."

The negative media attention was rising in proportion to Goop's reach. And Goop's particular excesses had generated some bona fide professional parodies. Goop's staff tuned in sometimes to a podcast called *Poog,* where comedians Kate Berlant and Jacqueline Novak discussed overwrought wellness trends. And journalist Gabrielle Moss released a book called *Glop: Nontoxic, Expensive Ideas That Will Make You Look Ridiculous and Feel Pretentious.*

All the attention only helped position Goop for its next phase, funded by a major infusion of outside cash.

CHAPTER 23

Steaming and Strategizing

I have always felt the harm of Gwyneth Paltrow is legitimizing conspiracy theories.

—Dr. Jen Gunter

By the summer of 2015, Goop employed around two dozen staff and was in the final stages of closing Series A funding. The staff was divided between the New York WeWork and Gwyneth's L.A. barn. Gersh oversaw New York and led a business team there, and Loehnen ran editorial in L.A.

Leadership meetings often took place in Gwyneth's Brentwood home. Loehnen, Gersh, and others assembled in the living room, shoeless (or with their shoes slipped inside elastic covers provided by the house manager). Gwyneth weighed in on most content decisions, raised money, and met face-to-face with staff. (She'd message them during the day and on weekends, expecting a prompt response. If she didn't get one, the next message would be "Where are you?") While Gersh would periodically insert herself, Gwyneth didn't seem all that interested in her advice.

To Gwyneth's credit, she quickly picked up certain aspects of business leadership, the same way she'd quickly picked up the harpsichord and archery for her nineties film roles. She learned the company's financials and understood, for instance, Goop's needs for a new technology build-out. But entrepreneurship exposed her to problems that the pampered confines of Hollywood stardom were designed to shield. Gersh used to tell her, "Business is a series of mistakes that need to be fixed; you're not going to get everything right." But to Gwyneth, mistakes felt insurmountable. In acting, she either filmed her scene right or she didn't. At Goop, she was quite hard on herself if something went wrong.

During leadership team meetings, Gwyneth sometimes brought in one of her gurus to hold a self-improvement workshop. At one such meeting, a facilitator asked the executives to take turns saying one thing they believed to be true about themselves but wasn't true of anybody else in the room. When it was Gwyneth's turn, she said with a smile, "I won an Oscar."

Her team's reaction amounted to a playful "Gwyneth, fuck off."

Gwyneth wasn't doing much acting during this period. One executive got the sense that she would have liked to do more, but she was in her forties now, and Hollywood didn't have many parts for her. *Mortdecai* came out in early 2015 to some of the worst reviews of Gwyneth's career, despite the talented ensemble cast, which included Ewan McGregor, Jeff Goldblum, and Johnny Depp in the lead role. It's unclear why she took it, but maybe it didn't seem like a bad idea to costar with Depp. The movie received a 12 percent on Rotten Tomatoes, and Gwyneth was nominated for a Razzie (the Golden Raspberry Award honoring the worst cinematic failures) for Worst Actress, but she lost out to Dakota Johnson for *Fifty Shades of Grey*.

People who knew Gwyneth well didn't understand why she accepted parts in so many movies that ended up flopping. When a friend asked her why she wanted to take a part after reading a script that didn't seem very good, Gwyneth said she thought the character was interesting. Or maybe she wanted to do movie after movie not just for money but also to stay in the public eye. One person who worked closely with her got the sense that she didn't know who she was if she wasn't written about.

.   .   .

LIFE IN THE Goop office followed certain protocols. While most employees called her "GP," those who pronounced "Gwyneth" wrong (Gwyneth made clear to new staff that her name was pronounced "Gwyn" like "pin" instead of "Gwen" like "pen") would get corrected and chastised by colleagues. When it came to lunch, the team would get their own wraps from Kye's or salads from La Scala. Thea Baumann, Goop's food editor who wrote recipes for the site, would also make Gwyneth's lunch. This was not a typical responsibility for a food editor, and Baumann, who had enough work as it was, came to seriously resent the arrangement, said someone familiar with her thinking.

The new editors Goop hired as it grew were pleased to find that the company didn't worry too much during this period about generating clickbait; they had enough sponsors, ranging from Fossil to Prada, who wanted to work with Goop because of Gwyneth and the wealthy audience she attracted. Gwyneth declined sponsorships that didn't suit her taste. ("There's not a pair of shoes I'd wear here," she said of one well-known mass-market shoe brand.) Though this limited the brands Goop could work with, that was okay, since, after all, Goop was in the business of curation.

Gwyneth was committed to covering products and experiences that translated her own tastes for her audience—however bizarre or inaccessible they might be. The Tikkun spa in Santa Monica, for example, was featured in early 2015 in Goop's Santa Monica city guide and the annual detox newsletter, with a focus on its vaginal steaming treatment: "You sit on what is essentially a mini-throne, and a combination of infrared and mugwort steam cleanses your uterus, et al. It is an energetic release—not just a steam douche—that balances female hormone levels. If you're in L.A., you have to do it."

The piece ran with "Goop" and a tiny image of Gwyneth's face as the byline. Though she hadn't written it, she had gotten the treatment with Gersh and had suggested Loehnen try it. Loehnen wrote up the spa for the site, and Gwyneth approved the story. It went up quietly at first—then *Fast Company* picked it up and the internet swarmed Gwyneth for, as the *Daily Mail* put it, "wax[ing] lyrical about steam-cleaning her private parts." The spa's owner Niki Schwarz recalled Gwyneth coming in to do the steam with celebrity friends, and telling her that the treatment "changed her life." Around the time Gwyneth promoted the steam in Goop, bookings for it doubled for at least six months.

Gwyneth later claimed she'd expected covering the steam to "cause a stir," but Goop staffers rarely knew in advance which stories or recommendations would attract outsize attention. While a few members of the media rushed to try the treatment for stories, others turned to medical experts. Ob-gyn Jen Gunter wrote about it on her blog, advising readers not to try it because it "is likely not beneficial and is potentially harmful," adding, "Ms. Paltrow and the people who push V-steams also need a little anatomy lesson because unless that steam is under high pressure (like with ejaculation) it's not getting from the vagina into the uterus." In 2019, the *Journal of Obstetrics and Gynaecology Canada* wrote up the case of a sixty-two-year-old woman who sustained second-degree burns after being advised to try vaginal steaming at home in an attempt to treat vaginal prolapse.

FEW GOOP CRITICS attracted more attention than Jen Gunter, who grew up in Winnipeg, Canada. When she entered medical school, Canada's restrictive abortion law was overturned, but the procedure remained stigmatized. She decided to go into women's health and studied abortion during her residency, believing that women should not be ashamed of their bodies and should be able to access the best possible care. Her passion for her work stemmed from, she said, "equality, because half the population isn't allowed to control their bodily function."

She later moved to the United States, where she noticed celebrities spreading health misinformation, the nascent internet serving as an accelerant. By the early 2000s, Suzanne Somers was advocating women take "bioidentical hormones" that weren't FDA-approved and other alternative treatments for breast cancer, including rejecting chemotherapy. There was also the anti-vaccine movement, boosted after Andrew Wakefield, a British anti-vaccine activist, published a study in 1998 showing a false link between vaccines and autism. Anti-vaxxer Jenny McCarthy went on *Oprah* in 2007 to blame her son's autism on vaccines and to tell parents to do their own research, infamously stating, "The University of Google is where I got my degree from."

To counter this type of misinformation, Gunter started a blog where she could share sound medical advice for her patients and anyone else who might be interested. She decided to examine Goop's claims about vaginal steaming after someone sent her a link. *The Huffington Post* interviewed her about it as a result of her blog post. People continued to send her Goop articles, so Gunter started occasionally checking Goop herself. Some of Goop's stories went so viral that she felt like she had no choice but to respond as a doctor and women's health advocate. Yet while her Goop criticism was widely read, Gunter said it accounted for less than 5 percent of her published content.

Gwyneth's advice to her staff in moments of controversy was always the same: Goop was starting interesting discussions, not offering the final word. And the team often felt as protective as Gwyneth did. Was it really that big a deal to write up a spa that offered vaginal steaming? They weren't the first outlet to publicize products and treatments of questionable value.

Plus, neither Gwyneth nor Goop's board nor its investors were concerned about these controversies. "This is what drove her to do the business. She thought, *I'm going to research things, recommend things, and if you want to go traditional, go see your GP. That's not what I'm going to do. I'm not going to tell you to get a checkup*," said a former executive. They viewed the audience as opting into Goop to hear what Gwyneth had to say, and if they wanted to hear traditional medical advice, they could go elsewhere. When *Fast Company* asked her about the vaginal steaming,

Loehnen said, "It feels good, it's not harmful—it's not like we're urging people to go out and buy AK-47s."

IN APRIL 2015, as part of a campaign to raise awareness and money for the Food Bank for New York City, Gwyneth's friend and former cohost Mario Batali asked her to live on twenty-nine dollars' worth of food for a week. "This is what $29 gets you at the grocery store," she tweeted on April 9, 2015, "what families on SNAP (i.e. food stamps) have to live on for a week." She selected a bunch of kale, a head of romaine lettuce, cilantro, a dozen eggs, an avocado, an ear of corn, a sweet potato, seven limes, a bag of brown rice, a bag of black beans, an onion, a tomato, a head of garlic, a jalapeño, and a pack of eighteen corn tortillas. Social media users were ruthless. "Yes poor people, Gwyneth Paltrow and her $280M net worth TOTALLY understands your plight to feed your family," tweeted one. "Gwyneth Paltrow will do the food stamp challenge for herself, but try feeding children that for a week. It's not that easy," posted another.

Gwyneth later wrote on Goop that she "only made it through about four days, when I personally broke and had some chicken and fresh vegetables (and in full transparency, half a bag of black licorice). My perspective has been forever altered by how difficult it was to eat wholesome, nutritious food on that budget, even for just a few days—a challenge that 47 million Americans face every day, week, and year." She included three "budget-conscious recipes" she had made, including black bean taquitos, black bean cakes with grilled corn salsa, and a brown rice, kale, and roasted sweet potato sauté with poached eggs.

GWYNETH AND FALCHUK had been careful about being seen together in public. That changed on the evening of Saturday, April 4, when they attended Robert Downey Jr.'s fiftieth birthday party in Santa Monica at the Barker Hangar, an airplane hangar turned venue, where paparazzi photographed them together as a couple for the first time. Wearing a suit and sneakers with no tie, Falchuk stepped out of a white Range Rover and placed his hand on Gwyneth's lower back, bare in her backless black top, as she carried in a large gift wrapped in striped paper.

The next night, she and Falchuk went out to dinner at Chinois on Main Street in Santa Monica, where, over lobster with curry sauce and black cod, they laughed and smiled and held hands.

Before her divorce from Chris Martin was finalized in 2016, Gwyneth expounded on the creation of a blended family at the BlogHer conference in 2015. "I'm very, very lucky in that I have a partner who's willing to do it with me in a really collaborative way. And I'm really *for* Chris and he's really *for* me," she said. "Our values are very much around the importance of family and the importance of those relationships, and I'm lucky that we're aligned in that way, and it's been hard and we've gone through really difficult times with it. But we've always said these children are our priority . . . so what that really means is even though today you hate me and you never want to see me again, we're going to brunch because it's Sunday and that's what we do . . . it's definitely imperfect, but it gets easier with time."

Though Gwyneth really committed to consciously uncoupling for the sake of her kids, she admitted to coworkers how eager she'd been to purge one relic of her marriage.

"I definitely didn't want that mattress around," employees heard her say at the Goop office. "I had to get that energy out of the house. I had to change that mattress. Ew."

TONY FLORENCE, A high-profile tech investor and co-CEO of venture capital firm New Enterprise Associates, saw firsthand the power of Goop. A company he'd invested in received a big sales spike after a Goop mention. He arranged a meeting with Gwyneth. "It was the first time I had seen a founder articulate a really big vision to use content to drive commerce," Florence said. He ultimately decided to lead the Goop Series A round of funding of $10 million, which closed by early August 2015.

Investors wanted Gwyneth to grow the business, and pushed her to do so. But they were never that hard on her, and left her to decide how best to expand Goop—which might not have been the best approach. But part of the appeal of investing was getting a taste of Gwyneth's world: sitting in her house for quarterly board meetings, eating the food she served, and being privy to her charisma.

With the cash infusion, Gwyneth made two important decisions: one, Goop would move out of the barn and into a full-time office space that would accommodate even more staff. And two, she would pull back further from acting. She had been doing around one movie a year since she'd had kids, but now she had investors to worry about. Plus, she hated wasting the day away waiting to film her scenes.

After moving out of the barn, the offices shifted first to a WeWork and then to a Santa Monica suite in squat gray bungalows at 2950 Nebraska Street. Finding the space was challenging, owing to Gwyneth's security needs. She often got followed driving to work, and needed an office where she could pull in the back instead of the front. Parking was still a nightmare, but Gwyneth had her own space marked with a black-and-white sign: "Reserved for G-Spot."

The new office had a test kitchen, meeting spaces, and ample room for desks. Gwyneth convinced Restoration Hardware to provide furnishings at no charge in exchange for setting up a shoot of the office for *Architectural Digest*. The accompanying story advised readers how to get the look—a palette of grays, dark wood, light pink, and gold accents—for themselves, and included links to RH.com. The bulk of the office furniture was hauled out so that the photos featuring Restoration Hardware products looked upscale and uncluttered. Most of the staff in fact worked at cheap particle-board desks that didn't appear in the shoot.

The office was stocked with "healthy" snack food, including nuts, hummus and pita chips, guacamole, flat pretzels, sea-salt crackers, and organic string cheese. Goop boasted of its kombucha on tap, but the office also had a machine by Juicero, which made four-hundred-dollar Wi-Fi-connected juicers that turned packets of prechopped fruits and vegetables into juice. Having raised $118 million, it closed sixteen months after launching. CNET would later call it "the greatest example of Silicon Valley stupidity." One employee recalled that each staff member was allowed two packets per week, which they had to check out from the office manager. Goop staff noticed that the machine was unnecessary, since you could just squeeze whatever was in the packets and get juice without the device.

THE SPRING FOLLOWING Goop's Series A, Gwyneth's third cookbook—*It's All Easy: Delicious Weekday Recipes for the Super-Busy Home Cook*—was to be published under Goop's very own imprint, Goop Press. No longer working with Julia Turshen, Gwyneth had cowritten the book with Goop's food editor Thea Baumann.

Seizing on Goop's and Gwyneth's popularity and reach, Grand Central Publishing had offered Gwyneth her own imprint in 2013, after the major success of her second cookbook, *It's All Good.* The books would become another way for Gwyneth to spread alternative health ideas that were increasingly—in no doubt owing to her influence—finding acceptance in the mainstream.

"The major issue is that you're legitimizing this pseudoscience," said Andrea Love. "Because this person is a celebrity, it gives them the appearance of legitimacy because they have the ear of the media, the ear of people in power, and they're getting amplified solely because they have a platform and not because they have any actual credibility."

Grand Central had agreed to publish books under Goop Press by authors in any of the subject areas Goop covered: sex, beauty, wellness, food, style. Authors could join the imprint through Goop or Grand Central, but both parties had to agree on the project, and both would receive a portion of the profits.

Sales of *It's All Easy* were around 84,000 copies and would drop again with her fourth cookbook, *The Clean Plate: Eat, Reset, Heal,* which sold just shy of 70,000 copies. Unlike with her previous books, Grand Central—unlikely to earn back the large advance they'd paid Gwyneth for the book—fretted over the declining sales.

Goop Press ended up being another platform for un-fact-checked Goop "experts" like Habib Sadeghi. In October 2015, Sadeghi published a Goop article titled "Could There Possibly Be a Link Between Underwire Bras and Breast Cancer??" Included in a special Goop newsletter "in honor of breast cancer awareness month," the story gave credence to a widely debunked 1995 theory linking the two. Dr. Jen Gunter eviscerated Sadeghi's claims in a post on her blog: "There is no science to back up a bra and breast cancer connection, never mind that the mechanism is biologically implausible. The myth has been debunked so many times I have lost track," she wrote. "It's so ludicrous that it should be funny, except some women will read this and be scared." In an interview, Gunter said, "It's the lowest of the low to scare people who have cancer and make them believe they caused their cancer." She added, "I have always felt the harm of Gwyneth Paltrow is legitimizing conspiracy theories."

A handful of medical experts from across the country reached out to Goop to say that the bra story was false and that they had been hearing from worried patients who had read it. An editor listened to their concerns—but that didn't stop Goop Press from publishing Sadeghi's book, *The Clarity Cleanse: 12 Steps to Finding Renewed Energy, Spiritual Fulfillment, and Emotional Healing,* which advocated traditional restrictive eating, including a four-day "mono-diet" limited to apples, brown rice, and sardines.

One person who worked closely with Gwyneth around this time said the negative response to Goop's wellness stories never seemed to bother her: "I think if you're going to be bothered by backlash, you can't do what she did."

Timothy Caulfield noted that the wellness industry had effectively co-opted "science-y language." He explained that Gwyneth and her favored experts talked about things like the "microbiome" or "quantum physics" to legitimize their claims. "She wants to position it within the scientific space, because she knows that most people recognize that science is how we understand our world, but at the same time, tries to have the marketing benefit of alternative ways of knowing," he said. "It's an extremely common theme on Goop."

Sadeghi, meanwhile, landed a segment with Megyn Kelly on the *Today* show, where he was called a "spiritual adviser to stars such as Gwyneth Paltrow and Penélope Cruz." (His book included blurbs from Cruz, Anne Hathaway, Demi Moore, Jessica Chastain, Tobey Maguire, and Cruz's husband, Javier Bardem.) Though the staff at Grand Central rolled their eyes at the pseudoscience, Sadeghi's book was one of the bestselling Goop Press titles, though only moderately successful by publishing standards, with just over 33,000 copies sold.

While Grand Central rejected some of Goop's author suggestions who were even more fringe than Sadeghi, Goop used the imprint to publish branded books like *Goop Clean Beauty* and *The Sex Issue: Everything You've Always Wanted to Know About Sexuality, Seduction, and Desire*, of which they sold 23,000 and fewer than 5,000, respectively. The collaboration eventually fizzled, and Goop Press migrated to publisher Rodale in 2021, but sales remained about the same.

While the imprint was unlikely to have been profitable for the publishers, Gwyneth had managed to enhance the halo of legitimacy around her favored gurus—no matter how dangerous or inaccurate their ideas—by turning them into published authors.

GWYNETH WAS ON a ski vacation at the Deer Valley resort in Park City, Utah, in February 2016 with Apple and Moses, then eleven and nine years old, and Brad Falchuk and his two children, when she experienced a collision with optometrist Terry Sanderson on the slope. Frightened, she got up and skied away. Sanderson claimed she'd callously fled the scene, but Gwyneth said she'd skied away out of fear after he ran into her back.

And Gwyneth had reason to be scared. Around two weeks before the accident, she was in a Los Angeles courtroom testifying in the trial of Dante Soiu, who had been accused of stalking her for the past seventeen years. Though Soiu had gone to a mental institution for several years after the 2000 trial, he'd been arrested again in 2015 for sending mail to her again.

During Gwyneth's two-and-a-half-hour testimony, she broke down in tears briefly when a prosecutor asked if she feared for her children's safety.

"I'm scared because the communications completely defy logic," she said. "I've been dealing with this for seventeen years with the communications from this man." The letters he wrote to her included discussion of her death and his intention to marry her. He sent pornography, clothes, earrings, and a WeightWatchers cookbook. Out of concern for Gwyneth's safety, Goop had a lockdown procedure in place in case somebody was stalking or threatening her.

Soiu pled not guilty to the new charges of felony stalking, saying on the witness stand that he "was very lonely" and "wanted to have a pen pal," and the jury acquitted him, concluding that he hadn't intended to scare Gwyneth, even if his behavior was abhorrent and frightening.

While the issues with Soiu receded into the background of her public life, Gwyneth's collision with Sanderson would become part of pop culture lore.

CHAPTER 24

Ridiculous but Awesome

There were times when people were very cruel about me and what I was trying to do. At a certain point, you think, *Gosh, this just can't be about me.*

—Gwyneth Paltrow

Gwyneth drew even more hatred in late 2015, when Goop launched a holiday gift guide called "Ridiculous but Awesome," a catchphrase that might well have announced the entire enterprise far better than "Nourish the Inner Aspect." The guide suggested a $90,000 trip to the edge of outer space and, for more budget-minded shoppers, a truffle slicer for $40 (though the white truffles themselves cost $175).

However over-the-top her taste, no one disputed that Gwyneth had an instinct for what Goop fans would buy. She approved every product in the Goop store, and her writers interviewed her about the recommendations so they could festoon the guide with her appreciations. She then oversaw multiple rounds of edits, and these, too, consistently impressed her staff—Gwyneth was as good an editor as some seasoned media professionals on her content team had encountered, in terms of product selection as well as copy.

The gift guides were such a big revenue driver that Goop eventually decided to stock and sell many items that would appear in them to maximize profits, rather than just linking out. Gwyneth used her friend group—as well as a larger network of wannabe friends—to get access to coveted brands. She obtained high-end products on consignment that other stores could not, like the Rolexes she got from Bob's Watches, owned by her friend Paul Altieri, allowing her to save money on holding high-end inventory. Goop's operations, like its gift guides, were often ridiculous—but, for the business, awesome.

GWYNETH MONITORED THE response to Goop's content for signs of what her readers would buy. For example, when a story about beauty products made without endocrine disrupters and formaldehyde brought a traffic spike in 2015, she had the idea for a "clean" beauty line. A mutual connection put Gwyneth in touch with Karen Behnke, founder of clean beauty brand Juice Beauty. Behnke went to meet with Gwyneth over cocktails in her Brentwood home, and they bonded over having mothers and daughters who loved skincare. They came up with a deal in which Behnke would invest seven figures in Goop, while Gwyneth would serve as a creative director and the face of a color cosmetics collection for Juice Beauty, which Behnke believed would bring valuable visibility to the line. Meanwhile, Juice Beauty would essentially allow Gwyneth to borrow the company's product development team to produce a Goop skin-care line faster than the company could create one on its own. Behnke was one of the first entrepreneurs to popularize "clean" beauty. But she and Gwyneth had different approaches when it came to branding and aesthetics—Gwyneth had a much more exacting aesthetic vision, and pushed Benhke to make ads that looked higher end than what Juice Beauty had been doing. When creating the line, Behnke met with Gwyneth every couple of weeks. Finding containers Gwyneth liked took about three months. Behnke would show her options, and Gwyneth would reject them, so Behnke would go back to her suppliers and ask for something more luxe. Gwyneth liked thick glass, for instance, but they couldn't use it because it was too heavy to ship. Ultimately, she settled on white ceramic, "which you rarely see because it's very expensive," Behnke said. The promise of Goop by Juice Beauty was that it wouldn't contain any chemicals that Gwyneth deemed harmful, like parabens, a selling point that would become ubiquitous in the next decade, often based on dubious claims of purity. Scaring readers into thinking their existing products contained harmful ingredients was an effective way to get them to buy "clean" ones from brands like Goop.

"If someone is calling something 'clean,' whether it's clean eating or clean beauty or clean whatever, that should be a red flag that you should not buy that product. Because either the person doesn't know anything about chemistry or formulation, or they do and they're intentionally misleading you to convince you to buy their product," said Andrea Love. She said that the fear of parabens originated from a poorly done, widely mischaracterized study, yet they're one of the most effective and safest cosmetic preservatives. Brands phasing out parabens has led to the rise of less safe, more allergenic preservatives and an increase in products contaminated with mold or bacteria, all of which can lead to infections, she added.

"This idea of 'clean' is one of the most powerful health halos out there," said Timothy Caulfield. "I think it's especially maddening when you hear it from the cosmetic industry . . . that is rooted in making you feel insecure about yourself, like you must constantly be improving. You're not good enough the way you are now. So we are going to charge you a little bit more for a product you don't need because we've made you feel insecure about who you are. That's the marketing strategy."

Goop wasn't sure how to launch Goop by Juice Beauty. They didn't know whether the products should live on Goop.com or have their own website. Gwyneth herself was unsure whether she wanted to be the face of it. Branding agency Crème Collective had experience working with other "clean" beauty brands and felt that Gwyneth should be the face, otherwise it might look like she didn't stand behind the products, among them $110 face oil, a $125 exfoliating mask, and $90 eye cream. At this early stage of the clean beauty market, Gwyneth could own and legitimize the line.

The look they came up with was aesthetically clean: black and white inspired by the line's packaging, with pared-down photos of Gwyneth's face. Crème needed an overall name for the campaign. Partner and brand strategist Therese Clarke came up with "good, clean goop," which became the tagline.

As Crème developed the campaign, they met with Gwyneth a couple of times. She had a sense of humor about herself, and they pitched pairing day-and-night creams with the copy "Conscious Coupling." Gwyneth thought it was funny but her team was afraid it was too polarizing. Crème mainly liaised with Goop's head of merchandising, Blair Lawson, who asked them to communicate with her and go directly to Gwyneth only if she had given them permission. This was something other senior leadership would do to manage who was talking to Gwyneth, though it's unclear if she demanded this or members of her team believed it essential.

Why wasn't exactly clear. While lower-level employees at Goop found her easy to work with once they got access to her, she was often hard to reach—senior executives seemed to shield her from those who ranked below them. Meanwhile, those executives jostled for her attention and struggled to understand what she wanted. The dynamic resembled that of her Spence friends, who jostled for her attention and sometimes struggled to understand why she would turn on them. Some of her employees were afraid of telling her that something she wanted to do wasn't a good idea, and of letting her hear that feedback from others.

Plus, Gwyneth had a habit of never telling someone to their face what she thought of them, but she couldn't resist sharing those unfiltered opinions with everyone else in her orbit.

CRÈME HAD A roughly hundred-thousand-dollar budget to create the ad campaign featuring Gwyneth for Goop by Juice Beauty. They scheduled the photo shoot at Smashbox Studios in Los Angeles and hired Gwyneth's glam team, including her stylist Elizabeth Saltzman and makeup artist Kate Lee. Gwyneth arrived at the shoot wearing slim-cut corduroy overalls in salmon pink, with her hair disheveled, recalled two people there. As with many of the photo shoots she'd done over the years, she seemed less than thrilled to be there and disinterested in talking to anyone. The team provided the playlist (no Coldplay) and menu (no gluten or dairy). Once Gwyneth's hairstylist Adir Abergel showed up, her mood improved.

When Gwyneth stepped in front of the camera, she didn't take a single bad picture. Usually, creative directors killed a bunch of photos from shoots like this. But Gwyneth knew all her best angles and could turn it on in an instant for the camera. Even bad photos probably would have sold product. Lawson had said, "You guys don't understand—if we just snap an iPhone photo of her in a sweater and post it on Instagram, we will sell out of the sweater."

Once the campaign was complete, the team was pleased that Gwyneth didn't look overly retouched: Her skin looked like her skin, her wrinkles slightly showing. In one image, her hair, which she usually wore stick-straight, was styled naturally wavy.

Gwyneth drew publicity for the launch that nascent, noncelebrity beauty brands could only dream of. *Vogue* ran a story about the line, and Gwyneth went on *The Tonight Show Starring Jimmy Fallon*. "I couldn't find products that were luxurious and really effective and help with, you know, wrinkles and all that were organic," she said. "I'm really into healthy food and wellness and stuff like that, and I think this is an extension of trying to eat well." She talked about how all the preservatives were "food-grade, so you could eat it, technically, if you wanted to." Fallon then produced a carton of McDonald's french fries from behind his desk, while Gwyneth laughed and held open a jar of cream. They each dipped a fry and ate it. "It's not bad," he said, laughing. "Better on your face, probably."

The public could buy it on March 1, 2016; as Behnke and two others recalled, the line met its initial sales goal of a few million in revenue a year. Blair Lawson said that the company tripled business from 2016 to 2017, following the launch of Goop by Juice Beauty, but Goop has always been circumspect about the finer details of its finances, and it's unclear how much of that growth was due to beauty. However, while Gwyneth still had to fulfill her obligations to Juice Beauty as the face of their color cosmetics line, Gwyneth was eager to make a Goop skincare line herself, without outside help.

One person familiar with her thinking said Gwyneth always believed she could execute something better than everyone else.

Besides, that was Goop: It was all about Gwyneth.

IN THE SPRING of 2016, shortly after Goop's Juice Beauty line launched, *Marie Claire* was planning its first-ever Power Trip, a "pop-up summit for badass girl bosses." The conference would fly a hundred female business leaders on a chartered flight from New York to San Francisco, where they'd hear "panel discussions about being a boss, being a brand, being a feminist, and being a disruptor." Gwyneth agreed to headline the event and forgo payment since the conference wasn't paying speakers, so long as they flew her private from Los Angeles. Among Gwyneth's other stipulations, filtered down through crisis publicist Matthew Hiltzik, no one was to address her when she arrived at her hotel, where she'd have a room to use before her talk. She wanted the hotel room temperature set at sixty-seven degrees. And she would only talk about Goop, not her previous career. She was still, with Hiltzik's help, trying to shift her public image to that of a serious businessperson, the kind who would appear on a *Forbes* cover instead of *Vogue*.

Her assistant Kevin Keating accompanied her on the trip. The plane coming from New York with Gwyneth's audience was delayed in the air by half an hour, organizers told Keating. He told *Marie Claire* that if they were any later than that, Gwyneth would have to pull out of the event. Before the audience arrived for Gwyneth's keynote interview with editor in chief Anne Fulenwider, she was cold, unsmiling, and refused to make eye contact with event staff. But when she got on the stage, she transformed. She talked about conscious uncoupling. She joked about being the target of online haters: "There were times when people were very cruel about me and what I was trying to do. At a certain point, you think, *Gosh, this just can't be about me.* This has to be a projection, or this has to be something else. There has to be some other energetic body behind this, because I'm just selling some fucking sweaters." It was one of her appealingly disarming moves: a Hollywood actress with her own giant brand, onstage at a conference called Power Trip, telling assembled business leaders how trivial and unthreatening her little project was.

GOOP CLOSED ITS $10 million Series B round in August 2016. The company had always planned to raise the money, since it needed to update Goop's technology, enabling products to be seamlessly purchased through editorial content. Hiltzik arranged for the *New York Post* to cover it. New Enterprise Associates had put money in again, and its head of internet investing, Tony Florence, told the paper that they were "thrilled with Goop's significant progress as a successful business, and are excited to be accelerating our investment behind Gwyneth as she works to realize her vision of building Goop into a global, next generation, direct-to-consumer platform."

Gwyneth said the funding would provide "enough runway to get us to profitability."

Gwyneth's life was very much in L.A. Going strong with Falchuk, she had put the three-bedroom Tribeca apartment she had bought in 2007 on the market for $14.25 million in March 2016. (It sold the following year for $10.7 million, after a new brokerage firm had cut the listing price to $9.95 million.)

Additionally, Goop revealed that Lisa Gersh was departing. The *New York Post* reported that she planned to stay in New York, where her family lived, and remain a "strategic adviser." Privately, Gwyneth seemed to have soured on Gersh. When Gersh ended up landing a job as CEO of the fashion label Alexander Wang, Gwyneth seemed dismayed, and was overheard saying to one staffer, "Why didn't they call to ask for a reference?"

This left Goop without a CEO. Geraldine Martin-Coppola, who had served as COO of ShoeDazzle and general manager of Fabletics, came on as president in October 2016. The assumption within the company was that Martin-Coppola would be empowered to support Gwyneth as president or maybe become CEO herself. But Gwyneth approached the board, including some of Goop's investors, to suggest herself for the CEO job. She had thought she'd needed a "grown-up" around to help her, but now she realized that "nobody knows what the fuck they're doing, and you can learn whatever it is that's specific to your business that you need to learn."

Gwyneth had strengths as Goop's leader: Her taste was impeccable, she was a media magnet, she had genuine culinary skills. But she also had weaknesses. She was nonconfrontational to the point where she didn't give people necessary feedback. When problems arose—say, something went wrong with a tech rollout—she became, one observer said, "childishly unhappy," occasionally to the point of tears, which was unhelpful. While her emotional reaction showed how deeply she cared about the company, people around her just wanted to fix the problems and move on. Also, she couldn't relinquish control, which meant she failed to empower experienced people to do what she had hired them to do.

The board agreed to give her the CEO job, and at an auspicious time. Goop ended up tripling its revenue in 2016 to an estimated $15 to $20 million.

But Gwyneth would prove unable over the next nine years to shepherd Goop into a period of sustained profitability and growth. She worked on the company—she was more than a CEO in name only—but it might have performed better if she'd served as a figurehead executive or pure creative lead, the way Jessica Alba did for Honest or Kim Kardashian did for her shapewear brand, SKIMS. Gwyneth wanted Goop to do everything instead of laser-focusing on, say, beauty. The problem with this strategy was that building out a team for each function—content, beauty, an events business that Gersh had wanted to start—was expensive. People around her believed that Gwyneth could compete in any category, but they also thought that she would be better off proving success in one first.

Next up was a clothing line.

THE ONE-OFF FASHION collaborations Goop had been doing were more like editorial content than a business strategy. The limited inventory created urgency and drove people to Goop.com. Goop had gone from selling one item at a time to selling mini-collections created in collaboration with established labels. In 2015, Gwyneth decided to level up again. She had seen the news that a label she liked, Band of Outsiders, was closing. She had worn its neo-preppy clothes on *Glee*, and had collaborated with the designer, Scott Sternberg, on a capsule line including a $995 jumpsuit, a $1,095 schoolboy blazer, and $295 button-down shirts. Gwyneth sent him a condolence message about Band and invited him to meet with her.

The two had coffee in the soothing gray-and-white kitchen with black accents and floor-to-ceiling glass doors that opened out onto Gwyneth's large, perfectly manicured lawn. She told him she had been working on a clothing line with another designer, but she wasn't happy with it—the clothes didn't feel like a brand.

From Sternberg's perspective, Gwyneth needed to start the whole project over, but she didn't seem to know that. "You don't even know what you need to do, because you need everything," he told her. The line would clearly be Gwyneth's vision, but she needed help from someone like Sternberg to execute it. Sternberg saw that Gwyneth had an infectious personality, a way of getting her staff excited about achieving her goals for Goop and encouraging them to experiment. He and Gwyneth came up with an arrangement in which he would design the line as a consultant and meet with her at her home every month or so.

They first had to create Goop's brand book, a compendium of visual references and inspiration from which every collection would stem; he asked her what words described the brand, then assigned images to each word. Gwyneth's dogs, a Maltese and a German shepherd, laid at their feet while they worked. There was an ease to the relationship. She connected him to a therapist (though he was never able to get an appointment). When he told her he was thinking about trying a cleanse, she opened up her cabinet. "Which one, darling?"

Sternberg understood that the line extended from Gwyneth's image, so eventually, they headed to her closet for inspiration. After all her years as an It girl, she had an incredible archive and pulled out terrific Prada and Calvin Klein pieces. She liked prep and clean femininity with menswear and military flourishes. "I would look at something," she recalled, "and think to myself, *I love the little puff sleeve, but I wish that the sleeves were three-quarter, I wish it had a collar, I wish it had buttons*, whatever."

Gwyneth had tried having the clothes made in Los Angeles, but the samples looked cheap. Sternberg suggested they source from Italy. He recommended an atelier he had used for Band of Outsiders; they also made pieces for Alaïa and Saint Laurent. The clothes would be expensive, but that didn't seem like an obstacle. So much of what Goop recommended—and what subscribers bought—was luxury. And since the business was direct to consumer, the prices could be lower than they might be at a high-end department store like Saks Fifth Avenue.

Goop launched the line, Goop Label (later shortened to G. Label), in the fall of 2016. Gwyneth decided to sell it like the capsule collections: Gwyneth told *Fast Company* that Goop would produce fewer than a thousand pieces of each design, with five items at most in each drop, though two people with knowledge of the volume said Goop actually produced an average of around eighty of each piece. The *Fast*

Company story reported that everything "was snapped up within hours of going live." But according to one former employee, that wasn't exactly the case—at least one item was slow to sell: a white leather "Classic G" tote bag that cost $285. Goop had hundreds of them lying around.

"Do I need to be photographed with it?"

"Yes, Gwyneth, that would fix the problem," a team member told her. She was, and the stock promptly sold out.

G. Label didn't need much advertising. Other brands and retailers constantly needed to promote new products to attract customers, but Goop's content did the work for them. And Gwyneth could offer an interview, and the result would be a whole story focused on her latest clothing launch. She landed features touting G. Label in *The New York Times*, *Fast Company*, and *Harper's Bazaar*. Items like the gray suit and the "Elise" blouse, standard-issue except for its subtle puff sleeves, sold well, but pieces Gwyneth wore consistently sold the best.

The launch of G. Label changed Goop's approach to fashion coverage. Laurie Trott, a fashion media veteran who had worked at *Who What Wear* and *Lucky*, signed on in early 2015 as fashion director. Trott looked at fashion through the lens of Gwyneth's sensibility, helping the buyers figure out what to sell, and working on website content. Gwyneth was involved in all the details. She approved every item Goop sold and signed off on models and photographers for the relatively modest fashion shoots. At some point, G. Label started doing well enough that Goop stopped staging fashion shoots for other clothes, once more bringing the brand back to Gwyneth.

EVEN AS CEO, Gwyneth was determined to remain the main source of Goop's product recommendations, and to preserve her own tastes as the primary aesthetic. She genuinely believed she was providing a service that few could. As CEO, she continued to tune out the scientists and skeptics. She saw Goop as a crusade for women's health. Though her main priority was always selling products, she had to spread gospel in order to maintain her perceived authority in the wellness market-place.

"I'm always the guinea pig to try everything. I've got to try them all. I love acupuncture. Also, I just heard of a service called a sound bath, which might be too hippie-ish even for the likes of me. It's some new healing modality. I might not be able to handle it," she told *The New York Times*. "But generally, I'm open to anything. I've been stung by bees. It's a thousands-of-years-old treatment called apitherapy. People use it to get rid of inflammation and scarring. It's actually pretty incredible if you research it. But, man, it's painful. I haven't done cryotherapy yet, but I do want to try that." (Cryotherapy would later make headlines when supermodel Linda Evangelista revealed that a form of it called CoolSculpting had permanently and painfully disfigured her.)

In 2017, Gwyneth talked about apitherapy again. "The doctor stings you [with a live bee] like it's an acupuncture needle. I had it done on my cesarean scar . . . I had some buckling in the scar, and it really evened it out," she said. When Goop began teasing its first live event, Gwyneth spoke in a promotional video about bee-sting therapy. "You're probably thinking this is one of those crazy upscale events where we drink kale smoothies and get stung by bees on purpose. And you're right," she said, "it is."

In October that same year, actor Gerard Butler was rushed to the hospital in anaphylactic shock after being injected with venom from twenty-three bees, which he had hoped would ease muscle aches. A woman in Spain who had been undergoing bee-sting therapy monthly for two years died the following spring of a severe anaphylactic reaction. Authors of a report about her death in the *Journal of Investigational Allergology and Clinical Immunology* warned that published evidence of the treatment's efficacy and safety was scarce and concluded, "[T]his practice is both unsafe and unadvisable."

While Goop couldn't box up bee-sting therapy and ship it to paying customers, the company went ahead with other products that experts advised against. In 2018, Goop recommended $135 coffee enema kits as part of its annual "detox guide." The kit, by Implant O-Rama, was "Dr. Junger's pick for those who know what they're doing," Goop wrote, linking out to a longer article about colonics in which Junger suggested the enema for anyone "doing a cleanse." The enema kit's website declared, "Coffee enemas can mean relief from depression, confusion, general nervous tension, many allergy-related symptoms and, most importantly, relief from severe pain."

In a segment about the kits on *The Late Show with Stephen Colbert*, he said, "I always say I can't start the day until my coffee's had me." Quoting an expert who said, "If you have a liver, your body is already getting rid of toxins," he continued, "In case it's unclear what you're doing, it's butt-chugging a venti."

The Mayo Clinic reported that coffee enemas had led to several deaths, while *The American Journal of Gastroenterology* documented a case of a severely inflamed colon in a sixty-year-old woman who had tried one.

As of 2025, the coffee enemas remained on the site.

Eventually, regulators took note. The National Advertising Division, a unit of the Better Business Bureau, investigated Goop's claims about products called Brain Dust and Action Dust from the brand Moon Juice, which cost thirty-eight dollars for a 1.5-ounce jar. Goop had claimed that the powder "encourages healthy metabolic function" and "maintains healthy systems for superior cognitive flow, clarity, memory, creativity, alertness and the capacity to handle stress." The dust links appeared in a story titled "GP's Morning Smoothie": "Gwyneth drinks this smoothie every morning, whether or not she's detoxing. Choose your Moon Juice moon dust depending on what the day ahead holds . . . brain dust before a long day at the office, sex dust before a date, etc."

Goop removed the offending claims and said in a statement that it "accepts the decision of the National Advertising Division and represents that the advertising at issue has been voluntarily and permanently discontinued."

. . .

FLUSH WITH CASH, Goop hired more people, including Nandita Khanna, who had worked at Condé Nast, Hearst, and J.Crew, as editorial director; and Elise Loehnen became head of content. But tension in the C-suite was now permeating the company's atmosphere. One employee who had worked previously in fashion and at Condé Nast—not typically nurturing environments—described Goop as one of the most difficult working environments they had ever encountered. "I never felt less well in my life than during my time there. I didn't take care of myself at all," the person said.

While Gwyneth presented a polished, happy image of Goop in the press, which gave the impression the company was a booming business, the office culture was noxious and chaotic, some employees from the time said. The problems stemmed from the C-suite, where executives struggled to navigate Gwyneth's impatience and perfectionism. But also, there was something about these women—all smart and ambitious and impressive in their own right—working for a celebrity that led them to treat one another like they were on *The Real Housewives*. They seemed threatened by each other, based on whom Gwyneth was favoring in a given moment (and she made it clear). Gwyneth could be warm and caring but also cold. Employees who worked up the nerve to go into her office were often met with impatience, an attitude of "What do you want? Get it over with. Let's move on." If an employee replied to one of her emails with "Thanks" or "On it," she'd tell them not to send those emails, because they were a waste of time.

Gwyneth was rarely harsh with a subordinate, but her capricious, indirect leadership style led to resentments. Two former executives explained that some of her direct reports got hooked on the warm light of her attention—hoping to become a friend or secure an invitation to her home in the Hamptons—and when Gwyneth's attention was withdrawn, executives turned on one another. Gwyneth's interests and allegiances were so unpredictable that currying favor was the only reliable way to secure one's position. The dynamic was subtle but damaging. If one person got too close to her, another would feel threatened, and that fear and distrust trickled down to lower-level employees. Just as she could sour on ideas, Gwyneth could sour on people, particularly those who got too clingy. Other employees were intimidated by her perfection, and reluctant to assert themselves. Either way, almost no one—Goop's board included—was willing to tell her no.

Gwyneth was also frugal when it came to both Goop's and her own expenses. The media industry was suffering, but Goop, despite its funding, had even fewer resources than competitors. Lacking a budget for freelancers, editors were overworked and underpaid. Writers had to create editorial content for multiple sections of the site and branded content for advertisers. Editorial staff opened their laptops as soon as they woke up and worked until they went to bed. One former employee took their laptop with them everywhere; if they got a Slack message while driving, they would pull over to answer it. Gwyneth expecting immediate answers from executives meant their direct reports had to provide instant answers, too. Gwyneth, who still signed off on every newsletter subject line, would occasionally call lower-level employees on weekends to request edits to stories. Her notes weren't unreasonable, but the rapid-fire timing made employees feel like they always had to be by their phone and computer. Some staff felt burnt out.

Some of the excess workload trickled down from Gwyneth's erratic management style. She'd ask her team to pursue ideas and then she'd lose interest, but the staff was expected to keep the ideas going. This was how, within a few years, Goop evolved into an online magazine, a direct-to-consumer business, a live events company, a beauty brand, a podcast, a fashion brand, and a television show. All the while, there wasn't a lot of tolerance for imperfection. Gwyneth wanted everything Goop did molded in her flawless image, and employees would work until two a.m. setting up wellness events until everything looked as impeccable and dreamy as one of Gwyneth's homes. When she found pee on a toilet seat at the office, she said in the Slack channel that "someone tinkled," adding, "Make sure to clean up after yourselves, I'd appreciate it."

While she would talk about how hard she was working, Gwyneth also seemed to take a lot of vacation time. Goop offered employees an annual two-week "Goopcation" meant to give all staff two weeks off each August—but also allowing Gwyneth to spend time with her kids in the Hamptons. Employees were allowed unlimited paid vacation days, but some felt like the Goopcation effectively discouraged staff from taking different weeks off. Gwyneth still sometimes sent Slack messages to her senior team during Goopcation, so employees—who were expected to respond—didn't feel like the offices were truly closed.

Not only was the pace and breadth of work unsustainable for employees, it would also prove unsustainable for Goop.

CHAPTER 25

Egg-sistential Crisis

Saying that you're ahead of the curve is a
common strategy for wellness gurus . . . It's a
completely absurd argument.

—Timothy Caulfield

Not content to limit retail operations to the internet, Goop
opened its first brick-and-mortar store, the Goop Lab, on
September 15, 2017, in the Brentwood Country Mart in
Santa Monica, where Gwyneth had shopped as a kid, and which was
now less than two miles from her Mandeville Canyon home. Designed
to resemble a "Bren51twood bungalow," the Goop Lab space was
another disarming fusion of commerce and coddling, with a living room
where customers were encouraged to sprawl out, an apothecary counter
to sample the products, a greenhouse, and a porch. Since the launch of
Goop by Juice Beauty, the company's revenue had tilted heavily toward
e-commerce, up to around $20 million from $6 million before the launch,
according to someone familiar with the numbers. Publishing and brand
deals had grown from around $12 million to $14 million, and Goop
continued to lead the industry in monetizing product recommendations
and drawing big sponsors. Cadillac spent $1 million with Goop on a
"dinner series," which involved Gwyneth or one of her friends hosting

dinners in five cities for invited influencer guests who would be driven there in Cadillacs. The partnership was covered everywhere from *The Wall Street Journal* to *Adweek* to *People*. Gwyneth cohosted one in New York City alongside Mario Batali, at his restaurant La Sirena. She didn't know anyone famous in Miami, so Goop staffers hosted a Gwyneth-less dinner gathering that brought in two hundred thousand dollars without even producing an It girl or influencer.

The physical stores had begun as pop-ups in Los Angeles and New York in 2014. Brands paid to get items featured there as part of an advertising buy. Gwyneth could easily get press for store openings, which meant companies that had paid to place products ended up featured as her favorite things in the media coverage. Brands could also pay to hold events in the stores. The email list was up to one million subscribers, and while only around twenty thousand of those purchased anything, someone familiar with the numbers recalled, 11 percent of that smaller group had a household income of over $1 million. Very few media outlets connected advertisers to that affluent a demographic.

When Goop decided to launch a travel app, an advertiser sponsored it with the promise that it would reach ten thousand downloads. "Call it G. Spotting," Gwyneth told an executive. "Everybody will make fun of me for being an idiot and we'll have the ten thousand downloads we'll need right there." Gwyneth had spent her career manipulating her own coverage, and she applied the same savvy to Goop, beating her competitors at their own game.

Condé Nast Traveler took the bait with a story that asked, "What sort of a name is G. Spotting? . . . [C]onsidering Goop was supposed to be a word that means nothing and could mean anything (her words, not ours), and she named her kid after a fruit, perhaps the app's name too hits the right spot." And G. Spotting hit its target.

This publicity strategy helped Goop without requiring Gwyneth to personally plug something, which was a crucial part of building a long-lasting celebrity brand. The company would be more valuable and have longer legs if it didn't rely on her to sell things. She said, "I'm not interested in building a celebrity business. I want Goop to be its own brand that can thrive and scale without my involvement at some point. I'm always careful about—the same way I'm the creative force behind this brand, any creative force, their brand will represent their likes and dislikes, whether it's Jenna Lyons [creative director of J.Crew] or the guys at Valentino or anyone."

FEW EMPLOYEES GOT the chance to go to Gwyneth's house. But a select group of roughly twenty did around 2017 for a workshop with Sadeghi and his wife on "the power of the question." Everyone went barefoot in her yard, which likely suited Gwyneth just fine, since she was a believer in "grounding." Also called "earthing," it involves touching bare skin to the earth. Goop had published an interview with an earthing "expert" who said it helped cure insomnia and lengthened the life of a hospice patient. (The story also linked out to earthing products for those who couldn't get outside, including an "earthing universal mat kit"—a black mat that plugged into the wall—to put under a desk during the workday and cost $59.99. There is no evidence that the mats have any effect.)

The Goop staff sat in a circle in the grass around Sadeghi. He instructed them to turn to each other and ask hard questions, the goal being to both talk and listen for an uncomfortable amount of time. "It was very strange," said someone who participated. "But everyone was very happy to be doing it." Rather than order catering for the event, Thea Baumann cooked. Often Goop's annual detox recipes, like the chicken kefta wraps included in the 2015 detox guide, were served at events like this.

The lunches Baumann made for Gwyneth and a small group of executives now delineated who was senior (those invited to lunch) and the rest (those who weren't). Gwyneth preferred that her food come from farmers markets or the upscale, exorbitantly priced, trendy grocery store Erewhon, where a quart of organic chicken bone broth cost seventeen dollars and a smoothie could run more than twenty. She believed it was easier to trust that their food was organic and "clean" versus, say, what Whole Foods sold.*

Gwyneth, who had been thin her whole life and wanted to stay that way, had food prepared accordingly for herself and those invited into her inner sanctum. The lunch would often be something light, like soup or a salad, and the executives would joke that they needed to go get a more filling meal afterward. Those who weren't senior enough to receive lunch would witness it carried to her across the office from the test kitchen: a perfect plate of vegetables and a poached egg, sometimes deposited on her desk with no acknowledgment from Gwyneth, who just kept working.

Gwyneth had close relationships with her food editors (after Baumann, Goop hired Caitlin O'Malley and Ana Hito) that blurred the lines between professional and personal. The food editors, who wrote Goop's recipes, worked directly with her until she tired of them for one reason or another. In the office, it was common knowledge that the food editors would go to Gwyneth's house after work and make her dinner under the guise of "recipe testing." When she and Brad Falchuk were living apart, the food editor would bring dinner to his house, too, which wasn't a light lift in L.A. traffic.

IN THE BEGINNING of 2017, Goop was expanding rapidly. It employed over seventy people and would soon hire thirty more. To accommodate the additional staff, the company leased a building adjacent to its bungalow offices that was decorated, like the rest of the office, to look like a Restoration Hardware showroom. It included a test kitchen; a conference room; and a long farmhouse-style table around which staff gathered for informal weekly all-hands meetings.

Around this time, Gwyneth became aware of jade eggs, which were

---

* That said, in 2025, Erewhon briefly closed its "tonic bar" after the Los Angeles County Department of Public Health, in what it called a "major violation," found cockroaches near where it stored its plastic cups and paper goods.

meant to be inserted vaginally as part of a wellness practice. Gwyneth first laughed, then tried one and decided that Goop should cover the eggs and (contextual commerce and all) start selling them.

Goop had originally only bought around six hundred eggs, half in quartz and half in jade. On January 12, Goop sent the newsletter featuring the story designed to promote them. Headlined "Better Sex: Jade Eggs for Your Yoni," it featured beauty editor Jean Godfrey-June's interview with Shiva Rose (described as a "beauty guru/healer/inspiration/ friend"), who said that the eggs had traditionally been "used by women in ancient China." She added, "Before I insert an egg, I'll do a ritual: I place it on a beautiful piece of fabric, light a candle, maybe even burn some sage." At the top of the story was a picture of two eggs, in rose quartz and jade, with a link to buy them for $55 or $66 on Goop.com.

Within three hours, the eggs had sold out.

EGG-RELATED BACKLASH QUICKLY followed. Among other critics, Jen Gunter had written an impassioned blog post denouncing the eggs that was going viral. Opening "Dear Ms. Paltrow," she wrote, "I read the post on GOOP and all I can tell you is it is the biggest load of garbage I have read on your site since vaginal steaming." Later, she coauthored a study published in the journal *Female Pelvic Medicine & Reconstructive Surgery* that found no evidence they were ever used in ancient China. Other medical experts weighed in with similar concerns. "Many people have this idea that if it's natural it must be good, useful, and not harmful," associate clinical professor of obstetrics and gynecology at Northwestern University Lauren Streicher, MD, told CNN. "To which I always say, arsenic is natural, but that's certainly harmful." "There are no studies or evidence to show that jade eggs help with orgasms, vaginal muscle tone or hormonal balance," Dr. Leena Nathan, an assistant clinic professor of obstetrics and gynecology at UCLA Health, told Fox News. "Jade does not result in hormonal changes even when inserted in the vagina."

With thousands of customers on the waitlist for eggs, staff frantically called Goop's wellness gurus in an attempt to source more. One former staffer remembered calling "a reiki hairdresser" and "a crystal shaman" in Gwyneth's network, ultimately somehow managing to find more.

Though Gwyneth believed in sharing with her audience treatments she was curious about or personally liked, and was open to the possibility that anything might result in a positive outcome, former executives said her biggest concern was Goop's bottom line.

GOOP CONTINUED TO draw attention for its bizarre and often easily disprovable claims. In June, the technology blog *Gizmodo* investigated a Goop product called Body Vibes, described as "a major obsession around Goop HQ." These were stickers that attached to the skin, intended to "rebalance the energy frequency in our bodies," Goop claimed, adding, "everyday stresses and anxiety can throw off our internal balance, depleting our energy reserves and weakening our immune systems." Goop also claimed that the stickers were made with the same "conductive carbon material NASA uses to line space suits so they can monitor an astronaut's vitals during wear." They cost $120 for a pack of twenty-four.

Gizmodo checked the claims with NASA, which said they "do not have any conductive carbon material lining the spacesuits." At *Gizmodo*'s request, Mark Shelhamer, former chief scientist at NASA's human research division, also took a look. "Wow," he said. "What a load of BS this is."

Goop first deleted the NASA-related copy from its post, and eventually removed the product entirely.

WHILE GWYNETH SEEMED to brush off these controversies, certain critics got to her. She felt Jen Gunter was notably profiting off of criticizing her. Loehnen tried to convince Gwyneth that she shouldn't fight directly with Goop's critics, that this would only make it worse. "You're punching down," she said. "Don't take the bait." But she would not hold back. On July 13, six months after the egg controversy began, Gwyneth posted on Twitter, "When they go low, we go high," quoting Michelle Obama's famous speech at the Democratic National Convention. She linked out to a statement from Goop, which did not cite Gunter by name but referenced a "San Francisco-based ob-gyn/blogger" described as "strangely confident."

The statement continued, "It is unfortunate that there are some who seem to believe that they already know it all, who pre-judge information before they've even taken the time to read or understand it, who believe that there is actually nothing left to learn, who believe that they, singularly, own the truth. That is troubling, and that is dangerous." It was signed "Team goop" and supported by letters from Goop experts Steven Gundry, a doctor and diet book author; and Dr. Aviva Romm, an "integrative women's and children's physician." Gundry, who has been alleged to have made unsupported medical claims about the supposed harms of the plant protein lectin, said he contributed a letter after Goop asked him for a response, because of the "profanity" Gunter had used, which he found "odd to see . . . from a fellow physician." In a subsequent letter headlined "12 (More) Reasons to Start a Jade Egg Practice," sexuality coach Layla Martin accused critics of "sexually shaming a woman for sharing her personal experience."

Gunter was in England when Goop posted the response on what happened to be her birthday. She looked at the story, saw that it was written by Gundry—whom she distrusted on his supplement peddling alone (Gundry noted he didn't sell the supplements at the office where he sees patients)—and Romm, and thought, *This is your A team?* "It was the funniest thing," she said. "I was just a chick with a WordPress, writing so my patients can get information." She couldn't believe that she, a mom of twins working full-time as a doctor, had gotten to Gwyneth this much with her blog. She was amused that Goop called her "strangely confident." "I'm like, really? I have a medical degree. I did a five-year residency in ob-gyn, I did a fellowship in infectious diseases, and I'm strangely confident about vaginal health. I'm the definition of the expert, really," Gunter said. "I guess you say whatever you need to, to protect your bottom line." *The Atlantic* called Gunter at three a.m., she recalled, asking for a quote.

By 2025, the jade and quartz eggs finally disappeared from the Goop store after being sold—no returns accepted—since 2017.

BONNIE PATTEN HAD become the head of Truth in Advertising in 2012, after working as a litigator in private practice for almost twenty years. A friend of hers had been inspired to start TINA.org after learning in law school that the Federal Trade Commission and other government agencies lacked the resources to regulate advertising claims. Thanks to the internet, deceptive claims were exploding. Patten had been representing doctors, hospitals, and corporations, and found the idea of working on behalf of consumers appealing.

She didn't focus at first on wellness businesses. TINA.org looked at every industry from automobiles to health care. But she started noticing that influencers were egregious practitioners of deceptive marketing, particularly when it came to wellness products like supplements.

Patten and her small team heard about the jade eggs the same way many consumers did—by reading about them online. One of her employees then took a hard look at Goop and the claims it was making on each of the numerous products in its store. According to Patten, they specifically looked for, and believed they found, "a pattern and practice of deception."

After an attorney reviewed the allegedly false claims Patten's team had identified, the group sent a letter to Goop on August 11, 2017, with their findings, requesting that Goop remove the deceptive statements, or else TINA.org would forward their complaint to regulators. Subsequently, TINA.org's legal director spoke to Goop's outside counsel, who said that the company needed more time to look at everything. As Patten understood it, Goop's outside counsel knew that they had sold items without a legal review. Goop made some slight adjustments to their product descriptions, including removing the claim that the yoni egg prevented uterine prolapse and that the Black Rose Bar (a type of soap) cured eczema and psoriasis. One claim that a Goop item could treat fertility was now attributed to "fans of the product." Patten was dissatisfied with the "minor tweaks."

On August 22, 2017, TINA.org escalated the matter by filing a complaint with two California district attorneys focused on health and wellness. Patten said, "Just because she's famous, that doesn't put her above the law."

THE LAST WEEKEND of June 2017, Gwyneth was on vacation with her kids in Europe when she took a phone call from Jodi Kantor, an investigative reporter from *The New York Times* who was looking into Harvey Weinstein's serial abuse of women and use of NDAs to cover it up. The year before, a *New York* reporter had been trying to do a similar story about Weinstein. At the time, Weinstein had urged Gwyneth not to talk. "I just really want to protect the people who did say yes" to sex with him, he told her. Gwyneth told him she wouldn't talk, and *New York*'s story never ran.

Now, during a conversation with Kantor recounted in the book she coauthored with reporting partner Megan Twohey—*She Said: Breaking the Sexual Harassment Story That Helped Ignite a Movement*—Gwyneth agreed to speak off the record. She wanted the story to come out, but she told them something her staff didn't see—that she was rattled by all the backlash plaguing Goop. As Kantor and Twohey wrote, "Privately, she was feeling crushed and unsure if she could handle any more controversy. She was certain that any story involving her, Weinstein, and sex was likely to be sensationalized, turned into the trashy celebrity scandal of the week."

With more than a hundred employees on her payroll, "I can't wreck the business," she told Kantor. She feared being dragged again would somehow hurt Goop. But she decided to tap her Hollywood network to see if she could find other women who would come forward, so that her account could be part of a larger story. About two weeks later, she frantically texted and called Kantor to say that Weinstein had invited himself to a party she was currently throwing at her Hamptons home. She was hiding in the bathroom as she made the call. Gwyneth had considered telling him not to come but had worried that would raise a red flag. He had arrived early, and she feared he'd come to confront her. She kept her assistant close throughout the party, and Weinstein left without incident. Kantor and Twohey came to the Hamptons a few weeks after that to encourage Gwyneth to go on the record about Weinstein's sexual misconduct in the Peninsula Hotel all those years ago. She was leaning that way but still wanted to do so as part of a chorus of women with stories about Weinstein. "I want to make sure that I'm not in any way at the focal point."

Rosanna Arquette, Angelina Jolie, and French actress Judith Godrèche shared similar stories in the piece, which the *Times* ultimately published in October 2017 with Gwyneth's revelation about Weinstein coming on to her in the hotel room, after she'd been cast in *Emma*. When later promoting their book about the investigation—which won a Pulitzer Prize, alongside Ronan Farrow's *New Yorker* piece—Twohey and Kantor reminded *Today* show viewers how crucial Gwyneth was in helping the story. Twohey said, "I think that many people will be surprised to discover that when so many other actresses were reluctant to get on the phone and scared to tell the truth about what they had experienced at his hands, that Gwyneth was actually one of the first people to get on the phone, and that she was determined to help this investigation—even when Harvey Weinstein showed up to a party at her house early and she was sort of forced to hide in the bathroom."

· · · ·

GOOP'S "EXPERTS" HAD helped guide the site toward the massive market for supplements after publishing enough stories on the subject to feel out demand for producing and selling their own line. Goop Wellness launched in 2017 with a cover story in *Women's Health* featuring Gwyneth, profiled by Goop's own Jean Godfrey-June. *Women's Health* had hired Godfrey-June to write the story, thinking she'd produce something revelatory about working for Gwyneth. But the piece was essentially an ad for the four supplement packets of six different pills that cost $90 for a one-month supply or $75 for a monthly subscription. The supplements were said to promote weight loss and increase energy. Godfrey-June interviewed Gwyneth over a stew she wanted following "an eight-day, goat-milk-only cleanse." Gwyneth said the supplements were designed to help women know what to buy in an already crowded supplement market. "It's almost impossible to navigate," she said. "We wanted to take the work out of it for you."

She went on, "I'm really interested in the impact of heavy metals and parasites on our bodies. I think they're two of the biggest culprits in terms of why we feel bad. I'm knee-deep in figuring out ways to clear them from the body, looking at all sorts of potentially weird modalities."

Gwyneth seemed to believe that her body was full of parasites, many acquired by eating sushi. Marion Nestle, the nutrition professor, noted, "Pretty much everyone is contaminated with metals, chemicals, plastics, and other potentially toxic substances. Even organic vegetables have traces of them. They aren't avoidable, although choosing organics can reduce them. I see this as a policy issue: We need the government to stop agricultural and industrial pollution so these things don't get to us in the first place." As to how consumers should view influencers who sell supplements, she said, "You should recognize that the influencer is trying to sell you something."

Doctors and medical experts worried about the proliferation of supplements, which are regulated by the FDA as food products but not with the same rigor as pharmaceuticals. "People are going to buy into this, and they're not going to trust trained scientists and health care providers who are telling them that these things aren't beneficial and they can cause harm," said Andrea Love.

Of course, expert sentiment didn't stop Goop from publishing a story in 2017 headlined "You Probably Have a Parasite—Here's What to Do About It," a Q&A with Goop guru Linda Lancaster, who advocated the eight-day raw-goat-milk "cleanse" to purge the parasites.

Noting that Truth in Advertising had labeled Goop's supplement claims deceptive, Gunter critiqued the supplements on her blog in August, after the launch had been publicized in *The New Yorker* and *The New York Times*, among other outlets: "GOOP specifically markets the non-existent adrenal fatigue to women and of course the supplements to treat it under the guise of feminism."

While Goop's staff included skeptics, many believed in the overall mission, used the company's products, and thought of Gunter as an uninformed scold who was capitalizing on her role as a Gwyneth antagonist. They believed that doctors like her lacked education on matters of nutrition and health and were attached to the orthodoxies of mainstream Western medicine.

"We would talk about something and the internet would freak out. And then, you know, six months later or two years later, it would be widely adopted," Gwyneth said in a 2022 CBS interview. As an example, she cited "the gluten-free thing . . . People thought that was totally nuts."

This deeply frustrated Caulfield: "Saying that you're ahead of the curve is a common strategy for wellness gurus . . . It's a completely absurd argument."

Goop claimed it sold a hundred thousand dollars' worth of supplements their first day on sale. "If we are selling it, it's because we love it," Gwyneth told a reporter. "If we've made it, it's the best."

HER CONFIDENCE WAS not enough to dissuade the California Food, Drug and Medical Device Task Force—comprised of prosecutors from ten counties across the state—from suing Goop in September 2018 for making allegedly unlawful health claims about the vaginal eggs and Inner Judge Flower Essence Blend, which Goop claimed could prevent "'shame spirals' downward toward depressive states."

Gwyneth chose to pay $145,000 to settle the suit and allow those who purchased the eggs within a set period to receive a full refund. She also hired people to remove from the site what the Santa Clara County district attorney's office called "advertised medical claims [that] were not supported by competent and reliable science." In a statement, Goop said it believed "there [was] an honest disagreement about these claims," but "the company wanted to settle this matter quickly and amicably. This settlement does not indicate any liability on Goop's part."

TINA.org was thrilled. Bonnie Patten felt like a check had finally been put on this company that had been operating like they were above the law, exploiting women's common health issues—tiredness, anxiety, the made-up "adrenal fatigue"—for financial gain.

Former Goop employees were dismissive of the legal action. Gwyneth, they argued, was being made an example of as a celebrity.

"Absolutely," Patten said. "For better or worse, our society believes that these superstars and influencers are credible, and they want to emulate their lifestyles. So people like Gwyneth can have an outsize impact on how consumers behave."

CHAPTER 26

Too Goop to Print

I thought *I* was batshit crazy!

—Gwyneth Paltrow

To open the first-ever In Goop Health conference, Gwyneth ascended a few stairs to a stage in Los Angeles on June 10, 2017, wearing a Vilshenko by Goop pink-and-white floral-print silk prairie dress. "Good morning!" she addressed the crowd, fiddling with her professionally smoothed hair before clasping her hands in front of her. "Oh wow . . . this is very overwhelming, and I'm so thrilled that you're all here."

She told her five hundred mostly white, mostly female guests wearing yoga pants and carrying expensive handbags how her father's illness had started her "journey to wellness." She introduced Dr. Habib Sadeghi—wrongly—as "the guy responsible for the term 'conscious uncoupling.'" He gave a nearly ninety-minute lecture on "cosmic flow," rambling on about "What makes water wet?" He ended with a plug for his book, but not before fifty or so "exasperated" women got up and left, reported the *New York Post*.

Although Gwyneth had become close with Sadeghi, she finally (possibly after this conference, one person in her orbit speculated) seemed to develop serious doubts about him, so she started to distance herself. However, Gwyneth was too nonconfrontational to tell some-one directly that she was moving on, so she would pass them to other staff to manage. The staff knew intuitively when she was about to phase a person out. As of 2025, Sadeghi's contributor page and some of his Goop articles turned up a 404 error on the site.

Over the course of the day, Gwyneth would share the stage with reality television personality Nicole Richie, actors Cameron Diaz and Lena Dunham, and fashion designer Tory Burch for a symposium that would showcase Goop's "most-trusted experts, can't-live-without-it products and, in true Goop fashion, their predictions for what the world will be buzzing about next." Attendees traveled from all over the country and the world for the summit, where they could start the day with a saline IV (Gwyneth loved IVs and sometimes had them administered during meetings in the office). Guests could then try out "sound bath meditation," "crystal therapy," a "meditation lounge with [cannabis brand] hmbldt and aura photography," and a "flower remedy station" where guests could "discover the floral salve for whatever is ailing you," as well as a "10-minute facelift" during which an organic sugar thread was inserted into the cheek. (Gwyneth told her staff she subscribed to this, along with a little filler, though she was open about disliking Botox, saying that it made her look "crazy" and "like Joan Rivers"; she endorsed Xeomin, a similar injectable for reducing forehead wrinkles.)

Goop sold tickets at three tiers, $500, $1,000, and $1,500, but revenue would also come from sponsors, including Tumi, Dyson, Tory Sport, Tropicana Probiotics, and Tito's handmade vodka, many of which had booths at the event. The summit's signature cocktail was "Goop Kool-Aid," made with olive juice, vermouth, a scoop of Vital Proteins collagen peptides, two martini olives, and Tito's.

Proceeds from the event benefited Good+ Foundation, started by Gwyneth's friend Jessica Seinfeld to fight family poverty. Goop staff were expected to volunteer. An editor who normally curated gift guides wrote copy for the selfie mirrors in the bathroom that were trendy at the time. Other editorial staff manned booths or covered the event for Goop, generating articles to satisfy sponsors. The roughly five hundred tickets sold out at all three price tiers.

The day ended with a panel discussion featuring Diaz, Burch, Richie, and Miranda Kerr, all focused on balancing work, family, and health. Kerr told the crowd she had recently used leeches to suck blood from her back in an effort to "detoxify." She continued, "I had a leech facial as well. And I kept the leeches. They're in my koi pond."

"Wow!" Gwyneth said, laughing. "I thought *I* was batshit crazy!"

THESE EVENTS WERE successful, but they took a toll on Goop's staff. The company hadn't sustained profitability, and Gwyneth was trying desperately to figure out how to do so. Taking venture capital meant she had to either scale her business enough to sell it to a much bigger company, or go public and, ideally, deliver her investors—and herself— a hefty payday. While the brand deals kept coming and product kept selling, overhead was increasing. To boost and diversify revenue, Gwyneth was constantly trying new things, like the summits, and a VIP travel service—an effort that was abandoned with no clear way to scale or monetize it. Goop was a start-up, after all, and many of the employees bought into the idea of hustle culture, but the volume of work was extreme even by that standard. There just never seemed to be enough people to handle everything.

Gwyneth also remained committed to projects that didn't bring in money, like Goop's travel guides, because they were part of the brand DNA. The travel team relied on contacts in various locations to provide insight on the best spots to visit, with Gwyneth throwing in ideas. She didn't micromanage the stories, but she made sure that her favorite places were included. If she went to a restaurant she liked, such as the steak house 4 Charles Prime Rib in New York, she'd drop it into the Slack channel. If she went somewhere she didn't like, she'd say it "sucked" and ask her team to take it out. When they decided to create a Hamptons guide, Gwyneth naturally had opinions. "I don't want Aerin included," she said, referring to Aerin Lauder's namesake store in Southampton.

VOGUE EDITOR IN chief Anna Wintour had become the artistic direc-tor of the magazine's parent company, Condé Nast, in 2013, which gave her oversight of all magazines in the portfolio, ranging from *Brides* to *GQ*. Wintour and Gwyneth were friendly, having crossed paths at the Met Gala now and then, and around 2017, Wintour invited her to Condé Nast to talk about the idea of collaborating on a print magazine.

"This is a terrible idea," Loehnen, who'd spent eight years working at Condé Nast, told Gwyneth. "You do not need to do this magazine. It's a dying medium."

"You're being negative," Gwyneth answered. *Vogue* had killed photo shoots of Gwyneth three times before finally putting her on the cover in 1996, and over a decade later, she still seemed to crave Wintour's approval.

Ad revenue was down across legacy media, and Condé Nast was looking for partners that could combine high-quality journalism with an appeal to high-end advertisers. As a luxury media brand, Goop made sense. Both parties would profit if the magazine worked. But the effort ended up being a disaster.

SEVERAL MONTHS BEFORE the magazine first came out, Gwyneth and Loehnen flew to New York to meet with editors in chief at Condé Nast who might be open to collaboration, according to three people who attended the meeting. The group convened in a wood-paneled conference room. Attendees included Elaine Welteroth from *Teen Vogue*, Will Welch from *GQ*, Adam Rapoport from *Bon Appétit*, Caro-lyn Kylstra from *Self*, and Wintour.

Condé editors in chief were used to commanding a degree of deference, but Gwyneth entered the room like the queen bee, and everyone seemed to soften in her direction. The meeting ended up being the Gwyneth show—she was alternately flirtatious and inscrutable, effusive and aloof. She also cursed a lot, complaining that the salad they had ordered her "tastes like shit." As one person there said, "It was like hearing Shirley Temple curse." But Gwyneth was just *fun*, and no one there seemed offended. The meeting was humming along when Wintour interrupted to say, "Gwyneth, do you know Carolyn? She's the editor in chief of *Self*, our health and wellness brand. Carolyn was telling me that she has some concerns about the way you do your reporting."

Self's ad sales team would work on *Goop*, but selling ads for *Self* was hard enough as it was. Kylstra had seen *Self*'s print issue close down, and she was constantly fighting to keep the brand alive and prevent more job losses. (*The New York Times* even called the *Goop* print edition "the presumptive heiress to the now-defunct print edition of *Self*.") Kylstra had been following Goop's health claims and had told Wintour before the meeting that associating with Goop could be risky for a company that also published respected, rigorous journalism in *Vanity Fair* and *The New Yorker*.

"You really need to make sure that they use fact-checkers," she told Wintour, "because they don't really use science. They're not using evidence-based medicine when they give advice, and they give health advice that can be problematic."

Wintour had a habit of asking people to repeat comments made in private to the people they concerned.

"I'm sure there are ways that we can collaborate," Kylstra said, directing the comment to Gwyneth. "We could do something around beauty or food. There's travel. I think one area where it probably doesn't make sense for us to collaborate is around health and wellness. We have a different approach to how we report, and we generally rely on evidence and evidence-based medicine when we're making recommendations, and your approach doesn't really align with our brand."

Loehnen spoke up first. "We get it. You guys are really old and conservative, and we are progressive. You guys serve that audience, we serve a different one."

That was the end of the pushback in that meeting, and the brief Vegas marriage between Condé Nast and Goop commenced.

WINTOUR AND GWYNETH got along well at first. Wintour would call her "baby" in meetings, greeting her on the phone, "Hi, baby."

Bob Sauerberg, Condé's CEO at the time, said, "It was a lovefest in the early days."

The impression on the Condé side, however, was that Goop wanted to take years-old articles from their website and repackage them for the magazine in hopes of giving them new life. An editor on Condé's special-issues team would spend two weeks polishing up a Goop piece, then send it to the magazine's fact-checkers, who would mark up all the unverifiable claims and send it back. The editor would delete those lines, or mitigate them, or qualify them—and try again.

Wintour told her team that *Goop* in print needed to be fact-checked at the same standard as all other Condé Nast titles. She told a *Vogue* editor she had assigned to work on it, "I don't want to be embarrassed."

Condé staff would try to chase down the writers of the old Goop stories and ask for their sources and research materials, often about some scientifically dubious process like lymphatic drainage massage or pet psychics. This was a typical magazine fact-checking process, but it seemed new to Goop. Condé's editors felt like they were making good-faith efforts to substantiate the stories only to find them falling apart under scrutiny. The editors would suggest new pieces, like something soft on Gwyneth's favorite Pilates studios, but Goop continued to put forward the wellness content.

Loehnen tried to mediate between the parties, but the real resistance seemed to be coming from Gwyneth. As recalled by one person who was involved, her attitude was "They don't get it, we have to do this to help women. This is the patriarchy. Medical funding sponsors research that helps men." Gwyneth appeared to really believe that Goop was finally illuminating truths that other outlets would not. But how to fact-check a story in which Anthony William, the so-called Medical Medium, talked to "Spirit" about cancer?

Beyond the fact-checking issues, *Goop* magazine had a leadership problem: No one seemed to know whether Wintour was in charge or Gwyneth. When someone from the Condé staff emailed Gwyneth directly about the magazine, as though she were a regular editor just like the rest of them, they were informed that all communications with her should go through her staff. Wintour, more particular about images than text, took issue with a pantsuit editorial *Goop* had produced. She and Gwyneth hashed it out in a way that Gwyneth probably wasn't accustomed to, given how scared her team was to tell her no. Gwyneth's reaction, which trickled down to the Condé staff, was "Who's running this magazine—Anna or me?"

And while Goop wanted to promote their products in the magazine, Condé Nast's sales team worried that advertisers wouldn't buy space in a magazine that only wanted to promote its own merchandise.

The first issue of *Goop* in print somehow came together, opening with a guide to the healing power of crystals, in which Gwyneth was a true believer: "To rid rooms of negative energy and keep energy vampires out of your life, call on amethyst. The stone is also used to help with addictions to things as varied as alcohol, shopping, and negative self-talk." Despite all the differences in approach, the magazine remained true to her aesthetic and her interests. The cover's tagline cleverly pre-empted the next round of outrage: "Earth to Gwyneth."

Wintour and her senior staff seemed happy with the cover image of Gwyneth, nude apart from a bikini bottom and covered in mud, but they were uneasy about visible nipples. The Goop team thought the nipples were cool and subversive. But Goop was a newsstand product now, and so the nipples were Photoshopped out.

When it came time to find a cover image for the second issue, focused on sex and love, a booking editor from *Glamour* put together an entire slideshow of possible subjects, including around two dozen diverse couples. In the end, Gwyneth decided she should be on the cover again, this time in the arms of Brad Falchuk. Inside the magazine, she wore an unmissably large blue sapphire on her left ring finger. The issue was being used to announce their engagement after Falchuk surprised Gwyneth with a proposal in Umbria, Italy.

The magazine partnership dissolved after the second issue.

"I think we had a natural coming apart," recalled Sauerberg. "I don't know that they fully appreciated the thoroughness that we went through in journalism and the kind of rules we had with photo shoots and the way we did certain things. I think they thought we were perhaps a little old-school." (A Goop source maintained that the partnership fell apart because Condé couldn't sell ads, which was true—demand from advertisers was low.)

Loehnen told *Women's Wear Daily* in August 2018 that Condé had failed to provide the Goop team with adequate data, which was why the magazine separated and was published independently. "There was no transparency around where it was being distributed and how it was selling, and in various markets, in various pockets, from a distribution standpoint, we really need to know that."

Gwyneth quickly lost interest in the magazine anyway. Goop published two more issues on their own, then moved on.

CHAPTER 27

The Gwyneth Problem

[I]t was often a struggle of, how do we make this somewhat
affordable to anyone?

—Former Goop employee

I f Gwyneth was plotting the acquisition of her company—
something that Goop executives were discussing—then turning Goop into a beauty brand was the right instinct. Celebrity
beauty lines were not yet in their Whac-A-Mole era, when a new
brand (Rare Beauty by Selena Gomez, Rhode by Hailey Bieber,
Pleasing by Harry Styles, the Outset by Scarlett Johansson, Fenty
Beauty by Rihanna) seemed to pop up every week. Gomez's line, led
by CEO Scott Friedman, a seasoned beauty executive, was "highly
profitable" in early 2024, according to *The Business of Fashion*, and
surpassed $400 million in sales in twelve months ended February of
that year. Yet Gwyneth's Goop Beauty failed to vault the company to
unicorn status.

Gwyneth was still learning how to launch and grow a product line
when Goop decided to get out of its partnership with Juice Beauty.
While the partnership had provided proof of concept for a proprietary line, it added three to six months to launch timelines and didn't
generate enough revenue, since profits were shared with Juice Beauty.

(Juice Beauty founder Karen Behnke, however, said the agreement was always supposed to come to an end.)

Gwyneth wanted Goop Beauty to be "clean," like the Juice Beauty products, look beautiful, and feel luxurious. Yet the team struggled to come up with something that wouldn't be obscenely expensive to customers. She chose a designer with experience in the film world to work on the packaging. Rather than applying stickers to the containers, she wanted everything to be directly decorated onto the jars. The designer would suggest expensive ideas, like hand-painted ombré containers versus something a machine could produce faster and less expensively. Goop staff feared him showing her things that she would fall in love with, leaving them to explain that those weren't affordable, factory-friendly ideas they could realistically produce and turn a profit.

Gwyneth continued educating herself about her industry. She told employees that she had stayed up late one night, reading about inventory terms. But an appropriate pricing strategy eluded her. Goop executives were okay with high prices—Goop wasn't trying to appeal to the masses. (Former employees said the customer wasn't all that clearly defined beyond "wealthy white women" between the ages of twenty-five and forty.) Gwyneth occasionally revealed how removed she was from the average shopper. For example, she couldn't understand why some of her staff took public transportation to work. When an employee drove out to Gwyneth's Hamptons house for a meeting with her, she offered the staffer a helicopter ride back, which the employee declined in part because they didn't know what they'd do with the car they had driven there.

Goop Beauty launched with a $125 exfoliator, $98 face cream, and $125 glycolic peel. Someone who worked at Goop with knowledge of the figures said each product cost around $25,000 to $100,000 to make, and in the beginning, each sold hundreds of units per month. (Goop would sell hundreds of units just from featuring products in annual gift guides.) Later launches included an orange-flavored drinkable vitamin C powder.

Gwyneth was Goop's most effective face and sales tool, but she needed to step back. She didn't particularly enjoy modeling in Goop ads and appearing in social media content to promote her product lines, and finding time on her calendar to schedule shoots was becoming even more difficult. Plus, her preferred hair and makeup people were too expensive. Her team had to photograph the clothing line on models, like Kirsty Hume (who married Gwyneth's ex-boyfriend Donovan Leitch Jr. and divorced him in 2014) and Missy Rayder, but none of them became an identifiable G. Label face in the way that Kim Kardashian's SKIMS line—valued at $4 billion in 2023—would successfully cast diverse celebrities ranging from Kate Moss to SZA.

Goop needed to find a way for G. Label to sell without relying on Gwyneth, but distancing the brand from her image was a struggle. She seemed to understand that being able to sell G. Label on a model who wasn't her would strengthen Goop. An overreliance on Gwyneth made the company a risky acquisition target. The second she decided she didn't want to bother promoting Goop, the way she'd abandoned so many of its projects, it would lose value.

BRAD FALCHUK'S FATHER, Kenneth, a retired Harvard Medical School professor, died May 3, 2018. At the office, Gwyneth was in a product prototype meeting with a staff member who claimed to be clairvoyant and had disturbed other colleagues by offering to contact their dead grandmothers. Gwyneth told the seer that Falchuk's father had passed away.

"He's really sad," she said.

"I'm sure he's going to come through one day and let you guys know he's okay," the employee said.

Gwyneth closed her eyes and answered, "Will you let me know when he does?"

CHAPTER 28

Vanilla Fish and Celery Juice

You wouldn't bring your car to get repaired by your accountant.

—Dr. Andrea Love

By early 2020, Goop employed more than 250 people. The company was doing multimillion-dollar deals with brands including Netflix and Forevermark diamonds. The site experienced its first million-dollar sales day. The In Goop Health summit had expanded to New York. And Gwyneth, believing Goop should have a campus like Google, decided to move the company to new offices in Santa Monica. "We needed to have more than one toilet for 80 people," she told *Architectural Digest*, which once again featured Goop's new office space. But now she had her own bathroom. "My one diva-ish request was for a shower because I'm always coming to the office fresh from exercising, and I need to do a lot of hair and makeup for asset creation." While the office was gorgeous, it was also absurdly large, taking up a city block in Santa Monica, home to some of the world's most expensive real estate. One former employee believed that, had Goop not leased such lavish office space, it would have been profitable sooner.

Goop garnered continuous media coverage, and outlets took Gwyneth seriously as a CEO, which made the company look like it was thriving. But according to former employees, the difficult dynamic in the office remained, and it wasn't clear how aware of it Gwyneth was.

"I (basically) walked away from a career where people kissed my ass to being grilled by a VC or my board," she wrote on LinkedIn, suggesting she wasn't perceptive to the reality that it was happening again at Goop.

Around this time, Gwyneth commissioned a set of inspirational posters in Goop gray and pink to remind the staff of a philosophy called the Collaborative Way, tenets of which include "honoring commitments," "acknowledge & appreciate," "listening generously," "being for each other," and "speaking straight." The posters were "everywhere," one person said—a reminder of Goop's values to live by—"which a lot of people did not." But perhaps because the staff hadn't been trained in the method, it didn't seem to help the office culture. When someone announced, "I'm going to speak straight," the person on the other end was advised to "listen generously." But as the tensions in the office increased, speaking straight often just signaled that someone was about to say something nasty.

Gwyneth hired Andres Sosa as chief marketing officer in 2018. He came to Goop from Net-a-Porter's TheOutnet.com, which was based in London, and his appointment was announced in *The Business of Fashion*. Gwyneth quickly became dissatisfied with his performance, though, and before long she was rolling her eyes and making her classic vomit face behind his back. Sosa left after seven months. There was so much turnover in this period that employees joked every Friday about who would be next to go. When she wanted an employee out, Gwyneth would ask members of the C-suite to find a way to handle it, sometimes demoting a person to a contract role. When one of them came to announce they were leaving, Gwyneth put on a surprised, sad face: "Aw, you're leaving?"

"She's an Oscar-winning actress," one executive reminded people, "so take it with a grain of salt."

WHEN GWYNETH WANTED to launch a new product, she relied on her own instincts instead of market research to try to understand what people would buy from Goop.

After the first Goop Glow drink came out, Gwyneth decided the next one should contain collagen to improve skin, and the flavor should be "birthday cake." The person overseeing the drink powder was prevented by a more senior executive from explaining to Gwyneth that collagen comes from the sea, which gives it a fishy flavor, and that normally, a company would consult with a flavor house about a taste to mask the fishiness. When the flavor samples came in, instead of tasting like birthday cake, it tasted more like "vanilla fish," said someone who tried it. Gwyneth's staff knew it was revolting and served her only half a shot, which she drank before approving the product. But customers were recommended to consume eight ounces per serving. The product sold poorly and ended up being given away in goodie bags handed out for free at promotional events.

THE SOMETIMES-TOXIC DYNAMIC in the office escaped press coverage for many years. Part of that was due to Goop having many employees sign NDAs, which left them terrified to talk about their experiences and Gwyneth. Part of it was due to Noora Raj Brown, the company's publicist, who was determined to both protect Gwyneth and to portray Goop as an established, durable company, and to shift its media strategy away from the reactivity of the early years. The company announced $50 million in Series C funding in early 2018, valuing it at $250 million. This represented a milestone for Goop, even if other celebrity brands continued to rapidly outpace it—Kim Kardashian's KKW beauty line, for instance, sold a 20 percent stake to Coty in 2020, valuing the brand at $1 billion.

Goop's media coverage was still dominated by its controversies. "Ultimately, we decided we couldn't change that cycle until we did something that would reset it," said Raj Brown. She thought Goop's $250 million valuation would finally show people that this wasn't "a blog or side hustle." But she needed to get the news out in the right way. She thought issuing a press release "wouldn't make any real waves." So Raj Brown arranged for a major magazine profile of Gwyneth in *The New York Times Magazine*.

With journalist Taffy Brodesser-Akner in tow, Gwyneth traveled to Harvard in late 2017 to speak to a class at the business school called the Business of Entertainment, Media, and Sports. Students were invited to ask Gwyneth questions about all aspects of Goop, from the clothing line to the newsletter. She told the class that Goop's controversies weren't designed to be clickbait. "It's a cultural firestorm when it's about a woman's vagina," she said. As Brodesser-Akner wrote, "The room was silent. She then cupped her hands around her mouth and yelled, 'VAGINA! VAGINA! VAGINA!' as if she were yodeling."

Brodesser-Akner went to Gwyneth's Brentwood house, where the two ate dinner together and smoked cigarettes. She interviewed Gwyneth in Goop's office and at the Carlyle hotel. Talking about her reporting later, Brodesser-Akner described the fact-checking process as unusually tense. Often subjects of profiles get scared when the fact-checking questions come through, Brodesser-Akner explained. "[A]s everyone knows and as you always try to prepare them, it's like, it's gonna seem incendiary, but her PR person's questions for me were like, 'How come we have not been asked for confirmation that the company is valued at $250 million?'—none of the questions were like, 'Is it true that Gwyneth Paltrow is the CEO of this company? How come we've only been asked about a cigarette?'" Brodesser-Akner said. "They thought that I was, like, taking her down for smok[ing] . . . I was gonna show the world that she's no health guru. She's a cigarette smoker."

In the end, the story didn't describe Gwyneth as CEO because it seemed unnecessary—as it might be unnecessary to describe Walt Disney as the founder of Disney. "[T]hey were very, very mistrustful of me," Brodesser-Akner said. "Like when it went to press, they were distancing themselves from me. They're like, 'I don't know, that doesn't sound right.' And luckily, I tape everything. I write everything down."

The story wasn't the usual puff piece about Gwyneth's warm smile and delicious cooking. It chronicled Goop's controversies, the accusations of quackery, but it also gave a clear, forceful expression to the other side: "Some would argue—her former partners at Condé Nast, for sure—that it is giving an unfiltered platform to quackery or witchery. O.K., O.K., but what is quackery? What is witchery? Is it claims that have been observed but not the subject of double-blind, peer-reviewed studies? Yes? Right.

O.K., G.P. would say, then what is science, and is it all-encompassing and altruistic and without error and always acting in the interests of humanity?"

Ultimately, Raj Brown talked about the story as a win. "[I]t was on the cover of *New York Times Magazine* that Goop was worth $250 million. The story had enough intriguing controversy for it to go viral—in some ways good and in some ways bad. But we were able to take control of the narrative by putting ourselves out there on our terms. It was a bit of a denouement for us."

While the article didn't put to bed the narrative that Gwyneth promoted pseudoscience, it announced to millions of *The New York Times* readers that Goop would soon hire a "full-time fact-checker" and had hired a lawyer to vet all claims on the site, along with an expert in nutritional science and a director of science and research. Putting that infrastructure in place helped Goop quiet the news stories about it publishing pseudoscience, Brown said in 2023: "Every wellness story got a real fact-check."

HOWEVER, IT'S NOT clear that Goop did hire a traditional, full-time fact-checker. Three former employees said the company didn't have fact-checkers during this period, one explaining that, in fairness, when Gwyneth mentioned it in the interview with the *Times*, she probably did not "understand the function of a fact-checker at a magazine." Another editor remembered a copy editor, who typically edits for grammar, taking it upon herself to fact-check some stories.

The company did hire experts to screen the content for any potential legal issues or dangerous misinformation. One was Dr. Susan Beck, a nutritional scientist with a PhD who joined the company in June 2018 as senior vice president for science and research. Goop made her available for an interview with *The Business of Fashion*, and she described a new "testing protocol" that would ensure every Goop product was free of heavy metals, allergens, microbials, and pesticides. "We are going to educate our consumers on what we test for, and why, as well as post our test results, which is something the FDA doesn't require and most companies do not reveal to their consumers."

But one of Beck's primary concerns was making sure Goop didn't break the law. Selling jade eggs was never the problem; the legal issue arose when Goop linked out from the interview with Shiva Rose saying that the eggs could cure various medical ailments. This potentially amounted to making drug claims about a product, which were regulated by the FDA. The regulations are not always well-enforced, but Gwyneth had become a lightning rod.

Beck also hired Gerda Endemann, who held a PhD in nutritional biochemistry from MIT, to vet claims made about products Goop was selling that could run afoul of the FDA, to fact-check both old and new articles on the site, and to write stories herself. She and Gwyneth aligned on how they thought about health coverage. People could go to WebMD instead of Goop for health advice, but Gwyneth and Endemann believed that research was dated—that Goop was on the cutting edge. And Gwyneth didn't look to other media outlets to validate Goop story ideas. She wanted to tell readers about treatments and research that weren't yet settled science. Meditation, for example, once was considered a fringe spiritual practice in the U.S. before experts agreed on its health benefits.

Gwyneth wanted to help people become early adopters, just like her. She repeated one specific anecdote to illustrate this in three different interviews around this time. "Forgive me if this comes out wrong," she said in one with *WSJ. Magazine*, "but I went to do a yoga class in L.A. recently and the twenty-two-year-old girl behind the counter was like, 'Have you ever done yoga before?' And literally I turned to my friend, and I was like, 'You have this job because I've done yoga before.'"

Endemann wrote about the benefits of seed oils. Gwyneth had told Endemann she believed they were unhealthy, but she was fine with Endemann publishing a story with the alternate view, which one Goop staff member said proved her willingness to share with readers what science knew. Endemann also wrote about the benefits of red-light therapy. "Clinical research has shown that red light triggers reactions in cells that support skin rejuvenation and boost smoothness, elasticity, and appearance." The story linked out to two red-light face masks available for sale in the Goop store for $299 and $435, and a "gemstone heat therapy mat" for $1,049. When it was originally published, the story bore a label at the top—part of a new tagging system—that read "SUPPORTED BY SCIENCE," which linked out to a study about red light. Readers who clicked the arrow below that brought up a new message: "There's sound science and published research supporting this concept." The nonprofit *Consumer Reports* reported that the American Academy of Dermatology said that while red-light treatment was effective when administered in a medical office on powerful machines, the less powerful at-home masks were expensive, might not lead to visible results for everyone, and were most effective if used for thirty to sixty minutes twice per day over four to five weeks. But readers didn't find that information in Goop.

This tagging system was ostensibly designed to let readers know which content had scientific backing. Stories that didn't were published under a different tag, such as "HYPOTHESIS AND EMERGING RESEARCH," which linked to drop-down text that read, "Some early observations support this concept (or parts of the theory), and there is scientific interest in elucidating exactly what's at work." Or "FAS-CINATING PHENOMENA": "These are concepts and practices that we're deeply curious about. They typically fall outside the realm of conventional biomedicine but really resonate with some." Goop staff went to Endemann to consult about the scientific literature, and they generally followed her recommendations, but she was uneasy about the "HYPOTHESIS" label: *If something isn't true,* she thought, *do you just publish it and call it a hypothesis?* Though she would have liked to tone down some claims, the editorial team didn't always want to.

Endemann disagreed with her colleagues about Anthony William, the Medical Medium, who drove considerable traffic to the site. (One former employee admitted, "We used him when we needed page views.") Since his stories didn't plug products, they didn't pose a legal risk. When Goop published an excerpt from his book *Medical Medium: Secrets Behind Chronic and Mystery Illness and How to Finally Heal,* they added a tag that read: "FASCINATING BUT INEXPLICABLE," later updated to

"FASCINATING PHENOMENA" with an editor's note stating, "We trust that you'll quickly understand that this medical medium is operating well outside the bounds of medicine and science."* (The article stated that the Epstein–Barr virus causes thyroid cancer, which infectious disease expert Dr. Adalja said could be misleading; while Epstein-Barr is a cancer-causing virus, it doesn't cause the primary types of thyroid cancer.)

Endemann was uncomfortable specifically with stories containing William's claims about celery juice. One about "healing foods" (published in 2016, before she started) claimed that celery could help cure fifty-three medical conditions, ranging from acne to pancreatic cancer. William doubled down on these statements in another piece on "the Virtues of Celery Juice," stating that "celery juice is . . . one of the greatest healing tonics of all time. I've seen thousands of people who suffer from chronic and mystery illnesses restore their health by drinking sixteen ounces of celery juice daily on an empty stomach." This coverage was credited in outlets like *The New York Times* and *The Atlantic* with starting a celery juice craze. The story brought in so much traffic, thanks in part to careful search engine optimization by Goop staff, that editors declined to change the stories, even after Endemann expressed her concerns.

Andrea Love, the microbiologist and immunologist, described herself as "at a loss" to explain the appeal of someone like William. "You wouldn't bring your car to get repaired by your accountant, because they don't know what they're doing." Love stressed that William lacks scientific training—the kind that would prevent a doctor from telling patients celery juice could cure many ailments—and that his advice, by steering people away from in some cases lifesaving treatments, has "caused tangible harm" to many people. "Because he's got this amplification by these celebrity voices, he has become mainstream," she added.

---

* Yet the tagging system seemed inconsistent. Filed under "ANCIENT MODALITIES," a 2016 Q&A with Durek Verrett (who married Norwegian princess Märtha Louise in 2024) reported that to become a shaman he had to "actually die" and then come back to life. Several outlets even reported that he may have suggested children got cancer because they wanted it. Gwyneth called him her "light in shining armor."

But William was just one of many "experts" spouting pseudoscience through Goop, which former editors stressed was publishing fewer fringe articles by this point. As one example, ex-staff cited "Goop PhD," a series of stories about women's health issues, such as polycystic ovarian syndrome, that were common but not widely covered.

Yet in its January 2018 In Goop Health summit in New York, Goop featured as a speaker the psychiatrist Kelly Brogan, who had called the idea that HIV causes AIDS a "meme" and written that "drug toxicity associated with AIDS treatment may very well be what accounts for the majority of deaths." Brogan was an anti-vaxxer who claimed to be able to cure people without drugs. Despite headlines in Jezebel, *Newsweek*, and the *New York Post* about her dangerous claims, Goop featured Brogan on its podcast eleven months later.

"If you are willing to sit down with an AIDS denialist, you don't need to tell me anything else about [Gwyneth]. To me, that tells me that she's objectively an awful human being. It means you just care about attention and profit and money," said Dr. Gunter.

The same summit featured Taz Bhatia, who wrote a blog post saying that parents should consider an alternate vaccine schedule for their children, for a host of non-scientifically backed reasons, including if they had used IVF. (The Centers for Disease Control and Prevention and the American Academy of Pediatrics advise against this.) Bhatia went on to be featured on Goop repeatedly, along with more mainstream outlets like the *Today* show.

In 2019, speaking at *Vanity Fair's* New Establishment Summit, Gwyneth acknowledged some mistakes as CEO but described these as financial rather than ethical. "I have learned so much. And so much by making such grave mistakes that have cost millions of dollars," she said without elaborating. (One former executive suspected she could be referring to the high cost of employee turnover, including hiring expensive people who didn't work out, and having a vesting structure that allowed employees to walk away with equity after a year, which chipped into Goop's cap table.) Regarding Goop's controversies, Gwyneth pointed out that bad press often increased traffic. "In many cases, it really benefits us, because, like, we rank number one or two in SEO for a number of these topics that are now really super-popular. Like, you know, detox and celery juice, for example."

After Goop helped bring William into the mainstream, journalists started investigating him. *Inverse* and *Vanity Fair* published stories about people who died after seeking William's medical advice. *Inverse* interviewed Kate Gallagher Leong, who'd paid three hundred dollars for an hour-long phone consultation about her son, who was suffering from conditions doctors couldn't diagnose. William told her she had passed the Epstein–Barr virus on to him in utero, and suggested she give him vitamins. He died forty-eight days later. *Vanity Fair* focused on one of William's most devoted followers, Stephanie Tisone, who told William and his associates about a large lump in her left breast, which was followed by a cascade of debilitating symptoms, including pain so severe she couldn't stand. William at one point told her she had shingles and advised she take vitamin C and lysine. Though he never told her not to see a doctor, and at one point texted her, "[D]on't be afraid of getting attention from a doc on the breast," one person who worked with him told her the lump was a "viral flare." As she underwent tests, William stopped replying to her messages. She had delayed seeking care for so long that by the time it was detected, she had stage IV metastatic breast cancer that had eroded her spine. When a doctor gave her the diagnosis, she wanted to check it with William, but he never responded.

Tisone died in November 2018 at thirty-eight years old, and friends and family blamed her belief in William for her delay in seeing doctors. The next month, the *Wall Street Journal*'s glossy *WSJ.* magazine asked Gwyneth about some of the controversies over Goop's wellness coverage.

"I'm so happy to suffer those slings and arrows, because if you look at the culture from then to now, people are so curious," she said. "It's so beautiful to see people feeling empowered by natural solutions or ancient modalities alongside science and medicine."

Gwyneth was never as close to William as she was to Sadeghi. But Goop still boosted his public profile. And his celebrity connections grew to include Kim Kardashian, Robert De Niro, and Demi Moore.

CHAPTER 29

First Comes Love,
Then Comes Branding

I wouldn't buy that candle.

—Martha Stewart

Friday, November 2, 2018, was a particularly stressful day for the Goop editors assigned to a story titled "The Wedding Party: GP x Brad Tie the Knot." Many of the vendors used for the wedding had donated goods and services, two Goop employees said,[*] so any missed credits in the story amounted to stiffing them. All of the brands and vendors were carefully documented in a "sourcebook" accompanying forty-eight photos of the event—everyone from the invitation calligrapher to the cocktail napkin designer. Goop had always been transactional, but Gwyneth hadn't yet applied that strategy to a life event this personal and of this magnitude.

· · ·

---

[*] At least one vendor asked to provide product for the wedding—who signed an NDA at planners' request—was too small to produce all the items requested; Goop agreed to pay a usage fee to help accommodate the necessary increase in production.

FOR HER FIRST marriage, Gwyneth hadn't had a big wedding or the accompanying festivities. This time, she indulged in extravagance. First came a bachelorette party in Cabo with friends, including Stella McCartney and Cameron Diaz, who reportedly chartered a jet for the occasion. Then a blowout engagement party with four hundred people thrown by Ryan Murphy at the Los Angeles Theater. One person who attended said the event was unbelievably gorgeous and ended with people smoking cigarettes and weed on the lower-level dance floor.

At the rehearsal dinner, which took place at Gwyneth's home in Amagansett, guests enjoyed Argentinian chef Francis Mallmann's "twelve-hour grilled pineapple," which dangled dramatically over a circle of burning logs, along with other "wood-fired dishes" that Goop noted were kept warm in cast-iron cocottes by Staub (a brand with which she'd had an endorsement deal). Gwyneth slipped into a couture white lace Valentino dress with cap sleeves—also a gift—and affixed a delicate, floor-skimming veil to the crown of her head to marry Brad Falchuk near the spot on her grounds where she had buried her father's ashes. Seventy guests, including Steven Spielberg, who filmed it, gathered to witness the wedding. Guests were shuttled around in retro-style Moke cars; drank gin-lemon-thyme cocktails served on vintage trays from L.A.-based "luxury tabletop" store Casa de Perrin; and sat on more furniture by Restoration Hardware. The servers wore aprons by a brand called Fog Linen. Another vendor saw their website traffic double once the wedding photos went live on Goop, though the extra visits didn't result in a noticeable sales spike.

Gwyneth's private life was now a stage for wellness and luxury. She took the same approach after completing a six-year rebuild of the home she purchased in Montecito for $4.9 million in 2016, which also featured furniture by Restoration Hardware and appeared in an *Architectural Digest* cover story in 2022. Much of Gwyneth's compensation came from brand endorsement deals. While she made endorsements independent of Goop, like Frederique Constant watches, two people familiar with the payment structure said brands that wanted to run media featuring Gwyneth on Goop would do a deal with Goop and a separate deal with Gwyneth's personal reps. (Sometimes she had Goop staff vet products she was considering promoting in these private, non-Goop endorsement deals.)

Falchuk, one observer said, "really likes being Gwyneth Paltrow's husband." The two waited to move in together until some time after the wedding. He would spend four nights a week at her home and the other three at the place he shared with his two kids from his previous marriage. Gwyneth said her intimacy coach, Michaela Boehm—whose résumé included a psychology degree, "spiritual explorations with Celtic Mysticism," and training in yoga and improv—endorsed the arrangement for bringing "polarity" into the marriage.

"Oh, all my married friends say that the way we live sounds ideal and we shouldn't change a thing," Gwyneth said. But they did it mostly to ease the transition for the kids.

Gwyneth remained committed to maintaining a good relationship with her ex-husband. She posted pictures on Instagram of Chris Martin and Falchuk having brunch together. Over Christmas in 2019, the three of them took a "family honeymoon" to the Maldives with Apple, Moses, Falchuk's two children, and Dakota Johnson, whom Martin was dating at the time. ("I adore her. She's a fantastic woman," Gwyneth said.)

Speaking at the 2023 In Goop Health, Gwyneth said, "I'm still very close with my ex-husband. We've sort of morphed it into a true family. I know it sounds really weird to say, but he's kind of like my brother now. And it's hard for people to understand, but I did really make a commitment that he would stay my family, and I think we suffer a lot less because of that. I think it's incredibly painful for a woman, when you've co-mingled your DNA with a man, if you have no contact and acrimony and nothing between you. So if you're able to, transmogrify that into a different type of relationship and family. That's what we've been able to do, thank goodness."

· · ·

ABSENT FROM THE wedding were some of Gwyneth's oldest friends from Spence, who were confused by her disappearance from their lives. Those who were invited included Derek Blasberg, a onetime *Vogue* employee whose friendships with celebrities like Kate Hudson and Gwyneth had helped turn him into an influencer with 1.6 million Instagram followers. (His partner Nick Brown's firm had also invested in Goop.) When Blasberg befriended Gwyneth, her old friends were surprised, given that he seemed like the type she would have made fun of years ago.

"When I first met him, I was a little dubious," Gwyneth admitted. "I was like, 'Are you a professional friend of celebrities?'... After ten seconds, I fell completely in love with him." Gwyneth's circle around this time also included Amy Griffin, wife of billionaire hedge fund founder John Griffin, whose firm, G9, also invested in Goop. (At first, Gwyneth told friends Griffin was one of her "disciples" and "wants to be me." But then she moved closer to Griffin and distanced from others.)

While staying at her Montecito home, Blasberg suffered what was alleged to have been Ozempic-induced (a detail that was later called into question by the *Daily Mail*) diarrhea in the bed of the guesthouse, then fled without telling her, leaving her housekeeper to clean it up. Gwyneth was appalled. Brown, his partner, called her to try to smooth things over, but Gwyneth was reportedly so offended that Blasberg hadn't apologized personally, said one person with knowledge of the events, that she ensured that the story leaked. She did this in part by sharing it at multiple dinner parties, said someone else with knowledge of the events. In a *Daily Mail* piece, a "source" later said that Gwyneth felt bad the story got out and "would like to eventually laugh about this with Derek, but currently there is still much embarrassment." In a 2025 *Vanity Fair* interview, asked directly about the incident, Gwyneth issued no denials.

AFTER SHE STARTED seeing Falchuk, Gwyneth's interest in sex seemed to pique, and she launched what she cast as a crusade to remove the stigma from women's sexuality. Goop's first sex issue, published in

2016, covered everything from "toxic" lubricant (Goop offered a "non-toxic" version) to "not-so-basic sex toys," like a $15,000 24-carat gold vibrator. Around January 2020, Gwyneth and Douglas Little, founder of fragrance brand Heretic, came up with an idea they thought was hilarious, someone familiar with their thinking said: the "This Smells Like My Vagina" candle, which Goop sold for seventy-five dollars. Unsurprisingly, reviewers and buyers wondered whether the candle smelled specifically like *Gwyneth's* vagina. In fact, the scent was composed of "geranium, citrusy bergamot, and cedar absolutes juxtaposed with damask rose and ambrette seed." It sold out in days.

The candle had gone so viral that Martha Stewart was called upon to respond. "She does that kind of that irritatingly—she's trying to [get] the public to listen to her, and that's great, I mean, let her do her thing," she said on *Watch What Happens Live with Andy Cohen* when a fan called in to ask for her take. "I wouldn't buy that candle." Host Cohen asked what she thought it said about America that the candle was sold out. "I think it's not America," Stewart replied. "I think it's a lot of guys who are horny."

Naturally, Gwyneth followed up with a candle called "This Smells Like My Orgasm."

AROUND 2018, GWYNETH'S next big idea presented itself: a Goop Netflix show. Producers thought at first it could be part reality show, depicting Goop behind the scenes, and they came into the office to find potential "characters" and get a feel for the setting.

Also around this time, Falchuk and Murphy lured Gwyneth to a different Netflix show they co-created, *The Politician*, in which she played the patrician mother of a high school student. Falchuk told Gwyneth that he had written the part just for her.

Despite its full name being *The Goop Lab with Gwyneth Paltrow*, the show about her workplace was supposed to position Gwyneth in the background of the Goop brand. Though she hosted the program, others on staff were filmed trying out various wellness treatments, ranging from cold therapy to energy healing. In the first episode, staff including Loehnen and Gwyneth's longtime assistant Kevin Keating take psychedelic mushrooms in Jamaica in an effort to work through personal trauma. Gwyneth dabbled in treatments like the cold plunge, but was not the primary test subject.

In its review of *The Goop Lab*, *Variety* wrote, "Paltrow is a compelling host—not giving too much of herself away, ever stopping short of pure endorsement of any topic even as she gives it air—on what is a carefully structured, elegantly built, compulsively watchable show about, mainly, complete nonsense." *The Guardian* called it "a dangerous win for pseudoscience." But the backlash to the criticism, the anti-institutional argument that Paltrow had been seeding for years, was also taking hold. In *The New York Times* opinion section, writers Elisa Albert and Jennifer Block asked, "So what underlies all the overwhelming, predictable, repetitive critiques?" Calling Gwyneth an "easy target," they pointed out that "just as there are wannabe gurus selling snake oil, there are irresponsible, unethical physicians, as well as physicians with a shameful incapacity for nuance or empathy. Reiki is not proven to shrink tumors in any double-blind trials, but it, along with yoga and mindfulness and acupuncture, is being used in integrative cancer therapy at major institutions all over the world, because there *is* evidence that it has benefits, and no adverse side effects." Regarding the yoni egg, they added that no users had reported any significant harm, which was more than could be said for some FDA-approved products, like the birth control device Essure and pelvic mesh.

Then–Food and Drug Administration commissioner Dr. Robert Califf might disagree. In April 2023, he said medical misinformation specifically was contributing to life expectancy in the U.S. that was three to five years lower than the average in fellow high-income countries. The sense of community that Goop fosters with its Netflix show and summits was key—this only "increases your susceptibility to health misinformation," said Timothy Caulfield. While one could view Goop as peddling expensive, harmless nonsense, it promoted the same troubling ideas as the anti-vaxx movement, like that "doing your own research" was better than trusting the medical establishment. Plus, with a platform so big and impactful, it seemed particularly irresponsible for Gwyneth and Goop to feature people with no medical training masquerading as doctors, helping to spread and legitimize their unfounded ideas.

TRUTH IN ADVERTISING checked in on Goop in 2020 and discovered the company was back to making allegedly deceptive health claims. Again they sent Goop a letter, and again some changes were made—but not enough. In a new complaint to California district attorneys, TINA.org accused Goop of deceitful marketing on products it claimed could "treat and/or mitigate the symptoms of several medical conditions, including anxiety, depression, OCD, hormone imbalances, and hair loss, as well as address the symptoms of excessive alcohol consumption." The yoni egg, for instance, was still listed as a treatment for hormone imbalance.

Mashable writer Brenda Stolyar interviewed Gwyneth at the launch of Jerusalem Venture Partners' International Cyber Center. Gwyneth was there in a vague capacity to represent women in tech and promote cybersecurity, but Stolyar wrote, "It was when I asked about Goop's role in disseminating questionable health advice in the era of fake news that the light and airy mood shifted just a bit."

"I think there's a lot happening in the media right now, in terms of trying to say we give health advice," Gwyneth told her. "Or they use the word pseudo-scientific, which drives me crazy, because pseudo-science is saying: 'This pillow will fix your back pain.' And we don't do that. If we're interested in something, we'll get an expert opinion and do a Q&A." She added that Goop doesn't "dole out any advice." This despite an advice column then running on Goop, called "Ask Gerda," with headlines like "Ask Gerda: Should I Take Vitamin C for Immunity?" Gwyneth said the criticism was "clickbait and bullshit . . . it's a cheap and easy way to try and drive traffic to these [news] sites."

California authorities didn't take further action against Goop (Bonnie Patten guessed this had to do with a lack of resources), and the jade-egg-related settlement the company had signed in 2018 expired in 2023.

Patten said that Gwyneth "designed the playbook for other rich and famous people to copycat Goop." In 2024, when TINA.org investigated allegedly misleading claims made on menopause products, it found that Gwyneth, along with celebrities including Serena Williams, Jennifer Garner, and Kate Walsh, had endorsed menopause supplements making allegedly false or deceptive statements. Gwyneth hasn't popularized "wellness" so much as "wellness for the rich," Patten said. "The regular workingwoman can't decide when she wants to take a break or make sure she gets her bath time in every evening . . . It's not possible to live the life of Gwyneth Paltrow. We can't afford her life or her solutions."

THOUGH THE CONTROVERSIES provided buzz for Goop, the company aimed to return money to investors, having raised $140 million, according to PitchBook. So Gwyneth tried once again to get more serious about profitability. Goop was making 70 percent of its revenue through product sales by March 2019, and Gwyneth decided the editorial work was distracting from that income stream. Consultants she'd hired to chart Goop's future told her that the site could get away with recycling far more of its articles without compromising revenue. So Goop started cutting editors, including those who had been making Gwyneth's lunch, leaving her to bring food from home or order in like her staff.

By 2020, Goop was valued at $433 million. After some budget cuts, the company was profitable for a short period that year, but it didn't last. "We've had profitable months, many of those, but I don't want to say full profitability until we have a full year," Gwyneth told *Fortune* in March 2025.

Elise Loehnen left in October 2020 to write the book *On Our Best Behavior: The Seven Deadly Sins and the Price Women Pay to Be Good*. She was one of at least 140 employees to depart within that two-year period, along with Goop's chief financial officer, chief technology officer, chief revenue officer, general counsel, and editor in chief, according to an analysis of LinkedIn data by *Business Insider*. And 140 may have been on the low end: Some employees cycled in and out so quickly they didn't even list their time at Goop on LinkedIn.

DJENABA PARKER WAS looking for her next move toward the end of 2020, after spending more than eight years at Red Bull, working her way up to senior vice president and general counsel of North America. Gwyneth was looking for a new general counsel, and got connected to Parker. In the midst of COVID lockdowns, the two talked on Zoom about a dual chief people officer/chief counsel role, and Parker felt like they clicked. They aligned on a desire to make Goop work for customers, but also employees.

There was a hitch, though. Parker was unable to work full-time in Los Angeles. "For the right talent, we'll work it out," Gwyneth told her. "I'm a true believer that women can do anything. Except triplets," she laughed.

After consulting, Parker started full-time in early 2021. To strengthen the culture, she worked with Gwyneth on the unsexy parts of the business: improving HR processes that were already in place by implementing regular formalized performance and compensation reviews, and assessing employee engagement. Then there was the fun stuff, like hosting weekly events for employees, ranging from sound baths to Solidcore Pilates sessions to cooking classes. Or the company might bring in a "matcha stand" or a spread of adaptogenic mushrooms or the famous Courage Bagels (plebeians often wait an hour to buy them in Los Angeles).

Parker said, "The food ones tend to be very popular."

. . . .

TWO DAYS AFTER her fiftieth birthday, Gwyneth boarded a plane for Italy and popped a Xanax. She was on her way to a cruise ship anchored near Rome, where she would headline an event called Goop at Sea, a collaboration with Celebrity Cruises. Dressed in a gray sweatsuit, Gwyneth took her seat onstage to speak to "holistic psychiatrist" Ellen Vora, between sips of green juice from a glass Evian bottle.

Gwyneth said she didn't "have anxiety" at the time but she "can tip into overwhelm and stress." This was a challenging period where she was staying up until three a.m. worrying about an impending recession, and how that might impact Goop. After fifty-one minutes, she got up, waved at the crowd, blew a kiss, and jogged away up the stairs.

To mark the birthday, she'd shared photos of herself nude on social media, covered with gold body paint (to honor her "golden jubilee"), and given an interview to *CBS News Sunday Morning*. Looking back on her early fame, she said, "You know, to reach that kind of, like, pinnacle at that age and have that much scrutiny and attention, and then it's like, no matter what you do after that, you can't really win, right? It's like you have a few years of it's, like, nothing's gonna live up to that. It's just a lot to hold."

Apple had just left for Nashville to attend college at Vanderbilt University. "I know it sounds nuts, but it feels almost as profound as giving birth," Gwyneth said. "As a woman, you turn fifty, and maybe we all give ourselves permission to be exactly who we are. And we stop trying to be what other people are expecting us to be, and you kind of exhale into this other thing."

CHAPTER 30

Ski You in Court

It's hard to overcome that kind of influence and power.

—Terry Sanderson

Terry Sanderson sued Gwyneth over their 2016 skiing collision for $3.1 million in damages, claiming that she'd been out of control and crashed into him, leaving him with brain damage and four broken ribs. In the January 2019 suit, he claimed that Gwyneth had skied away without helping him, and that a Deer Valley ski instructor had filed a false report to back up her story. She filed a countersuit saying that she "was enjoying skiing with her family on vacation in Utah, when Plaintiff—who was uphill from Ms. Paltrow—plowed into her back. She sustained a full 'body blow.' Ms. Paltrow was angry with Plaintiff and said so. Plaintiff apologized. She was shaken and upset, and quit skiing for the day even though it was still morning." The suit added that a Deer Valley instructor had seen the incident and vouched that Sanderson had skied into Gwyneth from behind, and that Sanderson's suit was an "attempt to exploit her celebrity and wealth." Gwyneth asked for damages of a dollar.

.   .   .

AFTER SANDERSON'S INITIAL lawsuit was thrown out, he reduced his demand for damages to $300,000. Now, the trial was on and teed up to be the celebrity farce of 2023. Sanderson said in a 2025 interview for this book that "there was no reaching out, no contact, no efforts by attorneys to resolve" the case out of court. "I think it was just her time to stand up to something."

Gwyneth seemed to support this view in comments she made roughly two years after the trial. "I have to say, the idea that someone could ski into your back and knock you down and sue you ... I was like, 'This is everything that's wrong with our legal system.'"

Sanderson's insurance company gave him lawyers to choose from for the trial, and he picked Kristin VanOrman over the men, partly because he thought she would be "on equal terms" with Gwyneth. However, he acknowledged, "That didn't turn out too well."

"This week marked the return of one of the most riveting shows featuring affluent white people, the limits of their kindness, the destruction they're capable of, and the power they wield," wrote Alex Abad-Santos on Vox. "Welcome to the second week of the Gwyneth Paltrow hit-and-run ski trial."

The trial was a bizarre spectacle merging Gwyneth's public, private, and professional lives. Before she stepped into the courtroom, she had gone viral for saying on a podcast with her latest favored wellness expert and self-described "functional medicine provider" Will Cole—while hooked up to an IV of "good old-fashioned vitamins"—that she often had just bone broth for lunch. She added, "I have used ozone therapy, uh, rectally" (a practice that involved shooting ozone—a toxic gas—into her rectum, which the FDA has warned against).

But her questionable wellness persona was quickly sidelined in court by her fashion: appropriately conservative, given the setting, but also noticeably wealth-signifying. On the first trial day, March 21, 2023, Gwyneth wore a loose cream-colored sweater with a funnel turtleneck that collapsed on itself just so, her hair down and straight, mostly tucked behind her ears. Her expression shifted from disbelief to concern as she listened to Sanderson's attorney Lawrence Buhler describe the accident in his opening statement. Buhler told the jury that Gwyneth slammed into him from behind, knocking him face down in the snow, then left without apologizing or identifying herself.

Gwyneth's lawyer, Stephen Owens, told a different story in his opening statement: Sanderson had skied into her from behind, causing their skis to interlock. He also said Gwyneth had stayed at the scene until ski patrol came and asked Sanderson, who was seventy-six, if he was all right. Owens argued that skiing is risky, and no one could be at fault in this kind of mishap.

Utah courts generally allow cameras, and the trial unfolded on an internet livestream, a performance like Gwyneth hadn't given in years, with the protagonist in sleek designer clothes that left everything around her—the lawyers, the courtroom, the spectators, the witnesses—looking acutely drab. Gwyneth wore G. Label cardigans, leather culottes that may have been Proenza Schouler White Label, a coat and sweater by the Row, and a pouf-sleeved black sweater and boots by Prada: a real-life illustration of the quiet luxury trend associated with shows like *Succession*, where the soft power of wealth eclipses everything that stands in its way.

Town & Country published a list of Gwyneth's identifiable trial outfits and included links to G. Label pieces; *GQ* declared she "dressed brilliantly for the court of public opinion"; BuzzFeed said, "Gwyneth Paltrow's courtroom attire slayed."

Sanderson said he wasn't paying attention to the media coverage. However, while his team had told him not to engage with the jury, he said at one point that he noticed Gwyneth looking over at a couple of young women jurors, smiling, and giving them a wink. "You could just see the fandom," he recalled. "You begin to realize she's a powerful force and nothing was going to change their mind."

Gwyneth took the stand on the fourth and fifth days of the trial. She testified that Sanderson had skied into her, his skis "forcing my legs apart, and then there was a body pressing against me, and there was a very strange grunting noise." She thought she was being sexually assaulted. But ultimately, she emphasized, she could not be responsible for Sanderson's fall or injuries because "Mr. Sanderson categorically hit me on that ski slope and that is the truth."

Her cross-examination was, at times, just silly. Gwyneth told the jury that she was merely "friendly" with Taylor Swift, but not good friends. (Sanderson's attorney compared the two since both filed lawsuits seeking a symbolic dollar in damages.)

"Is it true that you feel it's unfair that Mr. Sanderson has brought this case against you?" asked Sanderson's lawyer, Kristin VanOrman.

"I do," replied Gwyneth, more somber than indignant.

"And he has deterred you from enjoying the rest of what was a very expensive vacation?"

"Well, I lost half a day of skiing," Gwyneth replied.

VanOrman seemed as susceptible as any other civilian to Gwyneth's charms and fame.

Asked to give her height, Gwyneth answered just five foot ten. "I am so jealous!" VanOrman said.

"I think I'm shrinking, though."

"I have to wear four-inch heels just to make it to five-five," VanOrman said.

Gwyneth smiled. "Well, they're very nice."

TRIAL MEMES FLOODED the internet. People made T-shirts, mugs, baseball caps, and posters about losing half a day of skiing.

Sanderson's testimony was equally strange. He bizarrely imitated Gwyneth's scream during his description of the accident. A neurological expert had earlier told the court that Sanderson could no longer enjoy wine tasting following his injuries.

In cross-examination, Gwyneth's lawyer brought up an email Sanderson had written to his daughters after the accident, in which he'd said, "I'm famous."

"Did you ever say to me, I wrote 'I'm famous' because it's cool that I had a collision with a celebrity? Was that your thinking at the time? And you said yes, do you deny it?"

Sanderson replied, "Not if you have it on record, no I don't deny it. I don't remember it."

At the conclusion of the trial—which pitted Gwyneth against a "normal" person more visibly than anything may ever have in her public life—the jury found Sanderson at fault. After the verdict, on her way out of the courtroom, Gwyneth put her hand on his shoulder and said, Sanderson later told a reporter outside, "I wish you well."

The internet flooded with "I wish you well" and "Gwynnocent" memes.

Sanderson also told the press that suing Gwyneth was "absolutely not worth it." She was awarded legal fees, but did not recoup them (the *New York Post* estimated they could have cost around a million dollars). While Sanderson believed Utah law prevented Gwyneth from recouping legal fees in this particular case, District Court Judge Kent Holmberg did not explain why the matter of him repaying her fees, as she'd sought in the 2019 countersuit, was dropped.

In his February 2025 interview for this book, Sanderson stood by his story—that Gwyneth skied into him, causing injury and personality changes. He was still mourning not having skied since the accident. "These people that are powerful and wealthy tend to use what they can, I think, to stay in the spotlight," he said. "And it is good for business. It's good for Deer Valley for her to be there." He was still working on paying "lots of legal expenses." He added that he had received interview requests from the BBC, *Inside Edition*, and *Vogue* (which offered Sanderson "a full spread," he said), but he had declined all of them.

"It was hard for everybody in the family who lost a lot of sleep over it, and I'm sorry I put them through it," he added, echoing what medical experts had been dealing with for years when it came to Gwyneth: "It's hard to overcome that kind of influence and power, and that's the lesson I learned."

. . .

TO GWYNETH'S FANS and allies, the trial—which became two musicals, *I Wish You Well* and *Gwyneth Goes Skiing*—illustrated her greatest strengths: She was poised, self-aware, skillful in the way she described herself and played on public perceptions of her. But the ordinariness of a trial, the repetition, the blandness, and most of all the implication that she could have behaved like a petty, uncaring celebrity, also shook her. Her expression occasionally showed the strain of constantly summoning the ideal response, an effective balance of humility, charm, righteousness, and grievance. But most of that, as usual, got lost in the public reaction, the outrage and the adoration and the memes and the merch. And in the end, being accused of injuring someone led to an uptick in the sale of certain fancy sweaters.

"I was just getting dressed and going to a pretty intense experience every day," Gwyneth told *The New York Times*, in a story six months later pegged to Goop's fifteenth anniversary. "And the sartorial outcome was so weird to me. That whole thing was pretty weird. I don't know that I've even processed it. It was something I felt like I survived. Sometimes in my life it takes me a long time to look back and process something and understand something."

In October of that year, Goop did the unthinkable: It launched a beauty line available at Target and Amazon. Priced under forty dollars, it was called "good.clean.goop"—the same catchphrase pitched by Crème Collective years before, which ran as a tagline on their Goop by Juice Beauty campaign. The next month, Gwyneth traveled to New York for the Council of Fashion Designers of America awards to receive a prize for innovation, sponsored by her corporate partner Amazon Fashion. The same award had gone previously to Kim Kardashian for her SKIMS line. While in New York, Gwyneth attended Kardashian's launch party for the SKIMS Swarovski collaboration. She was paid $250,000 for the appearance, someone familiar with the terms said, which had been part of a $1.25 million deal with Swarovski that included Gwyneth wearing the brand a certain number of times.

She finished the year with a controversial appearance at the Red Sea International Film Festival in Saudi Arabia, for which she was paid, one person with knowledge of the amount said, $1.6 million. Many in Hollywood, having been collectively outraged five years earlier following the government's role in the murder of journalist Jamal Khashoggi, were now willing to take large sums from the kingdom, where homosexuality can be punishable by death. Will Smith, Michelle Williams, Chris Hemsworth, Johnny Depp, and Halle Berry also appeared at the festival.

Though the good.clean.goop launch was widely publicized, the following June, the news outlet *Puck* reported that it was in the bottom fifteen products in its category at Target, which had developed concerns over Goop's controversies. The retailer had been punished by customers for a recent Pride campaign, which sparked conservative backlash and a boycott that caused online sales to drop 10.5 percent that quarter, and they failed to promote good.clean.goop or give it prominent placement in stores, fearing how polarizing Gwyneth had become.

By that time, controversies over Gwyneth's and Goop's health claims had dampened in the press. Goop was still recommending things like "mouth taping," where people slept with their lips sealed shut to facilitate nose breathing for supposed health benefits, but it was publishing much less content without a robust editorial team. Plus, the media was harder to shock. The ideas that Goop had promoted were now all over the internet, being pushed and normalized by countless Goop-coded influencers, impossible to regulate or control. TikTok and Instagram were replete with videos of people pushing diets that involved eating raw meat, chugging raw eggs, and drinking raw (unpasteurized) milk. In 2024, Gwyneth said she put Raw Farm cream in her coffee; later that year, the California Department of Public Health halted the company's distribution after bird flu was found in its products, which were sold at Erewhon for twenty-one dollars a gallon. Andrea Love said, "The only thing that raw milk does is increase foodborne illnesses."

But this hardly seemed scandalous next to the people eating whole raw lamb kidneys to techno music on social media.

GWYNETH HAD REMAINED a strong leader of Goop as CEO in the sense that her board and staff could never really tell her no when she had expensive ideas. But Goop's expenses were so great that, finally, something had to give. In September 2024, Goop announced that it would cut 18 percent of its 216-person staff, or forty people, and focus only on beauty, fashion, and food. Goop Kitchen, an L.A.-based ghost kitchen concept run by Dom Food Group, was a bright spot in the Goop portfolio. As a licensing deal, Gwyneth didn't have to do much more than promote it. This perhaps illustrated a possible future for Goop—licensing the name for product lines, cutting expensive infrastructure, and allowing Gwyneth to collect checks. (A Goop board member privately described Goop Kitchen as the company's biggest moneymaker.) The money-losing parts of the business Gwyneth loved in the 2010s, like travel and wellness, would be deprioritized.

The changes were driven in part by Julia Hunter, the former CEO of fashion label Jenni Kayne, who had been hired to consult for Goop. When Hunter came in, Gwyneth was both excited about what she could bring to Goop and also less visible in day-to-day operations. Gwyneth was starting to revive her acting career, and took a vacation while Hunter, as far as staff could tell, just started cutting people. Someone from HR conducted at least some layoffs over group Zooms. Afterward, Gwyneth addressed her remaining employees through tears. She also reached out personally to some who had been cut with warm goodbyes. At first, the remaining team wondered how they would do all the work without their colleagues, but then Hunter told them they didn't need to make all that content anymore.

In November, Goop underwent a second round of layoffs, cutting ten more people, including beauty editor Jean Godfrey-June just shy of her ten-year anniversary at the company. Hunter believed Goop's editorial content wasn't all that necessary given the brand's direct marketing capabilities. But without the stories, employees wondered why people would go to the site. Hunter also insisted that Gwyneth appear in even more Goop ads, which also surprised Goop staff since Gwyneth disliked modeling so much.

But Hunter didn't last long. After giving an interview to *Puck* in late 2024, in which she discussed the myriad problems with Goop's business as she saw them (like how In Goop Health "bordered on cheesy"), she left. Noora Raj Brown, Goop's publicist of nearly ten years, departed around the same time.

Gwyneth, of course, had options beyond Goop. Axios reported she was raising $75 million for a venture capital fund she named Kinship Ventures, which aimed to invest in "early-stage consumer goods and technology companies." Gwyneth has avoided talking about it publicly.

In her March 2025 *Vanity Fair* cover profile, Gwyneth seemed to be trying to take control of the narrative that had been widely reported about Goop's apparent decline, both as a business and in terms of cultural influence, and its layoffs. "*I. Don't. Care,*" she insisted to writer Michelle Ruiz, regarding the stories. "My business is a good business and it's a strong business and the brand is strong." A spokesperson told the magazine that 2024 revenue had increased 10 percent from 2023, Goop Kitchen delivering 60 percent year-over-year growth—but declined (as usual) to say if the company was profitable. Having raised $140 million "to get to less than that in revenue is not good," said venture capitalist Anarghya Vardhana. However, someone familiar with Goop at this juncture said it was a real business—G. Label could reach $20 million in revenue in 2025—and the company would probably be fine. That said, Gwyneth didn't seem to be having all that much fun with it anymore.

Besides, endorsement deals were a big part of Gwyneth's income, with brands ranging from Copper Fit to Saint Laurent eager to work with her. Brands didn't care about Goop's controversies, said one person with knowledge of her endorsement work. Wherever she went, Gwyneth got publicity and online "impressions"—all brands wanted, really.

With Moses heading off to Brown University, Gwyneth listed her Brentwood home for $30 million in May 2024. The price was lowered to $24.9 million in October; the house then survived the devasting wildfires that tore through Los Angeles in early 2025 and sold that January for $22 million. She had her bigger place in Montecito, a solar-powered fourteen-thousand-square-foot property with a large swimming pool, guesthouse, and home spa. It was the mega-mansion she wanted for her kids and two stepkids, whereas the other house had just six bedrooms.

Despite having said she would "literally never" return to acting, news broke in September 2024 of Gwyneth's casting in a movie inspired by table tennis player Marty Reisman, with Gwyneth starring opposite twenty-three-years-younger Timothée Chalamet. Gwyneth worked from the set, taking calls with Djenaba Parker. "She's just got a lot of capacity to be able to run a company and still do those things," said Parker. When paparazzi photos of Chalamet kissing Gwyneth during a scene came out in the fall of 2024, they were a useful distraction from stories about Goop's layoffs. While the work led her to fall back in love with acting, said someone familiar with her thinking, she also knew that the added visibility would only boost Goop's sales.

As Gwyneth continued her parents' legacy, the cycle could repeat with her own daughter. Gwyneth had told staff that she wanted to build a business she could pass down to Apple, who one person said had "genuine interest" in Goop. She had worked at the company's Sag Harbor store and interned in the Los Angeles office. Save for social media posts here and there, Gwyneth had kept her kids out of the public eye, and the public wanted to know all about them. While Moses attracted attention for joining a band called Dancer, Apple seemed to draw much more interest. In early 2023, when she attended a Chanel couture fashion show, the media swarmed. Like her mother, she attracted negative coverage, such as when she appeared at the debutante ball in Paris the following year, and a TikTok of her seemingly interrupting a fellow debutante's photo op went viral, leading social media users to label her a "mean girl." (The interrupted debutante, Aliénor Loppin de Montmort, later said that Apple was "the nicest girl ever.") A couple months later, Apple was in the news again for appearing at a New York Fashion Week event for the cosmetics brand Hourglass. Fame lies within easy reach for her, just as it did for Gwyneth. Only, unlike when Gwyneth became famous in the nineties, being an actor or musician was no longer a prerequisite for stardom, something Apple could, in part, thank her mother for. Whatever direction she chooses, said CAA's Richard Lovett, "She's not going to be the next [Gwyneth], but she will be the original Apple."

After nearly twenty years as an entrepreneur, drowning in numbers and promotions and managerial headaches, Gwyneth may have been happy to return to the work that had started it all for her. She said that she had made a promise to her mother. Once she sold Goop and returned her investors' money, she would act in a play: "I don't think I can have this job forever."

By 2025—nearly two decades after Gwyneth sent that first Goop email—the wellness movement found a new figurehead in Robert F. Kennedy Jr. and a new community in his MAHA (Make America Healthy Again) initiative. Donald Trump's secretary for health and human services, Kennedy has spoken out against everything from red food dye to vaccines. He has promoted the inaccurate ideas that both expose children to harmful levels of toxins, and that vaccines specifically cause autism.

In that 2025 *Vanity Fair* cover story, Gwyneth doubled down on her belief in the superiority of raw milk, which she used as an example of something "where people say, 'Oh, this is pseudoscience.'" She followed the typical wellness playbook of making a big, powerful, for-profit industry the enemy: "[I]s someone going to invest in getting a data set around raw milk?" she asked. "It's not going to be the dairy industry, right?" Gwyneth seemed blind to the reality that the wellness industry was bigger, more profitable, and perhaps even more powerful than many industries it seeks to villainize. (In her newsletter, Dr. Jen Gunter noted that many researchers had provided the dataset—dating back to Louis Pasteur in 1864.)

It's hard not to see a connection between Gwyneth and Goop and Kennedy—a fellow raw milk drinker—and MAHA. By sowing distrust of vaccines and promoting potentially harmful treatments (like vitamin A for pediatric measles patients, which caused liver damage in some), Kennedy helps steer people toward alternative therapies and pseudoscience promoted by the wellness industry and companies like Goop. Both Kennedy and Goop have encouraged people to see danger in widespread toxins supposedly lurking in everyday life, while also encouraging people to do their own research on their medical issues. The resulting widespread interest in alternative solutions has helped turn the wellness industry into one that is around as big as the pharmaceutical and agricultural industries in the U.S. combined. Proponents of wellness have positioned it as necessary opposition to Big Ag and Big Pharma, conveniently ignoring the they've created: Big Wellness.

Wellness businesses can make the savviest practitioners rich. For instance, alternative medicine proponent Mark Hyman, who wrote the preface to Kennedy's 2014 anti-vaccine book *Thimerosal: Let the Science Speak*, and whom Goop has interviewed repeatedly. He earned nearly $29 million in 2023 from his wellness business, which included supplements, a podcast, books, and testing for chronic conditions that medical experts describe as useless at best, dangerous at worst.

"I think that the legacy of Gwyneth Paltrow is she showed that there's big money in wellness," said Dr. Gunter. "Imagine if she'd been out there talking about abortion access."

When Gwyneth started Goop in 2008, the wellness industry was so nascent it was barely even measured. One study valued the "global spa economy," which shows you how quaint our notions of wellness were then, at $255 billion in 2007. By 2023, the U.S. had the largest wellness economy in the world, valued at $2 trillion, with the global wellness industry reaching $6.3 trillion, according to data from the Global Wellness Institute. In 2023, the U.S. pharmaceutical industry was valued at just over $600 billion, while the U.S. agriculture industry reached $1.5 trillion. The U.S. has the world's fastest growing wellness industry, expanding 8.3 percent between 2019 and 2023. By 2028, the global wellness industry is expected to reach $9 trillion; if the U.S. wellness economy continues growing at the same rate, it would account for around a third of that.

Big Wellness is also not subjected to the same rigorous regulations as our pharmaceuticals, our health care, and our food, which has only aided its explosive growth. Meanwhile, trust in influencers like Gwyneth has only risen as that in institutions like the FDA falls.

As it stands now, Gwyneth will probably be remembered less for her film work than the longevity of her fame and what she chose to do with it outside of Hollywood. Her greatest cultural impact isn't popularizing Calvin Klein fashion or jade eggs or "I lost half a day of skiing" T-shirts—it's showing the world just how much consumers will spend and how much effort they would undertake for the luxury of being well, no matter what science tells us. Her innovation was packaging it gorgeously—as flowers and sunshine and beauty and good taste—when it's really about fear of unending sickness and toxins and parasites and death.

I asked scientific and medical experts why people buy into wellness when they seek it out as an alternative to for-profit industries they perceive as putting money over health, particularly when wellness is an enormous for-profit industry itself. Dr. Andrea Love said that once people join the wellness movement, through Goop or MAHA or another entity, "In many ways, it is a cult. It's this strongly held belief system that becomes part of their identity. And that by challenging it, you're now attacking them personally." She added, "Facts aren't profitable. And they're not sexy."

Goop's apparent decline, with reportedly flat sales in recent years, coincided with its decision to pull back from publishing articles, though it still sells expensive products that may make deceptive claims—and that experts wish people wouldn't buy. Maybe contextual commerce didn't work without enough context. In 2025, Goop's success seemed to rely more than ever on Gwyneth. Her byline had been appearing on all the newsletters. She was modeling in many Goop campaigns featuring its clothing line and beauty products. And she was the spokesperson for the company at girlbossy women's summits, where whatever she said generated a slew of news articles. Ironically, while her image had started out as an asset, it was now a crutch. Was it her ego that prevented her from letting go of being the face of Goop? Or did the company stand a chance only if she promoted it? Whatever it was, it doesn't bode well for Goop's future. Any company acquiring it risks Goop losing its value the minute Gwyneth might decide to move on to her next career, the way she moved on from her friends and her gurus.

"I just don't think Goop will ever be successful," said one veteran investor in the consumer-packaged-goods space. "Goop doesn't really need to exist." This investor didn't believe the company should have ever raised over $20 million. The funding allowed the company to spend out of control in pursuit of growth at all costs, as Gwyneth failed to empower seasoned executives who could have helped her get to a point where Goop could get acquired or go public. In ten years, it's easy to imagine Goop existing in a reduced form—just a small skincare line or just Goop Kitchen or just a licensing business.

Whatever happens with Goop, Gwyneth will be fine. She has a way of emerging victorious from any calamity, whether a bad movie or an embarrassing trial. She has convinced the public at every turn to buy whatever she's selling. But the victory she's experienced at every stage of her life isn't something that she can sell—or that anyone can buy.

ACKNOWLEDGMENTS

MANY PEOPLE HELP with a biography of this nature, and I am grateful to every single person who worked on this book or supported me along the way.

Pamela Cannon edited these words with thought and care over many hours, and advised me on many aspects of the reporting over the three years it took me to complete this book. Seeing *Gwyneth Goes Skiing* with you was one of my great joys of these past three years!

Aimée Bell, thank you for your wisdom and guidance throughout this process. Your advice, edits, and care for writers is unmatched.

Jennifer Bergstrom, you have been a wonderful supporter of my work for many years now, and I am so grateful to publish with you and your excellent team.

Thank you to Sally Marvin and Jill Siegel for your help and guidance with publicity. You are both such wonderful cheerleaders.

Karyn Marcus acquired this book and gave me my first book deal many years ago. Karyn, I remain indebted to you.

Sam Douglas edited the first draft of this book and was an essential partner in cutting the excess words along with helping me help the reader understand Gwyneth Paltrow as the very lucky and complex person she is.

Ben Kalin fact-checked the biography I wrote on Anna Wintour, which was an enormous job, and I was lucky to work with him again on *Gwyneth*. Ben, thank you for working so very hard to meet our deadlines and make sure every word of this book was checked with diligence and consideration.

Raquel Laneri helped me conduct research and interview sources about Anna, and I was fortunate that she came back to help me with Gwyneth, particularly cracking into her tight-lipped circle at Spence. Raquel, you are an excellent journalist and a great friend.

Thank you, Hanna Preston, for all your hard work getting this book over the finish line with unfailing attentiveness and positivity.

My agent Gillian MacKenzie: Thank you for advocating for me, advising me, providing notes, and being a friend through three books now.

I would be remiss not to acknowledge the journalists whose profiles of Gwyneth I cited numerous times, and whose work helped me immensely in further understanding this elusive subject: Charles Gandee, Michael Shnayerson, Taffy Brodesser-Akner, Cindy Pearlman, and Nancy Jo Sales.

Thank you most especially to the more than 220 people I interviewed who so generously shared their memories about Gwyneth and her various ventures with me, who confirmed facts, and more. Those of you who spoke on background who I cannot name, you have my utmost gratitude. I am especially indebted to those who spoke on the record: Amesh Adalja, Kurt Andersen, Steve Andrews, David Anspaugh, Peter Arnell, Susan Baerwald, Jack Baran, Caryn Bardunias, Dana Barron, Karen Behnke, Michael Besman, Anna Bingemann, Mark Bittman, Boaty Boatwright, Risa Bramon Garcia, Henry Bronchtein, Maggie Buckley, Jayne Campbell, Neil Canton, Timothy Caulfield, Russell Channon, Jerri Churchill, Paul Cummins, Glenn Daniels, Andy Davis, Angel DeAngelis, Debbie DeRango, Gil Donaldson, David Dorwart, Mike Espinosa, Barbara Factorovitch, Jennifer Fell Hayes, Preston Fischer, Linda Fisher, Channing Gibson, Rufus Gifford, Edes Gilbert,

Mark Gill, Paul Michael Glaser, Sharon Globerson, Wendy Goodman, Lee Grant, Jill Greenberg Sands, Michael Greif, Jen Gunter, Sam Hoffman, Billy Hopkins, Joanne Horowitz, Kathleen Huggans, Dylan Jay Hay-Chapman, Jane Jenkins, Kevin Jones, Michael Alan Kahn, Michael Kaplan, Kevin Kelley, Linda Kobler, Anne Kopelson, Neil Kraft, Deborah Lapidus, Amy Lauritsen, Jessica Leader, Jack Lechner, Christine Lemme, Alex Levi, Andrea Love, Richard Lovett, Eva Lund, Jill Mackay, Betsy Magruder, Carla McCloskey, Pat McCorkle, Grayson McCouch, Jennifer McCray Rincón, Debra Michals, Bonnie Monte, Al Shaw Ki Moore, Simon Moseley, Larry Moss, Maureen Murdock, Alyson Murphy, Gordon Naccarato, Greg Naughton, Nancy Nayor, Marion Nestle, Alessandro Nivola, Robert Nugent Jr., Michael O'Flaherty, Donna Ostroff, Djenaba Parker, Karen Patch, Bonnie Patten, Robyn Peterson, Charlie Pinsky, Carlo Poggioli, Michael Riedel, Tom Reilly, Reg Rogers, Ann Roth, Carol Rusoff, Terry Sanderson, Bob Sauerberg, Tyagi Schwartz, Phyllis Serfaty, Charlotte Sewell, Suzie Shearer, Yves Simoneau, Stephen Soucy, August Spier, Rachel Strugatz, Jill Taylor, Barry Teague, John Tinker, Mark Tinker, Kate Turley, Annemarie van Gaal, Anarghya Vardhana, James Warner, Paul Webster, and Richard Whelan.

My friends Christina Amoroso, Jill Du Boff, Patti Greco, Meredith Kahn, Kira Peikoff, and Dana Thomas, thank you for reading early drafts of this book and providing feedback and encouragement. Justin Ravitz, Charles Manning, Ashwini Anburajan, James Lim, Christene Barberich, Dara Kapoor: you are amazing friends and I couldn't have done this book without you.

My sister, Holly, and Mark, Jack, Kai, and Jett: those Austin visits are my best escape from the bubble of writing about and researching another person so intensely.

To my husband, Rick: you are the best supporter and reader of my work and I love you beyond words. My children, Colby and Lila: you are the joy of my life and make me proud to do what I do during the many hard moments that invariably come along with writing biographies like this. I love you both with all my heart.

Mom, your advice is always the very best. Thank you for reading early drafts and always finding a way to cut through all the bullshit. I don't think I would have the chutzpah to take on big, scary projects like this book if I wasn't your daughter. I love you more than I can possibly say.

NOTES

INTRODUCTION

1 Goop's weekly staff meeting: Background interviews with three sources.

1 sometimes tried to plant products: Background interviews with two sources.

1 An "energy clearing kit": Background interview; "Energy Clearing Kit," Goop.com.

1 However, the egg-shaped stone: Background interviews with two sources.

1 Goop expert Shiva Rose: "Better Sex: Jade Eggs for Your Yoni," Goop.com.

2 "It's no yolk!": Lisa McLoughlin, "It's No Yolk! Gwyneth Paltrow's Website Goop Is Selling Eccentric Stone Sex Eggs Which Improve 'Orgasms and Muscle Tone,'" *Daily Mail*, January 14, 2017.

2 "Gwyneth Paltrow wants you": Cassie Murdoch, "Gwyneth Paltrow Wants You to Put a Rock in Your Vagina. Seriously," Mashable.com, January 17, 2017.

2 Writing on her blog: Dr. Jen Gunter, "Dear Gwyneth Paltrow, I'm a GYN and Your Vaginal Jade Eggs Are a Bad Idea," DrJenGunter.com, January 17, 2017.

2 often drove to work: Background interviews with three Goop sources.

2 Goop now employed around seventy: Jean Godfrey-June, "Gwyneth Paltrow Doesn't Care What You Think About Vagina Steaming or Jade Eggs," *Women's Health*, March 8, 2017.

2 she stood in its newly annexed office . . . "incredible power," she said: Notes from someone who was in the meeting; background interview.

3 Habib Sadeghi, for instance: Dr. Sadeghi, "Could There Possibly Be a Link Between Underwire Bras and Breast Cancer??," Goop.com.

3 Linda Lancaster had proposed: "You Probably Have a Parasite—Here's What to Do About It," Goop.com, January 5, 2017.

3 Goop's primary worry: Background interview.

3 The following year, California . . . the same claims: Sandra E. Garcia, "Goop

Agrees to Pay $145,000 for 'Unsubstantiated' Claims About Vaginal Eggs," *New York Times*, September 5, 2018.

3   Gwyneth said in one meeting: Background interview with source in the meeting.

3   "She is fucking borderline brilliant": Background interview.

3   spitting up on: Charles Gandee, "The Luckiest Girl Alive," *Vogue*, August 1996.

4   once sexually harassed her: Jodi Kantor and Rachel Abrams, "Gwyneth Paltrow, Angelina Jolie, and Others Say Weinstein Harassed Them," *The New York Times*, October 10, 2017.

5   Gwyneth described as "abusive": Taffy Brodesser-Akner, "How Goop's Haters Made Gwyneth Paltrow's Company Worth $250 Million," *New York Times Magazine*, July 25, 2018.

5   more than 45 million: Brian Lowry, "Oscars Draw Big Numbers, Though Not as Big as Hoped," *Los Angeles Times*, March 23, 1999.

5   "It's not like I go out there": Helen Barlow, "The Talented 'Twins,'" *Sun Herald*, February 13, 2000.

5   "I can't pretend to be somebody": Maureen Callahan, "The Girl Who Fell to Earth—Gwyn's Sad Slide Down Goop Chute," *New York Post*, February 5, 2009.

5   "I would rather smoke crack": Drew Grant, "Gwyneth Paltrow Prefers Crack to Canned Cheese," Salon.com, July 8, 2011.

5   "I think it's incredibly embarrassing when": Emma Brockes, "Where the Heart Is: She Likes the Geeky Roles, but Not the Low Pay That Goes with Them," *The Guardian*, January 27, 2006.

5   "To have a regular job and be a mom": Lily Harrison, "Gwyneth Paltrow's Post-Split Plans: Actress Reveals She's Taking a Break from Acting to Focus on Her Kids," *E! News*, March 26, 2014.

5   "every pretty girl": Julie Hinds, "The Fat Pack: Stars Who Suit Up for Beefy Roles Rather Than Put on Real Pounds Draw Criticism," *Detroit Free Press*, July 24, 2001.

7   "My father always used to": Krista Smith, "Gwyneth in Love," *Vanity Fair*, February 2004.

7   hasn't experienced sustained profitability: Emma Hinchcliffe, "Gwyneth Paltrow Is Taking Goop Back to Basics," *Fortune*, March 17, 2025; Rachel Strugatz, "Gwyneth & Now," *Puck*, March 26, 2025.

8   Yet Goop had published many stories: Background interviews with three sources.

8   "I can be mean": Anita Singh, "Gwyneth Paltrow Admits: 'I Harbour Revenge,'" *Telegraph*, April 4, 2010.

8   Some simply move on: Background interview.

8   "She's very good at": Background interview.

CHAPTER 1: PERFECT PEDIGREE

10   "[Bruce] was one hundred percent": Author interview with Paul Michael Glaser, February 22, 2024.

10 Most mornings . . . had passed through their minds: Author interviews with Maureen Murdock, October 19, 2023; and Jillian Mackay, October 20, 2023.

10 The two-story school: Author interview with Paul Cummins, October 19, 2023.

11 Like many of her classmates . . . Gwyneth's stealing stopped: MacKay, interview.

11 an easygoing banker: Nels Nelson, "Banker Cherishes His Role as Father of a Blythe New Star," *Philadelphia Daily News*, October 31, 1969.

11 that she wanted to be an actress: Edgar Williams, "A Break for Blythe," *Philadelphia Inquirer Magazine*, December 3, 1967.

11 son of a milkman: Nelson, "Banker Cherishes His Role as Father."

11 Harry himself had been offered: Percy Shain, "For Blythe Danner, Motherhood and Stardom Made '73 a Great Year," *Boston Globe*, January 6, 1974.

12 but he turned it down: Robert Wahls, "Footlights: Blithe Spirit," New York *Daily News*, November 2, 1969.

12 Before meeting her father: Williams, "A Break for Blythe."

12 Young Blythe was aiming: Wahls, "Footlights: Blithe Spirit."

12 four-story house: Judy Klemesrud, "And Next Sunday She's Getting Married," *New York Times*, December 7, 1969.

12 When they moved from Philadelphia: Williams, "A Break for Blythe."

12 where teachers emphasized: "Educator Sees Man Marching to End of Map but Going On," *Journal–Every Evening*, October 23, 1957.

12 (he played piano): Tim Appelo, "Blythe Danner and Hilary Swank Soar in Caregiving Movie 'What They Had,'" AARP, October 1, 2018.

12 She received offers during college: William Wolf, "A Success 'Overnight,'" *Boston Globe*, November 16, 1969.

12 who couldn't cry on cue: William Glover, "Raves Aren't Rattling New Stars," *Sunday Home News*, January 4, 1970.

12 Blythe took random acting: Mel Gussow, "Blithe Spirit Flying High," *New York Times*, October 23, 1969.

12 The company was looking to cast: Peter Wynne, "A Ghostly Role for an Actress of Substance," *The Record*, March 27, 1987.

12 "I speak German": Williams, "A Break for Blythe."

12 "a perfect sense of alienation": Kevin Kelly, "A Harsh, Hard-Hitting Drama," *Boston Globe*, March 4, 1966.

12 She was earning $60 a week: Wynne, "A Ghostly Role."

13 Her next few roles: Wahls, "Footlights: Blithe Spirit"; Klemesrud, "And Next Sunday She's Getting Married."

13 and received excellent reviews: Mel Gussow, "Broadway's Newest Star: Blithe Spirit Flying High," *New York Times*, October 23, 1969.

13 She was offered her first: Mary Campbell, "Pinter Drama 'A Lesson in Entertainment,'" *Journal-News*, February 17, 1980.

13 Bruce went to Tulane: Author interviews with Paul Michael Glaser, February 22, 2024 and November 1, 2024.

13 successful real estate developer: Jean Wetherbee, "Town Gets $77,500 Settlement In Glen Oaks Development Suit," *Hartford Courant*, September 22, 1978.

14 A few months after graduation ... immediately attracted to Blythe: Author interviews with Preston Fischer, January 17 and 18, 2024, and October 30, 2024.

14 whom he called: Gussow, "Broadway's Newest Star."

14 "Nudity is great": Klemesrud, "And Next Sunday She's Getting Married."

14 One evening after rehearsals: Tim Murphy, "For Blythe Danner, New York Is Wistful, Energetic," *New York*, January 4, 2008.

14 As Glaser remembered it: Glaser, interview, November 1, 2024.

15 "[Bruce] did have a": Fischer, interview, January 17, 2024.

15 Blythe and Bruce were opposites: Glaser, interview, February 22, 2024.

15 It ran for all of two weeks: Jane Wollman Rusoff, "'Fockers' Co-Star Blythe Danner Delights in Grandchild, Workload," *Sacramento Bee*, December 24, 2004.

15 "The dialogue is all outline": Clive Barnes, "Honesty Not Enough to Carry Play," *New York Times*, April 1, 1969.

15 The summer of 1969: Gussow, "Broadway's Newest Star."

15 She described the role as: Klemsrud, "And Next Sunday She's Getting Married."

15 Two days before opening night: Jerry Parker, "The Gentlemen Prefer Two Blondes," *Newsday*, November 10, 1969.

15 flowers, and congratulatory telegrams: Wynne, "A Ghostly Role," *The Record*, March 27, 1987.

15 The next day, a *New York Times* reporter: Gussow, "Broadway's Newest Star."

16 "terribly depressed": Klemsrud, "And Next Sunday She's Getting Married."

16 She imagined settling down: Parker, "The Gentlemen Prefer Two Blondes."

16 "I don't think I ever will": Glover, "Raves Aren't Rattling."

16 She replaced the star: Parker, "The Gentlemen Prefer Two Blondes."

16 She treasured privacy: Helen Dorsey, "The Self-Images of the New Blythe Danner," *Sunday News*, May 12, 1974.

16 She learned not to read reviews: Wynne, "A Ghostly Role."

16 The afternoon of Sunday: "Paltrow—Danner," *Philadelphia Inquirer*, December 15, 1969.

16 his Jewish friends were surprised: Fischer, interview, January 17, 2024.

16 a date selected: Wolf, "A Success 'Overnight.'"

17 Blythe had been living: Klemsrud, "And Next Sunday She's Getting Married."

17 Friends had helped him strip ... Roland Meledandri: Fischer, interview, January 17, 2024.

17 a favorite among high-status Hollywood: David Andelman, "Roland Meledandri, 51, Designer of Men's Clothing for Celebrities," *New York Times*, July 21, 1980.

17 Bruce's ambition started to lead him: Glaser, interview, February 22, 2024.

17 While Bruce was struggling: Michael Decourcy Hinds, "Blythe Danner and Her Cross-Country Family," *New York Times*, May 15, 1981.

17 When she walked onstage: Dorsey, "The Self-Images of the New Blythe Danner."

17 "You can put things off": Wynne, "A Ghostly Role."

17 She feared getting caught up: "Blythe Danner Career Retrospective," *SAG-AFTRA Foundation Conversations*, November 30, 2015.

17 Bruce's career needed a boost: Fischer, interview, October 30, 2024.

18 By 1972, Blythe was: Wilson Morales, "*Catch Me If You Can*: An Interview with Steven Spielberg," BlackFilm.com, January 2003.

18 While Bruce thrived: Glaser, interview, November 1, 2024.

18 Blythe thought about: Jefferson Hack, "Gwyneth Paltrow Quizzed by Wes Anderson and Other Stars," *AnOther Magazine*, April 13, 2020.

18 Bruce was pushing: Smith, "Gwyneth in Love."

18 Blythe found doctors: Michael deCourcy Hinds, "Blythe Danner and Her Cross-Country Family," *New York Times*, May 15, 1981.

18 Spielberg became: Morales, "*Catch Me If You Can*: An Interview with Steven Spielberg."

18 "somebody else's skin": Wynne, "A Ghostly Role."

CHAPTER 2: NEPO-BABY ON SET

19 "I've known my whole life": Michael Shnayerson, "Today Belongs to Gwyneth," *Vanity Fair*, September 2000.

19 Gwyneth showed up on: Helen Dorsey, "The Self-Images of the New Blythe Danner," *Sunday News*, May 12, 1974.

19 Bruce had plenty of free time: Michael Decoury Hinds, "Blythe Danner and Her Cross-Country Family," *New York Times*, May 15, 1981.

19 "I was the nanny": "The Family Union," *Sunday Morning*, CBS News, February 17, 2001.

19 As an infant: Gwyneth Paltrow, *My Father's Daughter: Delicious, Easy Recipes Celebrating Family & Togetherness* (Grand Central, 2011), 14.

19 Gwyneth developed: Background interviews with two sources.

20 "Had I been more confident": Dorsey, "The Self-Images of the New Blythe Danner."

20 they filled with antiques: Johna Blinn, "Her Meat-and-Potatoes Man Gets Gourmet Fare," *Courier-Post*, May 15, 1974.

20 His friends said his work: Author interviews with Paul Michael Glaser, February 22, 2024; and Mark Tinker, February 7, 2024.

20 "from college and drink": Glaser, interview, February 22, 2024.

21 When the students moved out: Author interview with Robert Nugent Jr., November 2, 2024.

21 "I will be a tyrant.": Williamstown Theatre Festival archival video footage.

21 "elitist theater like Broadway": Bruce Husten, "Summer Theater," story accessed through collection of Nikos Psacharopoulos papers at New York Public Library.

21 But he did want celebrities: Author interview with Deborah Lapidus, November 7, 2024.

21 The festival had always: Author interview with Boaty Boatwright, February 14, 2024.

21 The final decision: Background interviews with two sources.

21 His staff understood why: Background interview.

21 she was terribly nervous: Jean Hackett, *The Actor's Chekhov: Interviews and Essays* (Smith and Kraus, 1995), 22.

21 She and Bruce drove: Georgia Dullea, "At Lunch With: Blythe Danner and Gwyneth Paltrow: Not Entirely Out of Character," *New York Times*, August 3, 1994.

22 wheel her: Author interview with Lee Grant, December 11, 2023.

22 everyone was drawn . . . local celebrity: Background interview.

22 chipmunk cheeks: Ellen Gray, "New Role as Real-Life Grandmother Doesn't Slow Blythe Danner," *Philadelphia Daily News*, December 23, 2004.

22 After sitting with her mother: Dullea, "Blythe Danner and Gwyneth Paltrow."

22 "knew that this was my thing": Cindy Pearlman, "Gwyneth Paltrow's Lucky Number: She's Glad to Be Starring in the New Film, 'Seven,' and Working with Morgan Freeman and Brad Pitt Isn't Too Bad, Either," *Austin American-Statesman*, September 15, 1995.

22 But as far as many casting directors: Author interviews with numerous Williamstown alumni.

22 Blythe just thought: Katie Couric: "Katie Couric Talks to Gwyneth Paltrow About Love and Her Recent Successes as an Actress," *Dateline*, NBC, January 24, 1999.

22 St. Augustine's was a small: Nancy Graham, "Private Schools Booming; Quality Given as Reason," *Los Angeles Times*, June 14, 1979.

23 A *Vanity Fair* story: Michael Shnayerson, "Today Belongs to Gwyneth," *Vanity Fair*, September 2000.

23 though faculty from the time: Author interviews with faculty, including Paul Cummins, October 19, 2023; and Maureen Murdock, October 19, 2023.

23 Students called teachers: Author interview with Carol Rusoff, October 21, 2023.

23 Book reports might be: Author interview with Jayne Campbell, October 20, 2023.

23 Gwyneth's drama teacher: Rusoff, interview.

23 Toward the end of 1977: Harry Harris, "Miss Danner, Ken Howard Reunited in 'Court Martial,'" *Philadelphia Inquirer*, December 1, 1977.

23 "backyard with a tree house": Charles Gandee, "The Luckiest Girl Alive," *Vogue*, August 1996.

23 Gwyneth made the walk every weekend: Ingrid Schmidt, "Gwyneth Paltrow Is Everywhere; The Scoop on Goop? Its Boss Chats About the Growing Empire of Stores, Products, Even a Magazine," *Los Angeles Times*, November 19, 2017.

24 Arnold Schwarzenegger bought: Arnold Schwarzenegger, *Total Recall: My Unbelievably True Life Story* (Simon & Schuster, 2012), 366, iBook; "'NYPD' Producers Seek Smits Sub," *San Antonio Express-News*, June 4, 1998.

24 "climb trees and be outside": Helen Barlow, "Dying to Be Herself," *Courier Mail*, February 12, 2000.

24 doorbell, then scamper off: Shnayerson, "Today Belongs to Gwyneth."

24 houses in the neighborhood . . . ultimate prize: "'NYPD' Producers Seek Smits Sub"; "Gwyneth Paltrow on Naked Photoshoot for 50th, TPing

Arnold Schwarzenegger's House & Goop Gift Guide," *Jimmy Kimmel Live*, ABC, November 1, 2022; Schwarzenegger, *Total Recall*, 359.

24 She would bring them with her: Ingrid Schmidt, "Creating Natural Beauty: Gwyneth Paltrow Is All Aglow About Juice Beauty Organics," *Los Angeles Times*, February 21, 2016.

24 "Gwyneth used to hold": Nadine Brozan, "Chronicle," *New York Times*, May 29, 1995.

24 Around age seven: Jay Carr, "Emma Gets a Clue: Gwyneth Paltrow Is About to Become a Star, Playing a Jane Austen Busybody While Dodging the Gossip of Real-Life Fame," *Boston Globe*, August 4, 1996.

24 "polite and well-behaved": Frank Rizzo, "Multiple Roles: Acting Together, Being Themselves Together," *Hartford Courant*, August 3, 1994.

24 "you have to be a child": Carr, "Emma Gets a Clue."

24 Blythe took Gwyneth to Beaufort: "For Paltrow, a life steeped in drama," *USA Today*, October 29, 1993.

24 "Gwyneth was in a school with": Mary Campbell, Associated Press, February 17, 1980.

25 On set, Blythe talked . . . and often opaque rejection: Background interview.

CHAPTER 3: CURTAIN CALL

26 "There was a sense": Author interview with Bonnie Monte, June 6, 2023.

26 The family would spend around: Author interview with Robert Nugent Jr., November 2, 2024.

26 which ran for three seasons: "St. Elsewhere Catches Hospital Flavor," *Boston Globe*, July 13, 1982.

26 Bruce caught plays . . . "Shoot me!": Author interviews with John Tinker, January 31, 2024 and November 13, 2024.

26 Blythe would bring Gwyneth and Jake: Author interview with Jennifer McCray Rincón, November 2, 2023.

26 Blythe was like royalty: Author interviews with numerous Williamstown sources.

27 During rehearsals, Blythe would say: Background interview.

27 That summer, Gwyneth was asked: Background interview.

27 Psacharopoulos thought of the: Interviews with numerous Williamstown sources, including Jennifer McCray Rincón, Bonnie Monte, Deborah Lapidus, and others, various dates.

27 The festival had an apprentice program: Author interview with Grayson McCouch, May 16, 2023; old apprentice application accessed through Nikos Psacharopoulos papers at New York Public Library.

27 When one of Gwyneth's peers: Background interview.

27 At the end of the season: McCouch, interview.

27 In 2021, the *Los Angeles Times*: Ashley Lee, "Inside the Battle to Change a Prestigious Theater Festival's 'Broken' Culture," *Los Angeles Times*, September 25, 2021.

27 The nepotism undergirding: Background interview.

28   She also befriended . . . fell out of touch: Nugent, interviews, March 15 and November 2, 2024.

29   Blythe often took: Background interview.

29   In a 1994 interview: Rizzo, "Multiple Roles."

29   On the first day of rehearsal . . . "where she would end up": Author interview with Bonnie Monte, June 6, 2023.

30   had a cast of sixty: Robert L. King, "Bringing 'The Greeks' to Williamstown," *New York Times*, July 12, 1981.

30   *The Greeks* was a grueling . . . watching the show: Background interview with someone who worked on the production.

30   Blythe let her daughter roam: Author interview with Michael O'Flaherty, November 7, 2024.

30   the Cabaret, a musical revue: Eileen Swift, "A Cultural Picnic in the Berkshires," *Newsday*, July 10, 1988.

30   Cabarets were the most exhilarating: Nugent, interview, March 15, 2024.

31   Starting at eleven thirty: Cabaret program accessed through Psacharopoulos papers at NYPL.

31   Cabarets were casual: O'Flaherty, interview.

31   the cleared-out area: Photos accessed through Psacharopoulos papers at NYPL; Nugent, interview, November 2, 2024.

31   Gwyneth and Blythe sang: Nugent interview, March 15, 2024.

31   Gwyneth performing that same number: O'Flaherty, interview.

31   "'She's got it. She knows'": Michael Shnayerson, "Today Belongs to Gwyneth," *Vanity Fair*, September 2000.

CHAPTER 4: SPENCE AND SENSIBILITY

32   "Not one person had": Background interview.

32   When Gwyneth was around ten years old: "Goop's Gwyneth Paltrow on Being Brave in the Face of Public Scrutiny at #BlogHer15 Creator's Summit:" *BlogHer*, August 5, 2015.

32   By the time she became: Author interview with Paul Michael Glaser, November 21, 2024.

33   Blythe decided: Charles Gandee, "The Luckiest Girl Alive," *Vogue*, August 1996.

33   after passing a required: Author interview with Kate Turley, February 28, 2025.

33   Wealthy, high-strung parents: Jane Mayer, "Prestige Nursery Schools: How to Get In," *Harper's Bazaar*, June 1983.

33   An old saying of these: Donald G. McNeil Jr., "Close to Home: What Might a Daughter Pick Up from 'Sex'?," *New York Times*, February 26, 2004.

33   "like the thoroughbred horse": Author interview with Jessica Leader, November 20, 2023.

33   Between classes, all the girls: Background interview.

33   Gwyneth arrived at Spence: Nancy Jo Sales, "A Star Is Bred," *New York*, July 29, 1996.

33 Boys from other schools: Background interview.

33 Her classmates couldn't understand: Caroline Doyle Karasyov, "The Private Side of Gwyneth," *Harper's Bazaar*, November 2001.

33 Many of the roughly fifty girls: Background interviews with several Spence sources.

33 On her first day, Gwyneth wore . . . "that striped shirt on": Plum Sykes, "The Power of a Fashion Icon: Gwyneth," *Vogue*, March 2002.

34 Gwyneth's arrival unsettled: Background interview.

34 "She established herself as": Turley, interview.

34 But other students seemed to feel: Background interviews with two Spence sources.

34 Alison Cayne, whose father: Background interview.

34 Gwyneth could be cruel: Background interview.

34 By eighth grade . . . splayed out around them: Background interviews with two Spence sources.

34 She found her crew: Karasyov, "The Private Side of Gwyneth."

35 They kept the Santa Monica home: Author interview with John Tinker, January 31, 2024.

35 But the girls at Spence: Background interviews with several Spence sources.

35 When they went to summer camp: Leader, interview.

35 One day in the locker room: Background interview; Sales, "A Star Is Bred."

36 That initial year at Spence: John Smyntek, "Names & Faces," *Detroit Free Press*, July 6, 2004.

36 Students would sneak past: Background interviews with two Spence sources.

36 "I was immediately drawn": Ty Wenger, "Gwyneth Paltrow: My First Times," *Marie Claire*, July 2005.

36 When she wasn't smoking: Background interview.

36 Desperate to get her to quit: Karasyov, "The Private Side of Gwyneth"; background interview.

36 "I smoked a pack a day": *Armchair Expert*, March 18, 2019.

36 Students weren't supposed to: Background interview.

37 Spence girls had to wear: Author interview with Edes Gilbert, May 9, 2023.

37 All the girls hiked: Author interview with Phyllis Serfaty, May 10, 2023.

37 but only Gwyneth: Background interview.

37 She'd wear a white top with: Gilbert, interview.

37 Gwyneth credited her school: Sykes, "The Power of a Fashion Icon."

37 By high school, Gwyneth had: Leader, interview.

37 "Suddenly, I was, like": Gandee, "Luckiest Girl Alive."

37 She was popular and cool: Background interview.

37 "I never wished I had": Cindy Pearlman, "Oscar Winner's Angst: Paltrow Says Big Moment Was Very Traumatic," *Chicago Sun-Times*, January 4, 2000.

37 In ninth grade: Background interview.

37 Spence was a demanding: Background interviews with several Spence sources.

37 Gwyneth had arrived unprepared: Gilbert, interview.

37 A former classmate recalled: Background interview.

37 "The girls there were": Gandee, "Luckiest Girl Alive."

38   She made it clear to her teachers: Background interviews with several Spence sources.

38   Two former faculty members: Serfaty, interview; background interview.

38   Some teachers remembered her as: Background interviews with several Spence faculty.

38   When Gwyneth was at . . . comfort for his family: Author interview with Mark Tinker, February 7, 2024.

39   "Bruce loved a fight": Author interview with Channing Gibson, July 20, 2023.

39   On *The White Shadow*: Tinker, interview, February 7, 2024.

39   He liked to ski: Author interview with Gordon Naccarato, July 28, 2023.

39   When he was out for dinner: Tinker, interview, January 31, 2024.

39   French Burgundies: Gibson, interview.

39   Where Blythe was careful: Tinker, interview, January 31, 2024.

39   The same was true of his personal: Tinker, interview, January 31, 2024; Gibson, interview; Tinker, interview, February 7, 2024.

39   In Los Angeles, he drove: Tinker, interview, November 13, 2024.

40   When Bruce flew: Gibson, interview.

40   Blythe tended to book coach: Tinker, interview, January 31, 2024.

40   purely for artistic fulfillment: Background interview.

CHAPTER 5: ACTING UP

41   "She's not trying": Author interview with Edes Gilbert, May 9, 2023.

41   When Gwyneth was younger: Author interviews with Bonnie Monte, June 6, 2023, and January 30, 2024.

41   her tenth-grade spring abroad: Jaime Peñafiel, "Azul & Rosa. Mi Semana," *El Mundo*, January 12, 2003.

41   In addition to savoring: John Hind, "Gwyneth Paltrow: 'Leonardo DiCaprio Would Tell Me How Dirty Meat Is. Now I Haven't Eaten Red Meat in 20 Years,'" *The Guardian*, April 20, 2013.

41   she learned to speak: Background interview.

41   She also adapted very well: Michael Shnayerson, "Today Belongs to Gwyneth," *Vanity Fair*, September 2000.

41   Back home, she entered: Charles Gandee, "The Luckiest Girl Alive," *Vogue*, August 1996.

42   Her bedroom was on: Author interview with Gordon Naccarato, July 28, 2023.

42   two golden retrievers: Author interview with John Tinker, January 31, 2024.

42   Often she would go: Background interviews with two Spence sources.

42   parties that Gwyneth would throw: Author interview with Edes Gilbert, May 9, 2023.

42   She started showing up late . . . stuffy institution of Spence: Background interview.

43   "She's just traditional" . . . "who was sexual": "Gwyneth Paltrow: Dangerous and Scintillating," *Literally! With Rob Lowe* podcast, July 23, 2020.

43   One day, Spence's rather humorless . . . clean it up: Background interview.

44   She fell for: Gandee, "Luckiest Girl Alive."

44   At one point, she dated: Background interview.

44   "boyfriend when I was 15": Nancy Jo Sales, "A Star Is Bred," *New York*, July 29, 1996.

44   the Danner-Paltrow household: Monte, interview, January 30, 2024.

44   One of Gwyneth's friends from the time: Background interview.

44   In a joint interview: "Gwyneth Paltrow and Bruce Paltrow Discuss Their New Movie, 'Duets,'" *Good Morning America*, September 13, 2000.

44   She found traveling with: "Gwyneth Paltrow: Kisses to All My Exes," *Call Her Daddy* podcast, February 16, 2024.

45   Blythe could be almost: Background interview.

45   Sometime in her junior year . . . "about meeting her own needs": Gilbert, interview.

46   Like Dawson, Gilbert: Gilbert, interview; author interview with Kate Turley, February 28, 2025.

46   "There was just something about her": Gilbert, interview.

46   When she was seventeen: "Happy Birthday, Gwyneth: A Timeline," Goop .com, September 27, 2022.

46   Starting in the ninth grade: Background interviews with several Spence sources.

46   Though she wasn't known as a drama nerd: Gilbert, interview.

46   Drama teacher Jennifer Fell Hayes: Author interview with Jennifer Fell Hayes, May 10, 2023.

46   In later interviews: Sales, "A Star Is Bred."

47   actress Kerry Washington: Helen Murphy, "Kerry Washington and Gwyneth Paltrow Once Performed Shakespeare Together in School," People.com, November 6, 2019.

47   But according to Fell Hayes: Hayes, interview.

47   By her senior year . . . fell closed onto her fingers: Author interview with Jessica Leader, November 20, 2023.

47   Spence required students: Background interviews, two Spence sources.

48   The spring of 1990 . . . "on the other's strengths": Debra Michals, "Beauty Heritage," *Harper's Bazaar*, August 1990; interview with Debra Michals, December 12, 2023.

49   During Gwyneth's senior year: Gilbert, interview.

49   Gwyneth told friends that Dawson: Background interview.

49   When a friend got into Barnard: Background interview.

49   When Gwyneth got rejected: Gandee, "Luckiest Girl Alive."

49   Gwyneth was admitted: "Happy Birthday, Gwyneth: A Timeline," Goop.com.

CHAPTER 6: MAJOR: HOLLYWOOD

50   "I was looking at her": Anthony Breznican, "Steven Spielberg: The EW Interview," *Entertainment Weekly*, December 2, 2011.

50   John Tinker joined Bruce: Author interview with John Tinker, January 31, 2024.

50   filming in nearby New Jersey: "Television Production Charts," *Hollywood Reporter*, May 15, 1990.

50   So by May 1990: "Zach Braff's First Pilot Was Way Too Much for CBS," *Late Late Show with James Corden*, CBS, March 15, 2022; author interview with Tyagi Schwartz, November 7, 2023.

50   Because of the stitches . . . fighting it that hard: Schwartz, interview.

51   Another member of the cast: Author interview with Dana Barron, November 1, 2023.

51   The *High* cast: Schwartz, interview.

51   in her senior yearbook: Spence yearbook, 1990.

52   Kevin Kelley directed her . . . didn't bother giving it: Author interview with Kevin Kelley, May 19, 2023.

52   In the audience was Joanne . . . also represented Bruce: Author interview with Joanne Horowitz, November 28, 2024.

53   One afternoon that summer: Author interview with Glenn Daniels, December 12, 2023.

53   As Boatwright remembered it: Author interview with Boaty Boatwright, February 14, 2024.

54   Williamstown's 1990 season . . . he'd walked away: Author interview with Christine Lemme, April 4, 2024.

54   As Nancy Nayor: Author interview with Nancy Nayor, September 23, 2023.

55   as Joanne Horowitz: Horowitz, interview.

55   as a casting director . . . fly Gwyneth out to Los Angeles: Nayor, interview.

55   From the first introduction: Background interview.

55   The studio agreed . . . "it was very true": Nayor, interview.

56   He later said . . . "you can't do it": Michael Shnayerson, "Today Belongs to Gwyneth," *Vanity Fair*, September 2000.

56   Nayor cast Gwyneth: Nayor, interview.

56   *The New York Times* called it: Caryn James, "A Period Piece in Search of a Period," *New York Times*, October 4, 1991.

57   she stayed in the guest bedroom: "Gwyneth Paltrow: Dangerous and Scintillating," *Literally! With Rob Lowe* podcast, July 23, 2020.

57   she declared a major: "Happy Birthday, Gwyneth: A Timeline," Goop.com, September 27, 2022.

57   where classes could be as small: Shnayerson, "Today Belongs to Gwyneth."

57   She wasn't there to work: Author interview with John Tinker, November 13, 2024.

57   Blythe had dropped her daughter: Michael Grossberg, "Intermission," *Columbus Dispatch*, May 10, 1992.

57   Gwyneth was focused on: Charles Gandee, "The Luckiest Girl Alive," *Vogue*, August 1996.

57   Gwyneth went to see it: Shnayerson, "Today Belongs to Gwyneth."

57   "Gwynnie the Pooh": Mitchell Fink with Emily Gest, "It's a Job to Dine for: Foodies Vie for Crix Job," New York *Daily News*, January 27, 1999.

57   "We were driving back": Breznican, "Steven Spielberg: The EW Interview."

58   "I was petrified": Diane Sawyer, "Gwyneth Paltrow Interview to Raise Her Profile in Attempt to Promote New Movie," *Primetime Live*, ABC, October 9, 2023.

58   Spielberg asked his: Email from Jane Jenkins to author, November 1, 2023.

58 Carla McCloskey worked: Author interview with Carla McCloskey, November 1, 2023.

58 On her first day at work: Author interview with Jerry Churchill, November 1, 2023; McCloskey, interview.

58 seemed to believe that her part: Schwartz, interview.

58 Someone on the publicity team: Background interview.

58 "I sort of gave up": Shnayerson, "Today Belongs to Gwyneth."

58 Casting director Pat McCorkle . . . "explain all that to her": Author interview with Pat McCorkle, April 26, 2023.

59 Once Gwyneth arrived: Author interview with Grayson McCouch, May 16, 2023.

59 This was a setting where: Author interview with Greg Naughton, April 10, 2024.

59 "I felt chided, like a child": Leo Seligsohn, "A Mother and Daughter at Work and at Play," *Newsday*, August 19, 1992.

59 Gwyneth played the role: Naughton, interview.

60 Blythe watched Gwyneth: Frank Rizzo, "Multiple Roles: Acting Together, Being Themselves Together," *Hartford Courant*, August 3, 1994.

60 One year Amy Irving: Author interview with Michael O'Flaherty, November 7, 2024.

60 Rob Lowe showed up: Background interviews with two sources.

60 Gwyneth sang: Naughton, interview.

60 "People would just get smashed" . . . couples in the world: McCouch, interview.

61 After *Picnic*, Rick: Shnayerson, "Today Belongs to Gwyneth."

61 Bruce honored the occasion: Alex Morris, "Gwyneth Paltrow Gets Real: 'I Know Who I Am, and I Own My Mistakes,'" *Glamour*, February 2, 2016.

61 She often did: Gwyneth Paltrow, *My Father's Daughter: Delicious, Easy Recipes Celebrating Family & Togetherness* (Grand Central, 2011), 15.

62 apartment she shared: Morris, "Gwyneth Paltrow Gets Real."

62 Over a roast chicken . . . "so mad about it": Schwartz, interview.

62 another friend confirmed: Background interview.

62 She picked up: Author interviews with August Spier and Eva Lund, July 26, 2023.

62 The co-owner August: Spier, interview.

62 Before Gwynth began: Lund, interview.

62 "sell out to get to that place": "For Paltrow, a Life Steeped in Drama," *USA Today*, October 29, 1993.

CHAPTER 7: FLESH AND BONE

63 "There is the perception that": Rhonda Richford, "Cannes Lions: Gwyneth Paltrow Admits to Trolling With Some Goop Items," *The Hollywood Reporter*, June 22, 2016.

63 In 1991, Esprit sent: Trish Donnally, "The Spirit Behind Esprit: Susie Tompkins' New 'Retail Activism,'" *San Francisco Chronicle*, September 26, 1991.

63 Gwyneth was on the audition: Author interview with Neil Kraft, April 27, 2023.

64 Esprit later said: Esprit, Facebook post, December 23, 2019.

64 Susan Baerwald was producing: Author interview with Susan Baerwald, May 31, 2023.

64 Her director, Yves Simoneau: Author interview with Yves Simoneau, June 23, 2023.

64 "You just cast me": Baerwald, interview.

64 "[W]e were having": Leo Seligsohn, "A Mother and Daughter at Work and at Play," *Newsday*, August 19, 1992.

64 "The only cruel thing": Eric Knutzen, "Blythe Danner, Daughter Put Love Aside for Tough Roles," *Boston Herald*, May 16, 1992.

65 $48,000: Charles Gandee, "The Luckiest Girl Alive," *Vogue*, August 1996.

65 $30,000 . . . "was so psyched": Ty Wenger, "Gwyneth Paltrow: My First Times," *Marie Claire*, July 2004.

65 Though she did carry: Baerwald, interview.

65 But a friend of Gwyneth's: Background interview.

65 "feels really right for me": Wenger, "Gwyneth Paltrow: My First Times."

65 Gwyneth arrived every day: Baerwald, interview.

65 She never seemed to Simoneau . . . "that was not there": Simoneau, interview.

66 Blythe remembered watching: Kevin Sadlier, "A Murder in the Family: TV Magazine," *Sun-Herald*, November 15, 1992.

66 "Gwyneth and me to play the roles": Knutzen, "Blythe Danner, Daughter."

66 "has that morbid curiosity": "TV Movie 'Cruel Doubts' Profiles Family Dysfunctions," CNN, May 14, 1992.

66 "a really chilling performance": Ann Hodges, "Deja View: 'Cruel Doubt' Covers Same Story as 'Honor Thy Mother,'" *Houston Chronicle*, May 15, 1992.

66 "a particular standout": Tom Walter, "NBC Tells 'Honor Thy Mother' Story Best," *Commercial Appeal*, April 26, 1992.

66 Gwyneth drove around: Author interview with David Dorwart, April 26, 2023.

66 a white Jeep: Ann Oldenburg, "Matchmakers Matchup," *USA Today*, August 21, 1996.

67 "One day I was thrilled": Harold von Kursk, "Picture Perfect," *Daily Telegraph*, July 11, 1998.

68 In *Flesh and Bone*, the role: Author interview with Risa Bramon Garcia, September 15, 2023.

68 "I was looking for a young girl": Robert Dominguez, "Pitt's Pal's Pendulum On Way Up," New York *Daily News*, April 21, 1996.

69 "My movie star": Seligsohn, "A Mother and Daughter at Work."

69 "ingenious": Karen Campbell, " 'By 'n' By' Is Sweet but a Little Rough Around the Edges," *Boston Herald*, August 25, 1992.

69 Gwyneth went up to Dorwart: Dorwart, interview.

69 But Horowitz's work: Author interview with Joanne Horowitz, November 18, 2024.

69 she traveled to Austin: John Clark, "Getting Gwyneth Right: She's Been Labeled Somebody's Daughter," *Newsday*, August 4, 1996.

69 The *Flesh and Bone* hairstylist: Author interview with Linda Kobler, May 19, 2023.

70 but the crew felt: Background interview.

70 "I couldn't believe that": *Late Night with Conan O'Brien*, CBS, November 2, 1993.

70 After filming *Flesh and Bone* . . . "*interest on that?*": Author interview with Tyagi Schwartz, November 7, 2023.

70 "was so hardcore": Tristan Kirk, "Gwyneth Paltrow: My Father Taught Me Hard Graft," *Telegraph*, December 30, 2014.

70 "There is the perception that": Rhonda Richford, "Cannes Lions: Gwyneth Paltrow Admits to Trolling with Some Goop Items," *Hollywood Reporter*, June 22, 2016.

70 Ed Zwick had dreamed of: Ed Zwick, *Hits, Flops, and Other Illusions: My Fortysomething Years in Hollywood* (Gallery, 2024), 141–42.

71 "the unnameable thing behind": Zwick, *Hits, Flops, and Other Illusions*, 150–51.

71 Four weeks out: Zwick, *Hits, Flops, and Other Illusions*, 153.

71 Zwick felt like he was: Background interview.

71 "yours, and you'll get those": "Gwyneth Paltrow: Dangerous and Scintillating," *Literally! With Rob Lowe* podcast, July 23, 2020.

CHAPTER 8: BIG BREAK

72 "She could access": Interview with Reg Rogers, December 6, 2023.

72 Larry Moss taught: Author interview with Larry Moss, June 28, 2023.

72 Gwyneth had missed: Michael Shnayerson, "Today Belongs to Gwyneth," *Vanity Fair*, September 2000.

72 She would lose out: "Gwyneth Paltrow: Dangerous and Scintillating," *Literally! With Rob Lowe* podcast, July 20, 2020.

73 "I was young": Shnayerson, "Today Belongs to Gwyneth."

73 When Gwyneth performed . . . "into a successful career": Moss, interview.

74 "impressive newcomer": Bob Strauss, "Couple Gets Down to 'Flesh and Bone,'" *Chicago Sun-Times*, October 31, 1993.

74 "holds the screen": Jay Carr, "Atmosphere brings 'Flesh and Bone' to Life," *Boston Globe*, November 5, 1993.

74 "plays Ginnie with a lusterless": Michael Wilmington, "'Flesh and Blood' Has a Full-Bodied Flavor That Is Marred by a Sappy Ending," *Chicago Tribune*, November 5, 1993.

74 "striking performance": Kenneth Turan, "'Flesh' Willing, but Plot Unable," *Los Angeles Times*, November 5, 1993.

74 "Ginnie is played with": Janet Maslin, "Building a Future on a Shaky Past," *New York Times*, November 5, 1993.

74 "people seeing you, recognizing you?": "Gwyneth Paltrow's First Talk Show Appearance," *Late Night with Conan O'Brien*, CBS, November 2, 1993.

74 "*before this movie came out*": Frank Rizzo, "Multiple Roles: Acting Together, Being Themselves Together," *Hartford Courant*, August 3, 1994.

75 In early 1994: "Keeping A-Prized," New York *Daily News*, March 7, 1994.

75 Gwyneth had moved: John Hind, "Gwyneth Paltrow: 'Leonardo DiCaprio Would Tell Me How Dirty Meat Is. Now I Haven't Eaten Red Meat in 20 Years,'" *The Guardian*, April 20, 2013.

75   one friend recalled: Background interview.

75   "the goods from when he was nineteen": Alex Cooper, "Gwyneth Paltrow: The Ultimate Dating Roster," *Call Her Daddy* podcast, May 2, 2023.

75   "He was vegetarian": Hind, "Gwyneth Paltrow: 'Leonardo DiCaprio.'"

75   *Vogue* bookings editor: Author interview with Maggie Buckley, February 20, 2024.

75   Wintour was not impressed: Anna Wintour, "Traumas of a Cover Girl," *Vogue*, August 1996.

76   Buckley hated to tell . . . as they would become: Buckley, interview.

76   For one of her *Vogue*: Background interview.

76   Gwyneth's name was floated: Kenneth Turan, "The List Begins with 'Schindler': As Nomination Ballots Make Their Way to Academy Voters, Two Things Are Clear," *Los Angeles Times*, January 9, 1994.

76   *Newsweek* profiled her: "New Faces for the New Year," *Newsweek*, January 10, 1994.

77   *The New York Times*: Janet Maslin, "Why Some People Aren't Smiling on Oscar Night," *New York Times*, March 20, 1994.

77   *Rolling Stone*: Peter Travers, "Oscar Blindness," *Rolling Stone*, March 24, 1994.

77   When the movie came: Jami Bernard, "Video Reviews: Flesh and Bone," New York *Daily News*, April 29, 1994.

77   Gwyneth did get: Todd McCarthy, "'Schindler's List' Gets a Sweep from Critics," *Chicago Sun-Times*, January 5, 1994.

77   Calvin Klein decided: Background interviews with two sources; "CK One Campaign: The Genderless Scent Will Have Sexless Ads," *Women's Wear Daily*, August 5, 1994.

77   "Real glamour is": André Leon Talley, "Period Drama," *Vogue*, September 1999.

77   He happily gave Gwyneth: Background interviews with two sources.

77   she couldn't believe: "New Faces for the New Year," *Newsweek*, January 10, 1994.

77   Thanks in part to Blythe's: Author interview with Gil Donaldson, July 18, 2024.

77   Actors depicted in: Background interview.

78   Every Tuesday: Author interview with Linda Kobler, May 19, 2023.

78   All the actors who played: Allan Kozinn, "Good History? Perhaps Not, But Good Music," *New York Times*, April 16, 1995.

79   She had been practicing: Kobler, interview.

79   "My French harpsichord": *Jefferson in Paris*, 1:10.

79   Merchant had a reputation: Background interview.

79   "throwing our clothes at each other": Bob Strauss, "Paltrow's Revolutionary Exposure," *Daily News*, April 6, 1995.

79   The exhausted, overworked: Background interview.

79   Gwyneth's family traveled: "Happy Birthday, Gwyneth: A Timeline," Goop.com, September 27, 2022.

79   Labrador retrievers, Anca and Holden: Georgia Dullea, "AT LUNCH WITH: Blythe Danner and Gwyneth Paltrow; Not Entirely Out of Character," *New York Times*, August 3, 1994.

79   For one film shoot: Author interview with John Tinker, January 31, 2024.

80   After their stay in Paris: Rizzo, "Multiple Roles."

80   Gwyneth found her way to the: "Happy Birthday, Gwyneth: A Timeline," Goop.com.

80   Yet *The Boston Globe*'s: Jay Carr, "'Jefferson' Delivers History Lesson Without Drama," *Boston Globe*, April 7, 1995.

80   The cast rehearsed in: Author interview with Reg Rogers, December 6, 2023.

81   But the hot, stuffy: Author interview with Michael Greif, November 12, 2023.

81   Blythe, whose turn as: Rogers, interview.

81   "The first three acts came": Greif, interview.

81   stepped in to shield her: Rogers, interview.

81   "She gets so panicked": Jennifer Beals, "Gwyneth Paltrow," *Interview*, September 1995.

81   "She could access" . . . about the day's rehearsal: Rogers, interview.

82   both got low marks: Malcolm Johnson, "Mostly Excellent Cast Moves Through Laughter and Tears in 'Sea Gull,'" *Hartford Courant*, August 6, 1994.

82   Ben Brantley wrote: Ben Brantley, "Chekhov, Picked Apart and Put Back Together," *New York Times*, August 12, 1994.

82   After Perry died in 2023: Gwyneth Paltrow, Instagram post, October 29, 2023.

83   One producer she worked with: Background interview.

83   If they bothered her: Background interview.

83   Right after *The Seagull*: Jesse Kornbluth, "Perfectly Paltrow," *Buzz*, August 1995.

83   Anspaugh had worked for . . . "She's got it": Author interview with David Anspaugh, November 5, 2023.

83   "slow, plotless, and relentless": Roger Ebert, "'Moonlight,' Becomes a Bore with Flaky Feminism," *Chicago Sun-Times*, September 29, 1995.

83   *The Boston Globe* wrote: Jay Carr, "Cliches dim 'Moonlight,'" *Boston Globe*, September 17, 1995.

83   And the *Los Angeles Times*: Jack Mathews, "'Moonlight' Fails to Capture a Promising Subject," *Los Angeles Times*, September 29, 1995.

84   It earned only $2.5 million: *Moonlight and Valentino*, as per Internet Movie Database.

84   Gwyneth never spoke: Anspaugh, interview.

84   "I kind of—how shall": Daniel Neman, "Taking the Lead: Paltrow Stars in Austen Story," *Richmond Times-Dispatch*, August 18, 1996.

84   "There's a part of us": Ingrid Schmidt, "Gwyneth Paltrow Talks Aging, Acting and Recession Fears at Goop Event," *Hollywood Reporter*, October 17, 2022.

CHAPTER 9: BRAD ROMANCE

85   "I don't think she was": Author interview with Michael Kaplan, November 9, 2023.

85 Around six months before . . . "a coffee table": Ione Skye, *Say Everything: A Memoir* (Gallery, 2025), ebook, 211–13.

86 "If you think about it": Background interview.

86 Leitch, who never seemed: Background interview.

86 Though Skye found: Skye, *Say Everything*, 213.

86 Not long before the trip: Krista Smith, "Gwyneth in Love," *Vanity Fair*, February 2004.

87 christened "the Class of 2000": "Special Hollywood Issue," *Vanity Fair*, April 1995.

87 At the photo shoot: Smith, "Gwyneth in Love."

87 Brad Pitt hadn't forgotten: Author interview with Anne Kopelson, September 18, 2023.

87 "This is the feel-bad": Bronwen Hruska, "Don't Call Him Sexy," *Los Angeles Times*, September 17, 1995.

87 Husband-and-wife producing: Kopelson, interview.

87 Gwyneth had tea: Author interview with Billy Hopkins, February 14, 2025.

87 The magazine was slammed: Karla Peterson, "Check this Mirror, Hollywood: You're not the Fairest of Them All," *San Diego Union-Tribune*, March 30, 1995.

88 However, she received another: Background interview.

88 The Kopelsons had worked: Kopelson, interview.

88 Gwyneth's part was small: Author interview with Michael Alan Kahn, February 26, 2024.

88 On one of those days . . . "love at first sight": Author interview with Michael Kaplan, November 9, 2023.

88 Gwyneth hadn't given: Charles Gandee, "The Luckiest Girl Alive," *Vogue*, August 1996.

88 Around that time, Gwyneth asked: George Rush and Joanna Molloy, "Paltrow May Have Joined Pitt List, Leaving Leitch in the Lurch," New York *Daily News*, February 23, 1995.

88 Her rep at the time: Rush and Molloy, "Paltrow May Have Joined Pitt List."

88 "for anything too serious": Skye, *Say Everything*, 213.

89 He had grown up in: Terry Gross, "Brad Pitt: 'Moneyball,' Life and 'The Stalkerazzi,'" NPR, September 22, 2011.

89 Once there, he took odd: Hruska, "Don't Call Him Sexy."

89 While *Se7en* filmed: *People* magazine's "Sexiest Man Alive" issue, January 30, 1995.

89 And yet Gwyneth: Kaplan, interview.

89 After a take . . . "before she arrived": Kaplan, interview.

89 "She's not like Nicole Kidman": Background interview.

90 The Pitt-Paltrow romance . . . "a surprise": Kaplan, interview.

90 Bruce, however, was: Author interview with Gordon Naccarato, July 28, 2023.

90 Now, as the tabloids: Martyn Palmer, "Gwyneth in Love . . . Again," *Daily Mail*, January 9, 1999.

90 By late February 1995: Rush and Molloy, "Paltrow May Have Joined Pitt List."

90   Gwyneth would learn quickly: "Goop's Gwyneth Paltrow on Being Brave in the Face of Public Scrutiny at #BlogHer15 Creator's Summit," *BlogHer*, August 5, 2015.

90   Paparazzi started showing: Author interview with Michael Kaplan, February 17, 2025.

90   The paparazzi were the primary: Background interview.

90   In April, just before: Jules Stenson, "Love You to Pitts! Brad's Tender Kiss for His New Girl Gwyneth as They Frolic Naked on Paradise Island: Brad Pitt Pictured Naked with Gwyneth Paltrow," *The People*, April 30, 1995.

91   The images ran again: Bo Emerson, "The Newsstand: Best Story," *Atlanta Journal-Constitution*, May 9, 1995.

91   After the trip, Pitt: "The Lunatic Fringe," *Miami Herald*, September 15, 1995.

91   Bruce, who had high standards: Author interview with John Tinker, November 13, 2024.

91   who found it annoying: Background interview.

91   However, back on the *Se7en* set: Kaplan, interview, November 9, 2023.

91   After the photos came out, Madonna: Mary Gabriel, *Madonna: A Rebel Life* (Little, Brown and Company, 2023), 703–4, Kindle.

92   Word had come down: Author interviews with Dylan J. Hay-Chapman, November 10, 2023, and Kathleen Huggans, November 17, 2023.

92   Anderson had offered: Sherri Sylvester and Jim Moret, "Dan Aykroyd to Star in New Sitcom," CNN, March 4, 1997.

92   and she would be paid . . . without any supervision: Background interview.

92   With no producers: Chapman, interview.

92   "He and I were very close": Jake Paltrow, "June Zero Q&A," Q&A, Quad Cinema, New York, June 29, 2024.

92   His fellow PAs thought: Chapman, interview.

92   Despite being a budding tabloid star: Huggans, interview.

93   Behind the closed door of her trailer: Author interview with Alyson Murphy, November 17, 2023.

93   "my friends or whoever": Jennifer Beals, "Gwyneth Paltrow," *Interview*, September 1995.

93   After a grueling: Chapman, interview.

93   Anderson was headstrong: Background interview with two sources.

94   When a cut was completed: Background interview.

94   Unwilling to implement edits: Kristine McKenna, "Knows It When He Sees It: Paul Thomas Anderson Got Hollywood's Attention with a Look at the '70s Porno-Film World," *Los Angeles Times*, October 12, 1997.

94   It made $224,000: *Hard Eight*, as per Internet Movie Database.

94   "a porno movie": John Clark, "Getting Gwyneth Right: She's Been Labeled Somebody's Daughter," *Newsday*, August 4, 1996.

94   "studiously vacant": Dave Kehr, "Tough Guy with a Soft Heart: 'Hard Eight's' Hard-Nosed Hero Is an Unlikely Agent for Reno-vation," New York *Daily News*, February 28, 1997.

94   "In one scene, Paltrow": James Verniere, "Just Say No Dice when 'Hard Eight' Rolls By," *Boston Herald*, March 14, 1997.

94 "her best role yet": John Anderson, "Mesmerizing Performances, Story Keep 'Eight' Rolling," *Los Angeles Times*, February 28, 1997.

94 Gwyneth repeatedly denied: "Gwyneth Paltrow Interview to Raise Her Profile in Attempt to Promote New Movie," *ABC News*, October 9, 2003; Rene Rodriguez, "Gwyneth Paltrow Former Enemies Clamor to Be Her Best Buddy," *Miami Herald*, May 3, 1996.

CHAPTER 10: PERIOD PIECE, POWER PLAY

95 "I have to say to Brad": Cindy Pearlman, "Spielberg Is Ready for Seconds," *Chicago Sun-Times*, June 26, 1997.

95 Mark Gill, Miramax's head: Author interview with Mark Gill, February 12, 2025.

95 Miramax staff had a saying: Background interview.

95 Gwyneth would later recall: Jodi Kantor and Megan Twohey, *She Said: Breaking the Sexual Harassment Story That Helped Ignite a Movement* (Penguin Press, 2019), ebook, 59.

95 "He was at the Toronto": Michael Shnayerson, "Today Belongs to Gwyneth," *Vanity Fair*, September 2000.

96 "something outstanding about her": Email from Harvey Weinstein, April 7, 2025.

96 "He was a bully" . . . behaved better when one was around: Author interview with Jack Lechner, August 1, 2023.

96 Gwyneth also encountered: Background interview.

97 Douglas McGrath, a former *Saturday Night Live* . . . Gwyneth as the lead: Background interview.

97 McGrath came from Midland: John Clark, "Getting Gwyneth Right: She's Been Labeled Somebody's Daughter," *Newsday*, August 4, 1996.

98 Weinstein, along with other: Background interview.

98 a character Austen described: Nancy Jo Sales, "A Star Is Bred," *New York*, July 29, 1996.

98 McGrath said, "No other studio": Elaine Dutka and John Clark, "Miramax Finds Success Breeds Admiration, Envy: Movies: The Company Revolutionized the Indie World, but It's Now Accused of Operating like a Major Studio," *Los Angeles Times*, January 30, 1997.

98 Matt Reeves had also: Background interview.

98 Miramax had hired him: Author interview with Paul Webster, September 19, 2023.

99 Reeves wanted Gwyneth: Clark, "Getting Gwyneth Right."

99 Gwyneth found the script: Sales, "A Star Is Bred."

99 Gwyneth's original deal: Background interviews with two sources.

99 She later described: Sales, "A Star Is Bred."

99 Meryl Poster, then senior vice president: Clark, "Getting Gwyneth Right."

99 Gwyneth saw Weinstein: Jodi Kantor and Rachel Abrams, "Gwyneth Paltrow, Angelina Jolie and Others Say Weinstein Harassed Them," *New York Times*, October 10, 2017.

99   She had been charmed: Kantor and Twohey, *She Said*, 59.

99   She loved his team: Kantor and Twohey, *She Said*, 60.

99   thought of themselves as: Background interview.

99   The appeal of working for Weinstein: Background interview.

100   After booking *Emma*: Kantor and Twohey, *She Said*, 60.

100   "I was a kid": Kantor and Abrams, "Gwyneth Paltrow, Angelina Jolie and Others."

100   Back in New York . . . "how we confronted with things": Amy Woodyatt, "Brad Pitt Opens Up About Fathers, Sons and Confronting Harvey Weinstein," CNN, September 18, 2019.

100   He told Weinstein something: Kantor and Twohey, *She Said*, 60.

101   "He leveraged his fame": *Howard Stern Show*, May 23, 2018.

101   After that confrontation: Kantor and Twohey, *She Said*, 61.

101   She later told *The New York Times*: Kantor and Abrams, "Gwyneth Paltrow, Angelina Jolie and Others."

101   Weinstein disputed her version: Weinstein, email.

101   Another Miramax source remembered: Background interview.

101   Though Gwyneth seemed: Background interview.

102   From then on, "he was": Kantor and Abrams, "Gwyneth Paltrow, Angelina Jolie and Others."

102   Weinstein mostly left the crew . . . "Gwyneth's best friend": Webster, interview.

102   At a press junket: Charles Gandee, "The Luckiest Girl Alive," *Vogue*, August 1996.

102   Gwyneth was chosen again: David Seidner, "Hollywood Power & Glamour: The 1996 Portfolio," *Vanity Fair*, April 1996.

103   *The Pallbearer* wouldn't be the last: Webster, interview.

103   In the summer of . . . moved Gwyneth and Pitt back in: Background interview.

104   Gwyneth received . . . where they were filming: Author interview with Russell Channon, February 6, 2024.

104   One day when he was: Background interview.

104   Haft had been told: Background interview.

104   "It turns out": "Gwyneth Paltrow Is Full of Regret While Eating Spicy Wings: Hot Ones," *First We Feast*, March 21, 2024.

104   It seemed to drive her costar Jeremy: Background interview.

105   Gwyneth grew to dislike: Background interviews with two sources.

105   Gwyneth arrived to shoot: Channon, interview.

105   Gwyneth appeared in a few scenes: Rob Brydon, "Ruth Jones," *Brydon &*, Apple podcast, June 12, 2024.

105   Gwyneth expressed doubts: Background interview.

106   he was a boy from Missouri: Karleigh Smith, "Inside Brad Pitt's Strict Religious Childhood and the Hardline Family Pastor Who Preaches Corporal Punishment," *Daily Mail*, September 23, 2016.

106   "Brad and I had very different": Pearlman, "Spielberg Is Ready for Seconds."

106   When Nancy Jo Sales profiled: Sales, "A Star Is Bred."

106   Some of Gwyneth's closest: Background interview.

106   Pitt had spent: Stephen M. Silverman, "Brad Pitt Opens Up About His Faith," *People*, December 1, 2020.

106 Pitt started questioning: Mick Brown, "'Angie and I Were Aiming for a Dozen': Brad Pitt on Kids, Marriage, and Being Directed by His Wife," *The Telegraph*, November 28, 2015.

106 Pitt was a welcome presence: Background interview.

106 The shoots were taxing: Channon, interview.

106 "I have such a battle": Jennifer Beals, "Gwyneth Paltrow," *Interview*, September 1995.

107 $327 million worldwide: *Se7en*, as per Internet Movie Database.

107 "I got a bit of heat": Gary Dretzka, "A Star Is Hyped: It's Hard to Be Cynical About 'Emma' Star Gwyneth Paltrow's Well-Choreographed Fame," *Chicago Tribune*, August 8, 1996.

107 "I mean, I would much rather be Robin": "Peach Buzz: Press Aide Gets Full Court Press," *Atlanta Journal-Constitution*, July 25, 1996.

107 "I don't really understand": Beals, "Gwyneth Paltrow."

108 The dailies were promising: Background interview.

108 Weinstein started talking: Jeannie Williams, "Allen at Home with Martha Stewart," *USA Today*, June 26, 1996.

108 He believed his indies could: Background interviews with two sources.

108 Gwyneth finally got her: Gandee, "Luckiest Girl Alive."

109 Wintour noted in that month's: Anna Wintour, "Editor's Letter: Traumas of a Cover Girl," *Vogue*, August 1996.

109 Editor in chief Kurt: Email to author from Kurt Andersen, December 19, 2023.

109 Top makeup artist Kevyn Aucoin . . . further friction: Background interview.

109 Aucoin's roughly five: Background interview.

110 The story leaked: "Showbiz News in Brief," *Sunday Mercury*, February 21, 1999.

110 The *New York* cover story ran: Sales, "A Star Is Bred."

110 *Emma* was released: Robin DeRosa, "Box Office," *USA Today*, August 5, 1996.

110 On August 9, it opened: "Williams' 'Jack' Jumps over the Box-Office Competition," *South Florida Sun-Sentinel*, August 14, 1996.

110 *Emma* went on to gross: *Emma*, as per Internet Movie Database.

110 "Paltrow, one of the canniest": Jamie Bernard, "In the Austen Found Dept., A Swell 'Emma': Gwyneth Paltrow Proves Her Meddle as the Timeless, Clueless Tinker Belle," New York *Daily News*, August 2, 1996.

110 "resplendent Emma": Janet Maslin, "So Genteel, So Scheming, So Austen," *New York Times*, August 2, 1996.

110 "He was a very difficult boss": Ramin Setoodeh, "Gwyneth Paltrow Talks About Her Biggest Fights with Harvey Weinstein," *Variety*, February 19, 2019.

111 Mark Gill, Miramax's then–marketing: Author interview with Mark Gill, February 12, 2025.

111 Another Miramax employee from: Background interview.

111 "I never had a problem": Setodeth, "Gwyneth Paltrow Talks About Her Biggest Fights."

111 Reflecting on their relationship: Kali Hays, "Gwyneth Paltrow, Oprah Talk Weinstein, #MeToo's Future in First Goop Podcast," *Women's Wear Daily*, March 8, 2018.

111 "I would say that the word *abusive*": Weinstein, email.

112 Around the time of *Emma's*: Background interview.

112 Gwyneth occasionally laughed about: "Gwyneth Paltrow Is Full of Regret While Eating Spicy Wings: Hot Ones," *First We Feast*, March 21, 2024.

112 Weinstein wanted Gwyneth . . . "it was an It moment": Author interview with Marcy Granata, March 7, 2024; Granata, email.

113 Now that she was famous . . . who worked in media: Background interviews with several sources.

113 leaning more on her friendship . . . "need to end this": Background interview.

114 cavernous living room: Braden Keil, "Fresh Prince N.Y.," *New York Post*, December 20, 2003.

114 In early 1997, when Miramax: Background interview; Peter Biskind, *Down and Dirty Pictures: Miramax, Sundance, and the Rise of Independent Film* (Simon & Schuster, 2004), 506, Kindle.

115 To friends who observed: Background interview.

115 While studios indulged movie stars: Gill, interview; background interview.

115 Weinstein had access: Gill, interview.

115 Anna Wintour told *Women's Wear Daily*: Lisa Lockwood, "Cover Stories: Sizzlers and Fizzlers," *Women's Wear Daily*, November 22, 1996.

CHAPTER 11: "IT" HAPPENS

116 "Gwyneth Paltrow got robbed": Background interview.

116 Gwyneth brushed off: Background interview.

117 Director Alfonso Cuarón: Art Linson, *What Just Happened? Bitter Hollywood Tales From the Front Line* (Grove Press, 2008), 90–111.

117 While Hawke would mingle: Author interview with Al Shaw Ki Moore, December 6, 2023.

117 "She hung out with us": Author interview with Angel DeAngelis, December 6, 2023.

117 Weinstein had a habit: Author interview with Mark Gill, February 12, 2025; background interview.

117 Gwyneth would roll her eyes: DeAngelis, interview.

117 whom she knew a little: Paul Willstein, "Raising New 'Expectations' a Novel Task," *Star Ledger*, February 10, 1998.

117 She expressed her discomfort: DeAngelis, interview.

118 Gwyneth and Hawke took a walk: Steven Smith, "Gwyneth Paltrow: Here And Now," *Los Angeles Times*, April 22, 1998.

118 "I'm so glad that I have": Bob Strauss, "Paltrow Believes in Twists of Fate," *Los Angeles Times*, February 1, 1998.

118 Gwyneth flew on a private plane: Author interview with Alex Levi, August 16, 2023; email to author from Barbara Factorovich, August 13, 2023.

118 One day, one of the young women: Levi, interview.

119 Pitt surprised her on: Alex Cooper, "Gwyneth Paltrow: The Ultimate Dating Roster," *Call Her Daddy*, podcast, May 3, 2023.

119 ring he had designed himself: Background interviews with two sources.

119 Gwyneth's friends for the most: Background interview.

119 By late January, they were reported: "Production Line," *Screen International*, February 14, 1997.

119 Columbia green-lit the project: Author interview with Kevin Jones, February 9, 2024.

119 On February 11, 1997, Harvey Weinstein . . . he'd failed her: Background interview.

119 Gwyneth was disappointed that she hadn't been: Background interview.

119 Miramax producer Paul Webster: Author interview with Paul Webster, September 19, 2023.

120 Gwyneth's Spence classmate Caroline Doyle: Background interview.

120 They played the happy couple: Background interview.

120 go to designer showrooms: Background interview.

120 Pitt and Gwyneth's Spence friend Julia Cuddihy: Background interview.

120 On the day of the launch event . . . on a desert island: Email to author from Annemarie Van Gaal, July 27, 2023.

121 British television actor Peter Howitt: Author interview with Richard Whelan, December 6, 2023.

121 Jill Taylor, who had signed . . . appointment at Calvin Klein: Interview with Jill Taylor, February 9, 2024.

122 One of the publicists on the brand's small team . . . cutting remarks about her: Background interview.

122 Gwyneth could call on designers like Klein . . . this kind of symbiosis: Background interviews with several sources.

122 In early 1997, in a show of solidarity: Roger D. Friedman, "Celebrities and Designers: Swatches Joined at the Seam," *New York Times*, December 29, 1996.

122 So when she asked . . . keep them: Taylor, interview.

123 The moment she finished that speech . . . along with "bollocks": Whelan, interview.

123 The young crew scrambled . . . and drink prosecco: Taylor, interview; Whelan, interview.

124 Gwyneth had turned her Miramax friends: Background interview.

124 she introduced the crew to her alternative burger: Taylor, interview.

124 With the help of her assistant: Author interview with Suzie Shearer, December 6, 2023.

124 Her tearful sessions in Aucoin's apartment: Background interview.

124 Kevin Jones flew to New York: Jones, interview.

124 he resented that Gwyneth: Anne Shooter, "Party Boy Pitt Splits with Girl Who Tried to Tame Him: Romance That Went from Brad to Worse," *Daily Mail*, June 18, 1997.

124 "burnt out": Rick Fulton, "Pitt's All Over! Heartless Hunk Brad Ditches His Golden Girl," *Daily Record*, June 18, 1997.

124 "nervous about such a serious commitment": Liz Smith, "Those Bawdy Spice Girls," *Newsday*, June 23, 1997.

124 two people recalled a rumor: Background interviews with two sources.

124　In her 2018 profile of Gwyneth: Taffy Brodesser-Akner, "How Goop's Haters Made Gwyneth Paltrow's Company Worth $250 Million," *New York Times Magazine*, July 25, 2018.

125　Asked about it the next year in *Vanity Fair*: Cathy Horyn, "A Commanding Lead," *Vanity Fair*, November.

125　"I fucked that up, Brad!": Sophia Amoruso, *Girl Boss*, Apple podcast, August 30, 2017.

125　"I definitely fell in love with him": *Howard Stern Show*, WXRK, January 14, 2015.

125　Kevin Jones was blindsided: Jones, interview.

125　"I've been chased by those": Steven Schaefer, "Putting 'The Game' into Play: Stars Ponder Princess, Paparazzi at Film Premiere," *USA Today*, September 5, 1997.

126　being chased by paparazzi: Background interview.

126　As requested, in September 1997, *Marie Claire*: Jeannie Williams, "Schwarzenegger's Own Heart-Pounder," *USA Today*, December 2, 1997.

126　Before the trip, a doctor had told her: Ty Wenger, "Gwyneth Paltrow: My First Times," *Marie Claire*, July 2004.

126　used her machete to whack: *The Rosie O'Donnell Show*, NBC, December 20, 2008.

127　She kept a diary of her time: "I Am Loopier Than I Thought . . . ," *Miami Herald*, November 29, 1997.

127　She slept on sand so hard: Wenger, "Gwyneth Paltrow: My First Times."

127　She saw a shark from the shore: Smith, "Gwyneth Paltrow: Here and Now."

127　She lit a fire one night: "Paltrow Brings a Little Weirdness to Editor Stint," *Chicago Sun-Times*, December 9, 1997.

127　The *Miami Herald* picked up: "I Am Loopier Than I Thought . . ."

127　While Gwyneth was reported to have met: Stephanie Kaloi, "Inside Ben Affleck's Past Romances with Jennifer Lopez and Gwyneth Paltrow," *People*, May 10, 2023.

127　she in fact met him alongside Miramax's: Background interview.

127　Raised in Cambridge: Stephen Galloway, "Confessions of Ben Affleck," *Hollywood Reporter*, October 10, 2012.

127　Affleck had started acting as a child: *Kelly Clarkson Show*, NBC, March 4, 2020.

127　His father was a playwright and alcoholic: Rebecca Aizin, "All About Ben Affleck's Parents, Chris and Tim Affleck," *People*, June 6, 2024.

127　Affleck himself was struggling: Aizin, "All About Ben Affleck's Parents."

128　"the smartest woman": "Names in the News," Associated Press, June 24, 1998.

128　her friends had reservations about him: Background interview.

128　She spoke openly about how much she enjoyed: Background interview.

128　"I'm a very sexual person": Caroline Doyle Karasyov, "The Private Side of Gwyneth," *Harper's Bazaar*, November 2001.

128　"technically excellent": "Gwyneth Paltrow: Kisses to All My Exes," *Call Her Daddy* podcast, February 16, 2024.

128　Calling the paparazzi an intrusive: Claudia Puig, "Plain Expectations: Stardom Sneaked Up on Gwyneth Paltrow," *USA Today*, February 20, 1998.

128　After breaking up with Pitt: Background interviews with two sources.

129 Gwyneth had helped set Ryder up: Jae-Ha Kim, "Dance Divas Grace Heart & Soul," *Chicago Sun-Times*, February 2, 1999.

129 Driver would later say: Robert Hofler, "Get Over It. (She Has.)," *Los Angeles Times*, July 26, 1998.

129 Gwyneth told her friends that Driver's: Background interview.

129 Once, when she was staying in a rented house: Background interview.

129 She told friends that after Ryder . . . "Vagina Ryder": Background interview.

129 Despite saying she wanted to keep: Author interview with Amy Lauritsen, October 20, 2023.

129 Director Andy Davis originally wanted: Author interview with Andy Davis, October 12, 2023.

130 Gwyneth was paid $3 million: Peter Biskind, *Down and Dirty Pictures: Miramax, Sundance, and the Rise of Independent Film* (Simon & Schuster, 2004), ebook, 417.

130 a $60 million budget: *A Perfect Murder*, as per Internet Movie Database.

130 She told Harvey Weinstein: Michael Shnayerson, "Today Belongs to Gwyneth," *Vanity Fair*, September 2000.

130 "Michael was constantly kidding": Jodi Applegate, "Gwyneth Paltrow Talks About Her New Movie 'A Perfect Murder,' *Sunday Today*, NBC, June 7, 1998.

130 had become concerned that she had gained weight: Amy Longsdorf, "Self-Image Isn't Everything for Gwyneth Paltrow: The Academy Award Winner Pokes Fun at Her Beauty by Wearing a Fat Suit in Her Latest Film, 'Shallow Hal,' *Wilkes-Barre Times Leader*, November 4, 2001.

130 *A Perfect Murder*'s ending was: Author interview with Henry Bronchtein, November 2, 2023.

131 Davis decided to film an alternate: Davis, interview.

131 someone who worked closely with Gwyneth: Background interview.

131 By the time they shot in London: Davis, interview.

CHAPTER 12: SHAKESPEARE IN LOVE, GWYNETH IN OVERDRIVE

132 "[T]he first lady of Miramax": Jeannie Williams, " 'First lady of our Hearts' in love with 'Shakespeare,'" *USA Today*, December 8, 1998.

132 had been delayed to avoid competing: Robert W. Welkos and Claudia Puig, "Company Town: 'Titanic' Embarks on 6-Month Side Trip: Delay: Paramount and Fox Push Back Release of Costliest Film Ever—$200 Million and Counting—to December, an Already Crowded Movie Season," *Los Angeles Times*, May 28, 1997.

132 "I just hope that people aren't mad": Claudia Puig, "Plain Expectations: Stardom Sneaked Up on Gwyneth Paltrow," *USA Today*, February 20, 1998.

132 In late January, she attended: Untitled article, *New York Post*, January 29, 1998.

132 Ben Affleck went: Background interview.

133 "sleazy": Jami Bernard, "Grating 'Expectations': Sleazy Tale's a Pip Squeak Compared with Dickens' Classic," New York *Daily News*, January 30, 1998.

133 "underwritten": Janet Maslin, "Tale of Two Stories, This One with a Ms.," *New York Times*, January 30, 1998.

133 "a complete failed film": Brent Lang, "How Alfonso Cuaron Went Back to Scratch to Rekindle His Career After 'Great Expectations,'" *Variety*, April 20, 2016.

133 "which is the wrong reason": Sherryl Connelly, "Paltrow Shuns Fame, Seeks 'Small Movies,'" *The Oregonian*, May 2, 1998.

133 "Unfortunately," *Variety* wrote: Todd McCarthy, "Misconceived Thriller: Toplines Lange as Mommie Dearest," *Variety*, March 9, 1998.

133 "I don't know what you're talking about!": Steven Smith, "Q&A: Gwyneth Paltrow: Here and Now," *Los Angeles Times*, April 22, 1998.

133 "her most winsome star turn": Stephen Holden, "Finding Love on the Road Not Taken," *New York Times*, April 24, 1998.

133 To celebrate *Sliding Doors*, Calvin: Larry Sutton and Marcus Baram, "Mariah's Ex Is Butterflying the Coop," New York *Daily News*, April 23, 1998.

133 Her friends worried when she would: Background interviews with two sources.

134 When Affleck was in Savannah: George Rush and Joanna Molloy, "Ben & Gwyn Spies Go Good Flinch Hunting," New York *Daily News*, July 16, 1998.

134 Novelist and screenwriter Marc Norman: Ed Zwick, *Hits, Flops, and Other Illusions: My Fortysomething Years in Hollywood* (Gallery, 2024), 116–130.

134 high turnaround price: Peter Biskind, *Down and Dirty Pictures: Miramax, Sundance, and the Rise of Independent Film* (Simon & Schuster, 2004).

134 But then he froze out Zwick: Biskind, *Down and Dirty Pictures*, 491–92, Kindle.

135 Madden then signed a deal . . . "Gwyneth, doesn't it?": Author interview with John Madden, May 6, 2025.

135 Gwyneth was burned out: Bruce Westbrook, "Actress Takes Time for Shakespeare," *Houston Chronicle*, December 28, 1998.

135 Two Miramax people remembered: Background interviews with two sources.

136 According to someone else who was close to her: Background interview.

136 "It was never sent to Winona": Harvey Weinstein, emails, April 7 and May 26, 2025.

136 Miramax sources didn't: Lechner, interview; and background interviews with several Miramax sources.

136 Certainly, John Madden . . . "very nervous": Madden, interview.

136 One Miramax producer: Background interview.

136 After a story about Gwyneth: George Rush and Joanna Molloy, "Jerry & Co. Liable to Affect Our Vital Seins," New York *Daily News*, October 30, 1997.

136 Gwyneth told friends that Ryder: Background interview.

137 in September, after reportedly looking at: Ruth Ryon, "'Gettin' Jiggy' in the Hills of Malibu," *Los Angeles Times*, April 25, 1999; "Los Feliz Library Big on DiCaprio," *Daily News of Los Angeles*, April 9, 1999.

137 At some point during: *Shakespeare*: Background interview.

137 Madden said Miramax expected: Madden, interview.

137 The budget increased: Background interview.

137   Gwyneth would practice: Background interview.

137   recalled her chewing gum: Background interview.

138   Gwyneth later said that she had: Ramin Setoodeh, "Gwyneth Paltrow on How 'Shakespeare in Love' Changed Her Life (and the Oscars) Forever," *Variety*, February 19, 2019; background interview.

138   When *The Sunday Times Magazine* sent: Dylan Jones, "I Interviewed Gwyneth Paltrow Once. Never Again," *Times*, March 22, 2024.

138   On set, Gwyneth was receiving . . . half a dozen times during filming: Background interview.

138   He was paying Gwyneth $2.5 million: Biskind, *Down and Dirty Pictures*, 493.

138   When Weinstein knew an actor: Background interview.

139   The crew later wondered: Background interview.

139   Madden suggested another reason . . . "rewarded with the Oscar": Madden, interview.

139   "She was an icon": Author interview, John Madden, May 6, 2025.

140   as likely stipulated in her contract: Background interview.

140   The crew had been told . . . like a happy place to her: Background interview.

140   When a reporter asked Affleck: Cindy Pearlman, "Ben Hits Big: Flying Solo, Affleck Gets Some Action," *Chicago Sun-Times*, June 28, 1998.

140   One person close to Gwyneth: Background interview.

140   "such an empty pursuit": Sherryl Connelly, "The Girl We Don't Quite Get," *Daily Telegraph*, July 28, 1998.

141   After Bruce released Brad Pitt: Interview with Kevin Jones, February 9, 2024.

141   He would need radical: Michael Shnayerson, "Today Belongs to Gwyneth," *Vanity Fair*, September 2000.

141   Plus, the news would likely lead to press: Diane Sawyer, "Gwyneth Paltrow and Bruce Paltrow Discuss Their New Movie, 'Duets,'" *Good Morning America*, ABC, September 13, 2000.

142   She later told *Vanity Fair*: Shnayerson, "Today Belongs to Gwyneth."

142   One Miramax producer remembered: Background interview.

142   She felt deep despair: Shnayerson, "Today Belongs to Gwyneth."

142   Gwyneth had joined: David Canfield, "The Talented Mr. Ripley at 25— Frank, Queer, and Ahead of Its Time," *Vanity Fair*, December 11, 2023.

142   Gwyneth, however, wasn't enamored: Background interview.

142   Ischia had no airport: Author interview with Steven Andrews, January 26, 2024.

143   In his hospital bed, Bruce: Author interview with Kevin Jones, February 9, 2024.

143   Gwyneth returned to Ischia: Andrews, interview.

143   When telling the history of Goop: "Happy Birthday, Gwyneth: A Timeline," Goop.com, September 27, 2022.

143   Andrews recalled Gwyneth: Andrews, interview.

143   Filming winter scenes, with heavy coats . . . how to sit: Author interviews with Carlo Poggioli, February 17, 2024; Ann Roth, February 17, 2024.

144   Ben Affleck—who wouldn't: Andrews, interview.

144   Her assistant was her Spence: Background interview.

144   "The actual work was cathartic": Bob Strauss, "The Talented Gwyneth Paltrow," *Tampa Bay Times*, December 29, 1999.

144 The audience in one test screening: Background interview.

144 Afterward, Weinstein debated: Interviews with Mark Gill, February 12, 2025; Jack Lechner, August 1, 2023; background Miramax sources.

145 $25 million: *Shakespeare in Love*, as per Internet Movie Database.

145 Madden remembered people at Miramax: Madden, interview.

146 Teri Kane, who worked for Marcy Granata: Background interview.

146 In a *New York Times* story: Alex Kuczynski, "The First Lady Strikes a Pose for the Media Elite," *New York Times*, December 7, 1998.

146 Clinton left: Background interview.

146 Five days later, Miramax held: Gill, interview.

146 "irresistible": Lael Loewenstein, "Shakespeare in Love," *Variety*, December 7, 1998.

146 "exquisite": Joel Siegel, "Shakespeare in Love," *Good Morning America*, ABC, December 8, 1998.

146 "If you want to see Audrey Hepburn": Rod Dreher, "Shakespeare's in Love . . . With Our Gwyneth! Paltrow Finally Comes Into Her Own as the New Audrey Hepburn," *New York Post*, December 11, 1998.

147 "Gwyneth Paltrow, in her first great": Janet Maslin, "Shakespeare Saw a Therapist?," *New York Times*, December 11, 1998.

147 "[T]he language isn't": Matt Lauer, "Actress Gwyneth Paltrow Discusses Her Latest Movie, 'Shakespeare in Love,'" *Today*, NBC News, December 11, 1998.

147 Gwyneth and Affleck broke up the next month: Background interview.

147 "I love men": Caroline Doyle Karasyov, "The Private Side of Gwyneth," *Harper's Bazaar*, November 2001.

147 On January 26, 1999, she attended the Golden Globes: Barbara De Witt, "Globes Glitter as Retro Styles Steal the Show," *Daily News of Los Angeles*, January 15, 1999.

147 "I like to think that was her": Weinstein, email.

148 "I'm human, so of course the idea": Westbrook, "Actress Takes Time for Shakespeare."

148 According to several people at Miramax: Background interviews with three sources.

148 Weinstein was nervous about: Background interview.

148 "hand-to-hand combat": Gill, interview.

148 He was probably the first person . . . "will you be voting?": Interview with Jack Lechner, August 1, 2023.

148 Weinstein was clear . . . by the end of it: Background interview.

149 "traumatic": Bob Strauss, "Genuine Gwyneth: Paltrow Deepens Her Craft in 'The Talented Mr. Ripley,'" *Daily News of Los Angeles*, December 24, 1999.

149 As Gill remembered it, Gwyneth: Gill, interview.

149 Miramax wasn't working hard: Background interview.

149 Weinstein would later be accused: Rebecca Keegan and Nicole Sperling, "*Shakespeare in Love* and Harvey Weinstein's Dark Oscar Victory," *Vanity Fair*, December 8, 2017.

149 To distinguish her performance: Background interviews with two sources.

149 During the media blitz, Weinstein: Background interview.

149 At one point, Stephen Huvane: Background interview.

149 "She might look like a WASP": "Meet Gwyneth Paltrowitch," *Jewish Chronicle*, January 29, 1999.

150 "It's not like I go out there": Helen Barlow, "The Talented 'Twins,'" *Sun Herald*, February 13, 2000.

CHAPTER 13: A FAMILY AFFAIR

151 "[T]hey're all in the room watching": Author interview with Kevin Jones, February 9, 2024.

151 Valentino Garavani and his partner: Background interview.

151 Gwyneth was always: Background interview.

152 Valentino and Giammetti were capable of friendship: Background interview.

152 *Duets* filming was delayed: Michael Shnayerson, "Today Belongs to Gwyneth," *Vanity Fair*, September 2000.

152 Radiation was so taxing . . . on the Vancouver set: Jones, interview.

152 *It's five thirty a.m.*: Amy Wallace and Robert W. Welkos, "The 71st Academy Award Nominations: They're on the Short List," *Los Angeles Times*, February 10, 1999.

152 Gwyneth and Bruce had: Author interview with Neil Canton, January 20, 2024.

153 Gwyneth called it "the opposite": Bob Strauss, "Genuine Gwyneth: Paltrow Deepens Her Craft in 'The Talented Mr. Ripley,'" *Daily News of Los Angeles*, December 24, 1999.

153 The crew filmed the strongest . . . escort Gwyneth to the Oscars: Jones, interview.

CHAPTER 14: THE OSCAR—AND THE CURSE?

154 "I felt like people": Cindy Pearlman, "Oscar Winner's Angst: Paltrow Says Big Moment Was Very Traumatic," *Chicago Sun-Times*, January 4, 2000.

154 "inevitable": Jami Bernard, "Expect Major Oscars for 'Pvt. Ryan': Otherwise, Most Races Are Wide-Open, with No Holds Barred," New York *Daily News*, March 21, 1999.

154 "would seem to be the shoo-in": John Anderson, "The Oscars: Scoping Out the Winners," *Newsday*, March 21, 1999.

154 The *New York Post* ran: "Designers Obsess over Gwyneth," *New York Post*, March 19, 1999.

154 the *Los Angeles Times* noted: Barbara Thomas, "The 71st Academy Award Nominations: Who Will Wear Whom?," *Los Angeles Times*, February 10, 1999.

154 Meanwhile, her grandfather Buster: Laurie Hibberd, "Actor Gwyneth Paltrow and Her Father, Actor-Director Bruce Paltrow, Discuss Their Film 'Duets' and Family Tragedies and Triumphs," *The Early Show*, CBS, September 22, 2000.

154 In private, Gwyneth shrugged off the hype: Background interview.

154 Just before the Oscars, Gwyneth said: Amy Wallace, "Oscars '99: Strangers in Good Company," *Los Angeles Times*, March 21, 1999.

155   Inside the Polo Lounge the Saturday: Interview with Mark Gill, February 12, 2025.

155   Gwyneth brought the house down: "$75M Laugh," *New York Post*, March 22, 1999.

155   Gwyneth got ready in a suite: Background interviews with two sources.

156   Various designers had been sending: Wallace, "Oscars '99: Strangers in Good Company."

156   "It was so funny": André Leon Talley, "Period Drama," *Vogue*, September 1999.

156   Gwyneth didn't have a stylist: "Gwyneth Paltrow Breaks Down 13 Looks from 1995 to Now," *Vogue*, July 30, 2019, 11:27.

156   Stephen Huvane approached: Background interview.

156   However, Lauren wasn't about: Author interviews with two Ralph Lauren sources.

156   she hadn't been eating much: Background interview.

156   Lauren became so frustrated: Background interview.

156   A night or two before: Background interviews with two sources.

156   She accessorized with a diamond choker: James Barron and Constance C. R. White, "Public Lives," *New York Times*, March 25, 1999.

157   The designers at Ralph Lauren: Author interviews with two Ralph Lauren sources.

157   Lauren himself was not: Background interview.

157   Gwyneth walked into the Oscars: Background interview.

157   "Judi's a lock": Author interview, John Madden, May 5, 2025.

157   Weinstein walked in: Author interview with Jack Lechner, August 1, 2023.

157   The Miramax team: Interviews with several Miramax sources.

157   Early in the ceremony, Bruce: Barron and White, "Public Lives."

157   *Shakespeare in Love* started winning: Background interview.

157   After Nicholson opened: Frank DiGiacomo, "A Tense Best-Picture Victory for the Miramax Mogul Who Stormed Oscar Beach," *New York Observer*, March 29, 1999.

157   Gwyneth later would say: Robert W. Welkos and Eric Harrison, "The 71st Academy Awards: Oscars 99. Backstage, Night of Firsts for Stars of All Ages," *New York Times*, March 22, 1999.

157   She later described the feeling: Joanne Schneies, "Gwyneth Grows Up," *Herald Sun*, February 19, 2000.

158   "I remember Blythe and I": Madden, interview.

158   He had flown out: Hibberd, "Actor Gwyneth Paltrow and Her Father."

158   Madden saw genuine emotion: Madden, interview.

159   considered himself "a weeper": Mike Davies, "Arts: A Little Paternal Paltrow Pride: Mike Davies Talks to Bruce Paltrow," *Birmingham Post*, November 16, 2000.

159   After the ceremony, Gwyneth met: George Rush and Joanna Malloy, "Looks Like a Real-Life Romeo for Gwyneth," New York *Daily News*, March 23, 1999; background interview.

159   Before she arrived, Weinstein had pulled: Background interview.

159   Gwyneth attended the Miramax party: Rush and Malloy, "Looks Like a Real-Life Romeo"; and background interview.

159 The Miramax party went so late: Author interview with Miramax executive at the party.

159 The next morning, Gwyneth headed: Background interview.

159 Weinstein sent Meryl Poster: Background interview.

160 The following day, Gwyneth went: Mitchell Fink with Emily Gest, "'Ashes' Set Too Much for McCourt to Handle," New York *Daily News*, March 25, 1999.

160 But true to his word, Weinstein sent: Background interview.

160 "Berkshires and lie in the grass": Amy Wallace, "Strangers in Good Company," *Los Angeles Times*, March 21, 1999.

160 "seemed destined for stardom": Robert Dominguez, "It Was Paltrow, Right from the Start," New York *Daily News*, March 22, 1999.

160 "She is magnificent, beyond supermodel": Karen Heller, "And the Winner for Best-Dressed at the Oscars?," *Philadelphia Inquirer*, March 22, 1999.

160 "impossibly lovely and graceful": Rod Dreher, "Miramax-imized Its PR Campaign," *New York Post*, March 22, 1999.

160 Now that she had won the Academy Award: Robert Dominguez and Michelle Caruso, "Gwyneth's Got It! Her Star's on the Rise After Oscar Triumph," New York *Daily News*, March 23, 1999.

160 Weinstein said that whatever: Jeannie Williams, "Celebs Whoop it up After Night of Pure Gold: All Is Not 'Vanity,' Much Is Miramax," *USA Today*, March 23, 1999.

160 *Shakespeare in Love* had earned: Nicole Sperling, untitled article, *The Hollywood Reporter*, March 1, 2005.

160 $289 million: *Shakespeare in Love*, as per Internet Movie Database.

160 Four days after the ceremony, *The New York Times:* Barron and White, "Public Lives."

161 Gwyneth was excited: Background interview.

161 She described being sick: Schneies, "Gwyneth Grows Up."

161 at her parents' house: Gwyneth Paltrow, *Wylde Moon* podcast, August 27, 2022.

161 "I think I had adrenaline poisoning": Pearlman, "Oscar Winner's Angst: Paltrow Says Big Moment Was Very Traumatic."

161 "I didn't want to leave the house": Joanne Schneies, "That Speech: Face to Face," *Daily Telegraph*, February 19, 2000.

CHAPTER 15: THE BACKLASH BEGINS

162 "[S]he would be easier": Michelle Goldberg, "Paltry Paltrow," Salon.com, April 2, 1999.

162 When Gwyneth returned to New York: Ruth Ryon, "'Gettin' Jiggy' in the Hills of Malibu," *Los Angeles Times*, April 25, 1999; "Los Feliz Library Big on DiCaprio," *Daily News of Los Angeles*, April 9, 1999.

162 On April 1, Salon.com called her: David Rakoff, "Glorious Gwyneth," Salon.com, April 1, 1999.

162 "The way the fluff media": Michelle Goldberg, "Paltry Paltrow," Salon.com, April 2, 1999.

163　By October, British tabloid *The People*: Shane Donaghey, "Ulster Man of the People: Grinning at Star Gwyn," *The People*, October 31, 1999.

163　The media and public backlash: Background interview.

163　"an invention of the press": Email from Harvey Weinstein, April 7, 2025.

163　He offered her $8 million: Background interview.

163　Gwyneth also successfully requested: Background interview.

164　"not where I want to be": Background interview.

164　Before the Oscars, she had started talking: Author interview with Alessandro Nivola, October 1, 2023.

164　But director Barry Edelstein: Background interview.

164　After Gwyneth approved Edelstein . . . "is so extreme": Nivola, interview.

165　Edelstein thought that Gwyneth: Background interview.

165　"a chance of getting a ticket": Michael Riedel, "Gwyneth Mania: Oscar Winner Takes Center Stage at Festival in Bucolic Williamstown," *New York Post*, August 10, 1999.

165　Meryl Streep, Paul Newman, and Joanne Woodward: Nivola, interview; George Rush and Joanna Molloy, "It's Back Behind Bars for Downey," New York *Daily News*, August 6, 1999.

165　she didn't give a single interview: Author interview with Michael Riedel, July 27, 2023.

165　E! sent a camera crew: Riedel, "Gwyneth Mania."

165　In the first moments of the show: Nivola, interview.

166　"you forget it's Gwyneth Paltrow": David Patrick Stearns, "Paltrow in Shakespeare, as You Like Her," *USA Today*, August 9, 1999.

166　*Newsday* and the *New York Post*: Sylviane Gold, "Just As You Like Her: Paltrow and Company Shine in Williamstown," *Newsday*, August 10, 1999; Donald Lyons, "With Paltrow, Plenty to Like in 'As You Like It,'" *New York Post*, August 10, 1999.

166　And *The New York Times*'s: Ben Brantley, "As Rosalind Grows, So Does an Actress," *New York Times*, August 9, 1999.

CHAPTER 16: A NEW ALTITUDE

167　"[S]he . . . made it quite clear": "Pals Snubbed by 'Snob' Gwyn," *Sunday Mercury*, June 4, 2000.

167　*Bounce* had started out with Universal . . . "get Ben and Gwyneth": Author interview with Michael Besman, January 23, 2024.

167　"to get Ben and Gwyneth": Background interview.

167　Though they'd broken up: Background interview.

168　"personal issues, get in the way": Jay Carr, "Movies: Catching Up with Ben Affleck: The Actor Talks About 'Bounce,' His Career, and, of course, Gwyneth Paltrow," *Boston Globe*, November 12, 2000.

168　Gwyneth chose to dye her hair brown: Besman, interview; background interview.

168　Weinstein wasn't happy: Background interview.

168　The hair color became a problem: Besman, interview.

168　When she was reportedly with: George Rush and Joanna Molloy, "Jerry to GOP: Enough Already," New York *Daily News*, October 12, 1999; "Camry Cutie Arrested in Brawl," *New York Post*, October 15, 1999.

168　she would wear: Background interview.

168　Gwyneth's and Oseary's spokespeople: George Rush and Joanna Molloy, "Gwyn & Guy Are Couch Pet-atoes," New York *Daily News*, October 15, 1999.

168　But their supposed romance was short-lived: Caroline Doyle Karasyov, "The Private Side of Gwyneth," *Harper's Bazaar*, November 2001.

168　But Weinstein was concerned . . . for Best Supporting Actress: Author interview with Steve Andrews, January 26, 2024.

169　However, others at Miramax: Background interviews with two sources.

169　Frank Rich did a big feature: Frank Rich, "America Pseudo," *New York Times*, December 12, 1999.

169　"a blank slate without the imagination": Jami Bernard, "'Ripley' Ripping Good Tale of Stolen ID: 'Talented' Cast Is Hit and Miss in Chic Thriller," New York *Daily News*, December 24, 1999.

169　*Vanity Fair*'s story celebrating: David Canfield, "The Talented Mr. Ripley at 25—Frank, Queer, and Ahead of Its Time," *Vanity Fair*, December 11, 2023.

169　She traveled around Europe: Background interview.

169　Even within her entourage: Background interview.

170　Yet Gwyneth had been generous: Background interview.

170　Warner Bros. loaned her: Michael Shnayerson, "Today Belongs to Gwyneth," *Vanity Fair*, September 2000; background interview.

170　When Kittenplan got married: Background interviews with two sources.

171　ABC reported that: "Madonna Wedding Details Uncovered," *ABC News*, December 28, 2000.

171　while a friend: Background interview.

171　"get in touch again": "Pals Snubbed by 'Snob' Gwyn."

171　Gwyneth did end up attending: Background interview.

172　"You know," he told her: Samantha Bee, "The Real Gwyneth Paltrow," *Harper's Bazaar*, October 11, 2016.

172　had no problem calling: Author interview with John Tinker, January 31, 2024.

172　"When you achieve the kind of fame": Jane Mulkerrins, "'I'm Very Much the Marrying Kind': Gwyneth Paltrow Talks Love, Success and Marriage Second Time Round," *Marie Claire*, October 3, 2018.

172　One hot June day in New York City: Anna Wintour, "Letter from the Editor: A Rich Moment," *Vogue*, September 1999.

172　the premier issue of *Talk* magazine: Patrick Demarchelier, "Gwyneth Paltrow Is a Bad Girl," *Talk*, September 1999.

173　Gwyneth was furious: Background interview.

173　That wasn't the last time Gwyneth: Background interview.

173　"There were certain favors that he": "Miramax Mogul Gets Mauled," *New York Post*, November 25, 2001.

173　"the Über-'It' Girl": Michael Shnayerson, "Today Belongs to Gwyneth," *Vanity Fair*, September 2000.

173　She was living in New York: Author interview with Michael Shnayerson, May 31, 2024.

174 The story was pegged to *Duets*: Shnayerson, "Today Belongs to Gwyneth."

174 The release had been pushed: Author interview with Kevin Jones, February 9, 2024.

174 The *Toronto Star* noted: Sid Adilman, "Film Festival a Game of Celebrity Hide-and-Seek," *Toronto Star*, September 5, 2000.

174 A Disney publicist then canceled . . . "can't comment on this kind of thing": Peter Howell, "Toronto Film Festival: Today's 'It Girl' Superstar Gwyneth Paltrow a Hard Catch," *Toronto Star*, September 11, 2000.

174 "has terrible taste in women": Background interview.

175 *Duets* would pull in $2 million: Robert W. Welkos, "Weekend Box Office: Olympics Lure Away Audiences," *Los Angeles Times*, September 19, 2000.

175 The ticket sales led the *Los Angeles Times*: Kenneth Turan, "Nothing Much to Sing About," *Los Angeles Times*, September 15, 2000.

175 And Salon.com's critic reported: Stephanie Zacharek, "Duets," Salon.com, September 15, 2000.

175 Affleck's addiction issues: Caroline Doyle Karasyov, "The Private Side of Gwyneth," *Harper's Bazaar*, November 2001; background interview.

175 "doesn't take Freudian analysis": Shnayerson, "Today Belongs to Gwyneth."

175 In 2001, Gwyneth participated in: Background interview.

175 Sheen helped arrange a room: Anne Marie-O'Neil, "Reality Check," *People*, August 23, 2001.

175 Affleck "brave" for going: Karasyov, "The Private Side of Gwyneth."

175 Gwyneth briefly dated . . . "dating a Catholic!": Background interview.

175 For his new movie about an eccentric . . . before he shot a single frame: Background interview.

176 The Tenenbaum children were supposed . . . "I knew who I was": Author interview with Karen Patch, January 23, 2024.

177 brands like Fendi and Miu Miu: Christian Allaire, "What Makes Margot Tenenbaum's Style So Good, Even 20 Years Later," *Vogue*, October 5, 2021.

177 "but make it more sad": Author interview with Sam Hoffman, January 23, 2024.

177 The atmosphere on set was mostly harmonious: Background interview.

177 Anderson wanted the cast to feel: Background interview.

177 One day Anderson was on set: Hoffman, interview.

178 Luke Wilson . . . everyone on the set knew: Background interview.

178 "I hate dates": Karasyov, "The Private Side of Gwyneth."

178 "hottest ticket": Lou Lumenick, "A Royal 'Flush' at New York Film Fest," *New York Post*, October 3, 2001.

178 "a woman who has everything": Todd McCarthy, "Style Dictates Content of 'Royal' Family Saga," *Variety*, October 14, 2001.

CHAPTER 17: FAT SUIT FIASCO

179 "I got a real sense": Julie Hinds, "The Fat Pack Stars Who Suit Up for Beefy Roles Rather Than Put on Real Pounds Draw Criticism," *Detroit Free Press*, July 24, 2001.

179 "don't have to do anything unladylike": Matt Lauer, "Gwyneth Paltrow Discusses Her New Movie 'Shallow Hal,'" *Today*, NBC, November 6, 2001.

179 Gwyneth had seen *Charlie's Angels*: Background interview.

179 Gwyneth felt some part: Caroline Doyle Karasyov, "The Private Side of Gwyneth," *Harper's Bazaar*, November 2001.

180 Gwyneth was nervous: Background interview.

180 Before the filming started: Background interview.

180 "I was helping him [Bruce]": Tracy Smith, "Gwyneth Paltrow Marks a Birthday Milestone with Tracy Smith," *CBS News Sunday Morning*, September 25, 2022.

180 Gwyneth set about trying to cure: John Hind, "Gwyneth Paltrow: 'Leonardo DiCaprio Would Tell Me How Dirty Meat Is. Now I Haven't Eaten Red Meat in 20 Years,'" *The Guardian*, April 20, 2013.

180 "I felt I could heal him": Holly Willoughby, "Gwyneth Paltrow," *Wylde Moon* podcast, August 27, 2022.

180 She began searching for a solution: Gwyneth Paltrow, *My Father's Daughter: Delicious, Easy Recipes Celebrating Family & Togetherness* (Grand Central, 2011), 16.

181 While there's scientific evidence: Author interview with Dr. Amesh Adalja, April 21, 2025.

181 this diet "to keep thin": Caroline Graham, "Breaking the Ice," *Daily Mail*, January 20, 2002.

181 "That was the beginning of people thinking": Elisa Lipsky-Karasz, "Gwyneth Paltrow Wants to Convert You," *Wall Street Journal*, December 4, 2018.

181 "I used to drink": Vanessa Grigoriadis, "Gwyneth Gets Real," *Talk*, December/January 2002.

181 "I don't think you could say": Adalja, interview.

181 "skip it unless I'm ill": Graham, "Breaking the Ice."

181 She'd bring two yoga: Grigoriadis, "Gwyneth Gets Real."

181 The Farrellys' crew had worked together: Background interview.

182 she weighed 350 pounds: Cesar G. Soriano, "They Plump for 'Klump' and Other Big Roles," *USA Today*, July 20, 2001.

182 She planned to walk around . . . "difficult to watch": Author interviews with Barry Teague, February 21, 2024 and December 11, 2025.

182 Before Gwyneth got to Charlotte: George Rush and Joanna Malloy, et al., "Gwyneth's Getting Her Head Together," New York Daily News, August 12, 2001.

182 "No one would even look at me": Andre Chautard, "'Shallow Hal' Fat Suit Not Just Skin-Deep," *Los Angeles Times*, November 7, 2001.

183 Gwyneth had a sign made . . . "Upper East Side of New York": Background interview.

183 Her costar Jack Black: Teague, interview, February 21, 2024.

183 At one point, crew members: Background interview.

183 "Sometimes she felt like she": Teague, interview, February 21, 2024.

183 During some scenes, Gwyneth wore . . . "when she gets older": Background interview.

184 never liked her legs: Background interview.

184 Gwyneth told friends and some of the crew: Teague, interview, February 21, 2024; and background interview.

185 "If you're overweight and you": William Keck, "Fat Jokes Figure Prominently in Farrellys' 'Shallow Hal,'" *USA Today*, November 8, 2001.

185 "Rosemary jumps into a pool"... "people understand": Alex Kuczynski, "Charting the Outer Limits of Inner Beauty," *New York Times*, November 11, 2001.

185 $23.3 million: "'Monsters, Inc.' Tops Box Office Again," United Press International, November 11, 2001.

185 Matt Lauer asked her: "Gwyneth Paltrow Discusses Her New Movie 'Shallow Hal,'" *NBC News*, November 6, 2001.

185 In an interview with *Entertainment Tonight*: Julie Hinds, "The Fat Pack Stars Who Suit Up for Beefy Roles Rather Than Put on Real Pounds Draw Criticism," *Detroit Free Press*, July 24, 2001.

186 $120 million more: *Charlie's Angels*, as per Internet Movie Database.

186 But the backlash didn't seem to bother: Background interview.

186 Weinstein remained eager: Author interview with *Talk* magazine source.

186 After the towers fell, and Manhattan: Grigoriadis, "Gwyneth Gets Real."

186 She was upset about the cover: "We Hear..." *New York Post*, November 13, 2001.

186 even though the editors had: Background interview.

186 When her friend Caroline Doyle's story: Amy Reiter, "Rehab Redux," Salon.com, November 5, 2001.

187 "He lied to me": Alison Boshoff, "The photograph Gwyneth says she didn't want the world to see!; Leading magazine insists Hollywood actress was happy to pose naked," *Daily Mail*, November 7, 2001.

187 She thought her boyfriend Luke Wilson's mom: Background interview.

187 When she signed on for a black comedy: "Harvey Weinstein Says He's a Pioneer for Women in Self-Pitying: 'I'm the Forgotten Man,'" *IndieWire*, December 15, 2019.

187 "paid than all the men": Rebecca Rosenberg, "Harvey Weinstein: I deserve pat on back when it comes to women," *New York Post*, December 15, 2019.

187 The original script was sharp and satirical: Author interview with Jack Lechner, August 1, 2023.

187 Five rewrites later, the film ... a crew member dutifully exclaimed: Author interview with Jack Baran, February 27, 2024; and background interviews with four other crew members.

188 (*New York Times*): Stephen Holden, "FILM REVIEW; Love and Other In-Flight Hazards," *New York Times*, March 21, 2003.

188 (*New York Post*): Lou Lumenick, "A Dim 'View'," *New York Post*, March 21, 2003.

188 "golden girl with the Midas touch": Jodi Kantor and Megan Twohey, *She Said: Breaking the Sexual Harassment Story That Helped Ignite a Movement* (Penguin Press, 2019), 62.

188 However, another Miramax source: Background interview.

188 Weinstein pinpointed the fracturing: Harvey Weinstein, emails, April 7 and May 26, 2025.

CHAPTER 18: LOSING BRUCE

189   "It's literally my worst nightmare": Donna Freydkin, "Paltrow Finds a New Peace," *USA Today*, October 14, 2003.

189   For the 2002 Oscars, where she presented: Rina Raphael, "Gwyneth Paltrow: 'I Should Have Worn a Bra' to 2002 Oscars," *Today*, March 1, 2013.

189   "Hollywood is a completely male-dominated": Andrew Buncombe, "Gwyneth Paltrow May Dump Macho Hollywood for Cultivated London," *Independent*, March 21, 2002.

189   "Frankly, I'm a little bit burned out": Jasper Rees, "Gwyneth Takes Centre Stage," *Daily Telegraph*, April 27, 2002.

190   "I would do anything": Rees, "Gwyneth Takes Centre Stage."

190   He was "flabbergasted": Author interview, John Madden, May 5, 2025.

190   Gwyneth took the part for: "Paltrow Nets Raves in Panned Play," Associated Press, May 18, 2002.

190   She flew over in the spring of 2002: Richard Simpson and Mira Bar-Hillel, "Gwyneth Becomes a Chelsea Girl as She Buys the GBP 1.25m Flat She Fell in Love With," *Evening Standard*, May 27, 2002.

190   She told an interviewer: Rees, "Gwyneth Takes Centre Stage."

190   Gwyneth's friends viewed her as too smart: Caroline Doyle Karasyov, "The Private Side of Gwyneth," *Harper's Bazaar*, November 2001; and background interview.

190   "Every time I do a play": Rees, "Gwyneth Takes Centre Stage."

190   "a completely dark place" . . . "any of this stuff": Madden, interview.

191   Before the play opened: Richard Ouzounian, "Gwynie," *Toronto Star*, September 13, 2005.

191   "she bowed down to it": Madden, interview.

191   "the theatrical gift": Michael Billington, "Review: Proof," *The Guardian*, May 16, 2002.

191   "makes an arresting impression": Paul Taylor, "Proof, Donmar Warehouse, London," *The Independent*, May 15, 2002.

191   "thoroughly deserved her standing ovation": Charles Spencer, "All the evidence you need that Gwyneth is a star," *The Telegraph*, May 16, 2002.

191   "Are you aware" . . . *How did that happen?*: Interview, Madden.

191   By the time Gwyneth's thirtieth: Background interview.

192   "I get to wear something": Plum Sykes, "The Power of a Fashion Icon: Gwyneth," *Vogue*, March 2002.

192   She enjoyed traveling with Valentino: Hamish Bowles, "A Midsummer Night's Dream," *Vogue*, September 2002.

192   Described as a "houseguest": Bowles, "A Midsummer Night's Dream."

192   Valentino took her on their yacht: Baz Bamigboye, "Gwyneth's Gown Causes a Splash," *Daily Mail*, August 30, 2002.

192   on the twenty-ninth, she attended: Vicki Woods, "Shining Through," *Vogue*, October 2003.

192   In September 2002, Gwyneth happened to be: Background interview.

192   when Gwyneth turned thirty: Woods, "Shining Through."

193   Blythe was filming: "Bruce Paltrow Dead at 58," United Press International, October 3, 2002.

193 The surgery and radiation had compromised: "Bruce Paltrow Directed 'St. Elsewhere,' 'Duets,'" Associated Press, October 4, 2002.

193 For her birthday, Bruce gave Gwyneth a letter: David Hochman, "Gwyneth Lets Her Guard Down," *Good Housekeeping*, February 2011.

193 After their time in Rome: Gwyneth Paltrow, *My Father's Daughter: Delicious, Easy Recipes Celebrating Family & Togetherness* (Grand Central, 2011), 122.

193 They toured the Uffizi Gallery: Victoria Newton, "Gwyneth Sees the Father She Idolised Die of a Heart Attack," *Daily Mail*, October 4, 2002.

193 At some point during the trip: Geraint Llewellyn, "Gwyneth Paltrow Reveals Her Father Passed Away During Trip to Italy," *Daily Mail*, December 12, 2022.

193 One night in Cortona, known for: Paltrow, *My Father's Daughter*, 122.

193 Within a day, she realized: Geraint Llewellyn, "'He Just Died on Me': Gwyneth Paltrow Reveals Her Father Passed During Her First Ever Trip to Italy," *Daily Mail*, December 13, 2022.

193 Gwyneth insisted, and Valentino: Background interviews with two sources.

193 When they got to San Camillo hospital: Diane Sawyer, "Around the Watercooler," *Good Morning America*, ABC, October 8, 2003.

193 she reportedly felt that Blythe: Background interview.

194 After the shock of her father's death: "The Stars and Valentino," Oprah.com, October 20, 2004.

194 Wearing dark sunglasses . . . her father had loved so much: Based on images of the events.

194 Caroline Doyle flew in: Background interview.

194 She had never felt pain like that: Holly Willoughby, "Gwyneth Paltrow," *Wylde Moon* podcast.

194 "I was so traumatized": Alex Morris, "Gwyneth Paltrow Gets Real: 'I Know Who I Am, and I Own My Mistakes,'" *Glamour*, February 2, 2016.

194 After the funeral, Gwyneth went: Willoughby, "Gwyneth Paltrow."

194 She was due to start work: Sawyer, "Around the Watercooler."

195 "I don't know how I got": Donna Freydkin, "Paltrow Finds a New Peace," *USA Today*, October 14, 2003.

195 she had pulled out of two movies: Woods, "Shining Through."

195 She had thought about having a baby: Background interview.

195 She asked Mary Wigmore: "Gwyneth Paltrow: Kisses to All My Exes," *Call Her Daddy* podcast, February 16, 2024.

196 his curly hair reminding her: Nicole Lampert, "Gwyneth wants breast surgery," *Daily Mail*, December 24, 2005.

196 Gwyneth liked morning yoga: Alison Boshoff, "The Odd Couple," *Daily Mail*, November 9, 2002.

196 Gwyneth rarely drank alcohol . . . "main thing again": Robert Hilburn, "Pop Music: Sincerely Yours: Coldplay's Mission," *Los Angeles Times*, June 29, 2003.

196 While Gwyneth was extroverted: Background interview.

197 Martin said it was inspired by: Larisha Paul, "Chris Martin: My Life in 10 Songs," *Rolling Stone*, October 3, 2024.

197 Gwyneth later said: *Howard Stern Show*, January 14, 2015.

197 Before *Sylvia* came out: "Gwyneth Hungry for New Hit," *New York Post*, June 16, 2003.

197 Plath's daughter, Frieda Hughes: Jamie Wilson, "Frieda Hughes Attacks BBC for Film on Plath," *The Guardian*, February 3, 2003.

197 Gwyneth described being . . . "who Sylvia Plath is": Woods, "Shining Through."

197 Shortly before Gwyneth traveled: Woods, "Shining Through."

197 It wasn't that Gwyneth feared: Background interview.

198 By August 2003, she was pregnant: "Beating Diabetes," *Tampa Bay Times*, November 3, 2012.

198 While filming *Proof*, Gwyneth was able to hide: Author interview with Jill Taylor, February 9, 2024; background interview.

198 who reflected her own fear: "Gwyneth Paltrow x Brad Falchuk: What's to Come," *The Goop* podcast, September 27, 2022.

198 The scenes were very long: Taylor, interview.

198 Martin made extended visits: Taylor, interview; author interview with Charlotte Sewell, February 9, 2024; background interview.

198 But one Miramax executive who had watched: Background interview.

198 And as she delivered these monologues: Bianca Betancourt, "Gwyneth Paltrow Reveals Why She Won't Return to Acting Anytime Soon," *Harper's Bazaar*, January 10, 2020.

199 Asked in 2003 which projects: "Scribe Goes Ga-Ga for Viggo," *New York Post*, December 1, 2003.

199 She was starting to find things: Betancourt, "Gwyneth Paltrow Reveals Why She Won't Return."

199 testified in court against a stalker: David K. Li, " 'Sick Fan' Terrorized Gwyneth for a Year," *New York Post*, December 20, 2000.

199 "I sound like a complete jerk": Freydkin, "Paltrow Finds a New Peace."

199 At the end of filming *Proof* in Chicago: Background interview.

200 knew his employees feared him: Jodi Kantor and Megan Twohey, *She Said: Breaking the Sexual Harassment Story That Helped Ignite a Movement* (New York: Penguin Press, 2019), ebook, 61.

200 "I had a really rough boss": *Quarantined with Bruce* podcast, December 8, 2020.

200 "She wanted to make": Background interview.

200 Weinstein recalled that Miramax: Weinstein, email.

200 On December 1, 2003, in New York City: Donna Freydkin, "It's No Stretch to Get Paltrow to this Benefit," *USA Today*, December 3, 2003.

200 Wearing a black silk and chiffon: Lloyd Grove with Elisa Lipsky-Karasz, "Giving 'Pregnant' Pause," New York *Daily News*, December 3, 2003.

200 Gwyneth went on *The Tonight Show with Jay Leno*: "Pregnant Paltrow to Marry Rock Singer?," *Western Mail*, December 6, 2003.

201 "sources" told the New York *Daily News* that Gwyneth . . . earned $150,000 worldwide: George Rush and Joanna Malloy, et al., "Bridal Sweet," New York *Daily News*, December 11, 2003.

201 Within two days, Gwyneth and Martin: Jenice M. Armstrong, "Christmas a 'Family' Affair in Jacko House," *Philadelphia Daily News*, December 12, 2003.

201 A judge later reportedly came to their bungalow: Nicole Lampert, "Gwyneth Marries in Secret at a Lonely Bungalow," *Daily Mail*, December 10, 2003.

201 The county clerk confirmed the marriage: "Gwyneth Paltrow and Coldplay Lead Singer Chris Martin Are Married," Associated Press, December 10, 2003.

201 a substantial diamond on a thin band: Krista Smith, "Gwyneth in Love," *Vanity Fair*, February 2004.

201 Two photographers jostled: Tara Conlan, "Coldplay Singer in Clash," *Courier Mail*, December 9, 2003.

202 In 2009, he told *60 Minutes*: "What Chris Martin said about Gwyneth Paltrow on *60 Minutes*," CBS News, March 14, 2014.

202 "You look at celebrity couples who": Smith, "Gwyneth in Love."

202 As Gwyneth pulled back: Sara M. Moniuszko, "Gwyneth Paltrow on Why She Stepped Away from Acting: 'It's Just Not Who I Am,'" *USA Today*, December 9, 2020; "Gwyneth Paltrow: Kisses to All My Exes," *Call Her Daddy* podcast, February 16, 2024.

202 She recalled her acupuncturist: Smith, "Gwyneth in Love."

202 In the spring of 2004, Gwyneth … "almost always connects to the heart": Vicky Vlachonis, *The Body Doesn't Lie: A 3-Step Program to End Chronic Pain and Become Positively Radiant* (HarperCollins, 2015), 6–8, iBook.

203 Whenever she believed something: Background interview.

203 Gwyneth's first birth was a harrowing: Tania Shakinovsky, "Gwyneth Splashes Out on a Pair of Pools so She Can Have Her Water Baby at Home," *Daily Mail*, March 3, 2004; background interview.

204 After around hour sixty-two: Diane Sawyer, "Weather," *Good Morning America*, September 16, 2004.

204 her doctor suggested an epidural: Jo Kelly, "Have You Noticed … Posh Mums Are Pushing Again," *Herald Sun Sunday Style Magazine*, February 27, 2005.

204 With the indecipherable murmurings: Dorian Lynskey, "Friday Review: Strange? Us?," *The Guardian*, August 26, 2005.

204 Apple Blythe Alison Martin was born: Vlachonis, *The Body Doesn't Lie*, 8; Steve Hartley and Dan Kadison, "Mom's Apple Cutie Pie: Gwyn Has 9-lb., 11-oz. Girl," *New York Post*, May 16, 2004.

204 Gwyneth had avoided publicly stating: Bill Zwecker, "On Stars' Advice, Julia Pulled a Little Due-Date Deception," *Chicago Sun-Times*, December 17, 2004.

204 photographers and reporters quickly: Hartley and Kadison, "Mom's Apple Cutie Pie."

204 Vlachonis to perform "cranial osteopathy": Vlachonis, *The Body Doesn't Lie*, 8.

204 a study in the journal *Pediatrics*: Paul Posadzki et al., "Osteopathic Manipulative Treatment for Pediatric Conditions: An Updated Systematic Review," *Pediatrics* 132, no. 1 (July 2013): 140–152.

204 Gwyneth and Martin were "900 miles": "Gwyneth Paltrow Gives Birth to Baby Girl named Apple," Associated Press, May 15, 2004.

204 About the name Apple: "Gwyneth Paltrow Reveals Why She Named Her Daughter Apple," *The Oprah Winfrey Show*, ABC, April 1, 2019.

204 Motherhood, she said, "is absolutely" … "very long time": Laura Benjamin, "Paltrow's Parade," *Daily Mail*, May 21, 2004; Jennifer D. Braun, "Jenny's Dish," *Star-Ledger*, June 22, 2004.

205 "What the press release should have said": Anita Quigley, "Why Are Celebrity Parents so Tasteless," *Daily Telegraph*, May 17, 2004.

205 "I don't know if it's a scandal": Harry Smith, "Gwyneth Paltrow and Jude Law Talk About Their New Film "Sky Captain and the World of Tomorrow," *The Early Show*, CBS, September 17, 2004.

205 For many years, Apple: "Baby Apples Come in Pairs," *New York Post*, May 18, 2004.

205 Five weeks after Apple's birth: William Keck, "Hollywood's Two New Moms Step Out for a Night," *USA Today*, June 21, 2004.

205 The media noted how slender: Donna Freydkin, "Paltrow Sweet on Baby Apple," *USA Today*, September 8, 2004.

205 Gwyneth went to a party: Farrah Weinstein, "Gwyn & Bear It—My Cupping Treatment Sucked—But That's the Idea," *New York Post*, July 10, 2004.

205 Though cupping is generally considered safe: Robert H. Smerling, MD, "What Exactly Is Cupping?," *Harvard Health Blog*, July 29, 2024.

205 Both CNN and CBS's *The Early Show*: "Fallout from Flawed Intelligence: 'Too Much Too Soon,'" *Anderson Cooper 360*, CNN, July 9, 2004; Harry Smith, "Michael Gaeta, Licensed Acupuncturist, Discusses the Alternative Pain Therapy Known as Cupping," *The Early Show*, CBS, July 12, 2004; Weinstein, "Gwyn & Bear It."

206 John Demsey was looking for a new face: Background interview.

206 Wintour called Demsey in February: Molly Prior, "The Art of the Deal: For Beauty Companies, Wrangling Celebrities Is an Expensive But Rewarding Sport," *Women's Wear Daily*, March 13, 2006.

206 In February 2005, the *Chicago Sun-Times*: Tom Long, "Oscar Winners Who Lost Their Golden Touch," *Chicago Sun-Times*, February 27, 2005.

206 Gwyneth had already been top of mind . . . "a sack of shit": Background interview.

207 The Lauder campaign was one of Gwyneth's cushiest: Lisa Lockwood, "Gwyneth Paltrow to Appear in New Dior Ad Campaign," *Women's Wear Daily*, November 9, 1999.

207 Damiani jewelry: "Gem Dandy," *New York Post*, September 24, 2004.

207 Not long before Apple was born: Nicole Lampert, "For the Teetotal Miss Paltrow, a Cheque for 3 Million Is Enough to Drive Her to Drink," *Daily Mail*, December 26, 2003.

207 "I think it's gross": Emma Brockes, "Where the Heart Is: She Likes the Geeky Roles, but Not the Low Pay That Goes with Them," *The Guardian*, January 27, 2006.

207 Instead of having to spend months: Lampert, "For the Teetotal Miss Paltrow."

207 The advertising work "allows me": Cesar G. Soriano, "Mommy and Mode," *USA Today*, May 23, 2005.

208 In 2006, *The Guardian* asked Gwyneth: Brockes, "Where the Heart Is."

208 Gwyneth also spent a lot: Background interview.

208 Gwyneth and Martin bought a five-bedroom: Laura Benjamin, "Gwyneth Moves to Be Nearer Her Therapists," *Daily Mail*, July 16, 2024.

208 Gwyneth sold her New York town house: William Neuman, "A Farewell to Pale Male and Lola," *New York Times*, June 26, 2005.

208 It came with four bedrooms: Braden Keil, "Gimme Shelter—Monster House," *New York Post*, September 17, 2005.

208 Stephen Huvane said that she: Neuman, "A Farewell to Pale Male and Lola."

CHAPTER 19: MASS APPEAL

209 "Don't you want to be": Marianne Garvey, "Gwyneth Gets Back into 'Action'!" *New York Post*, August 7, 2007.

209 Around 2005, to help mold: Author interview with Anna Bingemann, October 6, 2023.

209 Bingemann, an Australian whose daily: Elana Fishman, "Stylist Secrets: Anna Bingemann Talks Baubles, Wardrobe Basics, and Styling at Sea," *Marie Claire*, May 23, 2011.

210 paid to wear a particular label: Author interview with Anna Bingemann, October 6, 2023.

210 Valentino was shifting away: Background interview.

210 When the film version of *Proof*: Choire Sicha, "At this Point, It's Stardom Optional," *Los Angeles Times*, September 11, 2005.

210 "I couldn't be making a movie": Terry Lawson, "As Mother, Wife and Actress, Paltrow Embraces Quality," *Detroit Free Press*, September 18, 2005.

210 She didn't want to travel: Michelle Ruiz, "Gwyneth Paltrow on Motherhood, MAHA, Meghan Markle, Making Out with Timothée Chalamet—and Much More," *Vanity Fair*, March 18, 2025.

210 "an exceptional portrait of psychological": Kenneth Turan, "Woman on the Verge: Gwyneth Paltrow's Exposed and Vulnerable Performance Is the Heart of 'Proof,'" *Los Angeles Times*, September 16, 2005.

210 "demands our pity, our attention": Manohla Dargis, "Solving for X: Is She Crazy or a Math Mastermind?," *New York Times*, September 16, 2005.

210 after not having a nanny: Derek Blasberg, "V Collector's Club: Gwyneth Paltrow," *V Magazine*, June 27, 2020.

210 Blythe let it slip: Adam Malecek, "BTW," *Wisconsin State Journal*, December 4, 2005.

211 host Lou Diamond Phillips introduced Gwyneth: "Gwyneth Paltrow Confirms She's Pregnant Again," Agence France Presse, January 13, 2006.

211 Gretchen Mol appeared on the cover: Ned Zeman, "The Hazing of Gretchen Mol," *Vanity Fair*, September 1998.

211 "wasn't a fraction of the actress": Background interview.

211 Bingemann had her pick: Bingemann, interview.

212 With five bedrooms: Braden Keil, "Gimme Shelter," *New York Post*, October 19, 2006.

212 the house was large enough that guests: Background interview.

212 Kim Gieske helped Gwyneth: Background interview.

212 Gwyneth lost the Golden Globe: Mandy Stadtmiller, "Awards Were a Starless Night," *New York Post*, March 7, 2006.

212 After her terrifying first birth: Background interview.

213 On April 8, 2006, Moses Bruce Anthony Martin: "It's a Boy! Gwyneth Paltrow and Her Rocker Husband Chris Martin Welcomed . . . ," *Miami Herald*, April 11, 2006.

213 Gwyneth later explained: RedEye, "For Hitmaking Duos, Two Stars Are Better than One," *Chicago Tribune*, September 25, 2006.

213   Moses made his public debut: "Million Dollar Baby: $4 Million for Shiloh Baby Pix?," *ABC News*, June 7, 2006.

213   "I do not know how single mothers": Sarah Bailey, "The real Gwyneth Paltrow," *Harper's Bazaar*, September 2006.

213   Gwyneth was home with her two kids: "Paltrow Went Back to Work to Be a Better Mum," WENN, February 5, 2007.

213   "Don't you want to be in a movie": Marianne Garvey, "Gwyneth Gets Back into 'Action'!" *New York Post*, August 7, 2007.

213   "What happens if, one day": Julia Ellis, "'Proof' Positive," *Variety*, September 12, 2005.

213   Gwyneth had privately admitted: Background interview.

214   "fire came back to work": Plum Sykes, "Gwyneth's Guide to Life," *Vogue*, May 2008.

214   And if the movie was a hit: Eric Harrison, "Comic-Book-Based Films in Planning Stages," *Houston Chronicle*, June 18, 2007.

214   "feel like doing an indie film": Emlyn Travis, "Gwyneth Paltrow Says 'Iron Man' Felt 'Very Low-Tech' Compared to Marvel Now," *Yahoo Entertainment*, April 3, 2024.

214   Gwyneth credited director Jon Favreau: Plum Sykes, "Gwyneth's Guide to Life," *Vogue*, May 2008.

214   shoots occurred at all times: Background interview.

214   In early 2007, fewer than two years: Josh Barbanel, "Few Views Are Forever," *New York Times*, January 28, 2007.

214   She had bought a new 4,400-square-foot place: Josh Barbanel, "Apartment, Art in Itself, Hits Market for First Time Since 1920s," *New York Times*, January 14, 2007.

214   At a dinner party ... "deadly serious": Beth Wilson, "Paltrow Promotes 'Pleasures' Scent," *Women's Wear Daily*, August 20, 2007.

215   Batali texted Charlie Pinsky: Author interview with Charles Pinsky, June 23, 2023.

217. Never religious, Gwyneth had gone back and forth: Background interview.

218   Gwyneth was cordial: Author interview with Mark Bittman, May 31, 2023.

218   "I haven't eaten anything from": Stephen M. Silverman, "Gwyneth Paltrow Will Eat Her Way Across Spain," People.com, December 1, 2020.

218   Anthony Bourdain was on a panel: Doug Camilli, "Burberry Coats Its Endorsement Harry Potter Star with Classy Praise," *The Gazette*, June 13, 2009.

218   During the filming, Gwyneth would eat: Pinsky, interview.

218   During the second week of filming ... national print or broadcast ads: Pinsky, interview.

219   She talked about her interest: "Chef Mario Batali's Culinary Road Trip," Oprah.com, September 17, 2008.

CHAPTER 20: GOOP RISING

220   "I would rather die": Lloyd Grove, "Two Pen Pals in One Hill of a Feud," *New York Daily News*, August 23, 2005.

220 Stepping onto the red carpet: Jenny Feldman, "Did Gwyneth Forget Her Pants?," Glamour.com, June 19, 2008.

220 The insecurity she had long felt about her legs: Background interview.

220 "The coverage [of the Balmain look]": Author interview with Anna Bingemann, October 6, 2023.

220 "changing and changing and changing": Josh Duboff, "Tracy Anderson Describes the First Time She Met Gwyneth Paltrow," *Vanity Fair*, March 16, 2017.

221 "have a supermodel body": Judith Newman, "Join the Gwyneth Paltrow & Tracy Anderson Fit Club," *Redbook*, December 19, 2012.

221 Gwyneth had introduced Anderson: Josh Glancy, "Celebrity Trainer Tracy Anderson on Madonna, Gwyneth Paltrow and How to Get 'Skinny-Ripped,'" *Times*, January 7, 2018.

221 relationship reached a breaking point: Background interview.

221 Anderson later said that Madonna: Glancy, "Celebrity Trainer Tracy Anderson."

221 During the filming of *Iron Man* . . . "lady take it away": Background interview.

222 Gwyneth fit in training . . . "I ever had": Amy Spencer, "Tracy Anderson: Strong Is the New Sexy," *Health*, April 14, 2015.

222 "I would rather die than let my kid": Grove, "Two Pen Pals in One Hill of a Feud."

222 "Cancer has been the curse": "Why Meat Is off the Menu for the Paltrow Children," *Daily Mail*, February 19, 2007.

222 "Diet cannot prevent cancer": Alok Jha, "Evil Genes and Antifreeze: TV Gurus' Toxic Talk Put Under the Microscope," *The Guardian*, January 3, 2008.

222 In early 2008, Sense about Science: Marina Hyde, "Our Gilded Mountebanks Believe That Quackery Can Pass for Gravitas," *The Guardian*, January 5, 2008; Nic Fleming, "Stars Who Turn Fads into Fact," *Daily Telegraph*, January 3, 2008.

223 "It's interesting that many": Author interview with Amesh Adalja, April 21, 2025.

223 "never looked lovelier": Chris Tookey, "Man of Iron Defeated by a Rusty Old Plot," *Daily Mail*, May 2, 2008.

223 With nearly $100 million: David Germain, "'Iron Man' Take Tops $100 Million," *Star-Ledger*, May 5, 2008.

223 ended up grossing nearly $600 million: Germain, "'Iron Man.'"

223 Gwyneth sat at her kitchen counter: Bingemann, interview.

223 The Sunday night before Gwyneth . . . "We've got it": Interview with Anna Bingemann, October 6, 2023.

224 Gwyneth's representatives provided: Background interview.

224 which reported her income as $25 million: Lacey Rose, "Hollywood's Top-Earning Actresses," *Forbes*, August 11, 2008,

225 She was the sixty-seventh-highest-paid entertainer: Background interview; Rose, "Hollywood's 10 Top-Earning Actresses."

225 "certainly prioritized": Author interview with Richard Lovett, April 11, 2025.

225 decided to write a cookbook: Blasberg, "V Collector's Club: Gwyneth Paltrow."

CHAPTER 21: GWYNETH, INC.

226 "My life is good": Gwyneth Paltrow, Goop.com, September 2008.

226 Peter Arnell had spent his career: Author interview with Peter Arnell, April 10, 2024.

227 The way Gwyneth tells the story: Marshall Heyman, "Gwyneth Paltrow's Top Life Hacks, from Hiring Right to Wearing Jumpsuits," *Wall Street Journal*, February 22, 2018.

227 Goop was "an old nickname": Robin Roberts, "Gwyneth Paltrow: 'Iron Man 2,'" *Good Morning America*, ABC, April 30, 2010.

227 Goop@aol.com email address: Background interviews with two sources.

227 "not what I set out to do": Olivia Barker, "Classroom Yoga? Not a Stretch for Paltrow," *USA Today*, February 27, 2009.

228 Visitors to the site were greeted with: Early Goop website screenshots.

228 A weekly newsletter freed Gwyneth: "Goop's Gwyneth Paltrow on Being Brave in the Face of Public Scrutiny at #BlogHer15 Creator's Summit," *BlogHer*, August 15, 2015, 39:34.

228 "We're having an especially good": Caroline Bankoff, "Gwyneth Paltrow Trying Valiantly to be a New-Age Martha Stewart," *New York Observer*, September 23, 2008.

229 "the road ahead looks bumpy": Maria Russo, "Paltrow Wastes No Time: Goop Is Thin," *Los Angeles Times*, September 26, 2008.

229 Regarding the "See," "Go," "Do," etc. categories: "Paltrow Explains It All for You," *Star-Ledger*, September 24, 2008.

229 "a site for hemorrhoid cream": Claudia Connell, "Learning to Live Like Gwynnie," *Daily Mail*, November 27, 2008.

229 "Gwyneth has, to her extraordinary": Hadley Freeman, "Lost in Showbiz: This Woman Would Like to 'Nourish Your Inner Aspect,'" *The Guardian*, September 26, 2008.

229 "Lady, you should take": Kate Harding, "GOOPenfreude," Salon.com, December 5, 2008.

230 She forged ahead: "Gwyneth Paltrow Talks Aging, Acting and Recession Fears at Goop Event," *Hollywood Reporter*, October 17, 2022.

230 kitchen of her thirty-three-room mansion: Kathryn Romeyn, "Inside Gwyneth Paltrow's Real Estate Portfolio," *Architectural Digest*, April 19, 2023.

230 the email included recipes for turkey ragu: "Happy Birthday, Gwyneth: A Timeline," Goop.com, September 27, 2022.

230 Gwyneth's second newsletter: Elaine Liu, "Gwyneth's London," *Lainey Gossip*, October 4, 2008.

231 "I've had this crazy, amazing life": Robin Roberts, "Gwyneth Paltrow: 'Iron Man 2,'" *Good Morning America*, ABC, April 30, 2010.

231 Gwyneth suggested readers choose a uniform: Connell, "Learning to Live Like Gwynnie."

231 She also recommended a $1,850 Hermès: Maureen Callahan, "The Girl Who Fell to Earth: Gwyn's Sad Slide Down Goop Chute," *New York Post*, February 5, 2009.

231　Her recipes went from the humble banana-nut muffins: Rebecca Traister, "Gwyneth Paltrow: Let Them Eat Roasted Poussins!," Salon.com, February 13, 2009.

231　She told readers the Ritz: Paige Wiser, "Gwyneth Paltrow is BETTER than you, and she wants you to know it; Actress' Web site tells us how to improve our miserable existences," *Chicago Sun-Times*, March 12, 2009.

231　reservations at two popular Momofuku: Bob Morris, "Martha, Oprah . . . Gwyneth?," *New York Times*, February 21, 2009.

231　"I am who I am": Callahan, "The Girl Who Fell to Earth."

231　Many people said that Gwyneth really did want: Numerous background interviews.

232　she was almost forceful: Author interview with Kevin Jones, February 9, 2024.

232　"Recently I have found three doctors": Tirdad Derakhshani, "Sideshow: The Doctor Is Out at 'Doctor Who,'" *Philadelphia Inquirer*, October 31, 2008.

232　In November, Claudia Connell lived: Connell, "Learning to Live Like Gwynnie."

232　outfits that cost upward of three thousand dollars: Olivia Bergen, "Get Gwyneth's Look . . . for just £11,000," *Telegraph*, May 20, 2011.

232　"The Gwyneth Paltrow guide to spring fashion": Margot Peppers, "The Gwyneth Paltrow Guide to Spring Fashion," *Daily Mail*, March 21, 2013.

233　"I like to do fasts and cleanses": Hadley Freeman, "Comment & Debate: Toxins Are All in the Mind," *The Guardian*, January 6, 2009.

233　Gwyneth gave her first interview: Mary Cadden, "GOOP: It's a Portal into Paltrow's Life on GOOP.com," *USA Today*, January 7, 2009.

234　By February, around five months after: "Ad Wiz Backs Gwynnie's Goop," *New York Post*, February 28, 2009.

234　A *New York Times* piece: Morris, "Martha, Oprah . . . Gwyneth?"

234　"I remember once I also had a movie": Tania Bryer and Alexandra Gibbs, "Gwyneth Paltrow on Goop," CNBC, November 3, 2017.

234　Literary agent Luke Janklow: Laura M. Holson, "Not Exactly Bookish," *New York Times*, June 14, 2013.

235　The world rights to the book: Matthew Thornton, "Deals," *Publishers Weekly*, January 12, 2009.

235　what *Forbes* later estimated to be: Clare O'Connor, "Act Three for Gwyneth Paltrow," Forbes.com, May 18, 2011.

235　the publisher's sales force . . . Batali write the introduction: Background interviews with two sources.

235　"I always feel closest to my father": Gwyneth Paltrow, *My Father's Daughter: Delicious, Easy Recipes Celebrating Family and Togetherness* (New York: Grand Central Life & Style, 2011), 12.

235　Turshen worked with her in her kitchens: Gwyneth Paltrow and Julia Turshen, *It's All Good: Delicious, Easy Recipes That Will Make You Look Good and Feel Great* (Grand Central, 2013), 12–13.

235　Gwyneth wrote the headnotes . . . "just reading that," she said: Background interview.

236　"A couple of years ago I was asked". . . "for pregnant moms": James Tapper, "Gwyneth: I'm Seized with Fear That Shampoo Gives Cancer and ADHD to Children," *Daily Mail*, April 5, 2009.

237   Gavigan would go on to found: Reuters, "Jessica Alba-Backed Honest Company IPO Raises $412.8 million," CNBC, May 5, 2021.

237   He had been drawn to celebrity culture since: "Don't Steam Your Vagina, Don't Listen to Gwyneth Paltrow," *Postmedia*, February 3, 2015.

238   Caulfield decided to visit . . . the old broken-clock analogy: Author interview with Timothy Caulfield, September 27, 2024.

238   Her claim that cancer rates had increased: Tapper, "Gwyneth: I'm Seized with Fear."

239   "How can the sun be bad": Daniel Sperling, "Gwyneth Paltrow: 'How Can the Sun Be Bad for You?,'" *Digital Spy*, July 4, 2013.

239   "These pronouncements are more entertaining": Viv Groskop, "Gwynnie's Facebook of Revelation: Picnics, Pizzas, Now Religion," *Observer*, June 12, 2011.

239   "journalists are terrified of celebrities": Anamaria Wilson, "Gwyneth Paltrow: Myth vs. Reality," *Harper's Bazaar*, April 9, 2010.

239   "I started questioning being hired": "Gwyneth Paltrow: Being Hired as a Face," Bloomberg TV, March 6, 2015.

239   But also, Estée Lauder—Aerin Lauder . . . had never met him: Background interview.

240   Gwyneth and Martin had been together: Gwyneth Paltrow, "From the Archive," *Vogue UK*, September 27, 2022.

240   Her friends weren't all that surprised: Background interview.

240   Plus, being in a relationship with: Background interview.

241   Gwyneth was confirmed: Philiana Ng, "Official: Gwyneth Paltrow to Appear on 'Glee,'" *Hollywood Reporter*, September 27, 2010.

241   Ryan Murphy, who wrote the part: "New Details on Gwyneth Paltrow's Upcoming Glee Gig," *Us Weekly*, September 27, 2010.

241   Brad Falchuk, who had driven: Alex Bhattacharji, "Why Brad Falchuk Is Hollywood's Best-Kept Secret," *Wall Street Journal*, August 14, 2019.

241   "It was a very curious family": Batya Ungar-Sargon, "His Mom Ran Hadassah. His Brother Made 'Glee.' Now Evan Falchuk Is Going into Politics," *Tablet*, December 30, 2013.

241   He'd attended private school: Bhattacharji, "Why Brad Falchuk Is Hollywood's Best-Kept Secret."

242   "She's stunning and she's charming": Josh Duboff, "Gwyneth Paltrow Gets Real About Past Relationships," *Harper's Bazaar*, January 7, 2020.

242   "She's just off the rails a bit": Claudia Puig, "Gwyneth Stays 'Strong' on All Fronts," *USA Today*, December 17, 2010.

242   whom she got to know since Martin was close . . . she'd tell friends: Background interview.

242   "This story always makes me cry": Mickey Rapkin, "The Spellbinder: Gwyneth Paltrow," *Elle*, August 2, 2011.

243   In 2011, Goop reported reaching: "What's Goop?: Our History," Goop.com.

243   Venture capitalist Juliet de Baubigny: Taffy Brodesser-Akner, "How Goop's Haters Made Gwyneth Paltrow's Company Worth $250 Million," *New York Times*, July 25, 2018.

243 Through friends, Gwyneth met: "Goop's Gwyneth Paltrow on Being Brave in the Face of Public Scrutiny at #BlogHer15 Creator's Summit," *BlogHer*, August 5, 2015, 39:34.

243 Using her own money: Anjali Mullany, "Gwyneth Paltrow Goes to Market," *Fast Company*, September 2015.

244 Gwyneth had the opportunity to promote it early: Jeffrey Steingarten, "Beauty and the Feast," *Vogue*, August 2010.

244 "Once you get past your initial nausea": Drew Grant, "Don't Hate Gwyneth Paltrow's Cookbook," Salon.com, April 4, 2011.

244 Journalists continued to ask her about it: Roberts, "Gwyneth Paltrow: 'Iron Man 2.'"

244 When she did an interview with BBC: "Gwyneth Paltrow: 'I'd Rather Smoke Crack than Eat Cheese from a Can,'" *Mirror*, July 7, 2011.

245 more than one hundred thousand copies: As per BookScan.

245 One warm Sunday afternoon . . . and eating french fries: Paltrow and Turshen, *It's All Good*, 10.

246 so did her belief that every physical symptom: Background interview.

246 She blamed herself: Paltrow and Turshen, *It's All Good*, 12.

246 After her medical tests in London: Ibid.

246 Gwyneth had met him in 2007: Sheila Yasmin Marikar, "Gwyneth Paltrow's Goop Expands into Vitamins," *The New Yorker*, March 20, 2017.

247 Alongside the author's note: Gwyneth Paltrow, *My Father's Daughter: Delicious, Easy Recipes Celebrating Family & Togetherness* (New York: Grand Central, 2011), 6.

247 About a year after the book's publication . . . "of writing and cooking": Julia Moskin, "I Was a Cookbook Ghostwriter," *New York Times*, March 13, 2012.

248 "Love @nytimes dining section": Gwyneth Paltrow (@GwynethPaltrow), "Love @nytimes dining section but this weeks facts need checking," Twitter post, March 17, 2012.

248 "Every single recipe in the book": Raphael Brion, "Watch Gwyneth Paltrow Defend Her Cookbook on the Rachael Ray Show," *Eater*, March 23, 2012.

248 The reaction was a surprise at the *Times*: Background interview.

248 But the *Times* stood by Moskin's work: Proud, "Tipsy, Make-up Free and in Her Pajamas."

249 Charles Pinsky was working with Turshen: Author interview with Charles Pinsky, June 23, 2023.

249 Turshen was credited: Paltrow and Turshen, *It's All Good*, 252.

249 But she wouldn't collaborate: Background interview.

249 Around 2012, Alejandro Junger introduced Gwyneth: Paltrow and Turshen, *It's All Good*, 13.

249 Friends and colleagues wondered: Background interviews with several sources.

250 "There's almost the narcissistic quality": Caulfield, interview.

250 Gwyneth was constantly searching: Background interview.

250 she would ask them about their medical issues: Background interview.

250 Gwyneth had her whole family tested: Paltrow and Turshen, *It's All Good*, 13 and 76.

250 "There's a large body of evidence": Caulfield, interview.

251 "The body automatically detoxes": Email to author from Marion Nestle, October 16, 2024.

251 "orthorexia [an unhealthy obsession with health food] under the guise of health": Author interview with Andrea Love, February 13, 2025.

251 The recipes for *It's All Good*: Paltrow and Turshen, *It's All Good*, 34, 38, 39, 57, 96, 108, 125, 152, 178, 228, 252–53, 268, 243.

251 When *It's All Good* landed: Background interview.

251 "I have known many women": Paltrow and Turshen, *It's All Good*, 21.

252 Sadeghi wrote the book's introduction: Paltrow and Turshen, *It's All Good*, 8–9.

252 published an excerpt from the book: Jane Gordon, "Cover Story: An Exclusive Interview with Gwyneth Paltrow," *Daily Mail*, March 18, 2013.

252 something she had revealed in *Redbook:* Judith Newman, "Gwyneth Paltrow's Trainer Tracy Anderson Shares Her Top Weight-Loss Tips," *Redbook*, October 5, 2010.

252 In the newsletter, she reported that Apple: "The Dish List," *Boston Herald*, April 1, 2013.

253 "laughable Hollywood neuroticism": Esther Zuckerman, "Gwyneth Paltrow Has Written the Bible of Laughable Hollywood Neuroticism," *The Atlantic*, March 12, 2013.

253 The *New York Post* said it: Hailey Eber, "Starved for Attention! Gwyneth Paltrow's New Dairy-, Gluten- and Sugar-free Cookbook Is a Recipe for Ridicule," *New York Post*, March 12, 2013.

253 Yahoo! Shine calculated that her eating plan: Jennifer Mascia, "Healthy Eating on Just $300 a Day," *New York Times*, April 7, 2013.

253 "taking heat for being": Ibid.

253 *It's All Good* was an early example: Background interview.

253 two hundred thousand copies: As per BookScan.

CHAPTER 22: THE UNCOUPLING

254 "I really had the sense": Nell Scovell, "February Cover Girl Gwyneth Paltrow," *Marie Claire*, January 1, 2015.

254 first a yacht trip around Italy: "Gwyneth Paltrow Celebrates the Big 4-0 with Her Family in Italy," *Daily Mail*, September 27, 2012

254 then a party at London's swanky: "A Shower of Stars for Gwyneth Paltrow's Birthday Party," *Evening Standard*, October 4, 2012; Author interview, John Madden, May 6, 2022.

254 she threw a party at Elio's ... hadn't received an invitation: Kirsty McCormack, "Gwyneth Paltrow Is Joined by Beyoncé and Other Celebrities for 40th Birthday Dinner in New York," *Daily Mail*, October 2, 2012; background interview.

255 she was terribly anxious about turning forty: "Gwyneth Paltrow x Brad Falchuk: What's to Come," *The Goop* podcast, October 4, 2022.

255 "Sometimes it's hard being with someone": Mickey Rapkin, "The Spellbinder: Gwyneth Paltrow," *Elle*, September 2011.

255 "Regardless of what happens in our marriage": Jane Gordon, "An Exclusive Interview with Gwyneth Paltrow on the Health Scare That Inspired Her New Feel-Good Cookbook," *Daily Mail*, March 18, 2013.

255 Around a year before they announced: Background interview.

255 Gwyneth planned her return to the States . . . to sponsor her renovation: Windsor Smith, *Homefront: Design for Modern Living*, introduction by Gwyneth Paltrow (Rizzoli, 2015), 6–7; background interview.

256 "the newest—and arguably hottest": Peter Kiefer, "How L.A.'s Mandeville Canyon Became Hot with Hollywood," *Hollywood Reporter*, February 24, 2017.

256 By the time Gwyneth and CEO Seb Bishop: Background interview.

256 In 2011, Goop's revenue was nearly $130,000: "Goop Inc. Limited Directors' Report and Unaudited Financial Statements for the Year Ended 31 December 2012," available via Companies House.

256 *Radar* wrote that: "GOOP in Crisis! Gwyneth Paltrow's Lifestyle Company Bleeding Cash as CEO Quits Unexpectedly," *Radar Online*, April 21, 2014.

256 But the figures didn't necessarily: Background interviews with two sources.

256 When she went into the office: Background interview.

257 To test the site's selling power: Anjali Mullany, "Gwyneth Paltrow Goes to Market," *Fast Company*, August 3, 2015; background interview.

257 *Gothamist* was one of many outlets: "Are You Under a Size 8? Gwyneth Paltrow Has the Perfect $100 White T-Shirt for You!" *Gothamist*, July 5, 2012.

257 Once the newsletter touting: Background interview.

257 Gwyneth's manager's niece: Background interview.

257 Despite her non-Goop work obligations: Background interview.

257 "As we monetized and as we got into e-commerce": Samantha Grindell and Amanda Krause, "Gwyneth Paltrow Said She Had to 'Google Acronyms Under the Table' at Goop Business Meetings," *Business Insider*, September 11, 2024.

258 Gwyneth topped *Star* magazine's: "Gwyneth Paltrow Voted Most Hated Hollywood Star," *BANG ShowBiz*, April 16, 2013.

258 "I remember being like: Really?": Brodesser-Akner, "How Goop's Haters Made Gwyneth Paltrow's Company Worth $250 Million."

258 "I'm forty, I have two kids": Irving Oala, "'It's Pretty F-ing Awesome!'" *Daily Mail*, April 26, 2013.

258 "Stuff blows up": Manohla Dargis, "Bang, Boom: Terrorism as a Game," *New York Times*, May 2, 2013.

258 *Iron Man 3* made the: Ben Child, "Iron Man 3 Makes Second-Biggest US Debut of All Time," *The Guardian*, May 6, 2013.

258 "I'm never going again": "Gwyneth Paltrow Calls Met Ball 'So Un-Fun,'" *Hollywood Reporter*, May 9, 2013.

259 *Vanity Fair* editor in chief Graydon Carter: Graydon Carter, "The Paltrow Affair," *Vanity Fair*, March 2014.

259 Gwyneth was tired from promoting: Background interview.

259 According to someone close to Gwyneth: Background interview; Emily Smith, "Behind Paltrow's Feud with Vanity Fair," *Page Six*, October 22, 2013.

261 Carter sat on it: Carter, "The Paltrow Affair."

261 A takedown it was not: The draft of the *Vanity Fair* article provided by a source to the author.

261 "spawned a group of imitators": Joshua David Stein, "Gwyneth Paltrow's Goop Inspires Famous Imitators," *New York Times*, November 13, 2013.

261 "about living a very one-of-a-kind,": Lisa Nevin-Phillips," Blake Lively Launches Lifestyle Company, *British Vogue*, September 25, 2013.

261 Lively's site, Preserve: Alessandra Codinha, "Blake Lively Is Shuttering Preserve—Why She's Taking the News Public and What's Next," *Vogue*, September 2015.

261 accusations of racism: Leeann Duggan, "Oh, No: Blake Lively Pens an Ode to the Pre–Civil War South," *Refinery29*, October 13, 2014.

261 Deschanel's HelloGiggles was the exception: Alyson Shontell, "Zooey Deschanel's Startup Hello Giggles Just Got Bought by Time Inc. for Around $30 Million," *Business Insider*, October 19, 2015.

262 "there's something slightly misgynistic": Daniel D'Addario, "Gwyneth Paltrow on Comparisons to Other Actresses: 'There's Something Slightly Misogynistic About It,'" *Time*, June 4, 2015.

262 By 2013, Gwyneth had relocated: "What's Goop?," Goop.com.

262 The Goop team in London: Background interviews with two sources.

262 Elise Loehnen, a veteran ghostwriter: Background interview.

262 it would hit roughly 700,000: Lauren Sherman, "Gwyneth Paltrow's Contextual Commerce Play," *Business of Fashion*, May 29, 2015.

263 Within her first month, Loehnen had drafted: Mullany, "Gwyneth Paltrow Goes to Market."

263 Gwyneth approved the piece with the headline: Background interview.

263 on March 25, 2014, Loehnen listened: Gwyneth Paltrow, "Gwyneth Paltrow on Her Conscious Uncoupling Journey," *British Vogue*, September 27, 2022.

263 "We have been working hard for well over a year": "Conscious Uncoupling," Goop.com, March 25, 2014.

263 Gwyneth said she saw her divorce: "Gwyneth Paltrow: Kisses to All My Exes," *Call Her Daddy* podcast, February 16, 2024.

263 Gwyneth had heard about conscious uncoupling: Background interview.

263 he seemed to have heard of it from marriage and family therapist: Jeanette Settembre, "Goop Scoop 'Conscious Uncoupling' More than Pretentious Intention," New York *Daily News*, March 27, 2014.

263 Gwyneth liked the idea: Paltrow, "Gwyneth Paltrow on Her Conscious Uncoupling Journey."

263 "It was very challenging for me": "Gwyneth Paltrow's Candid Admission About Her Divorce from Chris Martin," Oprah.com, November 11, 2015.

264 "There was nothing dramatic or anything": Nell Scovell, "February Cover Girl Gwyneth Paltrow," *Marie Claire*, January 1, 2015.

264 "When I turned forty": *InStyle*, February 2017 via Megan Lasher, "Gwyneth Paltrow Doesn't Care What You Think About Her Lifestyle," *Time*, December 29, 2016.

264 She cared about what *certain* people: Background interview.

264 "I chose myself": "Gwyneth Paltrow: Kisses to All My Exes," *Call Her Daddy* podcast.

264 While some of Gwyneth's old friends: Background interview.

264   Martin was a little more candid: "Chris Martin Felt 'Worthless' After Split from Gwyneth Paltrow," WENN, November 9, 2018.

264   He had approved: Background interview.

264   Martin uncoupled himself: Justine Picardie, untitled article, *Harper's Bazaar UK*, February 2015.

264   "Tonight on *Nightline*": Dan Abrams, *Nightline*, ABC, March 26, 2014.

265   "The Goop has hit the fan": Howard Gensler, "Paltrow, Martin Split: The Goop Has Hit the Fan," *Philadelphia Daily News*, March 26, 2014.

265   CNN quoted a Twitter user: Lisa Respers France, "Gwyneth Paltrow and Chris Martin Announce Split," CNN, March 25, 2014.

265   Anne Perkins wrote in *The Guardian*: Anne Perkins, "Gwyneth Paltrow and Chris Martin's 'Conscious Uncoupling'—A Template for Us All?," *The Guardian*, March 26, 2014.

265   In the explainer companion story Goop published: Habib Sadeghi and Sherry Sami, "Conscious Uncoupling," Goop.com.

265   In her *Guardian* story, Perkins called it: Perkins, "Gwyneth Paltrow and Chris Martin's 'Conscious Uncoupling.'"

265   Gwyneth's friends and former employees contended: Background interviews with several sources.

265   "Any child whose parents": Author interview with Richard Lovett, April 11, 2025.

265   Goop.com received so much traffic: Eliana Dockterman, "Gwyneth Paltrow Backtracks on 'Conscious Uncoupling,'" *Time*, December 31, 2014.

265   "What I didn't understand": Elisa Lipsky-Karasz, "Gwyneth Paltrow Wants to Convert You," *Wall Street Journal*, December 4, 2018.

265   "It's much harder for me": Lily Harrison, "Gwyneth Paltrow's Post-Split Plans: Actress Reveals She's Taking a Break from Acting to Focus on Her Kids," *E! News*, March 26, 2014.

266   "Gwyneth Paltrow: Moms Who Work": Donna Freydkin, "Gwyneth Paltrow: Moms Who Work 9-5 Have It Easier," *USA Today*, March 28, 2014.

266   The *Today* show ran a segment: Kristen Dahlgren, "Actress Gwyneth Paltrow Is Taking Some Heat," *Today*, NBC, March 29, 2014.

266   The *New York Post* published an open letter: Mackenzie Dawson, "A Working Mom's Open Letter to Gwyneth," *New York Post*, March 27, 2014.

266   "As the mommy wars rage on": "Ending the Mommy Wars," *Goop* newsletter, May 8, 2014.

266   Appearing at the Re/Code conference in May: Lisa Respers France, "Gwyneth Paltrow Makes People Mad—Again," CNN, May 29, 2014.

267   Goop's travel guides: *Goop* newsletter, November 10, 2019.

267   Gwyneth traveled there with *Glee* producer: Iona Kirby, "Did Gwyneth Paltrow and Glee Creator Brad Falchuk Enjoy a Secret Rendezvous at Exclusive Utah Hideaway?," *Daily Mail*, August 3, 2014.

267   Though there was speculation that: Alison Boshoff, "She Always Insisted There Was No One Else in Her Life," *Daily Mail*, April 10, 2015.

267   The two had a lot in common: Background interview.

267   Early in Gwyneth's new relationship: Background interview.

268   They pounced again when Gwyneth wrote about Masaru Emoto: Gwyneth Paltrow, "Goop Mag #16," *Goop* newsletter, May 29, 2014.

268   Shortly after this missive, Gwyneth pulled back: Background interview.

268   "My dream is that one day": Mara Siegler, "Gwyneth Paltrow Is Uncoupling from Goop," *New York Post*, July 28, 2016.

268   "It's Gwyneth Paltrow's latest far-out": Deni Kirkova, "Gwyneth 'The Guru' Paltrow's Latest Health Tips," *Daily Mail*, July 18, 2014.

268 .   Gwyneth's byline hadn't appeared: *Goop* newsletter, July 17, 2014.

268   "I just didn't know what the fuck": Andrew Ross Sorkin, "Gwyneth Paltrow on Goop and Embracing Ambition, *New York Times*, November 6, 2019.

268   Lisa Gersh came to Goop from Martha Stewart: Christine Haughney, "Gwyneth Paltrow Hires Former Head of Martha Stewart's Businesses," *New York Times*, October 7, 2014; Deepa Seetharaman, "Gwyneth Paltrow's Goop names new CEO, plans e-commerce push," Reuters, October 6, 2014.

269   Her ideal "contextual commerce" business: Background interview.

269   As part of a partnership with J.Crew: Elisa Lipsky-Karasz, "Gwyneth Paltrow Wants to Convert You," *Wall Street Journal*, December 4, 2018; "Fall Fashion on Jcrew.com," *Goop Newsletter*, September 13, 2012.

269   Brands and retailers struggled: Background interview.

269   A healthy 8 percent: Mullany, "Gwyneth Paltrow Goes to Market."

269   The newsletter had nearly one million: Mullany, "Gwyneth Paltrow Goes to Market."

270   "reporting to no one": Ibid.

270   Gersh's main project . . . business supported by content; and Gwyneth: Background interview.

270   Around the time Gwyneth moved back to Los Angeles . . . "to have a company": Background interview; author interview with Anarghya Vardhana, June 19, 2024.

271   Gwyneth could be incredibly clever and charming: Background interview.

271   "scary. I have a very weird thing": "Gwyneth Paltrow on Starting Goop, Fund-Raising," *Women's Wear Daily*, April 30, 2018.

271   "I haven't eaten at Gwyneth's house": Allison P. Davis, "Goop and Gwyneth Are Martha Stewart Approved," *New York*, October 15, 2013.

271   "She just needs to be quiet": NET-A-PORTER magazine interview, via E. Alex Jung, "Martha Stewart Thinks Gwyneth Paltrow Should Stop Trying to Be Martha Stewart," *New York*, September 14, 2014.

271   "If I'm really honest": Jessica Derschowitz, "Gwyneth Paltrow 'Psyched' over Martha Stewart's Goop Diss," *CBS News*, October 8, 2014.

272   Leading up to Thanksgiving in 2014: Khushbu Shah, "Martha Mocks Gwyneth's 'Conscious Uncoupling' with Six-Page Pie Spread," *New York Post*, October 13, 2014.

272   Gwyneth had been working with: Background interview.

272   Gwyneth responded to Stewart's troll: "Jailbird Cake," Goop.com.

272   "I avoided you for twenty years": *Howard Stern Show*, January 14, 2015.

272   Goop's staff tuned in sometimes: Background interview.

CHAPTER 23: STEAMING AND STRATEGIZING

273 "I have always felt": Interview with Dr. Jen Gunter, January 13, 2025.

273 Goop employed around two dozen: "What's Goop?," Goop.com.

273 Leadership meetings often took place . . . in her advice: Background interview.

273 To Gwyneth's credit . . . if something went wrong: Background interview.

274 During leadership team meetings: Background interview.

274 One executive got the sense that she would have liked: Background interview.

274 People who knew Gwyneth well: Background interview.

274 One person who worked closely: Background interview.

275 those who pronounced "Gwyneth" wrong: Background interview.

275 the team would get their own wraps: Background interview.

275 Thea Baumann, Goop's food editor: Background interview.

275 The new editors Goop hired: Background interview; *Goop* newsletters, October 9, 2017 and December 6, 2016.

275 Gwyneth declined sponsorships: Background interview.

275 Gwyneth was committed to covering products: Background interview.

275 The Tikkun spa in Santa Monica: "Tikkun Spa," Goop.com

275 annual detox newsletter: *Goop* newsletter, January 1, 2015.

275 she had gotten the treatment with Gersh: Background interview.

276 then *Fast Company* picked it up: Anjali Mullany, "Gwyneth Paltrow Goes to Market," *Fast Company*, August 3, 2015.

276 "steam-cleaning her private parts": Heidi Parker, "'It's the Golden Ticket': Now Gwyneth Paltrow Waxes Lyrical About Steam Cleaning Her Private Parts in New GOOP Post," *Daily Mail*, January 29, 2015.

276 The spa's owner Niki Schwarz: Niki Schwarz email to author, April 22, 2025.

276 steam to "cause a stir": Mehera Bonner, "12 Things You Never Knew About Gwyneth Paltrow," *Marie Claire*, March 22, 2016.

276 While a few members of the media: Dana Oliver, "I Tried a Vaginal Steam Treatment, and Here's What Happened," *Huffington Post*, April 24, 2016.

276 Ob-gyn Jen Gunter wrote about it: Jen Gunter, "Gwyneth Paltrow Says Steam Your Vagina, an OB/GYN Says Don't," DrJenGunter.com, January 27, 2015.

276 In 2019, the *Journal of Obstetrics and Gynaecology Canada* wrote up: Magali Robert, "Second-Degree Burn Sustained After Vaginal Steaming," *Journal of Obstetrics and Gynaecology Canada* 41, no. 6 (2019), 838–39.

276 Jen Gunter, who grew up in Winnipeg, Canada: Author interview with Dr. Jen Gunter, January 13, 2025.

276 Suzanne Somers was advocating women: Liz Szabo, "Suzanne Somers' Legacy Is Full of Health Misinformation," *KFF Health News*, October 23, 2023.

277 Anti-vaxxer Jenny McCarthy went on *Oprah*: Jenny McCarthy, "Excerpt from *Mother Warriors*," Oprah.com.

277 *The Huffington Post* interviewed her: Oliver, "I Tried a Vaginal Steam Treatment."

277　Gwyneth's advice to her staff: Mullany, "Gwyneth Paltrow Goes to Market."

277　Plus, neither Gwyneth nor Goop's board: Background interview.

277　When *Fast Company* asked her: Mullany, "Gwyneth Paltrow Goes to Market."

278　"This is what $29 gets you": Gwyneth Paltrow (@GwynethPaltrow), "This Is What $29 Gets You at the Grocery Store—What Families on SNAP (i.e. food stamps) Have to Live on for a Week," Twitter post, April 9, 2015.

278　"Yes poor people": Caitlin McBride, "Gwyneth Paltrow Under Fire for Undertaking €29-a-Week Food Stamp Challenge," *Independent*, April 13, 2015.

278　Gwyneth later wrote on Goop: Gwyneth Paltrow, "My $29 Food Stamp Challenge—and the Recipes (& Brouhaha) That Ensued," Goop.com.

278　That changed on the evening of Saturday, April 4: Allison Takeda, "Gwyneth Paltrow, Brad Falchuk Debut Romance at Robert Downey Jr.'s Star-Studded 50th Birthday Party," *Us Weekly*, April 6, 2015.

279　The next night, she and Falchuk: Alison Boshoff, "She Always Insisted There Was No One Else in Her Life: Is This Man the Real Reason Gwyneth's Marriage Hit the Rocks?," *Daily Mail*, April 10, 2015.

279　"I'm very, very lucky": "Goop's Gwyneth Paltrow on Being Brave in the Face of Public Scrutiny at #BlogHer15 Creator's Summit," *BlogHer*, August 5, 2015, 39:34.

279　Though Gwyneth really committed: Background interview.

279　she admitted to coworkers: Background interview.

279　Tony Florence, a high-profile tech investor: Elisa Lipsky-Karasz, "Gwyneth Paltrow Wants to Convert You," *Wall Street Journal*, December 4, 2018.

280　He ultimately decided to lead: Mitos Suson, "Daily Funding Roundup, August 6, 2015," VatorNews.com, August 7, 2015.

280　Investors wanted: Background interview.

280　With the cash infusion, Gwyneth made two: Daniel D'Addario, "Gwyneth Paltrow on Comparisons to Other Actresses: 'There's Something Slightly Misogynistic About It,'" *Time*, June 4, 2015; background interview.

280　After moving out of the barn: Background interviews with several sources.

280　The new office had a test kitchen: Background interviews with two sources.

280　The accompanying story advised: Madeline O'Malley, "Get the Look of Gwyneth Paltrow's Office," *Architectural Digest*, May 17, 2017.

280　The bulk of the office furniture was hauled out: Background interview.

280　The office was stocked with "healthy": Background interviews with several sources.

281　Having raised $118 million: Katie Roof, "RIP Juicero, the $400 Venture-Backed Juice Machine," *TechCrunch*, September 1, 2017.

281　"the greatest example of Silicon Valley stupidity": Claire Reilly, "Juicero Is Still the Greatest Example of Silicon Valley Stupidity," *CNET*, September 1, 2018.

281　Goop staff noticed that the machine was unnecessary: Background interview.

281　"The major issue is that you're legitimizing": Author interview with Andrea Love, February 13, 2025.

281 Grand Central had agreed: Background interviews with two sources.

282 Sales of *It's All Easy* were around 84,000: Book sales figures as per BookScan; background interview.

282 In October 2015, Sadeghi published a Goop article: Habib Sadeghi, "Could There Possibly Be a Link Between Underwire Bras and Breast Cancer??," Goop.com.

282 Included in a special Goop newsletter: *Goop* newsletter, October 15, 2015.

282 "There is no science to back up a bra": Jen Gunter, "Hey Gwyneth Paltrow, a GYN Says Stop Scaring Women About Bras and Breast Cancer," DrJen Gunter.com, October 20, 2015.

282 "It's the lowest of the low": Gunter, interview.

282 A handful of medical experts from across the country: Background interview.

282 which advocated traditional restrictive eating: Tatiana Boncompagni, "Why a Detox Should Address More Than Just Food," *Well+Good*, December 26, 2017.

282 One person who worked closely with Gwyneth: Background interview.

282 Timothy Caulfield noted that the wellness: Author interview with Timothy Caulfield, September 27, 2024.

283 Sadeghi, meanwhile, landed a segment: "Could the 'Clarity Cleanse' Gwyneth Paltrow Takes Help You?," *Today*, January 15, 2018.

283 His book included blurbs from Cruz: Marisa Meltzer, "How Habib Sadeghi Became a Guru for the Goop Set," *Town & Country*, April 23, 2018.

283 Though the staff at Grand Central rolled: Background interview.

283 remained about the same: As per BookScan.

283 Gwyneth was on a ski vacation: "The Latest: Gwyneth Paltrow Says Lawsuit Without Merit," Associated Press, January 29, 2019.

284 Around two weeks before the accident . . . a WeightWatchers cookbook: "Gwyneth Paltrow Tells US Court She's Been Stalked by Man 'For Years,'" BBC News, February 9, 2016.

284 Goop had a lockdown procedure: Background interview.

284 Soiu pled not guilty: Anthony McCartney, "Jury Acquits Ohio Man of Stalking Gwyneth Paltrow," Associated Press, February 17, 2016.

CHAPTER 24: RIDICULOUS BUT AWESOME

285 "There were times when people": Mehera Bonner, "12 Things You Never Knew About Gwyneth Paltrow," *Marie Claire*, March 22, 2016.

285 The guide suggested a $90,000 trip: Goop archived Gift Guide, Goop.com.

285 However over-the-top her taste: Background interviews with several sources.

285 She approved every product in the Goop store: Background interview.

286 Gwyneth used her friend group: Background interview.

286 when a story about beauty products: Taffy Brodesser-Akner, "How Goop's Haters Made Gwyneth Paltrow's Company Worth $250 Million," *New York Times Magazine*, July 25, 2018.

286 A mutual connection put Gwyneth: Author interview with Karen Behnke, April 24, 2025.

286   Gwyneth had a much more exacting aesthetic: Background interview.

286   When creating the line, Behnke met: Behnke, interview.

287   "If someone is calling something 'clean'": Author interview with Andrea Love, February 13, 2025; Courtney Blair Rubin and Bruce Boyd, "Natural Does Not Mean Safe—The Dirt on Clean Beauty Products," *JAMA Dermatology*, December 2019, 1344–1345.

287   "This idea of 'clean' is one of the most powerful": Author interview with Timothy Caulfield, September 27, 2024.

287   Goop wasn't sure how to launch: Background interviews with two sources.

287   the products, among them $110 face oil: Molly Creeden, "The 6 Anti-Aging Products That Gwyneth Paltrow Swears By: Introducing Goop Skin Care," *Vogue*, January 2016.

288   Why wasn't exactly clear . . . hear that feedback from others: Background interviews with several sources.

288   Plus, Gwyneth had a habit: Background interviews with two sources.

288   Crème had a roughly hundred-thousand-dollar budget . . . styled naturally wavy: Background interview.

289   *Vogue* ran a story: Creeden, "The 6 Anti-Aging Products."

289   Gwyneth went on *The Tonight Show Starring Jimmy Fallon*: Chloe Bryan, "Gwyneth Paltrow and Jimmy Fallon Eat French Fries Dipped in Skin Care Products," Mashable.com, March 6, 2015.

289   Behnke and two others recalled: Background interviews with two sources; Behnke, interview.

290   Blair Lawson said that the company: Diane Haithman, "Blair Lawson: Goop Inc. (Style)," *Los Angeles Business Journal*, September 10, 2018.

290   One person familiar with her thinking: Background interview.

290   "pop-up summit for badass girl bosses": Jessica Pels, "Welcome to the Power Trip, Marie Claire's Pop-Up Summit for Badass Girl Bosses," *Marie Claire*, March 19, 2016.

290   Among Gwyneth's other stipulations: Background interviews with two sources.

290   Her assistant Kevin Keating: Background interview.

291   She talked about conscious uncoupling: Mehera Bonner, "12 Things You Never Knew About Gwyneth Paltrow," *Marie Claire*, March 22, 2016.

291   Goop closed its $10 million Series B: Claire Atkinson, "Gwyneth Goes West with Goop After $10M Infusion," *New York Post*, August 16, 2016; background interview.

291   "enough runway to get us to profitability": Brooks Barnes, "Gwyneth Paltrow Has a Fashion Business Now. It's Called Goop," *New York Times*, September 10, 2016.

291   Going strong with Falchuk, she had put: Amy Plitt and Tanay Warerkar, "Gwyneth Paltrow and Chris Martin's Tribeca Penthouse Sells for $10.7M," CurbedNewYork.com, June 26, 2017.

292   Privately, Gwyneth seemed to have: Background interview.

292   Geraldine Martin-Coppola, who had served: Background interview.

292   She had thought she'd needed a "grown-up" . . . "you need to learn": David Yaffe-Bellany, "Gwyneth Paltrow on Goop and Embracing Ambition," *New York Times*, November 17, 2021.

292 Gwyneth had strengths as Goop's leader: Background interviews with several sources.

292 Goop ended up tripling: Chantal Fernandez, "Inside Goop's First Print Issue," *Business of Fashion*, September 20, 2017.

292 She worked on the company . . . success in one first: Background interview.

293 The one-off fashion collaborations Goop: Background interview.

293 had collaborated with the designer, Scott Sternberg: "Exclusives," Goop.com.

293 soothing gray-and-white kitchen: Katherine Clarke, "Gwyneth Paltrow Sells Los Angeles Home," *Wall Street Journal*, January 17, 2024.

294 "I would look at something": Brooks Barnes, "Gwyneth Paltrow and Goop Go Into the Fashion Business," *New York Times*, September 10, 2016.

294 two people with knowledge of the volume: Background interviews with two sources.

294 The *Fast Company* story: Elizabeth Segran, "Gwyneth Paltrow on Why Her Monthly Capsule Collections Sell Out in Hours," *Fast Company*, October 24, 2016.

295 a white leather "Classic G" tote bag: Chantal Fernandez, "Goop Label, Inspired by Gwyneth Paltrow's Closet, Is Finally Here," Fashionista.com, September 12, 2016.

295 But according to one former employee . . . promptly sold out: Background interview.

295 G. Label didn't need much advertising: Background interview.

295 She landed features touting G. Label: Barnes, "Gwyneth Paltrow and Goop Go Into the Fashion Business."

295 *Fast Company*: Segran, "Gwyneth Paltrow on Why Her Monthly Capsule Collections Sell out in Hours."

295 *Harper's Bazaar*: Samantha Bee, "The Real Gwyneth Paltrow," *Harper's Bazaar*, October 11, 2016.

295 Items like the gray suit . . . for other clothes: Background interview.

296 "I'm always the guinea": Ben Shapiro, "Gwyneth Paltrow Shares Beauty Advice, Even Though Her Daughter Is the Expert," *New York Times*, April 4, 2016.

296 Cryotherapy would later make headlines: Jason Sheeler, "Linda Evangelista Shares First Photos of Her Body Since Fat-Freezing Nightmare: 'I'm Done Hiding,'" *People*, February 16, 2022.

296 "The doctor stings you": Stephanie Chan, "Gwyneth Paltrow Is Covered in Mud for First Goop Magazine Cover," *Hollywood Reporter*, September 8, 2017.

296 "You're probably thinking this": Stephanie Petit, "Gwyneth Paltrow Admits She Sometimes Doesn't Know 'What the F— We Talk About' on Goop," *People*, June 6, 2017.

296 In October that same year, actor Gerard Butler: Hannah Ellis-Petersen, "Gerard Butler: I Injected Myself with Bee Venom and Ended Up in Hospital," *The Guardian*, October 20, 2017.

296 A woman in Spain who had been undergoing bee-sting: Hannah Strange, "Woman Dies from Bee Sting Therapy Promoted by Gwyneth Paltrow," *Telegraph*, March 22, 2018.

296 In 2018, Goop recommended $135 coffee enema kits: Travis M. Andrews, "Gwyneth Paltrow's Lifestyle 'Detox Guide' Promotes Coffee Enema. Experts Say It's Bogus," *Washington Post*, January 8, 2018.

297 "I always say I can't": *The Late Show with Stephen Colbert*, CBS, February 22, 2018.

297 The Mayo Clinic reported that coffee enemas had led: Ashley Welch, "Goop Is Promoting a $135 Coffee Enema; Here's What Science Says," CBS News, January 8, 2018.

297 The National Advertising Division, a unit of the Council of the Better Business Bureau: Cathaleen Chen, "Under Scrutiny, Goop Embraces Science," *Business of Fashion*, August 24, 2018.

297 Goop had claimed that the powder: "GP's Morning 'Smoothie,'" Goop.com.

297 Goop removed the offending claims: "Lifestyle Site 'Goop' Says It Will Voluntarily, Permanently Discontinue Claims for Moon Juice 'Brain Dust,' 'Action Dust' Following NAD Inquiry," Targeted News Service, August 9, 2016.

298 Flush with cash, Goop hired more people: Alexandra Steigrad, "Gwyneth Paltrow's Goop Staffs Up, Adds Editorial Director," *Women's Wear Daily*, September 26, 2016.

298 "I never felt less well": Background interview.

298 While Gwyneth presented a polished . . . but also cold: Background interviews with several sources.

298 Employees who worked up the nerve: Background interview.

298 If an employee replied to one: Background interview.

298 Two former executives explained: Background interviews with two sources.

298 Gwyneth's interests and allegiances: Background interviews with five sources.

299 Gwyneth was also frugal: Background interview.

299 Writers had to create editorial content: Background interview.

299 Editorial staff opened their laptops: Background interview.

299 One former employee took their laptop: Background interview.

299 Some of the excess workload . . . as one of Gwyneth's homes: Background interview.

299 When she found pee on a toilet seat: Background interview.

300 While she would talk about how hard she was working: Background interview.

300 Goop offered employees an annual two-week "Goopcation": Background interview.

300 Employees were allowed unlimited paid vacation: Background interview.

300 Gwyneth still sometimes sent Slack messages: Background interview.

CHAPTER 25: EGG-SISTENTIAL CRISIS

301 "Saying that you're ahead of the curve": Author interview with Timothy Caulfield, September 27, 2024.

301 Goop opened its first brick-and-mortar: "Gwyneth Paltrow and Christian Louboutin Fete Opening of Goop Lab, Capsule Collection," *Women's Wear Daily*, September 15, 2017.

301 Since the launch of Goop by Juice Beauty: Background interview.

302 The partnership was covered: "The Scene at the Goop x Cadillac Road to Table Dinner Party," *Wall Street Journal*, August 3, 2016; Sheila Cosgrove Baylis, "We Tried It: Goop's $1300-Per-Couple Farm-to-Table Dinner Party in the Hamptons," *People*, September 12, 2017; Christine Birkner, "Cadillac Is Driving Goop Readers to Dinner with Gwyneth Paltrow and Mario Batali," *AdWeek*, July 19, 2016.

302 Gwyneth cohosted one in New York City: Ellen Thomas, "Gwyneth Paltrow, Mario Batali Host Dinner with Cadillac," *Women's Wear Daily*, July 21, 2016.

302 She didn't know anyone . . . in the media coverage: Background interview.

302 Brands could also pay to hold events: Background interview.

302 The email list was up to one million subscribers . . . "right there": Background interview.

302 *Condé Nast Traveler* took the bait: Jane Sung, "Gwyneth Paltrow Has a Travel App . . . and It's Called G. Spotting," *Condé Nast Traveler*, November 21, 2016.

302 And G. Spotting hit: Background interview.

302 "I'm not interested in building": Daniel D'Addario, "Gwyneth Paltrow on Comparisons to Other Actresses: 'There's Something Slightly Misogynistic About It,'" *Time*, June 4, 2015.

303 Few employees got the chance: Background interview.

303 Goop had published an interview: "Earthing: How Walking Barefoot Could Cure Your Insomnia & More," Goop.com.

303 The Goop staff sat in a circle: Background interview.

303 the chicken kefta wraps: "The Annual Goop Detox," Goop.com.

303 Gwyneth preferred that her food: Background interview.

304 Gwyneth, who had been thin her whole life: Background interview.

304 Those who weren't senior enough: Background interview.

304 Gwyneth had close relationships: Background interview.

304 In the office, it was common knowledge: Background interviews with several sources.

304 When she and Brad Falchuk were living apart: Background interview.

304 employed over seventy people: Jean Godfrey-June, "Gwyneth Paltrow Doesn't Care What You Think About Vagina Steaming or Jade Eggs," *Women's Health*, March 8, 2017.

304 like a Restoration Hardware showroom: "Tour Goop's California-Cool Headquarters," *Architectural Digest*, May 3, 2017.

304 Gwyneth became aware of . . . start selling them: Godfrey-June, "Gwyneth Paltrow Doesn't Care."

304 Erewhon briefly closed its "tonic bar": Amaris Encinas, "Erewhon's Santa Monica location cited by public health officials after cockroaches found," *USA Today*, April 16, 2025.

305 Goop had originally only bought: Background interview.

305 On January 12, Goop sent the newsletter . . . on Goop.com: "Better Sex: Jade Eggs for Your Yoni," Goop.com.

305 "Before I insert an egg": "Better Sex: Jade Eggs for Your Yoni," Goop.com.

305 Within three hours, the eggs: Godfrey-June, "Gwyneth Paltrow Doesn't Care."

305 Jen Gunter had written an impassioned blog post: Jen Gunter, "Dear Gwyneth Paltrow, I'm a GYN and Your Vaginal Jade Eggs Are a Bad Idea," DrJenGunter.com, January 17, 2017.

305 Later, she coauthored a study: Jennifer Gunter and Sarah Parcak, "Vaginal Jade Eggs: Ancient Chinese Practice or Modern Marketing Myth?," *Female Pelvic Medicine & Reconstructive Surgery* 1, no.1/2 2019: 1–2.

305 Other medical experts weighed in: Kristine Thomason, "Sorry, Gwyneth: Experts Advise Against Jade Egg to Strengthen Pelvic Muscles," *CNN Health*, January 27, 2017.

305 "There are no studies or evidence": Sara G. Miller, "Gwyneth Paltrow's Jade Eggs Are a Bunch of Baloney," Fox News, January 20, 2017.

306 "a reiki hairdresser" and "a crystal shaman": Background interview.

306 In June, the technology blog *Gizmodo* . . . eventually removed the product entirely: Rae Paoletta, "NASA Calls Bullshit on Goop's $120 'Bio-Frequency Healing' Sticker Packs [Updated]" *Gizmodo*, blog, June 22, 2017; "Wearable Stickers That Promote Healing (Really!)," Goop.com.

306 She felt Jen Gunter was notably: Background interview.

307 On July 13, six months: Gwyneth Paltrow (@GwynethPaltrow), Twitter post, July 13, 2017.

307 a statement from Goop . . . "women's and children's physician": "Uncensored: A Word from Our Doctors," Goop.com.

307 Gundry, who has been alleged: Author interview with Steven Gundry, April 26, 2025.

307 unsupported medical claims: James Hamblin, "The Next Gluten," *The Atlantic*, April 24, 2017.

307 In a subsequent letter: Layla Martin, "12 (More) Reasons to Start a Jade Egg Practice," Goop.com

307 Gunter was in England when Goop . . . asking for a quote: Author interview with Jen Gunter, January 13, 2025.

308 Bonnie Patten had become the head: Author interview with Bonnie Patten, October 24, 2024.

309 Goop made some slight adjustments: "TINA.org Takes Gwyneth Paltrow's Goop-y Health Claims to Regulators," TINA.org, August 22, 2017.

309 The last weekend of June 2017 . . . part of a larger story: Jodi Kantor and Megan Twohey, *She Said: Breaking the Sexual Harassment Story That Helped Ignite a Movement* (Penguin Press, 2019), 62, iBook.

310 About two weeks later, she frantically texted: Kantor and Twohey, *She Said*, 62–63.

310 Twohey and Kantor reminded *Today* show viewers: Laura Bradley, "How Gwyneth Paltrow Helped Break the Harvey Weinstein Story," *Vanity Fair*, September 9, 2019.

311 a cover story in *Women's Health* featuring Gwyneth: Godfrey-June, "Gwyneth Paltrow Doesn't Care What You Think About Vagina Steaming or Jade Eggs."

311 *Women's Health* had hired Godfrey-June: Background interview.

311 But the piece was essentially: Godfrey-June, "Gwyneth Paltrow Doesn't Care."

311 Gwyneth seemed to believe that her body: Background interview.

311 Marion Nestle, the nutrition professor: Email to author from Marion Nestle, October 16, 2024.

312 "People are going to buy into this": Author interview with Andrea Love, February 13, 2025.

312 Goop from publishing a story in 2017 headlined: "You Probably Have a Parasite—Here's What to Do About It," Goop.com.

312 "GOOP specifically markets the non-existent": "GOOP's Physician Branded Supplements Warrant a Closer Look," DrJenGunter.com, August 25, 2017.

312 While Goop's staff included skeptics: Background interviews with several sources.

312 "We would talk about something": "Gwyneth Paltrow on the Power of Turning 50," *CBS Sunday Morning*, CBS, September 25, 2022.

312 This deeply frustrated Caulfield: Caulfield, interview.

312 Goop claimed it sold: Taffy Brodesser-Akner, "How Goop's Haters Made Gwyneth Paltrow's Company Worth $250 Million," *New York Times Magazine*, July 25, 2018.

312 "If we are selling it": Booth Moore, "At Work with Gwyneth Paltrow: 6 Lessons in Business and Why She Gave Up Acting for Goop," *Hollywood Reporter*, May 16, 2017.

313 Her confidence was not enough to dissuade: Mike Snider, "Gwyneth Paltrow's Goop Settles Unsubstantiated Vaginal Egg Health Claims for $145,000," *USA Today*, September 5, 2018.

313 Gwyneth chose to pay $145,000: Amy B. Wang, "Gwyneth Paltrow's Goop Touted the 'Benefits' of Putting a Jade Egg in Your Vagina. Now It Must Pay," *Washington Post*, September 5, 2018.

313 She also hired people to remove: Background interview.

313 Former Goop employees were dismissive: Background interviews.

313 "impact on how consumers behave": Patten, interview.

CHAPTER 26: TOO GOOP TO PRINT

314 "I thought *I* was": Jenni Avins, "Inside the Goop Summit: A Disorienting Day of Jade Eggs and Sound Baths," *Quartz*, June 13, 2017.

314 To open the first-ever In Goop Health: Social media video of In Goop Health.

314 She told her five hundred mostly white: Maureen Callahan, "Exasperated Attendees Give Up on Gwyneth's Goop Summit," *New York Post*, June 12, 2017; Amy Kaufman, "Finding My Inner Goop: An Inside Look at Gwyneth Paltrow's First Wellness Summit," *Los Angeles Times*, June 25, 2017.

314 She introduced Dr. Habib Sadeghi: Andrea Mandell, "Gwyneth Paltrow's First Goop Health Summit Was Half Great and Half Cray," *USA Today*, June 12, 2017; and Maureen Callahan, "Gwyn Goes from Goop to Nuts: Inside Wacky Debut Health Summit," *New York Post*, June 13, 2017.

314   seemed to develop serious doubts . . . phase a person out: Background interview.

315   Over the course of the day, Gwyneth: Josh Duboff, "Gwyneth Paltrow Is Hosting Goop's First-Ever Summit," *Vanity Fair*, April 20, 2017.

315   start the day with a saline IV: Jenni Avins, "Inside the Goop Summit: A Disorienting Day of Jade Eggs and Sound Baths," *Quartz*, June 13, 2017.

315   Gwyneth loved IVs: Background interviews with two sources.

315   Gwyneth told her staff: Background interview.

315   though she was open about disliking Botox: Emily Kirkpatrick, "Gwyneth Paltrow Won't Do Botox Again, but She Will Endorse this Anti-Wrinkle Injectable," *Vanity Fair*, September 17, 2020.

315   sponsors, including Tumi: Christine Birkner, "Why Brands Are Clamoring to Work with Gwyneth Paltrow's Goop," *AdWeek*, April 20, 2017.

315   The summit's signature cocktail: Diana Bruk, "The Menu at the First Ever Goop Wellness Summit Is Very . . . Goop-y," *New York Observer*, June 9, 2017.

315   Proceeds from the event benefited Good+ Foundation: "Gwyneth Paltrow Pokes Fun at Herself in New Contest Video," WENN, May 20, 2017.

315   Goop staff were expected: Background interview.

315   An editor who normally curated gift guides: Background interview.

316   Other editorial staff manned booths: Background interview.

316   The roughly five hundred: Callahan, "Gwyn Goes from Goop to N."

316   "I had a leech facial as well": Avins, "Intravenous Hydration Drips, Celebrity Healers, and Crystal Therapy."

316   Gwyneth was trying desperately to figure out: Background interview.

316   Gwyneth was constantly trying new things: Background interview.

316   Goop was a start-up, after all: Background interview.

316   Gwyneth also remained committed: Background interview.

316   The travel team relied on contacts in various locations: Background interview.

317   Wintour and Gwyneth were friendly . . . Wintour's approval: Background interview.

317   Several months before the magazine: Background interviews with two people who attended the meeting.

318   "the presumptive heiress": Alexandra Jacobs, "Meet the Goopies," *New York Times*, June 14, 2017.

319   Wintour and Gwyneth got along: Background interview.

319   Bob Sauerberg, Condé's CEO: Author interview with Bob Sauerberg, September 20, 2023.

319   The impression on the Condé side . . . as all other Condé Nast titles: Background interview.

319   "don't want to be embarrassed": Background interview.

319   Condé staff would try to chase . . . its own merchandise: Background interviews with two people who worked on the magazine.

320   The first issue of *Goop* in print: "In the Clear," *Goop*, Fall 2017.

320   Gwyneth was a true believer: Background interviews with several sources.

320 Wintour and her senior staff . . . arms of Brad Falchuk: Background interviews with two people who worked on the magazine.

321 Inside the magazine, she wore: "The Give & Take," *Goop* newsletter, April 2018.

321 "I think we had a natural coming apart": Sauerberg, interview.

321 A Goop source maintained: Background interview.

321 "There was no transparency": "Goop Magazine out from Under Condé Nast and Digging for Data," *Women's Wear Daily*, August 17, 2018.

CHAPTER 27: THE GWYNETH PROBLEM

322 "[I]t was often a struggle": Background interview.

322 If Gwyneth was plotting the acquisition of her company: Background interview.

322 Gomez's line, led by CEO Scott Friedman: Priya Rao, "Beauty's Most Sought-After M&A Targets in 2024," *Business of Fashion*, January 6, 2024.

322 added three to six months: Background interview.

323 Gwyneth wanted Goop Beauty: Background interview.

323 Yet the team struggled: Background interview.

323 She chose a designer with experience: Background interview.

323 Gwyneth continued educating herself: Background interview.

323 Former employees said the customer: Background interviews with several sources.

323 couldn't understand why some of her staff: Background interview.

323 When an employee drove: Background interview.

323 Goop Beauty launched with: "Happy Birthday Gwyneth: A Timeline," Goop.com, September 27, 2022.

323 Someone who worked at Goop with knowledge: Background interview.

323 Goop would sell hundreds: Background interview.

323 Later launches included an orange-flavored: Faran Krentcil, "Gwyneth Paltrow Wants You to Take Shots," *Elle*, November 20, 2017.

323 Gwyneth was Goop's most effective face: Background interview.

324 At the office, Gwyneth was in a product prototype: Background interview.

CHAPTER 28: VANILLA FISH AND CELERY JUICE

325 "You wouldn't bring your car": Author interview with Dr. Andrea Love, February 13, 2025.

325 By early 2020, Goop employed: Marisa Meltzer, "Gwyneth Paltrow Has the Last Laugh," *Town & Country*, April 8, 2020.

325 The company was doing multimillion-dollar deals: Background interview.

325 expanded to New York: Kristen Tauer, "The In Goop Health Summit Comes to New York," *Women's Wear Daily*, January 29, 2018.

325 believing Goop should have a campus: Background interview.

325   decided to move the company: Mayer Rus, "Look Inside Goop's Airy Santa Monica Office," *Architectural Digest*, August 3, 2020.

325   it was also absurdly large: Background interview.

325   "I (basically) walked away": Gwyneth Paltrow, LinkedIn post, September 7, 2016.

326   Gwyneth commissioned a set: Background interviews with two sources.

326   "honoring commitments": The Collaborative Way website.

326   Gwyneth hired Andres Sosa: Chantal Fernandez, "Goop Hires First Chief Marketing Officer from YNAP as It Plots European Expansion," *Business of Fashion*, June 8, 2018.

326   Gwyneth quickly became dissatisfied: Background interview.

326   There was so much turnover: Background interview.

326   When she wanted an employee out . . . "a grain of salt": Background interview.

326   When Gwyneth wanted to launch: Background interview.

326   Goop Glow drink: "What Drinking Collagen Might Do for Your Skin," Goop.com.

327   The person overseeing the drink powder: Background interviews with two sources.

327   The company announced $50 million: Todd Spangler, "Gwyneth Paltrow's Goop Banks $50 Million for European Expansion," *Variety*, March 29, 2018.

327   Kim Kardashian's KKW beauty: Dave Sebastian, "Kim Kardashian West's Beauty Brand Valued at $1 Billion in Deal with Coty," *Wall Street Journal*, June 29, 2020.

327   "Ultimately, we decided we couldn't change that cycle": "Conversations Worth Having: Noora Raj Brown," Mixing Board, March 28, 2023.

327   With journalist Taffy Brodesser-Akner: Taffy Brodesser-Akner, "How Goop's Haters Made Gwyneth Paltrow's Company Worth $250 Million," *New York Times Magazine*, July 25, 2018.

328   Talking about her reporting later: Vanessa Grigoriadis, "Gwyneth Paltrow's Ski Trial | Part 3," *Infamous*, December 9, 2023.

328   The story wasn't the usual puff piece: Brodesser-Akner, "How Goop's Haters Made Gwyneth Paltrow's Company."

329   Ultimately, Raj Brown talked about the story: "Noora Raj Brown on the Hard Conversations Worth Having," Mixing Board.

329   While the article didn't put to bed: Brodesser-Akner, "How Goop's Haters Made Gwyneth Paltrow's Company."

329   Putting that infrastructure in place: "Noora Raj Brown on the Hard Conversations Worth Having," Mixing Board.

329   However, it's not clear that Goop: Background interviews with three former Goop employees.

329   "understand the function of a fact-checker": Background interview.

329   Another editor remembered: Background interview.

329   "We are going to educate our consumers": Cathaleen Chen, "Under Scrutiny, Goop Embraces Science," *Business of Fashion*, August 24, 2018.

330   But one of Beck's primary concerns: Background interview.

330   Beck also hired Gerda Endemann: Background interview.

330   She repeated one specific anecdote: Devon Ivie, "Why is Gwyneth Paltrow's Go-To Quote About Bitching Out a Yoga Studio Employee?," *Vulture*, January 5, 2019.

330   "Forgive me if this comes out wrong": Elisa Lipsky-Karasz, "Gwyneth Paltrow Wants to Convert You," *Wall Street Journal*, December 4, 2018.

330   benefits of seed oils: Gerda Endemann, "Are Seed Oils Like Canola Bad for You? We Review the Research," Goop.com, January 10, 2023.

330   she was fine with Endemann: Background interview.

330   the benefits of red-light therapy: Gerda Endemann, "How Do Red Light Devices Work?," Goop.com.

331   The nonprofit *Consumer Reports* reported: Perry Santanachote, "Do At-Home LED Face Masks Work?," *Consumer Reports*, April 1, 2024.

331   Stories that didn't were published under a different tag: "The Science and Mystery of Energy Healing," Goop.com, November 1, 2022.

331   Goop staff went to Endemann . . . disagreed with her colleagues about Anthony William: Background interview.

331   "We used him when we needed": Background interview.

331   Goop published an excerpt: "The Medical Medium—and What's Potentially at the Root of Medical Mysteries," Goop.com, November 5, 2015.

332   "We trust that you'll quickly understand": "The Medical Medium," Goop .com.

332   Endemann was uncomfortable specifically: Background interview.

332   One about "healing foods": Anthony William, "Spirit Says: Healing Foods," Goop.com.

332   William doubled down on these statements: "The Medical Medium on the Virtues of Celery Juice," Goop.com.

332   This coverage was credited in outlets: Dawn MacKeen, "Is Celery Juice a Sham?," *New York Times*, October 16, 2019; Amanda Mull, "Actually, You Can Just Drink Some Water," *The Atlantic*, November 4, 2018.

332   The story brought in so much traffic: Background interview.

332   "at a loss": Author interview with Andrea Love, February 13, 2025.

332   Filed under ANCIENT MODALITIES: "Notes from a Shaman: Moving Negative Energy and Why the World Is in Upheaval," Goop.com.

332   "who married Norwegian princess": Eve Crosbie, "Norway's Princess Märtha Louise marries a US man who says he's a 6th-generation shaman in a one-of-a-kind royal wedding," *Business Insider*, September 1, 2024.

332   "light in shining armor": Emily Jane Fox, "The Princess and the Shaman," *Vanity Fair*, November 12, 2020.

333   Yet in its January 2018 In Goop Health summit: Joseph Frankel, "HIV Doesn't Cause AIDS According to Gwyneth Paltrow Goop 'Trusted Expert' Doctor Kelly Brogan," *Newsweek*, December 29, 2017; Joanna Rothkopf, "Anti-Medication Goop Summit Expert Claims AIDS Treatment Kills and GMOs Cause Depression," *Jezebel*, December 2, 2017; Sara Dorn and Gwynne Hogan, "Gwyneth Peddles 'Dangerous Ideas' at NYC Goop Summit," *New York Post*, January 27, 2018.

333   "If you are willing to sit down with": Author interview with Jen Gunter, January 13, 2025.

333 The same summit featured Taz Bhatia: Dr. Taz, "Solutions for Living Healthy Naturally: Back to School Survival Series, Part Two: The Vaccine Debate Continues," Dr. Taz MD Integrative Medicine, website, September 3, 2013.

333 In 2019, speaking at *Vanity Fair*'s New Establishment Summit: Kenzie Bryant, "'It's Extremely Empowering to Just Be Yourself': Gwyneth Paltrow on Aging, Wellness, and Goop," *Vanity Fair*, October 22, 2019.

333 One former executive suspected: Background interview.

334 *Inverse* interviewed Kate Gallagher Leong: Rae Paoletta, "How Goop's Favorite 'Medical Medium' Uses Spirituality to 'Scam' the Sick," *Inverse*, January 10, 2018.

334 *Vanity Fair* focused on one of William's: Dan Adler, "The Medical Medium and the True Believer," *Vanity Fair*, April 26, 2023.

334 "I'm so happy to suffer those slings and arrows": Elisa Lipsky-Karasz, "Gwyneth Paltrow Wants to Convert You," *Wall Street Journal*, December 4, 2018.

334 Gwyneth was never as close to William: Background interview.

CHAPTER 29: FIRST COMES LOVE, THEN COMES BRANDING

335 "I wouldn't buy that candle": Andy Cohen, "Would Martha Stewart Buy Goop's 'My Vagina' Candle?," *Watch What Happens*, Bravo, January 16, 2020.

335 Friday, November 2, 2018: "The Wedding Party: GP x Brad Tie the Knot," Goop.com; background interview.

335 Many of the vendors used: Background interviews with two sources.

335 At least one vendor: Background interview.

336 First came a bachelorette party: Erika Harwood, "Gwyneth Paltrow Is Heading to Mexico with Cameron Diaz for Her Bachelorette Party," *Vanity Fair*, April 12, 2018.

336 Then a blowout engagement party: "Gwyneth Paltrow Offers Peek Inside 'Intimate,' Star-Studded Engagement Party with Sweet Photo," *People*, April 16, 2018; Ian Mohr, "Is Black-Tie Engagement Party Really a Surprise Wedding for Gwyneth and Brad?," *New York Post*, April 13, 2018; background interview.

336 One person who attended: Background interview.

336 At the rehearsal dinner: "The Wedding Party: GP x Brad Tie the Knot."

336 Valentino dress with cap sleeves—also a gift: Background interview.

336 buried her father's ashes: Ale Russian, "Gwyneth Paltrow Married Brad Falchuk Steps Away from Where Her Late Dad's Ashes Are Buried," *People*, October 4, 2018.

336 Gwyneth slipped into a couture . . . a brand called Fog Linen: "The Wedding Party: GP x Brad Tie the Knot."

336 Another vendor saw: Background interview with two sources.

336 She took the same approach: Mayer Rus, "Step Inside Gwyneth Paltrow's Tranquil Montecito Home," *Architectural Digest*, February 2, 2022.

336 like Frederique Constant watches: Roberta Naas, "Celebrity Interview: "Gwyneth Paltrow Talks about Time, Frederique Constant, Smartwatches, Charity and Goop," *Haute Time*, November 3, 2016.

336 While she made endorsements: Background interviews with two sources.

337 Sometimes she had Goop staff: Background interview.

337 Falchuk, one observer said: Background interview.

337 The two waited to move in ... "change a thing," Gwyneth said: Christa D'Souza, "The Goop Founder on the Great Power That Comes with Growing Older," *Times*, June 9, 2019.

337 But they did it mostly: Background interview.

337 She posted pictures on Instagram: @gwynethpaltrow, Instagram, November 26, 2017.

337 "She's a fantastic woman": D'Souza, " Goop Founder on the Great Power."

337 Speaking at the 2023 In Goop Health: Ingrid Schmidt, "At Goop Wellness Summit, Gwyneth Paltrow Talks Family, Power and Ex Chris Martin: 'He's Kind of Like My Brother Now,'" *Hollywood Reporter*, November 13, 2023.

338 Absent from the wedding were some: Background interview.

338 His partner Nick Brown's firm: Robert Tuchman, "How Success Happened for Nick Brown, Co-Founder of Imaginary Ventures," *Entrepreneur*, January 9, 2022.

338 When Blasberg befriended Gwyneth: Background interview.

338 "When I first met him": Alexis Swerdloff, "'Hiiii Derek,'" *The Cut*, August 10, 2016.

338 At first, Gwyneth told friends Griffin was: Background interview.

338 While staying at her Montecito home: Background interviews with two sources.

338 Blasberg suffered what was: Russ Weakland, "Gwyneth Paltrow Is 'Horrified' at Derek Blasberg Fleeing Her Hamptons Home After 'Catastrophic' Diarrhea," *Daily Mail*, July 15, 2024.

338 a detail that was later called into question: Russ Weakland, "Mystery Celebrity Who Fled Gwyneth Paltrow's Hamptons Home After Suffering 'Catastrophic' Diarrhea Is Revealed," *Daily Mail*, July 3, 2024.

338 Brown, his partner, called: Background interview.

338 She did this in part: Background interview.

338 In a *Daily Mail* piece: Weakland, "Gwyneth Paltrow is 'Horrified' at Derek Blasberg Fleeing Her Hamptons Home After 'Catastrophic' Diarrhea."

338 In a 2025 *Vanity Fair* interview: Michelle Ruiz, "Gwyneth Paltrow on Motherhood, MAHA, Meghan Markle, Making Out with Timothée Chalamet—and Much More," *Vanity Fair*, April 2015.

338 Goop's first sex issue: Hailey Eber, "The Inside Scoop on Mating, Dating and Relating: Does Gwyneth Even Like Sex?," *New York Post*, May 12, 2016.

339 Gwyneth and Douglas Little: Background interview.

339 reviewers and buyers wondered: Hadley Freeman, "Why Is Gwyneth Paltrow Selling a Candle That Smells like Her Vagina?," *The Guardian*, January 13, 2020.

339 Martha Stewart was called upon to respond: Andy Cohen, "Would Martha Stewart Buy Goop's 'My Vagina' Candle?," *Watch What Happens*, Bravo, January 16, 2020.

339 Naturally, Gwyneth followed up: Kathleen Hou, "Gwyneth Paltrow Is at It Again," *The Cut*, June 17, 2020.

339 Producers thought at first: Background interview.

339 Falchuk and Murphy lured Gwyneth: Lipsky-Karasz, "Gwyneth Paltrow Wants to Convert You."

339 Despite its full name being *The Goop Lab with Gwyneth Paltrow*: Background interview.

340 In the first episode, staff including Loehnen: "The Healing Trip," *The Goop Lab with Gwyneth Paltrow*, January 24, 2020, Netflix.

340 In its review of *The Goop Lab*, *Variety* wrote: Daniel D'Addario, "Gwyneth Paltrow's 'The Goop Lab,'" *Variety*, January 17, 2020.

340 *The Guardian* called it: Arwa Mahdawi, "Goop Has a Netflix Deal: This Is a Dangerous Win for Pseudoscience," *The Guardian*, February 8, 2019.

340 In *The New York Times* opinion section: Elisa Albert and Jennifer Block, "Who's Afraid of Gwyneth Paltrow and Goop?," *New York Times*, February 3, 2020.

340 Then–Food and Drug Administration Commissioner: Meg Tirrell, "Health Misinformation Is Lowering U.S. Life Expectancy, FDA Commissioner Robert Califf Says," CNBC, April 11, 2013.

340 The sense of community that Goop fosters: Author interview with Timothy Caulfield, September 27, 2024.

341 Truth in Advertising checked in on Goop in 2020: Beth Mole, "Goop Accused of More Deceptive Health Claims, Violating Court Order," *Ars Technica*, February 3, 2020.

341 Mashable writer Brenda Stolyar: Brenda Stolyar, "Gwyneth Paltrow Talks Goop Criticism and Customer Data Privacy," Mashable, February 5, 2020.

341 This despite an advice column: "Should I Take Vitamin C for Immunity?," Goop.com.

342 California authorities didn't: Author interview with Bonnie Patten, October 24, 2024.

342 In 2024, when TINA.org investigated: "The Menopause Deception Epidemic," TINA.org, October 7, 2024.

342 Goop was making 70 percent: Riley Griffin, "Gwyneth Paltrow's Goop Cashing in Despite 'Pseudoscience' Claims," *Business of Fashion*, March 18, 2019.

342 Gwyneth decided the editorial work: Background interview.

342 By 2020, Goop was valued: Madeline Berg, "Gwyneth Paltrow's Goop Is Cutting 18% of Staff as It Scrambles to Change Strategy," *Business Insider*, September 6, 2024.

342 After some budget cuts, the company: Background interviews with two sources.

342 "We've had profitable months": Emma Hinchcliffe, "Gwyneth Paltrow is taking Goop back to basics—and says her best source of business advice is her 'Fight Club' group chat of female CEOs," *Fortune*, March 17, 2025.

343 She was one of at least 140 employees: Berg, "Gwyneth Paltrow's Goop Is Cutting 18% of Staff."

343 Some employees cycled in and out: Background interview.

343 Djenaba Parker was looking . . . "very popular": Author interview with Djenaba Parker, March 13, 2025.

344 Two days after her fiftieth birthday: Lauren Oyler, "I Really Didn't Want to Go," *Harper's*, May 2023; Charlie Gowans-Eglinton, "I Went on Gwyneth Paltrow's Goop Cruise: This Is What I Saw," *Sunday Times*, October 14, 2022.

344   This was a challenging period: Ingrid Schmidt, "Gwyneth Paltrow Talks Aging, Acting and Recession Fears at Goop Event," *Hollywood Reporter*, October 17, 2022.

344   To mark the birthday, she'd shared photos: "Gwyneth Paltrow on Selling Goop Products, Her Kids Driving & Being Married to a TV Writer," *Jimmy Kimmel Live!*, ABC, October 31, 2022.

344   "You know, to reach" . . . "into this other thing": Tracy Smith, "Gwyneth Paltrow on Turning 50 and Goop," *CBS News*, September 25, 2022.

CHAPTER 30: SKI YOU IN COURT

345   "It's hard to overcome": Author interview with Terry Sanderson, February 25, 2025.

345   Terry Sanderson sued Gwyneth: "The Latest: Gwyneth Paltrow Says Lawsuit Without Merit," Associated Press, January 29, 2019.

345   She filed a countersuit: Chloe Melas, "Gwyneth Paltrow Files Countersuit in Skiing Case," CNN, February 20, 2019.

346   After Sanderson's initial lawsuit: "Gwyneth Paltrow's Lawyer Calls Utah Ski Collision Story 'BS,'" Associated Press, March 21, 2023.

346   Sanderson said in a 2025 interview: Sanderson, interview.

346   "I have to say, the idea": "The Gwyneth Paltrow Episode," *The World's First Podcast with Erin & Sara Foster*, April 24, 2025.

346   Sanderson's insurance company: Sanderson, interview.

346   "This week marked the return": Alex Abad-Santos, "All the Beauty and the Brain Damage of Gwyneth Paltrow's Surreal Ski Trial," Vox, March 30, 2023.

346   she had gone viral for saying on a podcast: Emily Leibert, "Gwyneth Paltrow Can't Even Record a Podcast Without a Vitamin Drip: 'I Love an IV!'" *Jezebel*, blog, March 15, 2023; Jane Herz, "Here's the Dangerous Truth About Gwyneth Paltrow's Rectal Ozone Therapy," *New York Post*, March 26, 2023.

346   But her questionable wellness persona . . . at fault in this kind of mishap: "LIVE: Gwyneth Paltrow Ski Crash Case: Day 1 Sanderson v. Paltrow," *Court TV*, March 21, 2023.

347   *Town & Country* published a list: Sophie Dweck, "Everything Gwyneth Paltrow Wore to Her Ski Trial," *Town & Country*, March 31, 2023.

347   *GQ* declared she "dressed brilliantly": Eileen Carter, "Gwyneth Paltrow Dressed Brilliantly for the Court of Public Opinion," *GQ*, March 30, 2023.

347   "Gwyneth Paltrow's courtroom": Pocharapon Neammanee, "Gwyneth Paltrow's Courtroom Outfits Were the Definition of Stealth Wealth," *BuzzFeed News*, March 30, 2023.

347   Sanderson said he wasn't paying attention: Sanderson, interview.

348   "Well, I lost half a day of skiing": "Gwyneth Paltrow's Bizarre Quote from Ski Accident Trial Goes Viral," News.com.au, March 27, 2023.

348   In cross-examination: "Gwyneth Paltrow's Attorney Grills Terry Sanderson Under Direct Examination as Last Defense Witness," *Law & Crime Network*, May 29, 2023.

349 Sanderson later told a reporter outside . . . "not worth it": "Terry Sanderson Reveals Gwyneth Paltrow's Message After Ski Crash Verdict," *ExtraTV*, March 30, 2023.

349 did not recoup them: Sam Metz, "Gwyneth Paltrow Won't Recoup Attorney Fees in Ski Crash Suit," Associated Press, May 1, 2023.

349 the *New York Post* estimated: Priscilla DeGregory, Natalie O'Neill, and Elizabeth Rosner, "Gwyneth Paltrow's Legal Fees Could Reach $1M, Says Lawyer," *New York Post*, March 31, 2023.

349 While Sanderson believed Utah law . . . "that's the lesson I learned": Sanderson, interview.

350 "I was just getting dressed": Marisa Meltzer, "Gwyneth Paltrow Looks Back at 15 Years of Goop and More," *New York Times*, September 30, 2023.

350 Gwyneth attended Kardashian's launch party: Background interview.

351 She finished the year with a controversial appearance: Background interview.

351 Many in Hollywood, having been collectively outraged: Tatiana Siegel, "Will Smith Got Paid $1 Million, Gwyneth Paltrow Even More to Heat Up Saudi-Hollywood Relations at Red Sea Fest," *Variety*, December 13, 2023.

351 Though the good.clean.goop launch: Rachel Strugatz, "As Goop as It Gets," *Puck*, June 19, 2024; Nathaniel Meyersohn, "Target Sales Fall for the First Time in 6 Years After Pride Month Backlash," CBS News, August 16, 2023.

351 "mouth taping": Kelly Martin, "5 Things That Improved Our Oura Sleep Scores," Goop.com, January 11, 2024.

351 In 2024, Gwyneth said she put Raw Farm cream: Cato Hernández, "Raw Dairy Farm Shut Down," LAist network, December 4, 2024.

351 Andrea Love said, "The only thing": Author interview with Andrea Love, February 13, 2025.

352 Goop announced that it would cut 18 percent: Kathryn Hopkins, "Goop Refocuses Business on Fashion, Beauty and Food, Resulting in Layoffs," *Women's Wear Daily*, September 5, 2024.

352 Goop Kitchen, an L.A.-based ghost kitchen: Background interview.

352 A Goop board member privately described: Background interview.

352 The changes were driven in part by: Background interview.

352 Goop underwent a second round of layoffs: Rachel Strugatz, "Gwyneth's Beauty Makeover," *Puck*, October 23, 2024.

352 Hunter believed Goop's editorial content: Background interview.

353 After giving an interview to *Puck*: Rachel Strugatz, "Gwyneth's Beauty Makeover," *Puck*, October 23, 2024.

353 Axios reported she was raising $75 million: Kia Kokalitcheva, "Scoop: Gwyneth Paltrow Is Raising a $75 Million Venture Capital Fund," Axios, March 2, 2023.

353 In her March 2025 *Vanity Fair* cover profile: Michelle Ruiz, "Gwyneth Paltrow on Motherhood, MAHA, Meghan Markle, Making Out with Timothée Chalamet—and Much More," *Vanity Fair*, March 18, 2025.

353 "to get to less than that": Author interview with Anarghya Vardhana, June 16, 2024.

353 G. Label could reach $20 million: Background interview.

353 Brands didn't care about Goop's: Background interview.

354 With Moses heading off to Brown University: Katherine Clarke and E. B. Solomont, "Gwyneth Paltrow Gets $22 Million for Her Los Angeles Home," *The Wall Street Journal*, January 27, 2025.

354 She had her bigger place in Montecito: Nick Welsh, "Gwyneth Paltrow's Montecito Mansion Opposed," *Santa Barbara Independent*, June 29, 2017.

354 with a large swimming pool: Mayer Rus, "Step Inside Gwyneth Paltrow's Tranquil Montecito Home," *Architectural Digest*, February 2, 2022.

354 It was the mega-mansion she wanted: Background interview.

354 Gwyneth worked from the set: Author interview, Djenaba Parker, March 13, 2025.

354 While the work led her: Background interview.

354 "genuine interest": Background interview.

354 worked at the company's Sag Harbor store: Tracy Smith, "Gwyneth Paltrow on Turning 50 and Goop," *CBS News Sunday Morning*, September 25, 2022.

354 interned in the Los Angeles office: Sara Nathan, "Is the Gilt Finally Wearing off Goop and Its Golden Girl Gwyneth Paltrow?," *New York Post*, November 24, 2024.

354 joining a band called Dancer: Rachel McRady, "Chris Martin and Gwyneth Paltrow's Son Moses Martin Reveals His Singing Talents at Concert," *E! Online*, November 14, 2024.

354 In early 2023, when she attended a Chanel: Christian Allaire, "Apple Martin on Attending Her First Fashion Show," *Vogue*, January 25, 2023.

354 such as when she appeared at the debutante ball: Charna Flam and Zoey Lyttle, "French Debutante in Viral Apple Martin Video Speaks Out About 'Mean Girl' Accusations (Exclusive)," *People*, December 6, 2024.

355 Apple was in the news again: Melissa Minton, "Apple Martin Kicks Off NYFW in Slinky Black Slip Dress and Red Lipstick," *New York Post*, February 6, 2025.

355 "will be the original Apple": Author interview with Richard Lovett, April 11, 2025.

355 had made a promise to her mother: Marisa Meltzer, "Gwyneth Paltrow Looks Back at 15 Years of Goop and More," *New York Times*, September 30, 2023.

EPILOGUE

357 Kennedy has spoken out against: Berkeley Lovelace Jr., "RFK Jr. Announces Plans to Remove Artificial Dyes from Nation's Food Supply," NBC News, April 18, 2024; Seth Mnookin, "How Robert F. Kennedy, Jr., Distorted Vaccine Science," *Scientific American*, January 11, 2017.

357 In that 2025 *Vanity Fair* cover story: Michelle Ruiz, "Gwyneth Paltrow on Motherhood, MAHA, Meghan Markle, Making Out with Timothée Chalamet—and Much More," *Vanity Fair*, March 18, 2025.

357 In her newsletter, Dr. Jen Gunter noted: Dr. Jen Gunter, "Gwyneth Paltrow's Dairy Delusion," The Vajenda newsletter, March 20, 2025.

358   It's hard not to see a connection: Aria Bendix, "RFK. Jr's Controversial Health Stances, from Vaccines to Raw Milk," NBC News, November 15, 2024.

358   vitamin A for pediatric measles patients: Teddy Rosenbluth, "Remedy Supported by Kennedy Leaves Some Measles Patients More Ill," *New York Times*, March 25, 2025.

358   around as big as the pharmaceutical and agricultural: "U.S. Wellness Economy Report," Global Wellness Institute; "U.S. Pharmaceutical Market Size to Reach USD 1,093.97 Billion By 2033," BioSpace, July 12, 2024; Steven Zahniser, "What is agriculture's share of the overall U.S. economy?," USDA, December 29, 2024.

358   alternative medicine proponent Mark Hyman: Brendan Borrell, "He Built a Wellness Empire While Adventuring with Robert F. Kennedy Jr.," *New York Times*, December 18, 2024.

358   "I think that the legacy of Gwyneth Paltrow": Author interview with Dr. Jen Gunter, January 13, 2025.

358   One study valued the "global spa economy": "The Global Spa Economy 2007," Global Spa Summit LLC.

358   U.S. had the largest wellness economy: "The Global Wellness Economy Reaches a New Peak of $6.3 Trillion—And Is Forecast to Hit $9 Trillion by 2028," Global Wellness Institute, November 5, 2024.

358   just over $600 billion: "U.S. Pharmaceutical Market Size to Reach USD 1,093.97 Billion By 2033."

358   $1.5 trillion: Zahniser, "What is agriculture's share of the overall U.S. economy?"

358   The U.S. has the world's fastest growing: "The Global Wellness Economy Reaches a New Peak of $6.3 Trillion—And Is Forecast to Hit $9 Trillion by 2028."

359   "In many ways, it is a cult": Author interview with Andrea Love, February 13, 2025.

360   "I just don't think Goop": Background interview.

ABOUT THE AUTHOR

Amy Odell is the *New York Times* bestselling author of *Anna: The Biography*, an in-depth examination of Anna Wintour, and the essay collection *Tales from the Back Row: An Outsider's View from Inside the Fashion Industry*. A veteran culture and fashion journalist, she is the author of the influential newsletter *Back Row*. Her work has appeared in *The New York Times*, *Time*, *New York*, and numerous other publications.